Niguma, Lady of Illusion

The Tsadra Foundation Series

published by Snow Lion Publications

Tsadra Foundation is a U.S.-based nonprofit organization that was founded in 2000 in order to support the activities of advanced Western students of Tibetan Buddhism, specifically those with significant contemplative experience. Taking its inspiration from the nineteenth-century nonsectarian Tibetan scholar and meditation master Jamgön Kongtrül Lodrö Tayé, Tsadra Foundation is named after his hermitage in eastern Tibet, Tsadra Rinchen Drak. The Foundation's various program areas reflect his values of excellence in both scholarship and contemplative practice, and the recognition of their mutual complementarity.

This publication is part of Tsadra Foundation's Translation Program, which aims to make authentic and authoritative texts from the Tibetan traditions available in English. The Foundation is honored to present the work of its fellows and grantees, individuals of confirmed contemplative and intellectual integrity; however, their views do not necessarily reflect those of the Foundation.

Tsadra Foundation is delighted to ally with Snow Lion Publications in making these important texts available in the English language.

Niguma, Lady of Illusion

Sarah Harding

Snow Lion Publications
ithaca, new york

Snow Lion Publications
P.O. Box 6483
Ithaca, New York 14851 USA
(607) 273-8519 www.snowlionpub.com

Printed in USA on acid-free recycled paper.

ISBN-10: 1-55939-361-0
ISBN-13: 978-1-55939-361-4

Library of Congress Cataloging-in-Publication Data

Harding, Sarah, 1951-
Niguma, lady of illusion / Sarah Harding.
p. cm. — (The Tsadra Foundation series)
Includes translations from Tibetan.
Includes bibliographical references and index.
ISBN-13: 978-1-55939-361-4 (alk. paper)
ISBN-10: 1-55939-361-0 (alk. paper)
1. Niguma, 10th/11th cent. 2. Śaṅs-pa (Sect)—Doctrines.
I. Niguma, 10th/11th cent. Works. English. 2010. II. Title.
BQ7950.N557H37 2010
294.3'923—dc22

2010015861

Designed and typeset by Gopa & Ted2, Inc.

Contents

Prayer to the Gurus of the Shangpa Lineage
by Tenga Tulku Rinpoche ix

Preface xi

Acknowledgments xv

Technical Notes xvii

Introduction 1

Niguma, the Ḍākinī of Timeless Awareness 1

Stories of Niguma 16

The Textual Tradition 22

The Shangpa Tradition 27

1. Stages in the Path of Illusion 37

Introduction 37

Stages in the Path of Illusion 54

Outline of the Commentary 85

Stages in the Path of Illusion: The Commentary 86

2. The Six Dharmas of Niguma 135

Introduction 135

Vajra Lines of the Six Dharmas 139

3. Mahāmudrā 143
Introduction 143
Vajra Lines of the Amulet Mahāmudrā 145
Vajra Lines of the Amulet Mahāmudrā (with Notes) 147
Naturally Free Mahāmudrā 150

4. The Three Integrations 153
Introduction 153
Three Dharmas to Integrate on the Path 155

5. Immortal and Infallible 161
Introduction 161
Glorious Immortal Great Timeless Awareness 163

6. Chakrasaṃvara 167
Introduction 167
Mandala Ritual of Glorious Chakrasaṃvara 170
Swift Accomplishment of Glorious Chakrasaṃvara 173

7. Hevajra 177
Introduction 177
Mandala Ritual of Glorious Hevajra 178

8. The Ḍākinī's Personal Instructions: Five Short Texts on Yogic Techniques 183
Introduction 183
Esoteric Instructions on Opening the Channel 185
Meditation on Channels, Prāṇa, and Such 186
Meditation on Inner Heat in the Path of Methods 187
Yoga of Meditation in the Path of Methods 189
Channel Chakras of One's Body 191

9. Niguma's Aspiration Prayer 193

Aspiration Prayer of the Sealed Word ("Kagyama") 193

Appendix 1. "The Basis of Everything" by Khyabje Kalu Rinpoche 199

Appendix 2. The Tibetan Text of *Stages in the Path of Illusion and the Commentary* 201

Notes 257

Abbreviations 307

Bibliography of Works Cited by the Author 311

Reference Bibliography 319

Index 351

Prayer to the Gurus of the Shangpa Lineage

by Tenga Tulku Rinpoche

Vajradhara, Niguma, Sukhasiddhī, Rāhula,
Vajrāsana, great adept Maitrīpa,
And Hidden Yogin Rāhula:
I supplicate the six sublime gurus.

Crown jewel of learned adepts, sublime Khyungpo Naljor,
Mokchokpa and Wöntön Kyergangpa,
Sangye Nyentön Chökyi Sherab and
Sangye Tönpa Tsöndru Senge:
I supplicate the lineage of seven jewels.

Nurtured by the sublime glorious guru
In this life and in all future lives,
Through the consummate realization of Five Golden Dharmas
May I gain the original sovereign state in one lifetime.

Preface

THE MYSTERIOUS NIGUMA was an Indian woman from Kashmir who probably lived in the tenth and eleventh centuries. Not only are the dates uncertain, but so too is almost everything about her. I will explore what there is to know and not to know about Niguma in the introduction. What does stand firmly as testimony to her existence, however, is her legacy of teachings, which form the very core of the Shangpa Kagyu lineage, one of the "Eight Great Chariots of the Practice Lineages" that were later identified as the main conduits through which experiential Buddhism spread from India to Tibet.[1]

The collection translated here consists of all of the works that are attributed to Niguma contained in the Tibetan Buddhist "canon," a total of seventeen separate texts, plus the only known biography from the collected texts in the Shangpa tradition.[2] Most of these are only a few pages in length, though their original verses gave rise to a whole body of literature in the Shangpa practice tradition. The exception is her master work, the *Stages in the Path of Illusion* (*sGyu ma lam gyi rim pa*), and its commentary (*sGyu ma lam gyi rim pa'i 'grel pa*). This is our main focus here, though the other texts will be briefly introduced.

Stages in the Path of Illusion depicts a spiritual journey, beginning with the point of departure, or "ground"—the underlying buddha-nature with its inherent potential for awakening. It takes us through the progressive journey common to Mahāyāna Buddhism, but with Niguma's distinctive twist of using the journey's illusory nature as our guide. That it is illusion is not in question. The crucial instruction is in the way to engage that insight to gain the goal of the journey, illusory buddhahood.

It could be said that Niguma is the mistress of illusion. Not only is her very nature as a historical person obscure in every way and her main and only treatise focused on that subject, but the other teachings for which she is most famous also reverberate with this theme. The two principal areas of practice in the tradition are the yogas based on the Six Dharmas of Niguma, with an emphasis on the illusory body and dream yogas, and the special Amulet Mahāmudrā, a practice of doing nothing. This twofold division of teachings represents the two universal approaches in tantric practice: the path of methods or techniques (*thabs lam*) and the path of liberation (*grol lam*), which focuses on the cultivation of a superior way of knowing (*shes rab*). The original verses or "vajra lines" (*rdo rje tshig rkang*) of these subjects are translated here. In the first category there are also five very cryptic instructions (*zhal gdams*) concerning yogic exercises associated with the practice of inner heat (*gtum mo*), one of the six dharmas. The mahāmudrā category includes an annotated version of the *Amulet Mahāmudrā* and a further instruction entitled *Naturally Free Mahāmudrā*.

Two other very important source texts of Niguma in this collection are *Three Dharmas to Integrate on the Path* (*lam khyer gsum*), which instruct the practitioner on how to integrate all appearances as the guru, the deity, and illusion in daily life, and *Glorious Immortal Great Timeless Awareness*, which contains teachings on the immortal and infallible nature of the mind and body.[3] Together with the six dharmas and mahāmudrā, these form four of the famed Five Golden Dharmas of the Glorious Shangpa that make up the core of the tradition, and that will be discussed later. The fifth golden dharma, that of the two Kecharī ḍākinīs, was not included in this canonical collection. However, deity visualization practice, known as creation phase (*bskyed rim*), is represented by the means of accomplishment (*grub thabs*) and empowerment conferral in the important tantric deity Chakrasaṃvara: *Swift Accomplishment of Glorious Chakrasaṃvara* and *Mandala Ritual of Chakrasaṃvara.*[4] Surprisingly, we also find another tantric text: the *Mandala Ritual of Glorious Hevajra*,[5] a practice that does not currently form part of the core Shangpa tradition. I will provide more context for the Shangpa literary and practice tradition in the introduction.

The collection is capped off by the lyrical prayer known popularly as Niguma's *Aspiration Prayer of the Sealed Word* or simply *Kagyama* (*bKa' rgya ma*), in which she prays to "become the protector, hope, and reinforcement for all sentient beings equaling space, their every desire and hope, whatever they are, satisfied by me exactly as they wish."

I would like to add my own altruistic aspirations, otherwise stranded in the realm of wishful thinking, to be carried by Niguma's powerful blessing so that the work of translating her teachings will help accomplish her profound prayer.

Acknowledgments

I AM MOST GRATEFUL for help and comments by Ācārya Lama Tenpa Gyaltsen in translating the *Stages in the Path of Illusion* and its commentary. We studied every word of it together. His knowledge and enthusiasm for the path-system in the mahāyāna tradition was indispensable. And that's not to even mention the help with Tibetan itself! Khenpo Tsering Gyurme of Surmang Dudtsitil Monastery worked valiantly for many months searching for the quotations, often reading whole sūtras by the dozen. I don't think any database will ever replace the Tibetan lamas' training in memorization and reading. Khenpo Tsering also made himself available at the drop of a hat for any questions regarding my research. I thank both of these lamas for their benevolent support. Some friends and colleagues helped by reading the manuscript and offering suggestions: Erin McCartney for a first reading of the introduction, Anne Blasing for a second, Steven Johnson for detailed cross-checking, and Robert Spellman for one final reading with an eye for style (who knew you were such a grammar nerd?). Lama Drupgyu, my friend and colleague in the three-year retreat and himself once a retreat master, helped to retrieve my long dormant memories of yogic exercises. We should all be grateful that someone remembers such things. I am also grateful for other friends that are now working under the auspices of the Tsadra Foundation, such as Ngawang Zangpo, Cyrus Stearns, Karl Brunnhölzl, and Richard Barron. Thank you for keeping in touch and adding to my knowledge when needed, which was often enough. Thanks go to graduate students Cory Leistikow and Daniel

Garbes for help with entering the Tibetan fonts, and to my entire 2008 Tibetan IV class at Naropa University for sharing my translation travails. Certainly I thank Sidney and Jeff at Snow Lion Publications for all of their work, and Michael Wakoff, who had the terrible task of copyediting. Thank you to my good friend, Bhutanese master artist Phurba Namgay, for the Niguma tangkha shown on the cover. Above all, I wish to express my deep gratitude to Eric Colombel, founder and director of Tsadra Foundation. If not for you . . .

Technical Notes

IN THE TRANSLITERATION of Sanskrit terms, I have deviated from standard practice to bring it slightly more into line with English by replacing *ś*, *ṣ*, and *c* with *sh*, *ṣh*, and *ch*, respectively. In addition, I have dispensed with diacritics altogether for certain Sanskrit terms that have found their way into English dictionaries, such as "samsara," "nirvana," "mandala," and so forth. When the Sanskrit word was retained in the Tibetan translation, I too have retained it rather than translating it into English. The phonetics for Tibetan names, places, and occasionally terms has been rendered in the closest approximation of pronunciation in English without burdening the reader overmuch with subtleties of dialect or bringing even more languages into the mix (except for the indispensable German umlaut: *ö*). The transliteration scheme developed by Turrell Wylie in "A Standard System of Tibetan Transcription" (1959) can usually be found in parentheses or in endnotes.

I consulted many editions of each text; the sources are quite ancient, and many errors have certainly found their way in to the copies over the centuries. One could even say that they are riddled with spelling and word mistakes. I chose to translate the version of each word that makes the most sense, taking into consideration context, commentary (written and oral), meaning, and frequency of occurrence. The variances are often noted in the endnotes if they are meaningful or problematic. This is not, however, a critical text study, and every "*te*" that should be "*de*" is not noted. As mentioned in the translations, several of the texts have additional interlinear notes that were added at some earlier time to clarify the original. If these notes were included in the canonical editions, then I included them in the English translation, indicated by using a smaller font. In the case of such notes from other editions besides the canon, I included in the endnotes only those that seemed helpful. Finally, where I needed to add words for clarification or grammatical purposes, they will be found in brackets.

Introduction

NIGUMA, THE ḌĀKINĪ OF TIMELESS AWARENESS

WHO WAS THIS phantasmic lady Niguma? I will include here the brief biography found in the *Golden Rosary of Shangpa Biographies*, but other than that, one finds only hints and guesses from other sources. For instance, here is a typical description from the great Tibetan master Tāranātha:

> The ḍākinī Niguma's place of birth was the Kashmiri city called "Incomparable." Her father was the brahmin Santivarman (Tib.: Zhi ba'i go cha). Her mother was Shrīmati (dPal gyi blo gros ma). Her real name was Srījñāna (dPal gyi ye shes). She had previously gathered the accumulations [of merit and wisdom] for three incalculable eons. Thus, in this life [as Niguma], based on the teachings of the instructions by the adept Lavāpa and some others, she manifested the signs of progress in the secret mantra vajrayāna, and attained the body of union. So her body became a rainbow-like form. She had the ability to really hear teachings from the great Vajradhara. Having become a great bodhisattva, her emanations pervaded everywhere and accomplished the welfare of beings.[6]

The elusiveness of Niguma is typical of the lore of the ḍākinī, the very embodiment of liminal spiritual experience. Additionally the difficulty of pinpointing historical information may well be due to the lack of ancient sources from India and the lack of concern about such mundane matters by the Tibetan masters who encountered her in dreams and visions and maybe in person. After all, when confronted with the blazing apparition of the resplendent and daunting dark ḍākinī bestowing critical cryptic advice, a background check would be rendered irrelevant. Indian Buddhist hagiographies are virtually unknown, whether of men or women.[7] In Tibet, where hagiography became a prolific genre in its own right, those of women were extremely rare, for all the usual reasons. It is in the experiences of those heroes who encountered the ḍākinī that one finds the most information, and these experiences are invested with the value of spiritual meaning. In the *Golden Rosary of Shangpa Biographies*, Niguma's life story consists of only six folios, and half of them contain a supplication prayer to her, while that of her disciple Khyungpo Naljor, called a "mere mention" (*zur tsam*), consists of forty-three folios, and those of her brother Nāropa, Tāranātha, Tangtong Gyalpo, and so forth where Niguma is mentioned are much longer than that. Even more distressing, I have discovered that half of the remaining half of Niguma's life story, the part that concerns her birthplace, appears to be directly lifted from a biography of Nāropa![8] Perhaps she is just an adornment of the lives of great saints, a figment of men's imaginations.

That, of course, is something one has to wonder and worry about in nearly all of the more ancient writings about ḍākinīs. The idealized image of a female messenger, awesome keeper of the great mysteries to be revealed only to the deserving spiritual virtuoso, is packed with power and intrigue for both male and female practitioners. Though unique in its particulars to Himalayan Buddhism, it is found in reminiscent forms throughout the cultures and religions of the world. The mystery of the ḍākinī herself will not be revealed because she is the very definition of mystery, and were she discovered by those other than mystics, it would not be she.

But what of the actual woman behind the image? In the case of a reportedly historical woman such as Niguma, we should be able to find at least some hint of a subjective story, something to convince us that she is more than the object or projection of the practitioner's realization. And more than the "other" of the male "self." We seek her as the subject of her own story.

Niguma's Home

Niguma's life does present us with a few crumbs. First of all, her birthplace is known to be in Kashmir, a hub of Buddhist tantric activity that probably was in close quarters with the Shaivite tradition and other forms of esoteric Hinduism. The specific town, or perhaps monastery, is called Peme (dpe med) in Tibetan, meaning "without comparison," translating the term "Anupama."[9] But we learn in her biography that this is not a real town, exactly, but one that has been created by an illusionist. So the first hard fact is already shaky. The story first mentions the creation myth, as it were, of Kashmir itself, a land that was once under water. According to Niguma's biography, the story takes place during the time of the previous buddha, Kāshyapa, though in other versions the story centers around Buddha Shākyamuni's time and his disciple Ānanda.[10] In any case, a disciple wished to build a temple in the area of Kashmir and stealthily negotiated with the subterranean beings, or *nāga*, who were tricked into "upmerging" and surrendering a large area of land. It reports that the residents were amazed, though in the same story in Nāropa's biography, it is the nāga themselves who were amazed. In any case, the amazed ones commission an illusionist to create a city, which he does based on the "blueprint" of the great celestial city of the gods called Sudarshana. But this talented architect-magician dies before he could dissolve the city, and so it remained. This, then, is Niguma's home town: a divinely inspired illusion.

Family and Friends

Niguma's family relationships are similarly elusive, particularly when it comes to her connection with Nāropa (956–1040),[11] her contemporary and a great adept whose teachings on the six dharmas that he learned from Tilopa spread widely in Tibet. The names of Niguma's parents given above by Tāranātha are indeed the same as the names of Nāropa's parents as given in his biography by Lhatsun Rinchen

Namgyal (1473–1557) and are similar in other biographies too.[12] These biographies tell the story of those parents' first child, Shrījñāna, and how they had to perform special supplications for a male child after her birth. We also have the name of Nāropa's wife, Vimalā or Vimalādīpī (Dri med pa or Dri med sgron ma), with whom he parted to pursue his spiritual career. Nāropa is sometimes said to be from Bengal in the east, but there is little evidence for this theory, and most authors locate his birthplace in Kashmir, along with Niguma.[13] There is even some evidence that Nāropa's well-known hermitage of Puṣhpahari, or Pullahari, commonly identified as being on a hillock west of Bodhgaya, may have been in Kashmir.[14] In Niguma's biography, it simply mentions that Nāropa was also in the area. Despite any misinformed discrepancies, it would seem to be quite clear that Niguma and Nāropa were sister and brother. Yet scholars, mostly Western, have insisted on suggesting that Niguma was his consort, perhaps his sister too, in a sort of tantalizing tantric gossip. Alas it may be the great translator Herbert Guenther who started the trend. In his introduction to *The Life and Teaching of Nāropa*, he makes a most puzzling allusion:

> [Nāropa's] wife seems to have gone by her caste name Ni-gu-ma, and according to the widely practiced habit of calling a female with whom one has had any relation 'sister' she became known as 'the sister of Nāropa.'[15]

Guenther cites *The Blue Annals* and the *Collected Works of bLo bzang chos-kyi nyi-ma*, an eighteenth-century Gelukpa scholar known as Tukwan Lama, as the sources where "Ni-gu-ma is stated to have been the wife of Nāropa." However, both sources state nothing so definitive. *The Blue Annals*, which devotes most of a chapter to the accounts of Niguma and her lineage, mentions her only as Nāropa's sister,[16] using the Tibetan word *lcam mo*, a combination of *lcam* (an honorific) and *sring mo* (sister). The second source similarly says only that she is Niguma's *lcam,*[17] as do all other sources in Tibetan that I have seen. A supplication to Niguma in the practice of the white and red Khecharī ḍākinīs uses the unambiguous term *sring mo*, calling her "the single sister of the awareness-holder."[18] Admittedly, the word *lcam mo* can be used as mistress or wife, particularly as the senior of several wives,[19] but given this bivalent meaning and the fact that we have the identical parents' names and the name of Nāropa's real wife, why on earth would one choose to translate it as "wife"? Even the translator Roerich does not do so in the *Blue Annals* and comments elsewhere that "in the ancient language *lcam* means always 'sister.'"[20] It does seem to be that tired old need to attribute a woman's worth to her mate that plagues the annals of history, coupled with the scholarly penchant for repeating the confident pronouncements of former scholars.

Another possible source of confusion pertains to a supposed meeting between Nāropa's Tibetan disciple Marpa and Niguma. In the introduction to the translation of Tsangnyön Heruka's biography of Marpa called *The Life of Marpa the Translator*, the following information is offered, repeating the relationship in an even stranger way:

> After attaining his first realization of mahāmudrā under Maitrīpa, Marpa returned to Nāropa. This time, Nāropa sent Marpa to receive teachings from Niguma, Wisdom (Jñāna) Dākinī Adorned with Bone ornaments. She was Nāropa's wife before he renounced worldly life to enter the dharma, and later she became his student and consort. Finally, she became a great teacher herself and her lineage of teachings was taken to Tibet (though not by Marpa) and continues to this present day. Unfortunately, our story here does not tell us very much about their meeting (xliii).

The Tibetan text reveals that Marpa was indeed sent on two separate occasions, first by Nāropa and later by Shantibhadra, to meet a certain ḍākinī called simply by the metonym "Adorned with Bone Ornaments."[21] Nowhere does it mention Niguma specifically by name in this or other biographies of Marpa. It is true that in later eulogies Niguma is described as wearing bone ornaments, but I believe this could be considered a regular wardrobe for ḍākinīs, whose options were generally confined to charnel grounds. Better evidence of their identity than similar attire would be that both Marpa's ḍākinī and Khyungpo Naljor's Niguma can sometimes both be found in the same great cemetery of

Sosadvīpa (Tib. Sosaling), said to be just to the west of Bodhgaya and the vacation spot of many a great master, including Padmasambhava. It was also, however, a famous ḍākinī gathering spot. In Marpa's biography, he finds the bone-decked ḍākinī on two occasions: once he receives the empowerment and instructions in the *Four Seats Tantra* from her, and a second time he receives a prophecy about meeting Nāropa (after he had already passed away).[22] Given the widespread prevalence, even requirement, of ḍākinī encounters on the spiritual path of yogis, this account gives us nothing to cling to. Moreover, there is no account wherein Niguma receives any teachings from Nāropa, though the similarity of the content of their teachings might lead one to believe otherwise. But how do we know that it was not the other way around—that Nāropa did not receive teachings from his big sister?

Teachers

The only piece of specific information about Niguma's teachers that I have from my sources is her connection with a certain Lavāpa, according to two accounts by Tāranātha. However Lavāpa is not mentioned by name in Niguma's *Life Story*, where it says only that "she directly saw the truth of the nature of phenomena just by hearing some instructive advice from *a few adept masters*." The only two named masters in the *Life Story* are Nāropa and Ratnavajra, and then only as cohabitants in Kashmir.[23] Again, the commonly held belief that Niguma received the six dharmas from Nāropa seems to be unsubstantiated. In fact, the *Blue Annals*, following a similar statement in Khyungpo Naljor's biography, quotes Niguma saying that "these six doctrines are known only to myself and Lavāpa."[24]

It is, however, difficult to identify this Lavāpa. Tāranātha provides some nice anecdotes of an ācārya Lavāpa in *The Seven Instruction Lineages* and discusses him again in his *History*.[25] He is also mentioned by Nāropa's guru, Tilopa, as one of his four human teachers and the one from whom he received dream yoga, or lucid clarity, depending on the account.[26] Some sources identify Ācārya Lavāpa with Kambhalapāda, one of the eighty-four great adepts (*mahāsiddhas*) of Indian Buddhism who is associated with the conversion activities in the west of

India.[27] Tāranātha does not seem to make this identity and we are left with a lack of information on this "Lavāpa of the East," other than that he is called "the lesser (that is, younger), or latter Lavāpa." Here is another version by Tāranātha, with its veiled jab at this unidentified Lavāpa:

> She listened for a bit to instructions from Lavāpa of the East, and after meditating for seven days together with the master himself, she became a ḍākinī of timeless awareness with a rainbow body. She manifested the realization of the eighth ground. It is said that Lavāpa of the East [did not gain the full rainbow body because he] left behind a palm-sized portion of the crown of his head. This Lavāpa is the lesser. The name Nigu accords with the Indian language, which is Nigupta, and it is said to mean "truly secret" or "truly hidden." In fact, it is the code-language of the ḍākinīs of timeless awareness.[28]

Code-Language

The symbolic or code-language of the ḍākinīs (*mkha' 'gro'i brda' skad*) is itself "truly hidden." Masters of meditation decipher these communications in moments of inspiration, but by the time we hear what they might be, they have already been translated and carry all the perils of that craft, including possible fraud. We can see a few indecipherable graphics called "ḍākinī code-letters" (*mkha' 'gro brda' yig*) in treasure texts, but even this is only a subcategory of the mystery code-language itself. In his commentary on the treasure text *Lamrim Yeshe Nyingpo*, Jamgön Kongtrul explains:

> A person endowed with the karmic continuation and destiny will, by means of a profound coincidence of place, time, and aspiration, be able to decode the symbolic meaning of these treasure letters that are nirmāṇakāyas, the vajra forms endowed with all eminent aspects, and establish them correctly in writing.[29]

Perhaps the ḍākinī code-language is beyond verbal communication, with its necessarily dualistic and designatory nature. But then why call it "language"? Symbolic communication is specifically distinguished from nonverbal transmission in the Nyingma tripartite transmissions of dzogchen teachings, where the symbolic lineage of the awareness-holders (*rig 'dzin brda'i brgyud pa*) falls neatly between the nonverbal lineage of the buddhas' "thought" or intention, and the aural lineage of ordinary people. Janet Gyatso suggests that the ḍākinī, in keeping with her playful character, is "working within language to subvert it, drawing attention to its own (dualistic) structures while never retreating outside its realm."[30] And certainly the esoteric teachings of the tantras themselves in their written form are known to be coded. After all, the common name for those teachings is "secret mantra" (*gsang sngags*). The ḍākinī code-language is a secret within that secret and seems to be reserved for the most profound and spontaneous experiences of only very gifted practitioners.

Tāranātha makes no attempt to tell us what the name "Niguma" really means in that language, leaving it rather to the initiated to find out.

In a similar way it is difficult to precisely identify Niguma's other attributes that recur in most sources, although they are reported as quantifiable facts. She had high-level realization, placing her in the "pure" (*dag pa*) or nondissipating (*zag med*) grounds, she attained the so-called rainbow body, and most famously, she could receive teachings directly from Vajradhara. What do these qualities actually mean, apart from being ways to impress us?

Pure Ground

The first attribute is at least locatable in the mahāyāna map to enlightenment, or road to glory, as some have put it. The milestones on this journey are a main subject in the *Commentary to Stages in the Path of Illusion* and will be discussed in more detail later. The division into anywhere from ten to fourteen levels or stations (literally "grounds" Skt. *bhūmi*, Tib. *sa*) has become somewhat standardized and carries designations of either pure or impure. The impure stages are the grounds up to and including the seventh since there is still the risk that someone of low acumen could revert to a lesser degree of enlightenment. The grounds from the eighth and up are pure grounds since there can be no reverting from them.[31] Tāranātha designates Niguma's position as on only the eighth ground. By her own admission (if indeed she is the true source of the commentary to the *Path of Illusion*), she states confidently: "The author is myself, one who dwells on the three pure grounds and has obtained authorization from Vajradhara."[32] The *Life Story* reveals more of a progression through these last pure grounds, culminating in the tenth ground, "Cloud of Dharma," so-called because, as it says in the commentary, "cloud-like great timeless awareness pervades throughout the sky-like dharmakāya." Here is her description from *Path of Illusion*:

> Then, in a single instant, amidst
> the great appearance of dharma and
> immeasurable light and dharma clouds and
> dharma appearance and dharma light of immeasurable
>   tathāgatas,
> the immeasurably great Cloud of Dharma is attained.[33]

After the culmination of the tenth ground, wherein the perfection of timeless awareness is achieved, there is the state of total awakening as a buddha. Different systems describe different ways that this final transformation occurs, as we shall see, and often further levels are enumerated. Twelve are described in *Path of Illusion*, but it seems that more levels were always being added, especially in the dzogchen tradition, making buddhahood ever more distant. In any case, awesome as Niguma's tenth-ground status appears, with its "twelve hundred sets of unimaginable qualities," she herself warns that "the difference between buddhas and bodhisattvas is like the difference in the waters of the ocean and in the hoof print of an ox."[34]

Rainbow Body

The language of the paths and levels in general is so dazzling as to render one impotent. Even the lowest of the impure grounds are unimaginable. Yet these specific statements on Niguma's status must be made for a purpose, or else one could just as well have said merely that she was really fantastic and leave it at that. One issue involves the technical verification of the other two traits that she boasts: the body of a rainbow and her lessons from Vajradhara. Descriptions of Niguma are all ephemeral because they are descriptions not of a person but of a yogic experience. Later visionary accounts of her, such as that of Tangtong Gyalpo, are of course out of this world. But even the supposedly "real-time" encounters described in the biography of Khyungpo Naljor are dreamlike, if not dreams in fact. Rainbows are one of the primary examples of phenomena that both appear distinctly and yet are insubstantial, so it is not surprising to hear that the ḍākinīs encountered in paranormal or liminal states of consciousness are described as being rainbow-like. Words could only point to such an experience by evoking in us a similar experience, and even then must fall tragically short. But far beyond a mere metaphor, the phenomenon known as "rainbow body" has produced considerable speculation and technically specific statistics—as though it truly existed. Perhaps the rainbow body is a poetic trope of mystical virtuosos used to communicate their innermost experiences. Whether this actually produced the attempt to identify and locate the phenomenon in the maps of spiritual progress cannot be known. But at least in some literature, the rainbow body is described quite specifically, one might even say concretely, as when Tāranātha weighs the exact portion of Lavāpa's body that did not rainbow-ize in the above story.

There is an enormous amount of material concerning the phenomenon of light that permeates almost all aspects of Buddhism, and it is not uncommon in other spiritual traditions as well. These many aspects are not irrelevant, but just too much to cover here, and I refer the reader to other sources.[35] For our immediate purpose, I could at least narrow the field by pointing out that the majority of the material in the Buddhist tradition concerns the nature of the mind, whether it be the light that describes its essence of clear awareness, or the light that is an actual perception of luminosity (either could be indicated by the Tibetan terms *gsal ba* and *'od gsal*). But the term "rainbow body" (*'ja' lus*) concerns an actual physical body that is transformed in its very nature into another kind of appearing phenomenon that is like a rainbow. The simple dictionary definition is "the corporeal body liberated into a body of light."[36] This sometimes occurs at death, in which case the corpse either disappears altogether, leaving only fingernails and hair, or else shrinks, a phenomenon known as "lesser rainbow body." This phenomenon has been reported throughout Tibetan history up to the present. For instance, a person who observed the funeral of Lama Norbu Dondrup, the teacher of the late Kalu Rinpoche, reported that his body had diminished to the size of a baby.[37]

In the dzogchen tradition, it is said to be the product of very specific and intentionally designed practices, unique to that tradition. According to the modern Tibetan master Namkhai Norbu, what occurs is that "instead of decomposing into its constituent elements in the usual way, [the body] dissolves into the essence of its elements, which is light."[38] However in certain other tantric traditions, such as Kālachakra, it can be the product of particular completion phase yogic practices that work with the subtle energetic body with its potential for enlightenment.[39] Again, it occurs based on inner heat practices in the Kagyu tradition:

> The ultimate attainment, like using quicksilver to transform iron into pure gold, is that the quintessence of the channels, energy currents, and vital essences will increase, gradually consuming the refuse and transforming the body into the actual rainbow body of inseparable form-emptiness, the saṃbhogakāya.[40]

It becomes clear that these are not just remarkable death stories, however astonishing. The Tibetan developments of the esoteric instructions concerning this phenomenon perhaps eventually grew into a way to identify the ultimate fruition of practice and hence to describe enlightened beings as well as the practitioner's effulgent experiences of them. Whether applied retroactively or not, the salient point of assigning the rainbow body to the great masters of the past, such as Niguma, would seem to be to explain their remarkable and *continuing* appearance in the lives of their devotees, long after their possible normal life spans. In some places, Niguma is even named "she with the deathless body of a rainbow."[41] About this on-going beneficence, Namkhai Norbu continues,

> But a practitioner who perfects and completes the fourth level of the Todgál [*thod rgal*] visions does not manifest death at all, and makes this transubstantiation while actually living, with none of the symptoms or phenomena of a physical death, gradually becoming invisible to someone with normal karmic vision. This level of realization is called the 'Great Transfer', and this is the realization that Padmasambhava and Vimalamitra manifested. Both the Great Transfer and the Body of Light [i.e., rainbow body] are in essence the same; it is just that, in the Great Transfer, one arrives earlier.[42]

Although that particular terminology is specific to the dzogchen literature, it must be that they refer to a similar or equivalent phenomenon, as do a variety of other terms such as "body of union" (*zung 'jug gi sku*), "vajra body" (*rdo rje sku*), and so on. Such terms are found mainly in the context of vajrayāna, and we don't find such language in the Indian mahāyāna delineation of paths and grounds.[43] Later, Tibetan scholars attempted to correlate the two vehicles of spiritual journeying. However, when and where the transmutation occurs in relationship to the mahāyāna path is difficult to pinpoint (as is befitting of an idea that intentionally indicates elusiveness). In the system of Highest Yoga Tantra, Jamgön Kongtrul mentions it in connection with the peak experience, which is the second ground on the third path.[44] According to the general correspondences of the five paths and ten grounds, this would not even be the first ground of a bodhisattva, which does not begin until the Path of Seeing. Again, in the same source, the term "rainbow body" is used in connection with the first ground in the Kālachakra system, but with the caveat that the term refers to an approximation of the ultimate accomplishment.[45] Finally we find it again in the final Path of Consummation as the ultimate achievement of enlightenment.[46] Another source, Dagpo Tashi Namgyal, similarly assigns it to the highest, or thirteenth, level.[47] What are we to make of these various assignments in relation to Niguma? Jamgön Kongtrul may be trying to clarify this in the following passage:

> It can be determined that the fruition aspect of tantra is twofold: the actual fruition and the nominal results. The actual fruition is that of supreme Vajradhara, the powerful state of mastery over all family types. The nominal results are those of the illusory body and of an ordinary being who has realized primordial unity. The latter case is the flawed embodiment of one who is still on the path of training, while the former is the flawless embodiment of timeless awareness of one who has reached the path of no more training. The illusory body is also termed that of "a master of awareness" and "rainbow body"; it constitutes a complete transcendence of the three realms.[48]

We have seen already that by all accounts Niguma was considered a bodhisattva of the pure grounds, that is, the eighth to the tenth grounds. Her rainbow body must be an attainment less than that of total buddhahood, otherwise it might be expected that her appearances were a manifestation of saṃbhogakāya, the body of total enjoyment, which is an embodiment of a buddha only perceptible by bodhisattvas with extremely pure vision, themselves abiding on the eighth ground or above. If that were the case, what would we make of the fact that she received teachings from the buddha Vajradhara? Why would she even need to do that? And what does it mean to say that? These questions are given added urgency in the biography of Khyungpo Naljor, who roamed India specifically in search of those who had "met the buddha."

Buddha Speaking

One might be surprised to find that the *Golden Rosary of Shangpa Biographies* begins with the "life story" of the buddha Vajradhara, incidentally by the same author as that of Niguma's biography.[49] "Life story" is a functional translation of *namtar* (*rnam par thar pa*) in Tibetan, which literally means "total liberation." We are accustomed to these accounts' tracing at least some trajectory of the aspirant's journey to the liberated state, so it is odd to find such a genre applied to an epitomized buddha. In this "biography," Vajradhara is described as the inner aspect of the buddha Shākyamuni. In this form, the Buddha taught the four classes of tantra to King Indrabhūti, "he" abides until the end of time, and he dwells in that mysterious place called the *bhaga* of the vajra queen.[50] As Shākyamuni, therefore, he in fact does make a spiritual journey that began with the initial arousing of the spirit of supreme awakening. This inner aspect is called Vajradhara because of "holding (Skt. *dhara*) the adamantine or vajra-like absorption of the nature of phenomena."[51] Buddhas have many dimensions. After presenting various enumerations of buddha-bodies or kāyas (*sku*), this text settles on the usual three: dharmakāya, the body of dharma, saṃbhogakāya, the body of perfect engagement, and nirmāṇakāya, the body of emanation. Vajradhara as buddha manifests all three. But which Vajradhara does Niguma meet? All indications point to the saṃbhogakāya Vajradhara, an actual findable buddha, the intermediary or liminal form of buddha that facilitates communication, not the all-encompassing spacious buddha-mind of dharmakāya. In Vajradhara's biography the question arises, "To whom do the three kāyas appear?" It is answered quite succinctly:

> The dharmakāya free of all embellishment [appears] in the meditative equipoise above the first ground. The saṃbhogakāya adorned with the signs and marks appears in the subsequent knowing on the three pure grounds. The nirmāṇakāya appears in the subsequent knowing up through the seventh ground and above the greater [ground] of the Path of Accumulation.[52]

It is interesting that the dharmakāya is accessible first, though specifically in meditation. It seems more profound, the ground of all buddha-bodies, and therefore more difficult to realize. But the keener realization is to meet the fully adorned and manifesting buddha, not in meditation but in the subsequent awareness after meditation—in "daily life" so to speak. In fact, according to this statement, the nirmāṇakāya, the actual Shākyamuni or other physical emanation, does *not* appear to someone dwelling *above* the seventh ground. In other words, the highest bodhisattvas dwelling on the three pure grounds only encounter the saṃbhogakāya. They know the manifest appearance of enlightenment, or perhaps that appearance *is* enlightenment.

It must be this saṃbhogakāya that is meant in the *Stages in the Path of Illusion: The Commentary* where the imminent attainment of the tenth ground is "to see the Body of the tathāgata [in] a fathom of light of a color like gold, completely surrounded by ten million billion brahmās."[53] And this must be why Khyungpo Naljor is so determined to find someone who has directly encountered the buddha. For if someone had perceived a buddha, that is, a saṃbhogakāya, it would indicate the highest of realizations, higher than even finding dharmakāya, which would be *merely* "abiding in one's own mind pure as space."[54] Although he has already met many great masters of India, Khyungpo Naljor wants to meet an actual person who moves in the world with constant and normalized awareness of all dimensions and who can move between those dimensions with ease. In other words, a traveler through space—a ḍākinī.

As much as I have searched for this ḍākinī named Niguma and hoped to find her as an actual person and the subject of her own story, it may have been in vain. The more I dig, the more elusive she becomes. No doubt I am looking in all the wrong places, in old books and dusty corners. Still, I hope that this might be more than another case of the female as a vehicle of meaning for men, or that, as one post-Buddhist feminist puts it, "the place of the male as subject is unconsciously protected, whilst creating a notion of fluidity around the concept of the female body."[55] I might have to admit, however, that she is primarily an important event in the lives of the men who saw her, rather than a historically locatable person. Those men, in any case, are really the only sources of information about her. Her own story, if it ever existed, is not to be found apart from the few details that I have explored here. Before providing the translation of her biography, therefore, let us see what a few of those masters have said of their encounters with Niguma.

STORIES OF NIGUMA

Khyungpo Naljor's Niguma

(This section is a summary based on the *Brief Life Story of Lama Khyungpo Naljor* found in the *Golden Rosary of Shangpa Biographies*, vol. 1, 59–143.)

After studying with many gurus in Nepal and India, the Tibetan yogi Khyungpo Naljor resolved to find someone who had met the Buddha face-to-face. He was directed to Niguma, who was reported to have received teachings from the great Vajradhara. Inquiring as to where she was at present, he was told that if one had pure perception, one could see her face anywhere, but those with impure perception might search up and down without ever finding her. That was because she dwelt on the pure grounds and had transformed to a rainbow body. "Pure grounds" are certainly a matter of perception, rather than location. Nevertheless, they said, she occasionally shows up in the forest of a great charnel ground, Sosadvīpa, to preside over the feast circles of ḍākinīs. Inspired, Khyungpo travels there immediately, while paying homage to the Buddha. He sees a dark ḍākinī hovering in the sky, bedecked in bones and holding a trident and skull-cup, dancing about and displaying various forms, appearing sometimes as one and sometimes many. Convinced it is she, Khyungpo requests teachings, but the ḍākinī is uncooperative.

"I am a flesh-eating ḍākinī," she says. "When my retinue arrives, you'll be devoured. Get out now."

Flesh-eating ḍākinīs may have been the original ḍākinīs of Indian lore, those scary females that populated the charnel grounds and other places where god-fearing people dared not tread. They constellate some of our greatest fears and are never far behind the more beneficent figures that entice and instruct the Tibetan adepts.[56] Here, the gimmick of terrorizing the aspirant as a test of determination is of course a common element in hero stories. At the same time, it is not entirely a ruse. The chimerical ḍākinī, or the energy she represents, could turn dangerous at any time and devour rather than nurture the practitioner. Khyungpo, undeterred, again requests instruction in secret mantra.

"To request secret mantra mahāyāna requires gold. If there's gold, I'll do it," the ḍākinī retorts.

Khyungpo offers her the nearly impossible amount of five hundred gold *srang*, but she just throws it about the forest.[57] At this point Khyungpo starts to wonder if she really is a flesh-eating ḍākinī since she does not want the gold. It is difficult not to speculate about the implication here: that a genuine ḍākinī would be greedy for gold, but apparently a flesh-eating ḍākinī is satisfied with—well, flesh.

The ḍākinī then glares into space to invoke her vast ḍākinī entourage, who begin constructing, in space, all the requisites for an empowerment, such as palace, sand mandala, and feast provisions. She then bestows the empowerments for the practices of illusory body and dream, tells Khyungpo to get up, and then transports him miraculously about twenty-five miles. There, in the sky above a golden mountain like the great Mount Avṛha,[58] the ḍākinīs perform the feast ceremony and dance about. The golden mountain has four rivers of gold pouring from the four sides, and Khyungpo asks if it can really be somewhere in India or if it is the ḍākinī's magical projection. To this she replies with perhaps the most famous verse associated with Niguma, reiterated in various ways in the *Path of Illusion:*

> This variety of desirous and hateful thoughts
> that strands us in the ocean of cyclic existence[59]
> once realized to be without intrinsic nature,
> makes everything a golden land, child.
>
> If you meditate on the illusion-like nature
> of illusion-like phenomena,
> actual illusion-like buddhahood
> will occur through the power of devotion.

Niguma then commands Khyungpo to recognize his dreams by means of her blessing, which he does indeed do. He continues to have the very dreamy experience of traveling to the land of gods and demigods, being swallowed whole by a gigantic demigod, and receiving the entire instruction on the Six Dharmas from Niguma. She even mentions, in his dream, that no one but he has ever received the complete teaching in one nap in all of India. What is never clarified is the starting point of the dream experience: whether it was from the time of being transported to the Golden Mountain or from his first encounter with the ḍākinī. He recognizes the dream only after she blesses him to so do. In any case, he now wakes up and "really" (*dngos su*) receives the guidance on the Six Dharmas again three times, along with a number of other instructions.[60]

In short, the story goes on to say, Khyungpo received boundless tantras, sādhanas, and instructions from this ḍākinī of timeless awareness. Ever insatiable, Khyungpo Naljor continues on his quest, offering pounds of gold to many more teachers. Again asking for one who has seen the Buddha, he is directed to the other principal ḍākinī in the lineage, Sukhasiddhī. That is another story, but with many similar elements. Of the twenty-eight or so Indian and Nepali gurus that are mentioned by name in Khyungpo Naljor's biography, seven of them are female. This fact is not emphasized in any way, and one might feel it to be quite normal and unremarkable. Female gurus in India, though certainly a minority, continue to be commonly accepted up to the present. Possibly it was in Tibet that it became such an exception.

Tangtong Gyalpo's Niguma

(This section on Tangtong Gyalpo is from "A Jewel Mirror in Which All Is Clear" by Lochen Gyurme Dechen, translated by Cyrus Stearns in *King of the Empty Plain* , 150–51. I have retained his translation.)

The great adept [Tangtong Gyalpo] then practiced these profound instructions [on Niguma's teachings received from living masters] in an isolated and pleasant wilderness hermitage. Many types of meditative concentration arose in his mind, so that he considered spreading this profound oral transmission in these glacial mountain ranges. At that moment a clear voice from the sky called out, "Son! Yogin!"

When he looked up into midair, in the center of a bunch of clouds, the famous Niguma, the ḍākinī of primordial awareness endowed with the power to traverse space and with the immortal form of a rainbow body, directly revealed her face to the great universal emperor of attainment known as Tangtong Gyalpo, "King of the Empty Plain," the thunder of whose fame totally fills the expanse of space. When she completely bestowed the four initiations in a great sublime mandala, he was filled with the youthful vitality of the four joys. At that time they fully engaged in the great secret practices, such as questions and responses, symbols and return symbols, and happily enjoyed the miraculous sensory objects of a ritual feast.

On that occasion, Niguma deciphered and fully instructed the great adept in each of the *Vajra Lines* by means of actual, implied, and hidden oral instructions. In particular, she bestowed the extremely profound transference practices of the infallible White and Red Khecarīs, together with instructions for enhancing them by means of two examples sealed by her command. When he put these into practice, he gained an inconceivable repertoire of attainments, such as the instantaneous display of countless physical forms in just a single moment, a clairvoyant knowledge of others' minds, and the ability to actually transfer [the consciousness] when he performed the transference for another person.

Later, on the peak of the famous glorious Riwoché in Latö Jang that was the adept's home, he was given permission by the ḍākinī and placed in writing the guidance manual for this profound path, the *Collection of the Essentials*, together with the affiliated texts. But the oral instructions for the transference practices of the White and Red Khecarīs, together with the illustration of the two examples, he taught with the tune of the indestructible *nāda*.[61]

Mokchokpa's Niguma

The following is translated from the *Golden Rosary of Shangpa Biographies*, and constitutes the second account there, immediately after that of Buddha Vajradhara. The two were authored by the same person, identified simply as "the vagabond Mokchokpa." An easy assumption would be to identify this with the principal lineage-holder after Khyungpo Naljor, Mokchokpa Rinchen Tsöndru (1110–1170), and indeed the name "Rinchen Tsöndru" is inserted as an interlinear note in this edition of the *Life Story*. Jamgön Kongtrul, however, specifically warns against making this mistake and identifies the latter Mokchokpa, Kunga Ö, as the author in two separate sources.[62] The current successor (*sprul sku*) to the Mokchokpa lineage says that this is another name for Jatang Kunga Yeshe (Bya btang Kun dga' ye shes), the second Mokchokpa.[63] Kongtrul's correction, if true, must apply to quite a long tradition of conflation. Lhatsun Rinchen Namgyal wrote, in 1503, that he had copied the *Life Story of Buddha Vajradhara* specifically from that of Mokchokpa Rinchen Tsöndru. In any case, we are getting used to certain vagaries when it comes to everything Niguma.

The Life Story of Niguma, Ḍākinī of Timeless Awareness[64]

Homage to all the holy gurus

> From the sky-like nature of the dharmakāya,
> Light rays of the sun-and-moon-like form-kāyas
> Illuminate the mental darkness of those to be tamed;
> I bow reverently at the feet of the holy guru.

With that, I would express here just a fraction of the life story of Niguma, the ḍākinī of timeless awareness.

The land of her birth was the great city called Anupama [Incomparable], located in Kashmir. That place, moreover, was a city emanated by an illusionist. The way in which it was emanated is this: During the time of the previous buddha, Kashyāpa, there was an arhat named Madhyāntika [Midday Sun].[65] At that distant time the entire area was covered by water. The arhat wished to build a vihāra in that country, so he requested land from the nāga king.[66] The nāgas said, "We will give you as much land as you can cover sitting in lotus posture." Then the arhat emanated a huge body there that covered all the territories of Kashmir. As the nāgas had promised, ground arose there and a vihāra called Amṛtabhāvana was built.[67]

The local people were truly amazed, so they sent for an illusionist.

That illusionist emanated the great city called Anupama, by using the example of the great [city of] Sudarshana.[68] But before the illusion could be dissolved, the illusionist was killed, and so it has remained until now. Everyone said that this city had no exact comparison to anything in the world, and so it was known as "Incomparable." There are even thirty-six hundred thousand beer maids there. That is why it is called special.[69] The great paṇdita Nāroṭapa and Ratnavajra[70] both lived there.

Now about the ḍākinī of timeless awareness herself. She was born as the daughter of the brahmin Shāntivarma [and the brahmini Shrīmatī].[71] She was Nāro Paṇdīta's sister and a member of the brahmin caste.

She had cultivated the path previously during three incalculable eons, and its continuity was actualized, so that in this life she directly saw the truth of the nature of phenomena just by hearing some instructive advice from a few adept masters. Her dissipating illusory body arose as the nondissipating kāya. Dwelling in the three pure grounds, she encountered the great Vajradhara in person. After she had fully received from him the complete four empowerments in the emanated mandala of secret mantra mahāyāna, she developed the timeless awareness of the understanding of all dharma doors—sūtras, tantras, esoteric instructions, treatises, and so on. She realized all phenomena the way they are and the way they appear in their multiplicity, and became a real bodhisattva dwelling on the tenth ground, Cloud of Dharma. Cognitive obscuration became more and more subtle until there was nothing left to eliminate. She was none other than a buddha, the epitome of the three kāyas.

Having perfected renunciation and realization for her own welfare, she continues to accomplish the welfare of others through the two form kāyas, benefiting whatever beings are to be tamed until the end of cyclic existence. In particular, she watches over the holders of the lineage with impartial compassion, blessing them and compassionately overseeing the success of their enlightened activity.

Even more specifically, on the great adept Khyungpo Naljor she fully conferred the complete four empowerments in the emanated mandala and gave him the oral transmission of unimaginable tantras and esoteric instructions. In particular, she gave many profound and vast pithy instructions that have the power to establish worthy recipients in the awakened state of manifest realization with one body in one lifetime. Niguma sealed this with the command that it not spread beyond a one-to-one lineage for seven generations. She then prophesied that the disciples and holders of this lineage would all go to the celestial realm, Khechara. Such is this very lineage that is exalted above others.[72]

This is the mere mention of the liberation story of the ḍākinī of timeless awareness, written for the realization of the lineage holders by the vagabond[73] Mokchokpa in the Glorious Monastery of Gyere Yangön.[74]

> By this merit may all persons who hold the lineage
> maintain themselves in the manner of the guru's life story.
> By the pure white virtue of writing this,
> may I and the sponsors, teachers, and students,
> and all sentient beings of the three realms,
> quickly attain unsurpassed awakening.

THE TEXTUAL TRADITION

The decision to limit the choices for this collection of Niguma's work to the selection in the so-called Tibetan Canon is somewhat random. The tendency to regard this canon as definitive is always tenuous. There are currently as many as ten known canons, and their formation and historical links to each other are not well documented, although research is proceeding. The most basic division in all cases is between the kangyur, the translated words of Buddha Shākyamuni in one form or another, and the tengyur, the translations of treatises by Indian authors such as Niguma that comment upon those 'original' words. With more than 5,250 texts, the Tibetan Buddhist canon contains the textual corpus of Indian Buddhism that was translated into Tibetan and which forms the foundation of the practice of Buddhism in the Himalayan region. The tremendous amount of literary output by Tibetans themselves is, for the most part, not included in the canons, where all sources are held to be Indian. Thus for a text to be included, or excluded, from any particular canon may be construed as a comment on its origin and even its authenticity, where authenticity is defined as having Indian origins. It almost goes without saying that the decisions about and preparations of the canons nearly a millennium after Buddhist teachings first reached Tibet were fraught with trouble, politics, biases, and, surely, some serious scholarship. The intricacies and implications of the process make for very interesting research but will not be explored here.

What is of interest to us is that not all of Niguma's works are included in all versions of the tengyur, and with one exception, they are most conspicuously missing from the widespread Derge Canon in its many editions.[75] The one exception is the short ritual practice of the deity Hevajra included in the Derge Tengyur, and set apart in the Peking Tengyur in a different volume than all the rest of her works. It is interesting too that, of all these texts attributed to Niguma, this is the only one not in common use in the living Shangpa tradition. The deity Hevajra, so important in the Kagyu and Lamdre lineages, plays only a small role in the Shangpa practice of Five Tantras' Deities, although the empowerment of Nine Emanated Deities of Hevajra was bestowed on Khyungpo Naljor directly by Niguma.[76]

I do not mean to read too much into this oddity. Simple omission is certainly a possibility when dealing with thousands of texts being compiled in different corners of a vast country, where communications moved at the speed of horses at best and printing was a matter of carving blocks of wood in mirror image for each and every page. I just present it here as a point of interest for further speculation. It seems to suggest that those tengyurs that do contain the majority "bundle" of Niguma's work, such as the Peking and Narthang Tengyurs, had access to local Shangpa collections while others did not. One might have expected the opposite, that is, that the corpus of Niguma's work would be in the tengyur printed in Derge, the physical center of the later eclectic movement (*ris med*) that played such a pivotal role in rescuing the Shangpa teachings from obscurity.[77] But it could be that the geographical location of the earliest Shangpa establishments in the far west of Tsang, far from the Derge cultural arena, played a role in this. Finally, given the obscurity of Niguma and her historicity, it is possible that the compilers of the Derge Canon had doubts as to the true Indic origins of these texts. In any case, we find them now only in the closely related Peking, Narthang, and Golden Tengyurs.[78]

Perhaps the earliest inclusion of Shangpa texts in a collection besides these tengyurs is to be found in the massive collection of Bodong Chokley Namgyal (1376–1451). It is said that he received a direct transmission from the two ḍākinīs Niguma and Sukhasiddhī, the two primary sources of the Shangpa tradition, at the age of sixteen, presumably in visionary experience.[79] Bodong's core collection, *The Compendium of Suchness* in four forms and 137 volumes, may be considered a sort of canon, although it also contains works by Tibetan authors. It forms the bulk of the Tibet House publication called *Encyclopedia Tibetica*, or *Collected Works of Bodong Chokley Namgyal*. Bodong's bold project, at which he succeeded, was to comment on everything conceivable and organize all the teachings of Buddhism in a comprehensive manner. Because of this style of organization by subject, the works attributed to Niguma are scattered among three separate volumes, interspersed with other works and Bodong's own exegeses on the subject.[80] We find there some of the works presented in this collection, as well as some of the instructional guides (*khrid yig*) on these practices also attributed to Niguma but left out of the tengyur.[81]

The Tibetan Buddhist Resource Center (TBRC) holds a copy of a two-volume handwritten manuscript of Shangpa texts found in the monastery of Sangak Choling in Kinnaur, a county in Himachal Pradesh bordering on Tibet.[82] Many of the Shangpa texts found in the tengyur are also included in these two volumes,[83] along with some very interesting and apparently unique texts from the lineage that need to be researched further. In addition TBRC holds a rare handwritten copy of the *Path of Illusion* and its *Commentary*, which I have also consulted for this translation.

Other sources for Shangpa texts include the collected works of past masters who received both the original teachings from lineage holders, called the "long lineage" (*ring brgyud*), and were granted further instructions and empowerments in direct visions of Niguma, called the short or "direct lineage" (*nye brgyud*). Of these, the most famous is the great adept Tangtong Gyalpo (1361?–1485), whose visions of Niguma are recounted above.[84] He did not write down the instructions that he received until Niguma granted permission in a third vision in 1458. They are known as the *Collection of the Essentials*, and with a set of related teachings formed a branch of the Shangpa Kagyu called the Tangtong Gyalpo Tradition (*Thang lugs*). They are contained in *Supplemental Texts to the Collected Works of Thang stong rgyal po Series.*[85]

In the Jonang tradition, Kunga Drolchok (1507–1566) is said to have received the long lineage many times and the direct lineage twice from Niguma in pure visions.[86] Since he also received guidance more than a hundred times in twenty-five lineages, his very diverse collection is called *Hundred Guides of Jonang* and is supplemented by sources and histories.[87] His immediate incarnation, the great Tāranātha (1575–1635), minces no words in describing his own mastery of these teachings. He made important contributions to the body of Shangpa literature that can be found among his *Collected Works.*[88] These include both histories of the lineage and probably the most widely used practice guides.

The works of both of these masters were included in the later collections of Jamgön Kongtrul Lodrö Thaye (1813–1900). This great eclectic savant gathered what he considered the most crucial of the Shangpa cycle of teachings in the collection known as *Treasury of Instructions.* They constitute two volumes (eleven and twelve) in the eighteen-volume edition. But only two of our original Niguma texts are included there: *Vajra Lines of the Six Dharmas* and *Niguma's Aspiration Prayer.* Mostly this collection contains works by later holders of the lineage and by Kongtrul himself. All of Kongtrul's own compositions related to the Shangpa tradition are found in his *Treasury of Extensive Teachings*, volumes eight and nine.

The definitive and probably final collection in Tibetan of Shangpa texts was gathered by the late great master and lineage holder Karma Rangjung Kunchab (1905–1989), better known in the west as Kalu Rinpoche. It consists of eleven volumes and is entitled *Indian Source Texts of the Dharma Cycle of Five Golden Dharmas of the Glorious Shangpa.*[89] A later title within the texts, however, admits "Indian *and Tibetan* Source Texts" and is more reflective of the actual contents since very few Indian texts are represented. Our current edition of this is based on the original work from Palpung Monastery in Kham, Eastern Tibet, where Kalu Rinpoche was the retreat master at Tsadra Rinchen Drak, the three-year retreat facility founded by Jamgön Kongtrul.[90] All of the works attributed to Niguma that I have translated here are included in that collection, with the conspicuous exception of the Hevajra sādhana. In addition there are copious compositions and commentaries from all lines of the Shangpa tradition, as well as sources from other lineages that are commonly used as practice material in the tradition.

At present this collection forms the primary source for all practice and is transmitted in its entirety through a series of empowerments and scriptural transmission by lineage holders up to the present. It forms the basis especially of the three-year retreat tradition from Palpung that Kalu Rinpoche continued in India and the West, and in which I was privileged to participate. Most recently, in September of 2008, the young incarnation Kalu Yangsi Rinpoche completed this same retreat based on these same teaching transmissions that were granted to him by the late Bokar Rinpoche, dharma heir of the previous Kalu Rinpoche. The next collection of Shangpa texts will be the highly anticipated English translation of necessary three-year retreat texts that was initiated by Bokar Rinpoche shortly before his passing on August 18, 2004.

Finally, a necessarily brief survey of some available titles in English thus far: In 1978 the scholar Matthew Kapstein wrote an article called "The Shangs-pa bKa'-brgyud: An Unknown Tradition of Tibetan Buddhism." Thanks in part to his own extensive research in this and other articles,[91] this is no longer an entirely appropriate title since the tradition has become rather well known. Well before that, George Roerich's translation of *The Blue Annals*, a historical work by Gö Lotsāwa Zhunnu Pal, was first published in 1949, and contains "The Book on Ko-brag pa and Ni-gu," a required unreadable reading. Then, the not-to-be-forgotten eccentric Yogi Chen received profound instructions in Shangpa practice from Kalu Rinpoche and wrote his own versions and translations into Chinese and sponsored English translations that are still available on his web site. The bibliographer Gene Smith wrote a short introduction to a new edition of the *Shangpa Golden Rosary* in the fifteenth volume of the Smanrtsis Shesrig Spendzod collection entitled "The Shangs pa Bka' brgyud Tradition," first published in 1970 and now found in his *Among Tibetan Texts*. Glen Mullin has presented the Shangpa teachings that were practiced by Gendun Gyatso in *Selected*

Works of the Dalai Lama 2: The Tantric Yogas of Sister Niguma.[92] More recently, at last, there are some entire books dedicated to bringing the tradition to modern readers. Nicole Riggs has translated most of the life stories mentioned above in *Like an Illusion*, and Ngawang Zangpo has provided translations of the spiritual songs of the lineage masters in the volume *Timeless Rapture*, which includes brief stories and translated praises as well. Additionally, some of the Shangpa practices are outlined by him in *Jamgon Kongtrul's Retreat Manual.* An important text used in the Shangpa tradition as a basis for preliminary practices called "Stages in the Path of the Three Types of Person" (*sKyes bu gsum gyi lam rim*) by Tāranātha has been translated as *Essence of Ambrosia* by Willa Baker. Finally, my translation of Jamgön Kongtrul's synopsis of Shangpa esoteric instructions constitutes chapter 5 in Jamgön Kongtrul, *The Treasury of Knowledge: Book Eight, Part Four: Esoteric Instructions.* The brief history of the lineage in the same book is a summary of Kongtrul's, which will soon be available in full in books two, three, and four of *The Treasury of Knowledge.*[93]

THE SHANGPA TRADITION

The story of the Shangpa literature itself of course does not actually reveal what the tradition represents. Through the centuries a distinctive body of practice has developed from these writings that I have been discussing. This body of practice is far from a lost tradition, as some scholars have suggested. At this point in history, it might be said that more practitioners outside of Tibet have had extended retreat experiences of this tradition than any other, due mainly to the activities of Kalu Rinpoche. While it is impossible to do justice here to all of the teachings transmitted in this tradition, I will nevertheless attempt a brief overview to provide a context for Niguma's writings and their importance in the lineage. Particular teachings will be presented more thoroughly in the translations later in the book.

The teachings of Niguma and other Indian masters were received primarily by the Tibetan Khyungpo Naljor, "Yogi of the Garuda Clan."[94] All the texts that are attributed to Niguma were in fact written down by him. Khyungpo Naljor was born in a Tiger Year, probably in the eleventh century, and is reputed to have lived for 150 years, an admittedly suspicious age.[95] It is said that Khyungpo Naljor, like many other founders of lineages, went to India and Nepal to seek out the great teachers:

> Khyungpo Naljor, endowed with five culminations, received the entire dharma treasury—the quintessence of the heart-mind—of one hundred and fifty scholar-adepts. These include four root gurus, thirteen especially exalted gurus, and two ḍākinīs of timeless awareness, Niguma and Sukhasiddhī, who had heard the dharma directly from Buddha Vajradhara. Although this scholar-adept Khyungpo Naljor had progressively studied the [traditions of] Bön and Nyingma and attained accomplishment, the time had come for the [fulfillment of his previous] aspirations for enlightened activities, so he went in search of the profound teachings of sūtra and tantra from the exalted country [of India].[96]

The vast number of teachings he received could be classified into three areas: those of exegesis, debate, and practice. According to Jamgön Kongtrul and textual evidence, only the last of these, the area of practice, has continued. However one might suggest that *Stages in the Path of Illusion: The Commentary* is an exception due to its exegetical character. The teachings of these 150-plus gurus are reduced to five cycles by Kongtrul and others:

> Thus, [Khyungpo] was the unique teacher in the Land of Snows who [provided] unlimited doorways to the dharma and was unrivaled in his enlightened activity. It is just unimaginable! Of all of these, it is only the quintessence of the heart of the last one—the stages of practice—that has lasted until the present day. This is known as the five dharma cycles that are the root of the golden dharmas of Niguma and Sukhasiddhī. That is, the five cycles of Niguma, Sukhasiddhī, Vajrāsana, Maitrīpa, and Rāhula, along with various miscellaneous precepts.[97]

Khyungpo Naljor returned to Tibet and established his seat at Zhangzhong in the Shang region of Western Tsang.[98] Henceforth he was known as the Guru of Shang, and the holders of his lineage became known as the Shangpa Kagyu. It must be noted again that the Tibetan word "kagyu" (*bka' brgyud*) generically means "lineage of Buddha's Word" and is often applied to lineages other than the famous Kagyu tradition founded by Marpa the translator. The Shangpa Kagyu stands as an entirely separate lineage, though it may be argued that in modern times it was swept into the political camp of the Karma Kagyu and shares some masters with that, and other, lineages.

It is reputed that Khyungpo Naljor had eighteen thousand disciples,[99] but in obedience to the specific injunction of Niguma, her teachings were not spread openly for seven generations. This is known as a one-to-one lineage (*gcig brgyud*), and thus it passed from Khyungpo only to his last main disciple, Mokchokpa Rinchen Tsöndrü (1110–1170), and thence sequentially to Wöntön Kyergangpa (or Chökyi Senge, 1143–1216), Sangye Nyentön (or Rigongpa, 1175–1247/1255?), and Drogön Sangye Tönpa (1207–1278). Sangye Tönpa was to be the seventh "jewel," counting the first as Buddha Vajradhara, from whom it is said Niguma received the direct revelations. And so the vajra seal of the one-to-one lineage was lifted by Sangye Tönpa in the thirteenth century. "Then," says Kongtrul, "the world of Jambudvīpa and its surrounding islands were filled with his adept disciples."[100]

From that time, the stream of Niguma's teachings flowed out through many channels, often becoming known as specific lineages within the Shangpa, such as Jonang, Jakchen, Samding, and so forth.[101] In addition, the continuing revelations of Niguma to later adepts in direct lineages added greatly to the streams of transmission and to the overall body of teachings. Though there are these many streams as well as different specialties and inherited teachings (*bka' babs*), the tradition remains quite cohesive. Tāranātha sums it up in this way:

> Although [Niguma's teachings] split into immeasurable different kinds of lineages, due to the fact of being preserved in the ḍākinī's *Testimonial*,[102] neither the word nor the meaning have ever been compromised. Since it is therefore

> uncontrived and uncorrupted, it remains on the highest pinnacle of all practice lineages. This cycle of all of Niguma's instructions in general maintains the perspective of all sūtras and tantras. In particular, it is the heart of the ultimate teachings of the five tantra classes. Even more particularly, and extraordinarily, it is believed to have extracted the essence of the *Saṃvara Ocean* and *Jewel Ocean [Tantras]*.[103]

There are several arrangements of the progressive path of practicing these instructions, such as the extensive, abbreviated, and very abbreviated.[104] However, the framework of the Five Golden Dharmas of the Glorious Shangpa that was passed down in a one-to-one lineage has become the most renowned, while several other practices have become signature Shangpa practices. Here is the short list of those practices.

The Five Golden Dharmas

These form the heart of the Shangpa spiritual practice and are so-called because of the enormous amount of gold that Khyungpo Naljor offered to receive them. They have been diagrammed in the mnemonic device of a living tree:[105]

> The roots are the six dharmas
> The trunk is mahāmudrā
> The branches are the three integrations on the path
> The flowers are the white and red Khecharī
> The fruit is immortal and infallible.

Empowerment

Niguma's original vajra lines come directly from the Buddha Vajradhara. Most of these are included in this collection and will be discussed later. As Niguma points out in *Vajra Lines of the Six Dharmas*,[106] a practitioner must first receive tantric empowerment in order to become spiritually mature and able to best benefit from the practices. This is the usual and necessary preparation for all tantric practice. It presupposes a deep connection with a guru or spiritual mentor who holds the specific lineage and is able to transmit it fully. The initiatory ceremony also involves the taking of pledges that in effect bind one to that preceptor in a sort of covenant (*dam tshig*; Skt. *samaya*). That relationship between the guru and disciple forms the working basis of practice. The primary empowerment required for this tradition comes from either the Five Tantras' Deities or from Chakrasaṃvara.[107]

Preliminaries

The preliminary practices originally seemed to consist of a single purificatory practice unique to the teachings of Niguma called "The Purifier, Hollow Interior of *A*." Though barely mentioned in the *Vajra Lines* and in several early texts by Khyungpo Naljor, it is elaborated in greater detail by later contributors such as Tāranātha.[108] The practice involves visualizing and reciting the syllable "*A*" (pronounced "ah") as it moves through the central channel and throughout the whole body (the hollow interiors) as purifying elixir, inseparable from the guru. It was traditionally presented as the preliminary of the Six Dharmas, specifically of inner heat,[109] perhaps much the same way as the practice of Vajrayoginī is said to prepare the subtle channels of the vajra body for the practice of inner heat yoga. Later the tradition developed along the lines of other sects in maintaining a four- or fivefold preliminary practice commonly known as "ngöndro" (*sngon 'gro*). In that system, the hollow interior practice takes the place of the Vajrasattva mantra practice.

The Roots: Six Dharmas

These consist of the same practices as its better-known cousin, the Six Dharmas of Nāropa. Khyungpo Naljor received the six dharmas several times from Niguma, the first time in a dream from inside the belly of a demigod. In the Shangpa tradition, they are given in verse with their defining characteristics, which can be found in the text translated later:

> The path of methods [of inner heat]— naturally blazing bliss-warmth.

Illusory body—naturally liberated desire and anger.
Dream—naturally pure sleep-delusion.
Lucid clarity—naturally clarified stupidity.
Transference—buddhahood without meditation.
Intermediate state—saṃbhogakāya of the victors.[110]

The Trunk: Amulet Mahāmudrā

This is the particular name given to the Shangpa mahāmudrā tradition not by Niguma herself but because Khyungpo Naljor treasured these teachings so dearly that he wore them constantly in a sandalwood amulet box around his neck. Concerning the more profound interpretations of the name, Tāranātha had this to say: "Other explanations of the term such as that the 'jewel of the awareness mind is inserted in the amulet box of method and wisdom' are just utterly meaningless gossip."[111]

These are the instructions on the core meaning of mental non-engagement (*yid la mi byed pa*). This particular system is also called "three naturally settled states" (*rang babs rnam gsum*) after the initial practice from Niguma of settling the body, speech, and mind in calm abiding and higher insight. Niguma's instructions are translated later in this book. The main practice is to become resolved about the nature of mind itself through the natural freedom from four faults, once that nature has been introduced. Khyungpo Naljor received this teaching from Maitrīpa.[112] The final practice is to maintain the recognition that one's own ordinary mind is the three kāyas of the buddha, as taught by Sukhasiddhī. Special enhancement practices are also associated with it.[113]

The Branches: Three Integrations

In this practice all sights, sounds, and thoughts are understood to be the nature of the guru, yidam, and illusion. This understanding is integrated in life and in a matter of months or years, the three kāyas naturally arise as clarity, emptiness, and great bliss.[114] Niguma's instructions on this are translated later in the book.

The Flowers: White and Red Khecharī

These practices concern white and red forms of Vajrayoginī. Khecharī (Tib. *mkha' spyod*) means to engage in space, synonymous with the Tibetan word for ḍākinī: *khandroma* (*mkha' 'gro ma*), "she who moves in space." Though Khyungpo Naljor reportedly received these teachings from Niguma, the source of the Vajra Lines for White Khecharī is attributed to Atīsha Dipaṃkara Śhrījñāna.[115] The source text for Red Khecharī includes the practice of transference to the Khechara realm at the time of death, instructions that are attributed to Lama Rāhula.[116] Transference teachings based on both ḍākinīs were also transmitted directly to Tangtong Gyalpo by Niguma in his first vision of her, and his teachings on them are well known. The practice is summarized by Jamgön Kongtrul as follows:

> The Conqueror, the Vajra Queen, as the radiance of sun and moon, is aroused through special supplications and the vital points of visualization. The *chaṇḍālī* (inner heat) of bliss-emptiness blazes up based on the release of passion at each of the chakras in the four places. Through those very supports, one comes to engage in the space of great unity.[117]

The Fruit: Immortal and Infallible

The instructions called "Mind and Body, Immortal and Infallible" are actually a combination of the precepts of the deathlessness of the mind that were transmitted to Khyungpo Naljor by Niguma, translated later in this book, and the instructions on the infallible nature of the body that are attributed to Virūpa. Essentially, mind is immortal because it is unborn. The body is merely inert matter and therefore death and other such designations are irrelevant. The realization of immortal body is achieved through thirty-two yogic practices.

Other Shangpa Practices

Six Dharmas of Sukhasiddhī

The other principal female guru of Khyungpo Naljor was Sukhasiddhī, another ḍākinī of timeless awareness. The tradition tells the intriguing story of her transformation from a sixty-year old housewife whose generosity to a beggar caused her expulsion from her home, to a stunning sixteen-year-old devotee of the beer-guzzling adept Virūpa.[118] She too had direct access to the Buddha as Vajradhara. Of the teachings that Khyungpo Naljor received from her, only the most profound Six Dharmas and the Mahāmudrā precepts of pure timeless awareness remain. These more or less parallel the similarly named practices of Niguma, though both systems are practiced separately by modern-day Shangpa practitioners.

Five Tantras' Deities

Khyungpo Naljor received the transmission in these five tantras many times, first individually from Vairochanarakṣhita,[119] and then as a combined practice from Vajrāsana, his principal male guru.[120] He also received the empowerments from Niguma and later in Tibet from Lama Rāhula.[121] The *Indian Source Text of the Glorious Five Tantras* is by Vajrāsana,[122] but this special practice of visualizing the five tantric deities in the five chakras of one's body is said to be originally from *Jewel Ocean Tantra*, a major source of many Shangpa doctrines.[123] It is often said that Khyungpo fully realized the five tantric deities in the five chakras of his body and even appeared to his disciple Mokchokpa in the company of those deities. The practice holds a special significance in the Shangpa tradition for this reason and also, no doubt, because it conveniently combines five of the most complex and weighty tantras in a single practice. According to Tāranātha, the six dharmas are the essence of these five tantras.[124] Kongtrul connects them with other important practices as follows: Hevajra is the culmination of inner heat; Chakrasaṃvara is the culmination of action mudra; Guhyasamāja is the culmination of illusory body and luminous clarity; Mahāmāyā is the culmination of dream; and Vajrabhairava is the culmination of enlightened activity.[125]

In the sādhana itself, Vajrāsana describes the practice as "the essence of all tantras gathered into one."

The Five Deities of Chakrasaṃvara

Niguma's texts translated later in this book cite the *Saṃvara Ocean Tantra* as the source of this tradition. Niguma imparted certain versions of the Chakrasaṃvara, especially the completion phase, to Khyungpo in their initial encounter and, like the mahāmudrā instructions, he kept them in the amulet around his neck. He also received the full practice shortly thereafter from a certain Hidden Yogin.[126] The practice text attributed to Niguma translated here is quite remarkable and considerably different than the one found in the later Shangpa tradition. The more usual visualization, such as that found in Kalu Rinpoche's daily practice,[127] involves Chakrasaṃvara with Vajrayoginī as the central deities in union surrounded by four ḍākinīs.

There is also a practice of visualizing just the ḍākinīs without Chakrasaṃvara called *Five Ḍākinīs* (*mkha' 'gro sde lnga*) in the Shangpa lineage. The relevant texts of this were arranged by Kongtrul, drawing on Tāranātha's *Mine of Jewels*, and seem not to date earlier than that, though it is described as an esoteric instruction of Khyungpo Naljor, received directly from the five ḍākinīs themselves and in turn from the Lion-faced ḍākinī.[128]

The Four Deities Combined

In the seeming fondness for simplifying practices, this creation phase practice groups four beloved deities into one visualization: Six-armed Mahākāla, Vajrayoginī, Avalokiteshvara, and Green Tārā, with one's guru as Vajradhara in the center. Thus it is considered a kind of guru yoga, bringing the practitioner's mind into union with that of the guru in many forms. Kongtrul explains in his guidance manual to this practice that these four deities first actually appeared to the great adept Shavari[129]and then were codified in a practice manual by Maitrīpa. Khyungpo Naljor apparently heard it from him, and it became known as the Blessing of Constant Four Deities.[130] However, the main source for this current transmission was again Lama Rāhula. After receiving it from him in Tibet, Khyungpo Naljor could be seen by his fortunate disciples actually manifesting as these four deities. There is also a practice of the four deities individually (*lha bzhi'i sgos sgrub*).

Six-Armed Mahākāla, "Chakdrukpa"

The special dharma protector of the lineage is six-armed Mahākāla, or the Swift Protector of Timeless Awareness, a wrathful emanation of Avalokiteshvara. The particular iconography of the protector is distinguished from the Gelukpa counterpart by having the right foot bent up at the ankle, rather than bent at the knee. There is also a peaceful, white Chakdrukpa specializing in prosperity. Khyungpo Naljor received these practices and empowerments from Maitrīpa in the Shavari line and from Rāhula in the Atayavajra line.[131] This wisdom protector also serves in the most treasured guru yoga practice called *Dwelling in the Heart*, where guru and protector are inseparable.[132] Tāranātha wrote a "biography" of Chakdrukpa and a history of the transmission that is found in the *Golden Rosary of Shangpa Biographies* after those of all the lineage lamas.[133] Maitrīpa's own story and explanation of the protector as told by him to Khyungpo Naljor is included in the latter's biography.

Extraordinary Practices

There are certain practices unique to the Shangpa tradition that have been passed down orally through the lineage and have historically been closely guarded. On his third trip to the West in 1977–1978, the late head of the lineage, Khyabje Kalu Rinpoche, decided the time was right to spread one of these practices. It is called Uncommon Calm Abiding and Higher Insight (*thun mon ma yin pa'i zhi gnas lhag mthong*). In addition to the common practices of calm abiding and higher insight, such as those found in the Karma Kagyu tradition, this version employs special visualizations involving abstract forms of the elements and the aggregates. In some sense they might be called the vajrayāna version of calm abiding and higher insight. Instructions are not found in the collections, but were spread far and wide by Kalu Rinpoche.[134]

Stages in the Path of Illusion 1

INTRODUCTION

NIGUMA AS the embodiment of illusion may be a distinctive and fascinating twist, but her emphasis on teaching illusion is at least as old as the Buddha. In sūtras and tantras beyond count the Buddha spoke of the illusory nature of all perceived phenomena, primarily as a way to cut through attachment. In the earliest sermons, a primary focus was in explaining the lack of intrinsic, findable existence in the person as an individual as well as in all other phenomena. Later this developed into the full-blown doctrine of emptiness (*śūnyatā*), based on mahāyāna sūtras known collectively as the perfection of wisdom (*prajñāpāramitā*). The philosophy based on those sūtras, madhyamaka, refuted every aspect of existence and nonexistence. Through the rigors of logic and reasoning, when followed to their conclusion, it is discovered that there can be no conclusion, and that things cannot be found. This approach, however, may not imbue the logician with the visceral experience of phenomena that may well be empty and yet undeniably appear clearly. How can one understand such an idea that is ultimately ineffable, a concept beyond conceptual mind?

THE MAGIC

The Buddha apparently thought that providing illustrations would be a way in to this mystery, a way to get a handle on it through the imaging mind rather than just through the intellect. This is why one finds discussion of examples or similes of illusion almost as much as discussion of emptiness itself and its integral ideas of contingency and impermanence. The two most common images are dream and illusion since both provide excellent metaphors of our general condition. Dream especially is considered a fortunate fact of human life. How else could we understand our range of reactive emotions to ultimately unreal events if we had not experienced them all in dreams?

There are well-known lists of eight, ten, and twelve similes of illusion, although there is considerable variation. A typical list of the eight examples of illusion consists of (1) dreams, (2) illusions, (3) hallucinations, (4) mirages, (5) moon reflected in water, (6) echoes, (7) fairy cities, and (8) emanations or projections. If extended to twelve, the most commonly added are (9) water bubbles, (10) lightning, (11) mirror reflections, and of course (12) rainbows, which were discussed in the introduction.[1] Further examples are eye disease, wheels made by a whirling fire brand, the reflection of trees in water, perceived hair-nets, water whirling about in a mirage, dim-eyed people in the dark, a corpse animated by a ghost, machines, clouds, stars, mirages in the air, reflections in the eyes, a barren woman's child, and many more. The popular *Diamond Sūtra*, for instance, states:

> As stars, blurred vision, candles,
> illusions, dew, bubbles,
> dreams, lightning, and clouds;
> so should all that is conditioned be seen.[2]

The term being translated as "illusion" is *māyā* in Pāli and Sanskrit. It appears as an item in all versions of the lists, as well as being the overall concept that each example is illustrating. As a specific term, "māyā" has a history of its own. In its earliest usage it seems to be precisely "deceit." For instance, in *The Path of Purification* (*Visuddhimagga*), a comprehensive summary of the doctrine and practice of the Pāli canon by the fifth-century Indian Buddhaghosa, it appears only as one of the many traits of a person of "greedy temperament," and as one of an even larger number of flaws that must be overcome for someone to be called "blessed" (*bhagavā*).[3]

Another interesting occurrence early on is in the name of the Buddha's mother, Queen Māyā. It would be tempting to draw some profound conclusions about the nature of women and the doctrine of illusoriness, but that must be a later doctrine as there is little evidence of it here. Rather, it seems to be a pleasant twist on its meaning as "deceit" in the sense of the beguiling charm that robs men of their good sense, like many such names for women.[4] The *Sūtra of the Vast Display* (*Lalitavistara*) on the life of the Buddha, says:

> Ravishing the heart like a magical creation,
> she is called Māyādevī, Goddess of Illusion.[5]

There is a particular sense that developed from the term "māyā" as deceit, which is evident in the lists of types of illusion: the idea of a magic show that is intentionally created by an illusionist. It has been variously translated as "mock show," "apparition," "magic show," "wizardry," "enchantment," "wonderment," and so on. Māyā was translated into Tibetan as *sgyu ma*, (from *sgyu*, "deceit"). This in itself can mean the illusionist as well as the illusion that he or she creates, though to be more specific the texts will use *sgyu ma mkhan* for the illusionist. The story is often told in the sūtras of a magician who uses sticks and stones to create an apparition, such as this one narrated in the *Sūtra That Unravels the Intent* (*Saṁdhinirmocana*):

> Child of good lineage, for example, a magician (*sgyu ma mkhan*) or a magician's able student, standing at the crossing of four great roads, after gathering grasses, leaves, twigs, pebbles or stones, displays various magical forms, such as a herd of elephants, a cavalry, chariots, and infantry; collections of gems, pearls, lapis lazuli, conch-shells, crystal, and coral; collections of wealth, grain, treasuries, and granaries.
>
> When those sentient beings who have childish natures, foolish natures, or confused natures—who do not realize that these are grasses, leaves, twigs, pebbles and stones—see or hear these things, they think: 'This herd of elephants that appears, exists; these cavalry, chariots, infantry, gems, pearls,

> lapis lazuli, conch-shells, crystal, coral, wealth, grain, treasuries, and granaries that appear, exist.[6]

The modern reader might feel a sense of incredulity that there were apparently magicians in ancient India who could produce such illusions and people who actually believed them, at least until they discovered the pebbles and sticks. Few people these days are fooled by magic shows, and so this may seem like an obscure example and an outdated simile. At the same time, few people believe that motion pictures are real, and yet the theater can be full of laughing, crying, or screaming people covering their eyes. Sometimes they have to purposefully remember that it is "only a movie." The metaphorical value of a movie is the same as that of a magic show.

Māyā in particular is an example of an illusion that is purposefully created, unlike the natural phenomena of the other similes, such as rainbows and mirages. This is an apt metaphor, then, for mind—the illusionist—that under the influence of habitual cognitive and emotional obscurations perceives reality as solid entities permanently fixed in their status as good, bad, or neutral, despite all evidence to the contrary. There is almost a sense of purposefulness in this creation of the magic show and then an intentional ignoring of its illusory status. One wants to believe in the show and wills it to be real—to provide entertainment, to corroborate emotional response, and to verify one's very existence.

The original Indian idea was that we are duped by māyā. The whole display of our senses has tricked us into believing it and thus seduces us into the world of suffering. And the illusionist is that old trickster, one's own mind. But when this illusory nature is recognized to be just that, one is released from the bondage of the magic show, at which time it becomes a wonderful spectacle, even a display of the unimpeded creativity and freedom of mind. Then māyā itself is both the medium for this realization and the expression of it. This conscious and intentional method of relating to all phenomena as illusion is thus cast in a totally positive light on the spiritual path, a complete turn-around from the original negative valuation of it as deceit. Now illusion is seen as illumination and opportunity. The nature of our relationship with it is the salient point, rather than its own nature, which certainly does not exist anyway, in any way. Āryadeva says:

> Since everything is an illusory display,
> it is possible to attain enlightenment.[7]

The transformation of the māyā concept from something to escape to something to engage may be loosely correlated with the shift of emphasis on understanding emptiness that emerged in the mahāyāna teachings. A further development may be seen in the vajrayāna teachings with the esoteric instruction known as Illusory Body (*sgyu lus*). This occurs as one of the Six Dharmas of Niguma and in other configurations of completion stage practices in many lineages.

According to Jamgön Kongtrul, there are four levels of illusory body practice.[8] (1) The *literal* practice is simply to understand all phenomena as the embodiment of illusion. (2) The *general* practice of illusory body is a more specific application of the similes in meditation to develop the understanding that all appearances lack true existence despite their appearance as real. In classical vajrayāna methodology, this will involve seeing oneself and the environment as deities in the mandala, still in conjunction with the eight or twelve similes. This is called the special or pure illusory body in the general sense. (3) The *hidden* sense of illusory body is the application in completion phase yoga of the realizations from the previous practices. This involves the dissolution of the energy currents (*prāṇa*) in the central channel and, ultimately, the appearance of a divine form based only on energy current and mind. This is the true goal of illusory body practice in the context of the six dharmas. (4) The *ultimate* illusory body is the same as the rainbow body and has already been discussed in the context of Niguma's level of attainment.

This range—and change—of the meaning of illusion is also expressed simply as illusion that is "impure" and "pure;" or "false" and "genuine." Thus the great Nyingma master Longchen Rabjam (1301–1363), in the commentary to his famous *Natural Ease in Illusion*, says:

> All dharmas of samsara, appearing to the mind, develop from the force of habitual propensity of the mind. Therefore

> that is called "erroneously conceived illusion." All dharmas of nirvana, appearing to timeless awareness, are the Bodies of the natural radiance of intrinsic awareness and appearances of timeless awareness; a spontaneous presence that is beyond things and characteristics of dharmas. Therefore that is called "genuine illusion."[9]

Longchenpa's text bears many resemblances to Niguma's treatise, *Stages in the Path of Illusion*. Indeed the autocommentaries to both works cite so many of the same sources that it seems either that one copied from the other (and if chronology and authorship are true, that would mean Longchenpa copied from Niguma), or that they both utilized the same earlier Indian sources. However, their general approach is quite different. Longchenpa's work is one of a trilogy,[10] each volume offering a method to rest and restore the mind: in the nature of mind itself, in meditative stability, or in illusion. In the latter, he discusses at length the application of practice through each of the eight similes of illusion. Each of the eight is further correlated with the eight qualities of dependently arisen phenomena mentioned in Nāgārjuna's famous opening verse in his *Root Verses of the Middle*.[11]

Niguma's treatise, on the other hand, speaks only of illusion as the over-all theory of illusion, which at the same time implies the one example of the magic show. She then shows how one must engage this perspective step by step to travel the bodhisattva path to enlightenment.

Stages of the Path

Stages in the Path of Illusion and its *Commentary* do not pursue the hidden or ultimate levels of illusory body except for the occasional verses. Niguma leaves this for the actual practice of illusory body in the context of the Six Dharmas. Rather, *Stages in the Path of Illusion* applies the attitude of realization indicated by Kongtrul's first and second levels of illusory body to the complexities of the bodhisattva's spiritual journey: the factors of enlightenment, perfections, paths, and grounds.

The idea of "path" (*mārga*, Tib. *lam*) is as central and ubiquitous in

Buddhism as the concept of emptiness. The multileveled structure of the spiritual journey may even seem ironic in light of those teachings on emptiness. Yet as soon as a goal was identified—freedom from suffering—then some way to get there from here had to be identified. The path theory has prominence of place in one of the earliest formulations of the Buddha: the four noble truths. There is suffering, it has a cause, removing the cause will eliminate the suffering, and there is a way to do that: "the path." The Buddhist path describes a journey from the bondage of ignorance to the freedom of complete awakening. Every teaching to be practiced that is attributed to the Buddha or to enlightened beings of all times and in all directions makes up the path. One could say that it is a synonym of "*buddhadharma*." It is not just a random grab bag of methods (though at times it certainly seems so) but is presented as an enlightened and exact formula of spiritual practice and patterns of behavior that progressively remove the factors that obstruct progress and develop the powers one needs to traverse the path to its end. Even though one might say that to wake up from the sleep of ignorance could happen in an instant, there is a gradual journey of many moments to get to that instant. And even though one might say that to reach the goal is to arrive at the starting point and know the place for the first time, there is still the attempt to impose a linear order onto the circular journey, to make sense of it. To ask "how far?"

The Buddha's teaching of the path to awakening is predicated on the one fact accepted by all Buddhists: that he himself had traveled it and was describing it from the vantage point of its destination. "This is how I got here, and therefore you could get here by that same route." Details of the path, in fact, seem to be originally based on the literature concerning the previous lives of the Buddha, in the same way that the ideal Buddhist aspirant is based on the Buddha as arhant and later on the Buddha in his former life as bodhisattva.[12] As the path descriptions grew—and grow they did, into what appears now as more of a maze than a road—two functions can be discerned: to be a source of faith and a source of guidance. The path is both *descriptive* (of what the Buddha, or any idealized person, did), and *prescriptive* (of what their followers should do). Distinguishing these two functions may help to understand the intimidating amount of material about the path. Sometimes, as in the most inclusive tripartite path description of ethical discipline (*śīla*), meditative absorption (*samādhi*), and wisdom or intelligence (*prajñā*), one can engage it as advice and undertake any number of practices that fall under those three headings to lead a wholesome life that tends toward spiritual development. Sometimes, as in the descriptions of even the first ground (*bhūmi*) of the bodhisattva, where one is capable of feats such as visiting a hundred buddha realms, one should perhaps simply appreciate that there are great beings with such powers. Because, as Donald Lopez puts it:

> That path was increasingly seen as more and more protracted, encompassing lifetimes of practice, finally reaching, in the Mahāyāna, the generally accepted length of three periods of innumerable aeons (which Har Dayal has kindly calculated for us at 384×10^{58} years).[13]

Finding one's way through the intricacies of path literature is no task for the timid. It has been the occupation of scholars since the beginning, all trying to make sense of it while adding lists upon lists. There is no point in repeating all of that here, as it would be, indeed, all of the buddhadharma. There are several recent publications that will provide readers with more than they will ever need to know.[14] But the subjects of Niguma's texts deserve at least brief mention. These subjects combine four enumerations that appear to have developed somewhat organically along separate lines and in various texts, and were later merged into one comprehensive map painstakingly configured by mahāyāna scholars (who were apparently unaware of the emptiness of categories).

The basis of it all should be mentioned first as the starting place of the path. This refers to the idea of an underlying stratum or foundation that supports all aspects of mind and perception, and so is termed literally the ground of everything or all-base (*ālaya*, Tib. *kun gzhi*). The concept of all-base was articulated in the yogāchāra philosophy developed primarily by Maitreya, Asaṅga, and Vasubandhu based on sūtras of the third turning of the wheel of dharma. Although not posited as a "self" or existent entity, it nevertheless is used in attempts to explain the continuity of karmic actions and as such is sometimes translated as "storehouse." It is a neutral base or ground on which everything occurs. It is the ground of timeless awareness and at the same time the basis of delusion, in which aspect it is known as "all-ground consciousness." As such, it is the base of an eightfold scheme of consciousness used by yogāchārins to describe human experience. There is an enormous range of interpretation of all-base; Niguma's version in her *Commentary* follows the classical yogāchāra description with a leaning toward what later became known as an "other-emptiness" viewpoint. In Niguma's teaching, it is the illusory basis upon which the illusory path proceeds to reach the illusory goal of realizing the illusoriness of that basis.

The thirty-seven factors or *dharmas* that are conducive to or concordant with awakening seem to have very early beginnings. They are mentioned throughout the early sūtras and in the abhidharma and are explained at length in *The Path of Purification*.[15] The list includes some very well-known concepts such as the eightfold path of the noble ones and the four foundations of mindfulness. They are as follows: Four foundations of mindfulness (1–4), four renunciations (5–8), four supports for miraculous activity (9–12), five faculties (13–17), five powers (18–22), seven branches of enlightenment (23–29), and the eightfold path of the noble ones (30–37). This represents just a slight shift of the progressive list in the theravādin tradition, where the eightfold path is listed before the seven branches of enlightenment.

The five paths (*pañcamārga*; Tib. *lam lnga*) are also an early development. They emerged as the predominant schema from among what Kongtrul calls "limitless classifications"; ways of dividing up the basic Buddhist path-theory.[16] "The Sanskrit word "mārga" (path) derives from the verbal root *mārg* (to seek; to search; to strive to attain; to go) and has a wide range of meanings, such as "way," "tracks" (of wild animals), "passage," "course," "channel," "range," "search," "inquiry," "manner," "method," "practice," and, specifically, "the way or path pointed out by Buddha for escape from the misery of existence."[17] Kongtrul explains that the "essence of 'path' (that on which one progresses) is that, through having entered it, it serves as a stepping-stone for progressing toward more superior mundane or supramundane states."[18] Niguma's own verse on the matter defines it as follows:

> Since calm abiding and higher insight
> are combined together,
> and since it is supreme,
> and one desires to arrive, it is called "path."[19]

And the commentary elaborates:

> The essence of the path is that it is the way of combining calm abiding and higher insight. The literal definition is that since one desires to arrive at supreme enlightenment it is called "path." The divisions are the path of accumulation, the path of joining, the path of seeing, the path of meditation, and the path of consummation.[20]

The ten (or so) grounds can be found in various enumerations in the scriptures.[21] The earliest mention of ten grounds may be the *Mahāvastu*, a compilation of stories and traditions about the Buddha.[22] There the ten grounds or levels (*bhūmi*; Tib. *sa*) occur in the context of the Buddha's previous life as the bodhisattva. This represents a pre-mahāyāna formulation and may or may not be the source of later classifications, as the ten mentioned in the *Mahāvastu* do not bear the same names as those of the later standardized lists found in mahāyāna sūtras such as the *Sūtra on the Ten Grounds*[23] and in treatises such as the *Bodhisattva Grounds*[24] composed in Sanskrit in the late fourth century by Asaṅga. In fact, in the *Entry into the Middle Way*, another classical treatise devoted to the subject, Chandrakīrti declares that the scheme is peculiar to the mahāyāna tenets.[25] The most commonly studied authoritative text on the matter is Maitreya's commentary on the perfection of wisdom, *The Ornament of Clear Realization*.[26]

The Sanskrit word "bhūmi" has several definitions depending on which etymology it is given.[27] In Tibetan it was translated as "sa," meaning literally "ground" and by connotation "level" or "stage." In her commentary to the following verses in *Stages in the Path*, Niguma states simply, "The literal definition is that since they are the support for all qualities or the basis for progressing higher they are called 'grounds.'"

> The combined calm abiding and higher insight
> that transcends the mundane
> as unfixated naturally arisen illusion
> is nonconceptual timeless awareness.
>
> Being the foundation of the pure qualities,
> and [because] one progresses higher, they are called
> "grounds."
> The divisions are Very Joyful and so on,
> with ten early signs that one should know.[28]

These verses also serve to remind us that the development of calm abiding and higher insight is, in short, the Buddhist path. The names for the ten grounds that have become standardized (though not in English translation!) in the mahāyāna are: Very Joyful, Stainless, Illuminating, Radiant, Difficult to Overcome, Manifest, Gone Far, Immovable, Excellent Intelligence, and Cloud of Dharma. The tenth ground, Cloud of Dharma, was traditionally equated with buddhahood, but as discussed earlier, there has been a tendency to add further and further levels in the vajrayāna tradition—now up to fourteen.

The six or ten perfections refer to qualities that a bodhisattva practices and develops on the path and ultimately "perfects." Thus there is both a sense of path and of fruition. In later Pāli texts a list of ten such perfections (Pāli: *pāramī*) were added to the canon, possibly as a retroactive addition from the mahāyāna.[29] They differ slightly from the mahāyāna list and include two of the four immeasurables: love and equanimity.[30]

In the mahāyāna, the formula of the six perfections "was evolved after a process of selection and experimentation."[31] The list is found throughout Sanskrit literature and makes up the main path of the bodhisattva once the thought of enlightenment has been aroused. In that sense it is comparable to the eightfold path of the noble ones in early teachings of the Buddha. The Sanskrit term *pāramitā* was translated into Tibetan as *pha rol tu phyin pa*, meaning literally "to arrive over there," which was perhaps suggested by the addition of the term "*ita*" (gone to the beyond). There are many variables, however, and there has been much discussion about the actual meaning and derivation of the term.[32] Consequently, there does not seem to be any adequate English translation to capture the full range of meaning, and one has to fall back on the deficient but easy term "perfection." Other options are "transcendent action," "transcendental virtue," highest perfection," and "complete attainment."

With some overlap of the earlier list, the six pāramitās are generosity, ethical discipline, patience, diligence, meditative stability, and wisdom. A common way to understand the six perfections in terms of the path and its result is to regard the regular practice of the first five—generosity and so on—as the actions that the aspiring bodhisattva must practice. When the sixth—the perfection of wisdom—is applied to those first five, then those practices become truly "transcendent" or "perfect" and are the actual fruitional qualities possessed by a noble bodhisattva, which is to say, one who traverses the bhūmis. Kongtrul also states that the six pāramitās bring about the unfolding of the modes of the ten bhūmis according to the ways of engaging cognition.[33]

At some point four more pāramitās were added to the list: skill in methods, aspirations, power, and timeless awareness. These four are obviously associated mainly with the higher levels of fruition. A marriage of numerical harmony was destined for these two lists of ten, the pāramitās and the bhūmis, which might not have been an accident. In the *Sūtra on the Ten Grounds*, the ten pāramitās are correlated one-to-one with the ten grounds. The common scheme of six perfections was perhaps expanded to ten precisely for this purpose.[34]

All of the Above

Thus begins the intricate process of spiritual cartography and matchmaking that occupies much of the mahāyāna literature. The thirty-seven factors conducive to awakening are lined up alongside a steady progression in the first three paths, the ten grounds are grafted on to the five paths beginning with the onset of the third path, and the perfections are perfected in a steady sequence on the grounds. The whole map is fine-tuned even further by adding subcategories and levels within each of the five paths; thus there are the lesser, intermediate, and greater levels of the Path of Accumulation, and so forth. It is unfortunate that the ancient writings did not include charts, such as the one presented on pages 52–53,[35] which make the path-map easier to visualize.

Why and Wherefore?

As the subject progresses in complexity, the question constantly arises "to what end?" Although one might master the correlations of the chart, how does one actually apply the information to one's own path? For if one cannot do that, it certainly seems to be an exercise in frustration.[36] The idea is often presented that the complexity of the proposed path reflects the complexity of the defilements that it purports to purify.[37] This sounds true but still begs the question whether knowledge of such minutiae actually aids the purification process or confounds it. Certainly examination of defilements is de rigueur for Buddhists. Yet how important is it to identify and even name the process and one's location in a sort of Buddhist GPS? The question is especially pertinent given that the mahāyāna list in particular seems to be referencing something we can only hope to achieve, even at the very initial stages. The process of trying to apply the categories to oneself and one's own journey seems fraught with the dangers of straying into error, developing arrogance, and just plain wasting time.

As I suggested before, one can gain the benefit only if one distinguishes those aspects that are meant to be applied as personal practices now, "starting from where you are," and those that might inspire confidence in and credulity toward great spiritual beings. In suggesting these two modes of understanding the topic, I am not saying that the inherent ability of all beings to attain buddhahood is in doubt. I am just seeking a way through the maze of endlessly proliferating path-categories toward the exit light of what must somehow be edifying knowledge. Here is another, perhaps similar, way elaborated by Robert E. Buswell, Jr. and Robert M. Gimello in the foreword to their collection *Paths to Liberation*:

> It may well be that the persistent Buddhist tendency to elaborate on the path by dividing it into multiple and further subdivisible stages, although perhaps begun as a kind of "cartography" of the terrain of Buddhist religious experience, led retrospectively to creation of a spiritual pedigree for the ideal person such as might render that person worthy of emulation by others. Thus the process of mārga construction, whereby the path is built step by step, may be said to define a necessary stage in the evolutions of a tradition, viz., the stage of transition from the category of the particular, the idiosyncratic, or the biographical to the category of the universal and the generic. In this way the experience of one person is made accessible, in principle, to all. By organizing experience into sequences of stages, the transcendent goal presumed to have been achieved by spiritual exemplars at the source of the tradition is objectified, codified, and made available to ordinary Buddhist practitioners. The detailed ordering of experience that these schemata of the path provide offers practitioners an explicit guide to achieving the original and archetypal goal for themselves. The path thus mediates between the enlightened and the unenlightened.[38]

Nothing to Get Hung About

And if that doesn't work, well, you might try viewing the path as illusion.

This would not be a new concept. As mentioned before, the simile of illusion covers everything and has been used to qualify the Buddhist path specifically at least since the appearance of the perfection of wisdom sūtras. For example, in the *Perfection of Wisdom in Eight-thousand Lines*, the dream/illusion simile is used to describe the four stages on the path of the arhants, as well as of pratyekabuddhas and buddhas:

> Children of gods, all dharmas are like illusion, like dream. Stream-winning is also like illusion, like dream. The fruition of stream-winning is also like illusion, like dream. In the

> same way once-returning and coming back with its fruition, nonreturning and its fruition, and arhants are also like illusion, like dream. Arhanthood itself is also like illusion, like dream. Pratyekabuddhas are also like illusion, like dream. Pratekyabuddhahood itself is also like illusion, like dream. Genuine complete buddhas are also like illusion, like dream. Genuine complete buddhahood is also like illusion, like dream.[39]

In the commentary to the *Stages in the Path of Illusion*, Niguma cites a similar passage in the *Perfection of Wisdom in Eighteen Thousand Lines* that names all thirty-seven factors of enlightenment as being like illusions and dreams. But what is the point of analyzing the path down to its tiniest track if anyway it is just illusion?

Illusion gives us the perfect metaphor to make sense of the reality of emptiness and appearance; of primordially present awake awareness and an impossibly protracted path to enlightenment. In a way it is the naming of the area between paradoxes, of the creative space in the tension of opposites. The path makes sense only on the level of illusion: a journey that must be negotiated, carefully and with determination, but treading lightly and lightheartedly without becoming trapped in the doldrums of believing in it. The path and its fruition exist only as illusion, but without that marvel there is no path and no fruition. Then you are stuck. The difference between being stuck in samsara and free in nirvana is only the illusory journey on the illusory path. Careful, lest it disappear or solidify.

5 Paths	10 Grounds	10 Perfections
1. Path of Accumulation a. lesser		
b. intermediate		
c. greater		
2. Path of Application a. warmth b. peak		
c. acceptance d. supreme dharma		
3. Path of Seeing	1. Very Joyful	1. Generosity
4. Path of Meditation	2. Stainless 3. Illuminating 4. Radiant 5. Difficult to Overcome 6. Manifest 7. Gone Far	2. Ethical discipline 3. Patience 4. Diligence 5. Meditative stability 6. Wisdom 7. Skillful method
5. Path of Consummation	8. Immovable 9. Excellent Intelligence 10. Cloud of Dharma	8. Aspiration 9. Power 10. Timeless awareness

37 Factors Conducive to Enlightenment

four direct applications of mindfulness

1. of the body
2. of sensations
3. of the mind
4. of phenomena

four [aspects of] genuine renunciation

5. not to generate vice and unvirtuous factors that have not yet arisen
6. to renounce those vices and unvirtuous factors that have arisen
7. to generate virtuous factors that have not yet arisen
8. to keep and increase the virtuous factors that have arisen

four supports of miraculous ability: meditative absorptions distinguished by

9. determination
10. diligence
11. intention
12. conduct (or analysis)

five faculties

13. faith
14. diligence
15. mindfulness
16. absorption
17. wisdom

five powers

18. faith
19. diligence
20. mindfulness
21. absorption
22. wisdom

seven branches of enlightenment

23. mindfulness
24. revealing phenomena
25. diligence
26. joy
27. agility
28. absorption
29. equanimity

eightfold path of the noble ones

30. genuine view
31. genuine thought
32. genuine speech
33. genuine completed action
34. genuine livelihood
35. genuine effort
36. genuine mindfulness
37. genuine absorption

STAGES IN THE PATH OF ILLUSION

Sanskrit: *Māyādhanakramanāma*
Tibetan: *sGyu ma lam gyi rim pa* (*"Gyuma Lamrim"*)[40]

Homage to all buddhas and bodhisattvas.

1. I pay homage to you, mind itself:
primordial lucid clarity by nature,
[satisfying] all needs and desires,
like a wish-fulfilling jewel.

2. For the benefit of others I will explain
Stages in the Path of Illusion,
the central theme that is the quintessence
of the minds of the ocean of victors.

3. Beginningless basic space itself,
primordially nonexistent illusion,
is the seed of all phenomena,
the buddha nature, and virtue.
It is known as the essential base of all.

4. If those endowed with excellent faith, diligence,
 and devotion
meditate on the illusion-like [nature]
of illusion-like phenomena,
illusion-like buddhahood will manifest.

5. So listen well as I duly explain
the five paths and ten grounds [as illusion].

6. The entire animate and inanimate [world]
and whatever appears to the five senses
is all the empty appearance of the deity's Body.[41]
The deity's Body is limitless illusion.

7. The wise should take into practice
all the factors of enlightenment
as inseparable from the illusion of the deity's Body.

8. The stages on the five paths and ten grounds
are traversed on the strength of devotion.
The sublime vital point of the tantras' intention
is never to be separate from the guru's manifestation.

9. Thus, the extraordinary practice
[is to experience] all the sights and sounds of phenomena
as the nature of the deity and guru.

10. Shapes, colors, the five poisons,
and types of accomplishing activity[42] are the five buddha
families.
Whatever appears is appearance and emptiness:
creation and completion and their unity.

11. One should know [this through] the purifying vase[43]
[empowerment],
the secret [empowerment of] inseparable white and red [essences],
the third [empowerment which is the] aspect of bliss,
and the fourth inexpressible [empowerment].

12. Where there is bliss, clarity, and nonthought,
there the three kāyas are naturally arising.
Clarity without concept is twofold knowledge.

[The Paths]

13. Since calm abiding and higher insight
are combined together,
and since it is supreme,
and one desires to arrive, it is called "path."

[The Path of Accumulation]

14. The Path of Accumulation
is to renounce vice, however small,
and take up virtue, gathering accumulations
in order to realize the illusion of the nature of phenomena.

15. There are greater, intermediate, and lesser levels,
each formulated with further fourfold division:
four mindfulnesses, four renunciations,
and four supports of miraculous action.

16. Carelessness and impaired mindfulness cause downfalls.
Therefore mindfulness is explained first.

17. To practice mindfulness and awareness of
the illusion of inseparable appearance-emptiness
of this heartless body *as* the Victor's Body
is the direct application of mindfulness to the body.

18. The reference-points of pleasure, pain, equanimity,
and the sensations of all designated phenomena
understood as [mere] sensation
are the direct application of mindfulness to sensation.

19. All phenomena are mind,
yet mind will not be found inside or outside.
Mind not existing at all [except as] illusion
is the application of mindfulness to the mind.

20. Shrāvakas and pratyekabuddhas
label all things as phenomena.
[To know them as] random labels of mere names
is the application of mindfulness to phenomena.

21. Suffering is caused by nonvirtues.
Since those who desire freedom from it
regard all nonvirtue as though it were poison,
there are four genuine renunciations.

22. In order not to generate vice and unvirtuous factors
that have not arisen,
arouse determination, effort, and attention
to fully engage in what is genuine.

23. In order to renounce vice and unvirtuous factors
that have arisen,
arouse determination, effort, and so forth;
understand it the same as above.

24. In order to generate virtuous attributes
that have not arisen,
energetically arouse determination,
effort, and so forth, as above.

25. In order that virtuous attributes that have arisen may remain
and increase without any diminishing,
and not be lost or wasted,
arouse determination and so forth as above.

26. As for "arousing determination not to generate
vice and unvirtuous factors
that have not arisen,"
the proper mental engagement is to
practice with whatever appears as illusion.
Thus unvirtuous factors will not occur.

27. Furthermore, "vice and unvirtuous factors"
are whatever is incongruous

with ethical discipline, meditative absorption, and wisdom.
The mental engagement is that
in order to renounce those nonvirtues,
determination and so forth must be developed.
That is the idea of the first genuine renunciation.

28. Furthermore, the "unvirtuous factors"
are desirous attachment, angry aggression,
and unaware dullness.
The mental engagement is
[contemplation] on foulness pacifying desire,
love pacifying aggression, and
[contemplation of] interdependence pacifying stupidity.
Knowing that they are without intrinsic nature
pacifies all afflictive emotion.
That is the idea of the second genuine renunciation.

29. In order to generate virtuous factors that have not arisen,
the determination to accomplish buddhahood
by developing determination and effort
is the root of all roots of virtue.
The practice of mental attention is the supreme virtue.
That is the idea of the third genuine renunciation.

30. In order that virtuous factors that have arisen not diminish
or be wasted, arouse determination,
effort, mental attention, and engage the genuine.
The practice of illusion [regarding] the roots of virtue is that
by dedicating them to [attaining] omniscience,
rather than remaining in the three realms,
ultimately they will never be wasted.
That is the idea of the fourth genuine renunciation.

31. Those who desire to cross the ocean of suffering
of cyclic existence and arrive at the ground

that transcends misery
[need] the four absorptions of miraculous activity.

32. All phenomena are like illusion.
Unafraid of unreal, unlimited phenomena,
renouncing them, one is determined.
That is the absorption of determination.

33. When practicing the illusion of a determined goal,
once worldly attachment is discarded
and sloth abandoned, one is endowed with diligence.
Then it is the absorption of diligence.

34. With that unceasing diligence,
mind is without reference to anything inside or out.
Free of fixation, one-pointed focus on illusion
is the absorption of mind.

35. With that one-pointed absorption,
integrating unreal illusion on the path
during all moving, walking, lying down, and sitting,
is the conduct, so it is [the absorption] of conduct.[44]

36. The absorption of conduct and the others are all called
"the meditative absorptions that are the support of miraculous
ability
having the volition of renunciation."

37. The nature of meditative absorption
is to support miraculous activity.
Without fixation all mistaken factors
are genuinely renounced
and turned into virtue and genuine virtue.

38. Not to conceive even those virtuous factors
makes one free of concept,

so absorption is the nature of the miraculous.
Through that stainless, sublime path
one arrives in the genuine place,
so they are called "supports of miraculous activity."

39. The signs on the Path of Accumulation are faith and diligence,
and since ethical discipline is pure, the sense faculties
shun even the slightest misdeed.

40. One knows that external objects of desire and aggression
arise in oneself and are not "other"
and that that arising itself is illusion.
Day and night one's conduct is that of total renunciation.
The habitual patterns of intense determination arise.

41. By applying these former habitual patterns
to the things that appear in this way,
one does not conceive of them as permanent or real.
No doubts about their lack of reality ever arise.

42. Even if doubt does arise,[45]
one knows all composite phenomena to be impermanent,
[since even] the web of existence will disintegrate.
What need is there to make sure?

43. Therefore letting go of self-fixation,
the root of the suffering of cyclic existence,
that person will definitely find happiness.
Nonhumans will see and make offering and praise.

44. The period from when someone first generated the aspiration
of previously developed determination
until the arising of the timeless awareness of warmth
should be known as the Path of Accumulation.

[The Path of Application]

45. Since the [realization] of impermanent illusion from the
   Path of Seeing
is applied now, it is called "the Path of Application."
[It consists of] the absorptions of warmth and peak.
There are five faculties.

46. Doing no nonvirtue even to save one's life,
having faith in the powers, fearlessness,
emptiness, and the meaning of illusion:
that is called the faculty of faith.

47. Practicing the illusion [of what one has] faith in,
continually familiarizing oneself with it,
and arousing the faculty of diligence:
that is called the faculty of diligence.

48. Mindful of illusion that has come of diligence
so that it does not go to waste,
while abandoning all attachment to real existence:
that is the faculty of mindfulness.

49. Absorption in the illusion of mindfulness and determination
becomes one-pointed and without distraction.
Since absorption is included in one-pointedness,
that is the faculty of absorption.

50. That illusion that is included in absorption
is distinctly revealed by wisdom
that knows all phenomena to be without intrinsic nature:
that is the faculty of wisdom.

51. They are called the five faculties because
everything inconsistent with them is overwhelmed.

52. By practicing in this way
all phenomenal sights and sounds in the daytime
arise as the experience of unreal illusion.
Through time, body, and visualization [practices],
Dreams are recognized in an isolated place.[46]

53. However many dreams are dreamt,
they do not transcend four habitual patterns.[47]
The power of training with virtue, nonvirtue, and neutrality
produces the great timeless awareness.

54. Therefore those endowed with intelligence
[regard] dreams as golden.
Containing virtue and nonvirtue,[48] one practices accepting
and rejecting,
and applies the meaning of illusion to dreams.

55. Just recognizing that it is a dream is warmth.[49]
"Warmth" because it is the early sign of
the fire of illusion arising naturally without concept.

56. Form and so on are inseparable appearance-emptiness,
without increase and decrease—thus illusion.
When that illusion occurs naturally
for a bit in a dream, it is the peak.

57. Connecting mindfulness, determination, and devotion,
with the vital points of blending and transferring,[50]
when waking up from sleep
and recognizing one's former dream,
meditate on it as being no different than waking deluded
appearances.

58. Furthermore, without opening the eyes
decide that the pictures of your memories,

perceptions, and thoughts are illusory dreams
and then practice with intense determination.

59. When deluded perception occurs, train again and again.
Meditate that the outer environment and all beings within it
are the residence and residents [of the mandala],
and that this itself is illusory dream.
It is most crucial to train in this again and again.

60. With intense weariness leave behind
the fascination with hapless cyclic existence[51]
and this deceitful seducer: appearance.
With fierce determination discard it for the essence.[52]

61. Without mentally releasing this life,
whatever one does will be meaningless suffering.
Many attendants and servants are like an anthill.
Possessions are the same as passing clouds.

62. Even living in a jungle, one is just like a parrot,
clever in the designations of wildlife.
Therefore those who are thoughtful
should not be attached to this world.

63. Experience the sights and sounds of daily life
determined that you have fallen asleep.
There is no difference whatsoever
in actual perceptions and dreams.
To the unrealized they appear as two;
but there is nothing other than that.

64. The signs of warmth are that the notion of the reality
of the five aggregates is countered by illusion,
there are no hesitations or doubts
about the genuine profound meaning of illusion,
and oneself and others are joined to virtues.

65. One's body and so on are naturally endowed with loving mind,
and one does not come under the power of sleep and torpor.
Since latent habitual patterns of afflictive states are conquered,
one is possessed of the mindfulness and awareness of illusion.

66. The signs of the peak are that clothes, seat, and so on
do not develop odors and
the body is free of parasites inside and out.
Without avarice, body, speech, and mind
are without deceit and remain in isolation,
which stabilizes [practice] and sustains joy.[53]

67. There are five powers in the meditative absorptions
of [the levels of] acceptance and supreme dharma:

68. The power of faith when practicing illusion with faith and devotion
is such that even if a devil emanated in the form of a buddha
and dissuaded one with "this is not the dharma,"
one would not be subject to conversion.

69. The power of diligence in the diligent [practice of] illusion
is such that the forceful power of steadfast reliance
disables gods [and others] from turning one away
when reaching the ultimate ground.

70. The power of mindfulness that is generated
in the undistracted mind [focused on] the meaning of illusion
that cannot be distracted by thoughts
or disrupted by emotions is the power of mindfulness.

71. Meditative absorption in illusion free of concepts
without fixation on any objects of attachment and aggression
attains the power of isolation from busyness
and is the power of meditative absorption.

72. Wisdom knows that all phenomena
are illusion, without intrinsic existence.
That which liberates worldly ones arises from wisdom
and is the power of wisdom.

73. They are called "five powers" because
discordant factors do not move them.

74. Acceptance is lack of fear of the profound meaning
of illusion that appears yet is free of fixation.
Through training and increasing lucid dreaming,
if one is not afraid, then it is acceptance.

75. The signs are that in all daily activities
one is possessed of illusion's meaning and,
while accepting the illustrations by words,
the real meaning is willingness to be born in hell.

76. One is not affected by perverse dharma,
and will not come under the power
of all the devils who fake the dharma.

77. Even in dreams all phenomena
are known to be the dream itself.
Those are the signs of acceptance,
and not to fully fall into the three bad existences.

78. Once dreams are recognized, if the deity's Body
arises naturally just for a moment,
there is no question of recognition in the intermediate state.
The same will be true for illusion.

79. All phenomena, free of arising and ceasing,
becoming illusion is [the level of] supreme dharma.
Realizing all dream objects as one's own mind,
is mundane supreme dharma.

80. The signs of supreme dharma are that, in all activities,
whatever one does is for the welfare of beings,
and the activity that pleases the buddha
is free of all entanglement of attachments to this life.

81. The poison flowers of the eight worldly concerns
are genuinely liberated in illusion itself.
Once dreams are recognized, luminous clarity is realized.
That is what conquers the intermediate state.

82. From warmth up through mundane supreme dharma
is known as the Path of Joining.

[The Path of Seeing]

83. In the last moment of supreme dharma,
nonconceptual timeless awareness of the Path of Seeing
is the natural arising of illusion
that has the characteristic of being incontrovertible.

84. Seeing what was not seen before
is the timeless wisdom of the Path of Seeing.
The seven branches of enlightenment
are the meditative absorption on the Path of Seeing.

85. Since illusion, which is beyond intellect,
involves no deliberate application of mindfulness,
all phenomena are seen as nonentities.
This is the mindfulness branch of enlightenment.

86. Practicing illusion-like experience
with regard to all illusion-like phenomena,
there is no frame of reference for truly existent phenomena,
virtuous, nonvirtuous, or indeterminate.
This is the direct revealing of phenomena branch of
enlightenment.

87. Since all concepts are eradicated
in illusion, which is free[54] from all fixation,
striving without accepting or discarding phenomena
is the diligence branch of enlightenment.

88. Since joy and sorrow are eradicated
with regard to illusion, which is free from rejection or
acceptance,
joy about habitual phenomena is not aroused in the disciplined
mind.
This is the joy branch of enlightenment.

89. Because there is no reference point to whatever one
references—
since illusion has no existence in essence—
there is mental agility regarding all phenomena.
This is the mental agility branch of enlightenment.

90. Even illusion itself is not truly existent.
The realization that follows the eradication of phenomena
does not reference [even] the mind.
This is the meditative absorption branch of enlightenment.

91. Illusion, which dwells nowhere,
creates no dependency, attachment, or bondage.
No concern with phenomena
is the equanimity branch of enlightenment.

92. Once accustomed to that meditative absorption,
from day through half the night
all aspects of appearance and sound
will arise as illusion, without intrinsic existence,
limitless appearance inseparable from emptiness.

93. Just as bubbles arise and dissolve
back into the sparkling sea,

so thought bubbles also
cannot be anywhere else
except[55] in the ocean of phenomena's nature.
So rest at ease without rejecting or accepting.

94. At that time the fog of conceptual patterns
becomes baseless and cannot disturb.
Having generated certainty and conviction,
one gets used to [just that] without adding or subtracting anything.

95. Having engaged this by blending it with devotion,
the deity's Body [appears] clearly without concept,
blissful without fixation and free of craving,
naturally arisen, naturally liberated, and uncompounded.

96. Lucid clarity, omniscient yet free of concept,
occurs in sleep, dream, and the intermediate state,
or else in lucid dreaming or naturally arising;
this saṃbhogakāya lasts as long as one does not waver.

97. Day and night blend inseparably
and whatever appears is endowed with three constants.[56]
If one then practices without distraction,
making offerings and supplications,

98. one will attain stabilization of
emanations and transformations in dreams
and train in the creativity of illusion
with [everything] from buddhas to bugs.

99. Once the nonreferential illusory body is actualized,
illusion, deities' Bodies, and manifest clarity become inseparable,
and the lucid appearances increase.

100. Having similarly traversed through to objective
appearances,[57]
one hundred and twelve [Path of] Seeing eliminations are
eliminated.
One becomes clairvoyant and joyful,
while frightening appearances occur.

101. The signs that the lucid appearance of illusion has arisen
are that during sleep or otherwise,
in one second, lasting a mere instant,
twelve hundred qualities occur.

102. One enters the equilibrium of a hundred absorptions,
sees the faces of a hundred buddhas,
listens to the teachings of a hundred buddhas,
shakes a hundred world systems,

103. visits a hundred buddha realms,
fills a hundred realms with light,
matures a hundred sentient beings,
opens a hundred dharma doors,

104. remains for a hundred eons,
penetrates a hundred past and future lives,
and issues a hundred emanated bodies,
each surrounded by a hundred teaching attendants.

105. Since one can relinquish even life for the sake of dharma,
sense pleasures become allies.
Perfecting the four kinds of generosity,[58]
one does whatever one can of the remaining [perfections].

106. Attaining the [first] ground, one is free of the five fears:
lack of sustenance, death, lower realms,
criticism, and [troublesome] retinue.
Being without fear, anxiety is abandoned.

107. Thus all sights and sounds from the realization
arise as unreal illusion through realization.

108. If, in daytime and in dreams,
the habitual tendencies of confusion are not purified,
one does not abide even on the eighth ground—
no need to mention the Lotus-endowed.

109. Therefore, [regarding] the various appearances,
if one does not involve mental fixation
in the brilliant clarity of the five sense consciousnesses,
then that is clarity and emptiness inseparable;
the natural appearance of illusion without attachment.

110. All the phenomena of dreams
are realized as great bliss clarity-emptiness without fixation.
That timeless awareness on the Path of Seeing
is explained as the sign of a nonreturner.

111. One should know that the Path of Seeing
[extends] from the supreme dharma until the second ground.

[The Path of Meditation]

112. The Path of Meditation means nonconceptual illusion.
Since seeing becomes familiar, it is the Path of Meditation.
The grounds are from the second to the tenth.
The mental engagement in meditative absorption
is the eightfold path of the noble ones.

113. All phenomena of samsara, nirvana, and so forth,
are all equal in illusion.
Free of all reference points of a view,
it is the genuine view.

114. All thoughts of anything at all
are genuinely liberated in illusion itself.
Totally eliminating all thoughts
is genuine thought.

115. Words that are free of self-other concepts,
and ritual expressions that cause the realization
of the equality of all phenomena in illusion
are genuine speech.

116. Completed action becomes exhausted:
freedom from all limitations—
positive, negative, compounded, uncompounded—
is genuine completed action.

117. Any livelihood that is free from harming or violence,
that purifies violence toward beings,
and arrives at ultimate benefit of oneself and others
is genuine livelihood.

118. Total attention of the mind for the purpose of
accomplishing
the meaning of illusion that is profound and free of elaboration,
and the persistence of undaunted effort
is genuine effort.

119. One's own naturally arising illusion
affords no opportunity for interference
from devils, nonvirtue, and deviations;
this is genuine mindfulness.

120. Self and other are equal in illusion,
all phenomena are totally pure in illusion;
attaining omniscience in that very moment
is genuine meditative absorption.

121. The grounds are from the second, Immaculate,
through the tenth, Cloud of Dharma.
There are four hundred and fourteen Path of Meditation
eliminations.

122. Sorcery, miraculous powers, and so on develop;
the signs and qualities of these nine grounds
should be learned from the section on the ten grounds.

123. Whatever is attained after the Path of Seeing
up until the tenth ground is the Path of Meditation.

[The Path of Consummation]

124. Illusion totally liberated from all obscurations
is genuine, perfect buddhahood.
When other phenomena do not impede
the swift attainment
of that unsurpassable enlightenment,
it is known as the path of no obstacle.

125. Once all obscurations are eliminated on the Path of
Meditation,
in the last of the final stage of the tenth ground,
the most subtle of subtle fixations on illusion
are known as cognitive obscurations.

126. Alternatively, it is the obscuration of believing
the excellence of ultimate view.[59]
To eliminate that very obscuration
there is vajra-like meditative absorption.

127. Unfixated clarity-emptiness great bliss,
uncompounded naturally arising luminous clarity,
comes from the force of blessings.
Like torchlight illuminating gold coins in a dungeon,

the most subtle of subtle obscurations are naturally purified
by unimpeded ability.

128. Then uncompounded basic space itself
and timeless awareness are not two.
The complete purity of afflictive emotion and cognition
is the dharmakāya endowed with two purities.

129. Kāyas are support and accumulation
and pervasive and naturally existing.
Without change, birth, or characteristics,
all buddhas are dharmakāya.

130. There is no constructing or dwelling,
yet the two kāyas arise naturally from
the force of previous merit accumulation, thought of awakening,
aspirations, and creation phase.

131. Thus, in the palace of the Akaniṣṭha,
Saṃbhogakāya Vairochana Vajradhara
fully possesses the excellent major and minor marks.

132. The stainless kāya of appearance-emptiness, free of
 elaboration,
together with a host of bodhisattvas,
proclaims with unbroken continuity
the sounds of mahāyāna dharma without limits.

133. Nirmāṇakāya arises naturally to tame whomever
in place, time, teacher, retinue, and so forth,
according to the interests of those to be tamed.
An unimaginable array
manifests in forms of this and that.

134. Until the ocean of samsara is emptied,
like a lotus unsoiled by the swamp

or like a wish-fulfilling tree or jewel,
they ripen and liberate sentient beings.[60]

135. The dharmakāya free of birth and cessation is attained
through accumulation of awareness and completion phase.
Great bliss of three kāyas inseparable is attained
through two accumulations and creation-completion
 inseparable.

136. In short, from the sky-like dharmakāya,
the rainbows of form kāyas arise naturally.
Without discursive thought, everything is known;
inseparable natural freedom and spontaneous presence.

137. Essence itself and complete enjoyment
and emanation are the activity of dharmakāya.
If you would like elaborations on any
eloquent explanations of these four,
you should respectfully consult and learn from
the sūtras and the works of Lord Maitreya.[61]

138. Here practice is the primary concern.
Designations are like mirages.
Therefore, with no spare time in life,
mentally abandon this world.
Relying on an excellent holy guru,
you should actualize realization.

139. This life is short; things to know are many.
Moreover, one's lifespan is uncertain,
so like a goose drinking milk,[62]
take what you need.

140. For as long as ideas exist,
there is no end of vehicles.

When ideas are no more,
there is no vehicle, and no expression.

141. The signs of the paths and grounds vary
according to differences in the force of familiarization,
and to differences in seniority [in practice].
[There are differences in the] external objects, perceived objects,
perceived essence, and qualities that are attained.

142. The stages of external miraculous emanations
of arhants with or without adornments,
in the early or later part of life, and so on,[63]
should be learned from the sūtras and tantras.

143. From the end of the continuum of the tenth ground
until twofold wisdom produces the four kāyas
that are spontaneously present for oneself and others
should be known as the Path of Consummation.

[The Ten Grounds]

144. Now listen while I explain well
the ten grounds of a bodhisattva.

145. The combined calm abiding and higher insight
that transcends the mundane
as unfixated naturally arisen illusion
is nonconceptual timeless awareness.

146. Being the foundational support of the pure qualities,
and [because] one progresses higher, they are called "grounds."
The divisions are Very Joyful and so on.
There are ten early signs that one should know.

147. These are the defining characteristics of the ten grounds:
The meaning of illusion free of limitations and beyond intellect

that was not seen before becomes manifest,
and one's purpose is attained, so joy is born.
Therefore [the first ground] is called "Very Joyful."

148. The host of physical, verbal, and mental delusions
are realized as illusion since they are unborn.
Since ethical discipline is free of faults' stain,
[the second ground] is called "Stainless."

149. Appearance, sound, and all phenomena
arise as illusion with no fixation on their clarity.
Since the power of timeless awareness illuminates,
[the third ground] is therefore called "Illuminating."

150. That light of lucid appearance without fixation
is also nonexistent illusion.
Since radiating light burns up afflictive states,
[the fourth ground] is called "Radiant."

151. All fixation on the truth of remedial eliminations
turns into illusion that is genuine and unreal.
Since this subdues the difficult-to-tame afflictive states,
[the fifth ground] is called "Difficult to Overcome."[64]

152. All phenomena of samsara, nirvana, and so on
are indivisible, unlimited illusion.
Since the intrinsic nature becomes manifest,
[the sixth ground] is called "Manifest."

153. All phenomena are genuinely liberated in illusion,
while nonreferential compassion performs all purpose.
Since this is far from the [grounds of] shrāvakas and
pratyekabuddhas,
[the seventh ground] is called "Gone Far."

154. Illusion is beyond intellect and effort;
great naturally arising spontaneous presence.
Since afflictive emotion has no power to move it,
[the eighth ground] is called "Immovable."

155. However many phenomena one fixates on,
they are liberated in illusion itself.
Since intelligence is expansive and unhindered,
[the ninth ground] is called "Excellent Intelligence."

156. The illusion of the two accumulations in union
attains mastery over enlightened activity.
Since clouds of awareness pervade the dharmakāya sky,
[the tenth ground] is called "Cloud of Dharma."

157. The ten grounds are ten perfections.
This is the order of which goes with which:
First, mainly generosity is perfected,
while the remaining are accomplished as much as possible.
Second is the perfection of ethical discipline.

158. Third is done by patience.
Fourth is the perfection of diligence.
Fifth [attains] meditative stability.
Sixth the perfection of wisdom.

159. Seventh is method.
Eighth is the perfection of aspirations.
Ninth [attains] power.
Tenth the perfection of timeless awareness.

160. The characteristics of the ten perfections
will be explained without mistake.
In seeking timeless awareness, one dedicates
the roots of virtue to sentient beings in generosity.

161. To pacify all anguish of afflictive emotion
ethical discipline [is practiced].
Love and compassion for sentient beings
without malice is patience.

162. Insatiable perseverance
in the quest for virtuous factors is diligence.
Possessing an unregretful mind for the actualization
of omniscient timeless awareness is meditative stability.

163. When what is intrinsically unborn
is actualized, it is wisdom.
The timeless awareness of the victors
is accomplished by skillful method.

164. When the activity of timeless awareness
is really accomplished, it is aspiration.
No interference in the path continuum
from opposing forces and evil hordes is power.

165. This realization of phenomena just as they are
is held to be the perfection of timeless awareness.
The bodhisattvas become buddhas
on the tenth and eleventh grounds.

166. One should know about the obscurations
of twenty-one delusions.

167. Whoever is deluded has the delusion of fixating on
something.
Therefore totally eliminating any fixation
on all the phenomena on the grounds,
one must realize illusion without fixation.

168. If somehow one becomes fixated on that mere illusion,
then that too must be eliminated.

Beyond the existence or nonexistence of illusion,
elimination, acquisition, negation, and affirmation are free
in themselves.

169. The conventional reality of fixation on something
is naturally liberated without fixation—beyond intellect.
Therefore getting used to nonfixation on all phenomena
on the grounds purifies all obscurations.

170. The stages of naturally arising realization
and the stages of the signs will arise.
With realization of the meaning of naturally arising illusion,
the three spheres are totally pure and generosity is effortless.[65]

171. At all times of day and night,
naturally arising illusion-like [experience] occurs.
Furthermore, the meaning of omnipresent and pervasive
illusion of the realm of phenomena is realized.

172. There are twelve hundred clear appearances.
Outer and inner signs are as before.[66]

173. At Stainless, illusion and
the deity's Body without attachment is the stainless kāya.
Beyond ideas of going, coming, existing, and not existing,
this itself is the excellent support of familiarization:
The natural arising of illusion as the realm of phenomena itself
is the realization of the sublime meaning.

174. The signs are that, whether day or nighttime,
in a single instant,
one enters the equipoise of powers of absorption,
and twelve hundred [other qualities that] one should know.

175. At Illuminating, lucid clarity and
the deity's Body of great bliss are inseparable.

[In waking] clarity and dream time itself,
in order to tame immeasurable sentient beings,
unimaginable Bodies of deities naturally arise,
filling the realms and proclaiming the dharma.

176. The meaning that is similar to the cause
is that all phenomena are realized as the realm of phenomena.
One enters the equipoise of a hundred thousand absorptions,
and other [qualities of] a hundred thousand that one should know.

177. At Radiant, since the deity's Body
is effortlessly familiar, one becomes free
from the poison of strife and effort.

178. The meaning of the absence
of total fixation in the realm of phenomena is realized.
There are twelve [sets of] one billion,
such as entering into equilibrium and so forth.

179. On the ground Difficult to Overcome,
from within the realization that all phenomena are unborn,
unrestricted, nonreferential compassion [manifests]
the great seal of the deity's Body for others' sakes,
becoming inseparable during all activities.
Everything in the realm of phenomena
is realized to be undifferentiated from others.[67]

180. There are twelve [sets of] ten billion,
such as entering the equipoise
of ten billion absorptions
in a single instant.

181. On Manifest, all the causes and results
of samsara and nirvana become manifest.
The deity's Body of interdependent origination

arises in lucid clarity without fixation on clarity.

182. All intense afflictive states and perfect purity
are realized to be undifferentiated in the realm of phenomena.
There are twelve [sets of] one trillion,
such as one trillion meditative absorptions.

183. In the Far ground, all phenomena
are the Body of illusion without arising or ceasing;
the limitless great bliss of unity.
In all activities of day and night
recollection in that absence of attachment is attained,
which is known as being a "nonreturner."

184. The meaning of no differentiation in the realm of phenomena
and phenomena's defining characteristics are realized.
There are twelve [sets of qualities],
such as entering in the equipoise of ten sextillion.

185. On the Immovable ground, day and night
lucid clarity as the deity's Body without effort
arises naturally in aspects similar to saṃbhogakāya,
and refines illusion in the array of pure lands
of the buddhas of the ten directions and three times.

186. Like the totally pure spontaneously present sky,
the realm of phenomena without increase or decrease
is a sign of attaining power over the pure realms.

187. In a single instant one attains absorptions
equal to as many atoms as there are
in one hundred trillion worlds;
there are twelve such sets.

188. On the ground of Intelligence, lucid clarity
and phenomena[68] are limitless, uncompounded,

free of going and coming, birth and death, rejecting and
accepting;
beyond utterance, imagination, and description, unborn,
and without the duality of meditated object and meditation.

189. Like the pure sky without clouds,
the meaning of the timeless awareness
of unimpeded confidence is realized.

190. In a single instant one enters the equipoise
of absorptions equal to the atoms
in one million infinite buddha realms;
there are twelve such [sets of qualities].

191. On the Cloud of Dharma, the union of two accumulations,
nonabiding, without abiding, lucid clarity
is the natural, totally pure, nonconceptual kāya,
known vividly without fixating thoughts.

192. Beyond mind, free from the limits of reference points,
like the sky without arising or ceasing,
pure as space without defining characteristics,
beyond utterance, imagination, description, and intellect.

193. In all times of day and night,
the sublime inseparable appearance-emptiness, bliss-emptiness,
arises without increase or decrease;
the meaning of the power of enlightened activity.

194. This is truly a lord of the tenth ground
whose empowerment conferral is amazing;
the greatest of all in the three realms.
Placed on the lion throne of fearlessness,
empowerment is conferred by great light rays
and the hands of the victors of the ten directions.

195. Then, in a single instant, amid
the great appearance of dharma and
immeasurable light and dharma clouds and
dharma appearance and dharma light of immeasurable
tathāgatas,
the immeasurably great Cloud of Dharma is attained.

196. In that final existence,
cognitive obscurations are thoroughly eliminated
and vajra-like absorption is realized.

[The Fruition]

197. According to inner [tantra], the lord of the eleventh ground
receives the immaculate mahā-empowerment[69]
in the infinite palace of the Queen of Akaniṣṭha,
and realizes the lucid clarity of vajra absorption.

198. The twelfth, passionless Lotus-endowed,
the genuine buddha is the buddha there,
while an emanation attains awakening here.

199. The difference between a buddha and bodhisattvas
is similar to an ocean and [water in] an ox's hoof print.
Even the qualities of the three pure grounds
cannot be measured or evaluated;
what need to mention measures or descriptions
of the qualities of total omniscience?

200. As the sky is to the earth,
a hair's tip can indeed be measured.
The victorious one's ocean of qualities
cannot be described in an immeasurable eon.

201. In this way, traversing all the grounds,
like iron transmuted by burning,

afflictive states become nonconceptual mentation,
the five sense consciousnesses become fivefold timeless awareness,
the all-base transmutes into the ultimate kāya:
nondissipating, unconditional great bliss.

202. Basic space and timeless awareness being not two,
spontaneously present enlightened activity is uninterrupted:
a great natural arising without limits.

203. With the prediction and proper compilation of sūtra and tantra,
the words of this *Stages in the Path of Illusion*
were arranged without contradiction or confusion
in accordance with [my own] practice experience.

204. By that vast and immaculate virtue,
may all beings pained by suffering,
having trained well in the stages of illusion,
attain the great lucid clarity.

The Essential Stainless Stages in the Path of Illusion by Niguma, the ḍākinī of timeless awareness, is complete. It was translated by the ḍākinī of timeless awareness herself and Lotsāwa Lendarma Lodrö. Afterward, I, Khyungpo Naljor, received it and put it into practice.

mangalam

OUTLINE OF THE COMMENTARY

I. Homage and Author's Statement
- A. The Homage
- B. The Promise
- C. The Source Texts That Fully Clarify the Meaning

II. The Base
- A. The All-Base
  - 1. All-Base Consciousness
    - a. All-Base Consciousness as Indeterminate Lucid Empty Pure Awareness
    - b. All-Base as the Seed of Everything
    - c. All-Base Is Where Latent Habitual Patterns Ripen
    - d. How the All-Base Consciousness Is Presented
  - 2. Afflictive Mentation
  - 3. Mental Consciousness
  - 4. Consciousnesses of the Five Senses
- B. The Four Empowerments

III. The Path (Thirty-seven Factors of Enlightenment)
- A. Brief Presentation
- B. Extensive Explanation: The Five Paths
  - 1. The Path of Accumulation
    - a. The Lesser Path of Accumulation (Four Mindfulnesses)
    - b. The Intermediate Path of Accumulation (Four Renunciations)
    - c. The Greater Path of Accumulation (Four Supports)
  - 2. The Path of Application
    - a. Warmth and Peak (Five Faculties)
    - b. Acceptance and Supreme Dharma (Five Powers)
  - 3. The Path of Seeing (Seven Branches of Enlightenment)
  - 4. The Path of Meditation (Eightfold Path)
  - 5. The Path of Consummation
  - 6. The Ten Grounds

IV. The Fruition: Buddhahood

STAGES IN THE PATH OF ILLUSION: THE COMMENTARY

Sanskrit title: *Māyādhvanakramavṛitti-nāma*
Tibetan Title: *sGyu ma lam gyi rim pa'i 'grel·pa zhes bya ba*

I. Homage and Author's Statement[1]

Homage to all buddhas and bodhisattvas.

Vajradhara, ocean of victors,
Having bowed at your feet,
I write this clarification of *Stages in the Path of Illusion*
According to the teachings of sūtra and tantra.

These days one may ask what constitutes an unerring treatise that faithfully ascertains the meaning of the authentic word of the victorious ones. [It must consist of] the authorship, the source, the composition, the reason, the necessity, and the clarification of meaning.[70]

As for the first, the author is myself, one who dwells on the three pure grounds and has obtained authorization from Buddha Vajradhara. As for the source, it is taken from direct experience and many sūtras and tantras. The composition is *Stages in the Path of Illusion*. The reason was the inspiration to benefit sentient beings. The necessity is the release from the clutches of the devil, which is the fixation on all the phenomena of samsara and nirvana. The clarification of meaning is the homage that dispels obstacles, the promise to complete it, and the source texts that clarify the meaning.

1. I have inserted the headings in bold as a guide for the reader. I have also inserted the verse numbers in brackets that are keyed to the verse numbers in the source text. The verse numbers are only a rough guide as to which verses in the root text Niguma is commenting on; she does not comment on every verse in the root text (so there are some gaps), and she does not always comment on the verses in the order given in the source text (so the numbers are not always consecutive).

A. The Homage

[1] First of all, this precious jewel of the mind itself is worthy of homage since it is the source of all one's needs and desires once it has been polished by the two accumulations. The Great Brahmin [Saraha] said:

> One's own mind is the seed of everything.
> It bestows the fruits of our desires
> For anything in existence or beyond;
> Homage to the wish-fulfilling jewel of the mind.[71]

Alternately, resting the mind in the great bliss of unfixated lucid emptiness without the whole network of fixating views is the most sublime of all homage. It says in the *Vajra Garland*:

> Like putting water into water,
> or like putting butter into butter,
> seeing one's own timeless awareness
> by oneself—that is the homage here.[72]

B. The Promise

[2] Placing myself in abject obedience[73] to all the truth-telling sages, I make this promise as if it were a royal decree.

C. The Source Texts That Fully Clarify the Meaning

[3–4] From the *Actualization of Timeless Awareness Extensive Tantra*:

> Meditating on the illusion-like [nature]
> Of illusion-like phenomena
> in the illusion realm of phenomena, the all-base,
> illusion-like buddhahood manifests.
>
> There is no other realization than this
> in the five paths and twelve grounds.

> The meaning of base and its inherent fruition
> are inseparable in profundity and breadth.[74]

What does that mean? [Primordial] unity is ascertained in the abiding base just as it is, the practice of unity is the path that is the nature of method, and actualized unity arises naturally as the result.

II. The Base

Regarding [primordial] unity as the base just as it is, there is the all-base and the four empowerments.

A. The All-Base

What does it mean to say "the abiding base just as it is"? [It refers to] the all-base consciousness, the afflictive mentation, the mental consciousness, and the five sense consciousnesses.

1. All-Base Consciousness

To classify that all-base consciousness further, there is the all-base as indeterminate awareness, the all-base as the seed of everything, the all-base where latent habitual patterns ripen, and how the all-base consciousness is presented.

a. All-Base Consciousness as Indeterminate Lucid Empty Pure Awareness

The Fully Illuminated Essence Sūtra states:

> The all-base that is lucid, empty pure awareness
> is known as indeterminate.[75]

That lucid, empty all-base is neither one nor many, but rather a unity. In the *Stainless Essence Sūtra* it says:

All-base, lucid, empty, indeterminate,
being neither one nor many,
is the unity of empty and nonempty.
At that time it is the seed of all phenomena.[76]

When the lucid, empty awareness is covered by the latent habitual patterns of karma, it is like the example of the waxing and waning moon. The all-base revolves in the constituent of sentient beings, but since it is without increase or decrease, it is naturally lucid clarity. It says in the *Dense Array of Adornments*:

This all-base of embodied beings
is covered by the habitual patterns of karma.
Like the light of the full moon
that illuminates millions of realms,
and hovers around the Supreme Mountain,
[yet it is] not destructible like real objects.
Likewise mind and consciousness and mentation
certainly revolve around the constituent of sentient beings
[but do not increase or diminish it].
It is always light by nature.[77]

b. All-Base as the Seed of Everything

Virtuous, nonvirtuous and indeterminate latent habitual patterns accumulate upon the all-base and become seeds. From the same source:

All-base that is constituted by various forms[78]
is the abode of all consciousness.
The all-base with its latent habitual patterns
is the seed of everything.[79]

From that, the seeds of previous habitual patterns give rise to subsequent ones, as stated in *Illuminated Essence*:

> Since the previous latent habitual patterns give birth to subsequent ones, it is the "seed."[80]

How did those latent habitual patterns accumulate? *Dense Array* [*of Adornments*] explains:

> Immature beings impute samsaric forms
> that are without beginning in that realm.
> Negative tendencies and karmic conditions
> accumulate latent habitual patterns beginninglessly.[81]

How do these two—the beginningless all-base and the latent habitual patterns—cohabit? The *Fully Illuminated Essence* states:

> Just as gold is to tarnish,
> the all-base is to habitual patterns.

Also it is like river stones and algae, as stated in *Adornments*:

> Just as the stones in the depths of the water
> are completely enwrapped with algae,
> so the all-base consciousness
> is said to be stained by latent habitual patterns.[82]

c. All-Base Is Where Latent Habitual Patterns Ripen

The subtle habitual patterns of virtue, nonvirtue, and neutrality that are overlaid on the all-base ripen from subtle into grosser [patterns] and then fully ripen into each of the six kinds [of ordinary beings]. It says in the *Fully Illuminated Essence*:

> Virtue, nonvirtue, and in between;
> habitual patterns ripen into six kinds of cycling beings.

d. How All-Base Consciousness Is Presented

All-base is fully conscious in its empty-clarity, the nature of light. From [this] aspect of pure awareness,[83] it is called "all-base consciousness." It states in *Sections on Grounds*:[84]

> The clarity of all-base consciousness is fully conscious as nonconceptual consciousness. Consciousness itself in its clarity is without concept.[85]

All-base consciousness does not conceive of external objects that are truly existent. Therefore, the scope of its frame of reference is unlimited. Moreover, since it becomes the basic support of all samsara and nirvana, it is not differentiated from total perfection (*rnam byang*). As it says in *Adornments*:

> No different than total perfection,
> all-base cannot be differentiated.
> If it could be differentiated
> then all-base would not be permanent.[86]

And in *Illuminated Essence*:

> Since the all-base becomes the base of everything,
> it is therefore the base of total perfection.

Other sūtras iterate this as well. In them, the basic space of beginningless time is called "the base constituent" (*gzhi khams*). It says in the *Journey to Lanka*:[87]

> The basic space of beginningless time
> is the base of all phenomena.
> Because that exists, all beings
> will attain nirvana.

Again, the all-base or buddha nature (*bde bar gshegs pa'i snying po, sugatagarbha*) is described in the *Highest Continuum*:

> The [buddha nature] constituent is one that is beginningless.
> Because that exists, all beings will attain nirvana.[88]

And again, in *Adornments*, the all-base or buddha nature is described thus:

> The base of all the various grounds
> is buddha nature; virtue is also that.
> That nature is also termed all-base,
> which was taught by the tathāgata.
> But feeble-minded people do not understand
> [buddha] nature known as the all-base.[89]

It is also called "the appropriating consciousness,"[90] "base of the body," "base of all," and "mind support," as in the *Sections on Grounds*:

> That consciousness thus grasps this body and takes possession of it and then it is also called "the appropriating consciousness." Since it has become the base of this body, it is called "all-base." Since it is indeterminate it is also called "a sentient being" because all the consciousnesses come about based on that.[91]

There are limitless synonyms given in the sūtras, such as beginningless time (*thog ma med pa'i dus*), pure awareness (*rig pa*), basic space (*dbyings*), constituent (*khams*), all-base (*kun gzhi*), suchness (*de bzhin nyid*), realm of phenomena (*chos dbying, dharmadhatu*), heart (*snying po*), the body of dharma (*chos sku, dharmakāya*), unborn (*ma skyes pa*), all-base consciousness (*kun gzhi'i rnam shes*), the base support pervading sentient beings (*sems can kun khyab gzhi rten*), lucid emptiness (*gsal stong*), indeterminate (*lung ma bstan*), the house of the light of pure awareness (*rig pa 'od kyi khang pa*), the abiding base (*gnas pa'i gzhi*), and so forth. The mantra tradition also explains many synonyms, such as causal continuum (*rgyu'i rgyud*), base continuum (*gzhi'i rgyud*), quintessence continuum (*bcud kyi rgyud*), supporting continuum (*rten pa'i rgyud*), all-continuum (*kun gyi rgyud*), beginningless continuum (*thog ma med pa'i rgyud*), core continuum (*snying po'i rgyud*), and so on.

To be learned in the secrets of the all-base and mind and consciousness without confusion about the meaning of the names that are thus explained endlessly in the sūtras and tantras as synonyms for all-base is to be unconfused about all Buddhist teachings and to fully master them. This is taught in the *Sections on Grounds Sūtra*.[92]

2. Afflictive Mentation

The mentation with afflictive states[93] is that which fixates on the self with no reference to the all-base consciousness that is lucid, empty pure awareness, the nature of light.

3. Mental Consciousness

The mental consciousness (*yid kyi rnam par shes pa*) is so-called because it fixates on outer and inner phenomena, or objects. As it says in the *Journey to Lanka*:

> Mind is the all-base consciousness.
> The thought of "I" is the afflicted mentation.
> Whatever it is that fixates on objective reality,
> is called "mental consciousness."[94]

4. Consciousnesses of the Five Senses

The consciousnesses of the five senses (*sgo lnga'i rnam par shes pa*) are the eye consciousness that apprehends form, ear [consciousness] that apprehends sound, nose [consciousness] that apprehends smells, tongue [consciousness] that apprehends tastes, and the body [consciousness] that apprehends tactile sensations. Since it is aware and conscious of those objects in that way, it is it is held to be consciousness. Furthermore, mind [as] all-base is indeterminate. Mentation with afflictive states is unvirtuous. Mental consciousness is both virtuous and unvirtuous. The *Journey to Lanka* states:

> Mind is wholly indeterminate.
> Mental [consciousness] becomes both
> [because when] consciousness[95] arises,
> it is virtuous and unvirtuous.[96]

There are ten virtues of the mental [consciousness]. The nonvirtues of mental [consciousness] are six primary afflictive states and twenty secondary afflictive states.[97] Therefore, this mental [consciousness] can be both virtuous and unvirtuous. The consciousnesses of the five doors of the sense organs are indeterminate. It is also taught this way in the *Sublime Absorption Sūtra*:

> Mind is indeterminate.
> The afflicted one is unvirtuous.
> Mental [consciousness] is both virtue and vice.
> The five sense doors are indeterminate.[98]

B. The Four Empowerments

The basis of secret mantra is the four empowerments, as stated in the *Actualization of Timeless Awareness*:

> The tantric basis is the four empowerments
> because they are the basic support for creation and completion.[99]

And from *Secret Ḍākinī*:

> Tantra is the essence of the four empowerments;
> [both] the subject and the medium are tantra.[100]

All of that was the exposition on how the base abides.

III. The Path

Next, to explain the nature of the methods or the path of unity[101] with its corresponding signs. There is both a brief presentation and an extensive explanation.

A. Brief Presentation

The factors of enlightenment are presented as inseparable from illusion and dream. From the *[Sūtra of the Perfection of Wisdom in] Eighteen Thousand [Lines]*:

> Children of gods, the applications of mindfulness are like dreams, like illusions. In the same way, the genuine renunciations and the supports of miraculous powers, the faculties, the powers, the branches of enlightenment, and the noble eightfold path are all like dreams, like illusions. Children of gods, the ten powers of a tathāgata are similarly like dreams, like illusions. Likewise, the four fearlessnesses, the four modes of specific genuine awareness, great love, great compassion, and the eighteen distinct qualities of a buddha are like dreams, like illusions.[102]

The *Array of Sacred Oaths Subsequent Tantra* says:

> Lord of Secrets, [Vajrapani], realize that the five sense support objects
> and all other categories—the palace residence and
> the resident forms of deities—are like illusions.
> Know that in the same way those residences and residents
> are also inseparable from the factors of enlightenment.
> Thus those residences and residents are also
> the nonduality of illusion and the factors of enlightenment.
> They are not divisible into two.[103]

[8] From those, the path becomes sublime. The paths and grounds are traversed through months and years of guru devotion. As said in the *Actualization of Timeless Awareness*:

> Stages of the grounds and paths
> are traversed through months and years of guru devotion.
> If one is never apart from the guru's manifestation,
> then one will dwell together with all buddhas.[104]

The *Array of Sacred Oaths* says:

> By six months of unwavering devotion
> the ground of Vajradhara is attained.[105]

[10] The same thing is expressed in the fifty sections of tantra.[106] Furthermore, all appearance exists as the five families. By taking that as the path and meditating on it, appearances need not be dispelled by other [methods]. That is to adhere to the sacred oath of secret mantra. It says in the *Array of Sacred Oaths of the Five Families*:

> Nirvirana Vishkambin, whoever wishes to abide by the sacred oaths of the five families should understand the shapes of all phenomena as the five insignia. Know the various colors as the five families. Similarly, the five elements, the five aggregates, the five afflictive states, and the variety of sentient beings should be known as the five families. Thus the various shapes, colors, elements, aggregates, afflictions, and beings are the five families without any duality; they are not divisible into two.[107]

The form of the deity, whether created in ritual or self-arising, is creation phase in its appearing aspect and completion phase in its empty aspect; by nature an inseparable unity. From *Actualization*:

> The deity's form that purifies the ordinary
> is creation phase from the aspect of its appearance

and completion phase from the aspect of its emptiness.
This is taught in this way as inseparable.

And from the same source:

All things are appearance and emptiness inseparable.
Creation and completion and their unity;
there is not a single phenomenon that is not creation and completion.
This is the way that enlightenment is taught.

[12] The clarity of the deity's appearance is taken on the path as nirmāṇakāya, the bliss as saṃbhogakāya, and the nonconceptuality as dharmakāya. From the *Array of Sacred Oaths*:

> The clarity of phenomena is nirmāṇakāya. The nonconceptuality of that is dharmakāya. Because that freedom from concept is joyful, it is the saṃbhogakāya. This is the way enlightenment has been taught.

In this way, the nonconceptual wisdom of the clarity of all phenomena is the timeless awareness of the path that is like the first day of the new moon. The timeless awareness of the fruition is like the full moon. It says in the *Vimalakīrti Sūtra*:

Whoever dwells in sublime meditative absorption
[experiences] clarity without concept
and comprehends vividness while not having conceptual thought.
The timeless awareness of the path and fruition
grows like the new moon becoming full.[108]

In this way, taking appearances and deities and the factors of enlightenment as inseparable from illusion on the path should be understood through mastering the victor's sūtras and tantras.

B. Extensive Explanation: The Five Paths

Experience and the five paths and ten grounds are inseparable from illusion.

[13] The essence of the path is that it is the way of combining calm abiding and higher insight. The literal explanation is that since one desires to arrive at supreme enlightenment it is called "path." The divisions are the Path of Accumulation, the Path of Application, the Path of Seeing, the Path of Meditation, and the Path of Consummation.

1. The Path of Accumulation

[14] The essence of the Path of Accumulation is to abandon vice and to earnestly undertake the practice of virtue. It is defined as the gathering of the accumulations for the purpose of realizing the nature of phenomena (*chos nyid*; *dharmatā*).

[15] There are three divisions: the lesser, intermediate, and greater paths of accumulation.

a. The Lesser Path of Accumulation

[16] Since carelessness and impaired mindfulness are the cause of downfalls, the meditative absorption on the lesser Path of Accumulation involves four direct applications of mindfulness.[109] In the *Sūtra of Bodhisattva Dṛdhramati*,[110] Dṛdhramati asks, "Bhagavan, how should one meditate on the four direct applications of mindfulness?" The Bhagavan answers:

> [17] Dṛdhramati, you ask how a bodhisattva practices the direct application of mindfulness of the body in scrutinizing the body. You should examine individually the body's past limits, future limits, and present occurrence. Alas! Examining this body [that arises from] causes and conditions [one finds it] to be impermanent and changing, like an illusion. In this body there is nothing to call "mine." You must impart heart to this body that has no heart. What is that heart? It is

to accomplish and attain the Body of the Tathāgata. That is the direct application of mindfulness of the body.

[18] Dṛdhramati, you ask how one should practice the direct application of mindfulness of sensation to sensations. Any sensation is pertinent: pleasant sensations cause joy, painful sensations cause hatred, and those that are neither cause dullness. Train [in considering that] all of your sensations are like an illusion and without intrinsic nature. Teach the dharma so that all sentient beings can cut the continuity of sensation. For what reason? Realized sensation is blissful. Unrealized sensation becomes painful. Therefore, the wisdom that all the sensations in all mental images, mental engagements, and all designations of possible phenomena are like an illusion is the direct application of the mindfulness of sensation.

[19] Dṛdhramati, you ask how one should practice the direct application of mindfulness of scrutinizing the mind with the mind. Mind, once it arises, is perishing—it does not abide. It is not that once you have initially engendered mind it then abides. No matter what, it does not abide. Therefore mind does not see mind. Thus, the defining characteristic of the mind is that it is like an illusion. Since therefore there is no [real] defining characteristic, you should rest without fixation. That is the direct application of mindfulness to mind.

[20] Dṛdhramati, you ask how one should practice the direct application of mindfulness of phenomena by scrutinizing phenomena. Other than anything being emptiness, without attributes, and without aspirations,[111] do not imagine that there is even a speck of existing phenomena. While looking at that phenomenon and abiding, by genuinely seeing the nature of phenomena, you are genuinely not actually seeing the nonphenomena. As for what is called "the direct application of mindfulness [to phenomena]," the Buddha said that all labels of the multiplicity of phenomena are mere names. You will not find anything inside or outside [corresponding to] names or phenomena. So freedom from

extremes and truly existent phenomena is the direct application of mindfulness to phenomena.

b. The Intermediate Path of Accumulation

[21] Furthermore, on the intermediate level of the Path of Accumulation, one comes to regard vice and nonvirtue as toxic since they are the cause of suffering. In order to renounce them, there are meditations on the four aspects of genuine renunciation.[112] Dṛdhramati asked, "How should one regard the four aspects of genuine renunciation?" The Bhagavan answered:

> [22–25] Dṛdhramati, you ask about the fourfold path of a bodhisattva. In order not to generate vice and unvirtuous factors that have not yet arisen, one develops determination, makes effort, initiates diligence, takes control of the mind, and fully engages in what is genuine. In order to totally renounce those vices and unvirtuous factors that have arisen, one develops determination and the rest, as before. In order to generate virtuous factors that have not yet arisen, one develops determination and the rest, as before. In order that the virtuous factors that have arisen may remain, continually increase, not diminish, and not be wasted, one develops determination and the rest, as before.
>
> [26–27] Dṛdhramati, "vices and unvirtuous factors" are those things that are incongruous with ethical discipline, meditative absorption, and wisdom. The things that are incongruous with ethical discipline are impaired ethical discipline and all those factors that will cause it to become impaired. Those things that are incongruous with meditative absorption are whatever distracts the mind and impairs meditative absorption. Those things that are incongruous with wisdom are impaired views or holding one's own views as supreme, factors that will obscure the genuine [view]. The mental engagement is to develop determination, make

effort, initiate diligence, take control of the mind, and fully engage in what is genuine in order to renounce unvirtuous factors. That is the first genuine renunciation.

[28] Furthermore, those so-called unvirtuous factors are called "desirous attachment," "angry aggression," and "unaware dullness," arising from any cause. The mental engagement is to pacify desire with [the meditation on] foulness, aggression with love, and stupidity with [meditation on] interdependence. By the distinct revelation of any afflictive emotion, it is "renounced." Whatever is renounced will no [longer] be found, and that is the second genuine renunciation.

[29] "To develop determination, make effort, initiate diligence, take control of the mind, and fully engage in what is genuine in order to generate whatever virtuous factors have not yet arisen" [means] determination in the immeasurable virtuous factors that are to be accomplished and putting that into practice through complete control of the mind. This is the root of all the roots of virtue, and it is the third genuine renunciation.

[30] In order that the virtuous factors that have arisen may remain, continually increase, not diminish, and not be wasted, one must dedicate all the roots of virtue to enlightenment. For what reason? By dedicating absolutely all the roots of virtue to omniscience without [applying them] to remaining in the three realms, then nothing whatsoever will be wasted. This is the fourth genuine renunciation.

c. The Greater Path of Accumulation

[31] Then, on the greater Path of Accumulation, which is the nature of meditative absorption, there are meditations on the four supports of miraculous ability.[113] Dṛdhramati inquired, "Bhagavan, how should one regard the four supports of miraculous ability?" The Bhagavan answered:

Dṛdhramati, there are four in the path of the bodhisattva. What are those four? The meditative absorption of determination that is the support of miraculous ability which has the volition of renunciation, the meditative absorption of diligence that is the support of miraculous ability which has the volition of renunciation, the meditative absorption of intention that is the support of miraculous ability which has the volition of renunciation, and the meditative absorption of conduct[114] that is the support of miraculous ability which has the volition of renunciation.

[32] Dṛdhramati, whoever [knows] all phenomena to be nonexistent and like illusion, without any frame of reference, free of fixation, [that person] is without fear or anticipation of fear [concerning phenomena], and is joyous and enthusiastic, which generates determination. That is the meditative absorption of determination.

[33] Dṛdhramati, whoever possesses the determination of one-pointed faith abandons the endeavors of all worldly concerns and resists everything that causes sloth, all the while maintaining constant diligence. That is the meditative absorption of diligence.

[34] Dṛdhramati, whoever, through possessing the uninterrupted effort of effort, has one-pointed intention concerning mind's intrinsic nature of lucid clarity, which has no established existence whatsoever or frame of reference[115]—that is the meditative absorption of intention.

[35] Dṛdhramati, whoever possesses one-pointed meditative absorption engages in all the four periods of moving, walking, sitting, and lying down without ever leaving that meditative absorption—that is the meditative absorption of [engaged] conduct.

[37–38] Furthermore, Dṛdhramati, why are these called "supports of miraculous activity"? It is because those meditative absorptions cause one to renounce all mistaken factors, engage genuine virtue, arrive at a genuine place, and

> progress. [In that sense] the nature of the meditative absorption is called "the support of miraculous activity."

[39][Aspects of] the lesser Path of Accumulation that are partially concordant with liberation are that the special outlook of faith in the Jewels and the special faith from the distinct revelation[116] of all phenomena arise in one's stream of being. The conducive aspects of the intermediate [level] are the birth of diligence and enthusiasm with reference to the six perfections. The aspect conducive to liberation on the greater [Path of Accumulation] is the birth of frequent, short nonconceptual meditative absorptions in one's stream of being.

[40–43] In this way, the signs of the four [aspects on the] three [levels]—[or] twelve [in all]—on the Path of Accumulation is that once the pure ethical discipline refrains the doors of the senses from any impropriety, one shuns even the slightest evil misdeed. Therefore one understands that all external hateful enemies come from oneself and that there is no self and no other. That which is renounced are the ten nonvirtues accumulated through the three poisons.

[44] The parameters of the Path of Accumulation are from the first thought of the preliminary determination until the arising of the timeless awareness of warmth.

2. The Path of Application

[45] The essence of the Path of Application is the unity of calm abiding and higher insight. The literal explanation is that since it applies to the Path of Seeing, it is called the "Path of Application" (*sbyor lam*). The divisions are four: warmth, peak, acceptance, and supreme dharma.[117]

a. Warmth and Peak

The defining characteristic is [meditative] warmth since there is an early sign (*snga ltas*) of the fire of nonconceptual timeless awareness from the Path of Seeing. Alternatively, it is warmth since one realizes that all the afflictive states that have arisen are baseless or without intrinsic nature.

It is the timeless awareness of the peak [experience] since the roots of virtue increase, or since one has a slight realization without fixation of the clarity-emptiness of the factors of total perfection.

The meditation that mentally engages this are meditations on the five faculties[118] at the time of warmth and peak. Concerning that, Dṛdhramati asked, "Bhagavan, what are the five faculties." The Bhagavan answered:

> Dṛdhramati, on the path of the bodhisattva there are five. What are those five? The faculty of faith, the faculty of diligence, the faculty of mindfulness, the faculty of meditative absorption, and the faculty of wisdom.
>
> [46] What is the faculty of faith? This concerns the actual faith in the genuine view for a worldly person involved in cyclic existence. When such a person would not commit vice even to save their life for fear of the fully ripening consequences of action, and enters into the conduct of a bodhisattva, and harbors no doubts when hearing about emptiness, absence of characteristics, the powers, fearlessness, and other qualities of a buddha, [but experiences only] joy, then that faith is the faculty of faith.
>
> [47] What is diligence? To generate the power of diligence in whatever dharma one has faith in is the faculty of diligence.
>
> [48] What is the faculty of mindfulness? To [apply] the power of mindfulness to whatever dharmas were diligently gathered so that they are not lost is the faculty of mindfulness.
>
> [49] What is the faculty of meditative absorption? To apply the power of undistracted, one-pointed meditative absorption to whatever dharma has been retained through the faculty of mindfulness of those dharmas is the faculty of meditative absorption.
>
> [50] What is the faculty of wisdom? To examine those dharmas that have been retained through the faculty of mindfulness of whatever dharmas, and to thus know that

all dharmas are like illusions and totally nonexistent is the faculty of wisdom.

[64] In general there are twenty signs of abiding in the four [levels of] the Path of Application. First, the ten signs of warmth, according to Maitreyanātha:

(1) Countering form and so on,[119]
(2) the expiration of doubts,[120]
(3) nonleisure,
(4) dwelling in virtue oneself,
(5) establishing others in it also,
(6) [practicing] generosity and so on as support for others,
(7) no hesitation about the profound meaning,
(8) loving [actions] of the body, and so on,
not accompanied by the five obscurations,[121]
(9) all latent tendencies conquered,
(10) mindfulness, and awareness.[122]

From the *Actualization of Timeless Awareness*:

Illusion-like direct experience
is in small part the warmth of timeless awareness.
Sometimes the teaching of timeless awareness of conduct
increases the direct experience.

[66] Four signs of the peak [experience] are taught by Maitreya:[123]

Clean clothing and such,
parasites and such not occurring on the body,
mind free of deception, assuming abstinence,
and eliminating avarice.[124]

Even in dreams all phenomena
are seen to be like dreams, and so forth;
signs of arrival at the peak of application.
They were held to be twelve.[125]

From the *Latter Ocean Tantra*:

> When once a dream is recognized
> the yogin is blissful for a fortnight.
> Gods, nāgas, and gandharvas make offerings and praise.
> Heroes and ḍākinīs actually gather 'round.
> It is the ship of liberation from the sea of bad existence.[126]

b. Acceptance and Supreme Dharma

[67] Then there are meditations on the five powers on the [levels of] acceptance and supreme dharma. Dṛdhramati asked, "Bhagavan, what are the five powers?" And the Bhagavan answered:

> Dṛdhramati, there are five on the path of the bodhisattva. What are those five? They are the power of faith, the power of diligence, the power of mindfulness, the power of meditative absorption, and the power of wisdom.
>
> [68] What is the power of faith? It is to be unintimidated by anyone at all with regard to that in which one has faith and one-pointed interest. [For instance], if a devil came and transformed into a buddha right in front of you and said, "Yours is not the [true] dharma," and [tried to] convert or avert you, you would not lose [that faith] or [try to] escape. Moreover, [even] the four great elements that can change things could not divest you of that power that is focused in the power of faith. That is the power of faith.
>
> [69] What is the power of diligence? Whoever has undertaken diligent [application] and through the force of the power of steadfast adherence to whatever virtuous dharma it is, maintains such power of diligence until that goal is achieved, so that no one at all would be able to turn one away from it—that is the power of diligence.
>
> [70] What is the power of mindfulness? It is an undistracted mind in the direct application of mindfulness to any

and all phenomena. That is, the power of mindfulness that no afflictive emotion can overwhelm. If that mindfulness is not defeated by afflictive emotion, then it is the power of mindfulness.

[71] What is the power of meditative absorption? With conscientious mindfulness that is not overwhelmed by afflictive emotion, wherever one dwells is isolated from busyness. One does not get involved in the notion of fixating on all those objects of attachment and aggression, such as form and so on. Being totally nonconceptual about any phenomenon is the attainment of the power of isolation from busyness. That is the power of meditative absorption.

[72] What is the power of wisdom? Fully knowing all mundane and supramundane phenomena through the power of wisdom, that which liberates worldly beings from cyclic existence arises from the power of wisdom and timeless awareness. Therefore it is called "the power of wisdom."

[73–74] Why are they called five powers? As the five faculties stabilize, their power increases, so they are called "powers" (*stobs*).

[75–76] The signs of acceptance, according to Maitreya:

> Proceeding by possessing the nature of phenomena,
> seeking hell for the sake of sentient beings,
> impervious to others' misguidance,
> and as to devils expounding alien paths,
> realizing that they are "devils."[127]

[77–79] From the *Questions of Four Girls*:

> Having stayed alone in the forest
> and taken up the practice of phenomena as illusion,
> the various dreams are known as dreams
> and one abides in acceptance, free of bad existence.[128]

[80] [From *Ornament of Clear Realization*:]

> The single sign of supreme dharma
> is conduct that pleases Buddha.
>
> Through those twenty signs
> abiding in warmth and peak
> with acceptance, and supreme dharma,
> one will not turn back from perfect enlightenment.[129]

From the *[Sūtra of] Kumāraprabha**:

> Free of all worldly attachment,
> whoever possesses the altruistic mind
> pleases the victorious ones
> like no other dharma.[130]

[82] The eliminations are the same as before: [the ten unvirtuous actions accumulated through the three poisons.] The parameters are from the timeless awareness of warmth up until supreme dharma.

3. The Path of Seeing

[83] Now I will explain the Path of Seeing. The essence of the Path of Seeing is that the meaning of the four noble truths lacks a frame of reference. The literal explanation is that the Path of Seeing is the direct seeing of the nature of phenomena that was not seen before.

There are four divisions: suffering, its cause, its cessation, and the path. The defining characteristics of the divisions are to see suffering and the other truths as emptiness, which is the acceptance of the knowing of phenomena.[131] Additionally, the subsequent moment of knowing sees that emptiness in an expansive way. It is that seeing of the nature of phenomena that is the Path of Seeing. The realization of thinking that both the acceptance and knowing of phenomena are the infallible causes of attaining enlightenment is the acceptance of subsequent knowing of the four truths. The arising of decisive certainty that such realization is unmistaken is the acceptance of the subsequent knowing of the phenomena of the four truths.[132] That is seeing with the timeless awareness of the Path of Seeing. Those are differentiated by four degrees of [seeing] the extent of the nature of phenomena: lesser, greater, still greater, and much greater.

[84] The mental engagement of the meditative absorption [involves] the seven branches of enlightenment.[133] In the *Questions of Matisambhava Sūtra**,[134] Matisambhava* asks, "Bhagavan, how should one regard the seven branches of enlightenment?" The Bhagavan responds:

> [85] Matisambhava, since one neither recollects nor deliberates anything, all phenomena are empty of their own characteristics. To see all phenomena as in essence nonexistent is the genuine mindfulness branch of enlightenment.
>
> [86] Matisambhava, since one [sees that] there is no established existence to virtue, nonvirtue, or neutrality, all designations of phenomena have no frame of reference and are illusion-like. This is the revealing phenomena branch of enlightenment.
>
> [87] Matisambhava, since one totally eradicates concepts about phenomena, there is actual realization of the path without accepting or discarding the phenomena of nirvana or the three realms, freedom from fixation, enthusiasm, nondiscursive interest, and sustained effort. This is the genuine diligence branch of enlightenment.
>
> [88] Matisambhava, since one totally eradicates all joy and sorrow, joy about habitual phenomena is not aroused, and intense afflictive states are removed. This is the genuine joy branch of enlightenment.
>
> [89] Matisambhava, since one has not even an atom of reference point to any phenomenon that one references, the extreme physical and mental agility [with regard to] all phenomena causes the mind to abide in meditative absorption without obscuration or reference point. This is the genuine extreme agility branch of enlightenment.

[90] Matisambhava, since one totally eradicates or realizes the fixation on all phenomena, the mind does not reference anything at all. When the mind rests in equipoise on anything, the realization of phenomena occurs. But if the mind does [not] rest in equipoise, it is not it.[135] And if the mind rests in equipoise that is not the equipoise of awakening, it is not it. In this way, the placement in equipoise free of fixation is the genuine meditative absorption branch of enlightenment.

[91] Matisambhava, one does not abide in phenomena whatsoever, nor depend [on them], nor attach [to them], nor bond [with them]. Mind does not fixate on phenomena at all—happy, sad, or in between. Without being carried away by all the mundane phenomena, once one is possessed of the equanimity that is genuinely not preoccupied with all phenomena, it is a joy. This is the genuine equanimity branch of enlightenment.

Matisambhava, this is how you should regard the seven branches of enlightenment.

[100] Thus by the power of that absorption, one directly sees the nature of phenomena, and when endowed with the clairvoyant powers, knows heartrending joy. Ever pure in conduct, one can transform this body for beings and give up one's life for dharma. The intelligent [experience] this on the Path of Seeing; it is explained as the sign of a nonreturner.

[101–5] In addition to that, twelve hundred qualities will also develop.

[106] It says in the *Flower Ornament Sūtra*:

> As soon as one attains that ground one is free of five fears:
> lack of sustenance, death, criticism, lower realms, and [troublesome] retinue.[136]
> Free of those fears, one finds nothing causing anxiety.
> This is because the self does not dwell there.[137]

One should understand the freedom from these five fears.

There are one hundred and twelve eliminations on the first Path of Seeing.[138] In particular, the six imputed [or acquired] afflictive states.[139] These are ignorance, desire, pride, anger, doubt, and [mistaken] views.[140]

There are five views [to be eliminated]: the view of the transitory collection [as a self], fixation on extremes, perverse views, holding views as paramount, and holding one's ethical discipline and deliberate conduct [as paramount].[141] Adding those five views to the five nonviews of ignorance and so on makes the ten afflictive states.[142] In the desire realm, those ten afflictive states of views [and nonviews] occur [in relation to] each of the four truths, so that there are forty. In the higher realms—the form and formless realms—[because they are] without anger, there are nine [afflictive states] connected with each of the four truths. This makes nine times four, or thirty-six, for the form realm and nine times four, or thirty-six, for the formless realm; seventy-two in all.[143] Adding the forty of the desire realm to that, we get the one hundred and twelve factors that are eliminated on the Path of Seeing.

This is how they are eliminated: The greatest of the great afflictive states to be eliminated on the Path of Seeing are like a great darkness, and the least timeless awareness dispels them like a candle. Again, as above, they are eliminated by the four truths and by the realization of no-self, which eliminates them all at once.

[110] The way it is viewed in the truth of Mantra is taught in the *Actualization of Timeless Awareness*:

> The great bliss of action-mudra
> releases the channel knots of fixation on valid existence in daytime,
> and releases the channel knots of confusion at nighttime.
> This is the way enlightenment is taught.

And from the same source:

> The great bliss of the mudra's bliss,
> direct seeing of the nature of phenomena,
> occurs through the guru's kindness.
> This is known as the primary truth.

[95–99] From the *Array of Sacred Oaths*:

> By day the illusions of appearance-emptiness
> and at night the deity's dream forms arise naturally.
> When one remains focused on that,
> it is the saṃbhogakāya of the victors.
> In a moment nirvana is attained in the intermediate state;
> what need to mention abiding there continuously.
> It is the same with illusion and lucid clarity.
> One need not speak of anything else.

The *Illuminated Timeless Awareness Latter Tantra* states:

> Any pure realms of the ten directions
> are refined by the array of bodies in dream.
> The qualities of the first ground
> come from that and nothing else.[144]

[108] Again from the same work:

> If, in daytime and in dreams,
> the habitual tendencies of confusion are not purified,
> one does not abide even on the eighth ground;
> no need to mention the Lotus-endowed?[145]

And in the *Sūtra of Brahmānanda**, it says:

> The qualities of the grounds and paths
> should be realized during the occasion of dreaming.[146]

[111] The parameters are from the supreme dharma [at the end of the Path of Application] through the Path of Seeing.

4. The Path of Meditation

[112] Now I will explain the Path of Meditation. The essence of it is totally nonconceptual timeless awareness. The literal explanation is that [it is called] "the Path of Meditation" (*sgom lam*) because after one has seen the truth of the nature of phenomena [on the Path of Seeing], one must become familiar (*goms*) with it.[147]

The divisions are the nine grounds, such as the [second] ground Stainless and so on.[148] The mental engagement of meditative absorption [involves] the eightfold path of the noble ones.

> Matisambhava asked, "Bhagavan, how should one regard the eightfold noble path of a bodhisattva?" And the Bhagavan answered:
>
> [113] Matisambhava, the equality of all phenomena is the genuine view. So the view [that there exists] the self or the person or the sentient being or the life-force or emptiness does not produce the genuine view. To be free of all views, from the least reference point of a view up through nirvana, whether superior, average, or inferior—that is the genuine view.
>
> [114] Matisambhava, whatever thought [one has, one should] eliminate thoughts. One who is skilled in the higher insight that incorporates calm abiding eliminates thoughts of good and bad phenomena, thorough thinking, and all discursive thought. Not thinking of anything, no thoughts at all, no thoughts even about what is genuine—that is genuine thought.
>
> [115] Matisambhava, whatever words [one utters should] not hurt oneself or others. They should not cause afflictive states in oneself, nor cause afflictive states in others. Words that induce the certain realization[149] of the equality of all phenomena—that is genuine speech.
>
> [116] Matisambhava, any action that is exhausted with no more to accomplish is a completed action. That is, action

that pacifies afflictive states, that is not done to inflame afflictive states, any action that is free of afflictive states, and is not done to arouse afflictive states, free of all complete actions that are positive, negative, or mixed and that are not accomplished—that is genuine completed action.

[117] Matisambhava, not to accumulate afflictive states is genuine livelihood. That is any livelihood that does not hurt oneself or hurt others and that achieves the purpose of the dharma—that is genuine livelihood.

[118] Matisambhava, effort is for accomplishing the dharma that is profound, free of elaboration, and uncompounded. Real, genuine persistence that includes mental attention, determination, diligence, and being undaunted in that purpose is genuine effort.

[119] Matisambhava, any mindfulness should afford no opportunity to all the afflictive states. That includes the mindfulness of the branches of enlightenment [such as the direct application of mindfulness to] the mind, mindfulness of the immeasurables, and mindfulness of the six perfections. Any mindfulness that affords no opportunity to the devil, any mindfulness that does not turn into the wrong path, mindfulness that is like a sentinel that allows no opportunity for all of the unvirtuous phenomena of the mind and mental events—that is genuine mindfulness.

[120] Matisambhava, from the equality of the self comes the equality of all phenomena. Since the self is totally pure, all phenomena are totally pure. From the emptiness of the self comes the emptiness of all phenomena. One genuinely enters into that equipoise. Any genuine meditative absorption knows everything through the wisdom of mind moments. The all-knowing timeless awareness [attains] actual genuine perfect buddhahood—that is the genuine meditative absorption.

Matisambhava, that is how one should regard that eightfold noble path of the bodhisattva.

[121–22] The signs that occur after one has mastered the profound meaning and become familiarized and stabilized are that one comes to possess force and miraculous powers. From the second through the tenth grounds twelve hundred unimaginable qualities arise.

The [factors] that are eliminated on the Path of Meditation are divided into six latent afflictive states that one is born with.[150] What are those six? They are ignorance, desire, anger, pride, the view of the transitory collection [as a self], and the view of fixating on extremes.[151] For the desire realm, if we divide each of those six into great, medium, [and small, and each of those in turn into great, medium, and small, such as greater great, greater medium, and so on], then there are nine [divisions] in each. The timeless awareness that eliminates them is also divided into nine [aspects] of great, medium, [and small]. So nine [divisions] of six makes fifty-four.[152]

In the form realm anger has been discarded, so for the [remaining] ones, the five afflictive states of the first meditative stability each have nine divisions that are eliminated by nine timeless awarenesses (great, medium, and so on). Nine times five is forty-five. In the second, third, and fourth [meditative stabilities], there are forty-five each, making one hundred and eighty.

In the formless realm also there are forty-five for each of the [realms]: forty-five in the perception-field of Infinite Space, and in the same way for the other three fields—Infinite Consciousness, Neither Presence nor Absence, and Nothing Whatsoever[153]—there are forty-five each, totaling one hundred and eighty. In that way, two [times] one hundred and eighty is three hundred and sixty. Adding the fifty-four of the desire realm on top of that makes four hundred and fourteen eliminations on the Path of Meditation.

5. The Path of Consummation

Now the explanation of the Path of Consummation.[154] It states in the *Sūtra of Teaching the Unimaginable*:

> [124] Child of a good family, what is the Path of Consummation? In the swift attainment of unsurpassable

enlightenment, if no other phenomena interfere, then it is called "the path without obstacle."

[125–26] What is that, child of a good family? Once all the obscurations have been eliminated by the path in which one meditates, the very most subtle of subtle obscurations in the last of the continuum of ten grounds are conquered by the unhindered ability of the vajra-like meditative absorption.[155]

[127] And from the *Highest Intention Tantra*:

Unfixated clarity-emptiness great bliss,
uncompounded naturally arising luminous clarity,
the bliss of the secret stamens,[156]
comes from the force of blessings.

Like torchlight illuminating gold coins in a dungeon,
the most subtle of subtle obscurations are conquered
by the ability of natural purity and natural freedom.
This is the secret sphere of activity.[157]

What is that buddha that is purified of cognitive obscurations in that way? The *Highest Timeless Awareness Tantra* says:

[128] The uncompounded basic space itself
and timeless awareness are not two.
The complete purity of emotional and cognitive [obscurations]
is the dharmakāya endowed with two purities.
[129] Without change, birth, or characteristics,
all buddhas are dharmakāya.
[130] There is no constructing or dwelling,
yet the two kāyas arise naturally from
the causes and conditions of the former thought of awakening,
accumulation of merit, aspirations, and creation phase.

[131] In the palace of Akaniṣṭha,
Vairochana saṃbhogakāya Vajradhara
fully possesses the excellent major and minor marks.
[132] The stainless kāya of appearance-emptiness is beyond examples:
the perfect inseparability of bliss-emptiness free of attachment.
Buddhas surrounded by bodhisattvas
proclaim with the natural sounds of the unborn,
the dharma of inseparable bliss-emptiness without limits.
[133] The place, time, teacher, retinue, and so forth
of nirmāṇakāya arise naturally to tame whomever,
taking forms that tame whomever is to be tamed.
[134] They ripen and liberate [beings], faultless like the lotus,
or like a wish-fulfilling tree or jewel.[158]

[135]Again, from the *Highest Intention [Tantra]*:

Creation phase is characterized by bliss.
In that the two [form] kāyas develop.
Dharmakāya comes from completion phase.
It is taught in this inseparable manner.

[136–37] Saṃbhogakāya arises or comes from dharmakāya, and nirmāṇakāya from saṃbhogakāya. It says in the *Sublime Golden Light Sūtra*:

For example, lightning occurs based on the empty sky. [The appearance of light is based on the lightning]. In the same way, the merit-kāya[159] appears based on the dharmakāya, and the nirmāṇakāya appears based on the merit-kāya.[160]

There is this enumeration of three kāyas that in essence are not three. In short, the rainbow-like form kāyas arise in the sky-like dharmakāya, knowing without concepts the state of absolutely all that is to be known, knowing everything vividly without thought. It is sky-like dharmakāya endowed with the beautiful bodies of the form kāyas.

The essence of dharmakāya is threefold: it is uncompounded, spontaneously present, and those [traits] cannot be affected by outside conditions. The essence of rupakāya is also threefold: it has knowledge, love, and ability. In that vein, Maitreya said:

> Spontaneously present and uncompounded,
> and not realized through external conditions,
> it has wisdom, love, and ability.[161]

If you are interested in further elaborations—such as the way the four kāyas are established from the five timeless awarenesses, and [how] the four kāyas come from creation and completion and from the two accumulations, and how the four kāyas are established from the four empowerments—then these should be learned from the many sūtras and tantras.

[138–39] Here, [we are concerned with] teaching the experience of one-pointed practice and summarizing without contradiction the intent of the sūtras and tantras. There is no spare time to know the unreachable limits of everything to be known and all approaches.

[140] In the *Journey to Lanka* it states:

> For as long as ideas exist,
> there is no reaching the end of vehicles.
> When ideas are no more,
> there is no vehicle, and no expression.[162]

[143] The parameters of the Path of Consummation are from the last continuum of the tenth ground through the four kāyas with their enlightened activities.

6. The Ten Grounds

[144] Now I will explain the progression of the grounds.

[145] The essence of the grounds is supramundane higher insight free of duality.

[146] The literal explanation is that since they are the support for all qualities or the bases for progressing higher, they are called "[progressive] grounds" (*sa, bhūmi*). It says in the *Ornament of the Sūtras*:

> Since measureless elementals are [made] fearless,
> [and] those measureless ones
> are endowed with progress and go higher,
> they are therefore held to be "grounds."[163]

[147] The divisions are ten grounds, such as Very Joyful. The defining characteristics of each of the ten grounds [are described] in *Sublime Golden Light*:

> Child of a good family, for what reason is the first ground called "Very Joyful" (*rab tu dga' ba*)? It is because it is the first time that the supramundane mind that was not seen before becomes manifest, and thus one attains excellent meaningful thoughts. [Becoming very greatly joyful[164]], the first ground is called "Very Joyful."
>
> [148] The second ground is called "Stainless" (*dri ma med pa*) because the stains of the subtle downfalls and all of the mistakes and faults in ethical discipline are purified.
>
> [149] The third ground is called "Illuminating" (*'od byed pa*) because there is immeasurable timeless awareness of the absence of characteristics and absence of mental engagement,[165] and the light radiance of the timeless awareness of meditative absorption is incapable of being moved or outshined by anything at all, and because one abides in the retention of recollecting what was heard.
>
> [150] The fourth ground is called "Radiant" (*'od 'phro ba*) because that fire of timeless awareness [166] burns up all afflictive states and the firelight of meditation on the factors of enlightenment radiates [and grows].
>
> [151] The fifth ground is called "Difficult to Overcome" (*sbyang dka' ba*) because of the difficulty of mastering the methods of meditation and sublime timeless awareness,

and because of taming the difficult-to-tame afflictive states that are to be eliminated on the Paths of Seeing and Meditation.

[152] The sixth ground is called "Manifest" (*mngon du gyur pa* or *mngon sum pa*) because all habitual phenomena become manifest without interruption, that is, all mental engagement in the absence of characteristics is made manifest.

[153] The seventh ground is called "Gone Far" (*ring du song ba*) because the nondissipating phenomena are uninterrupted and with the mental engagement in the absence of characteristics there is long-lasting meditation in the absorption of total liberation, totally pure and unhindered. Also because one has gone far from the shrāvakas and pratyekabuddhas.[167]

[154] The eighth ground is called "Immovable" (*mi g.yo ba*) because of attaining mastery of the meditation on mental engagement in the absence of characteristics whereby the afflictive states have no power to move it.

[155] The ninth ground is called "Excellent Intelligence" (*legs pa'i blo gros*) because of gaining the power to teach dharma in all its aspects and, being without misdeeds, there is unhindered attainment of extremely expansive intellect.

[156] The tenth ground is called "Cloud of Dharma" (*chos kyi sprin*) because cloud-like great timeless awareness pervades throughout the sky-like dharmakāya.[168]

The early signs of the ten grounds are described in the *Sūtra of Teaching the Unimaginable*:

Child of a good family, the early sign of the first bodhisattva ground is that the bodhisattva, the great being, sees the world systems of the three thousand-fold universe of world systems completely filled with ten million [times] one hundred thousand billion treasures. Child of a good family, such is a bodhisattva, a great being.

Child of a good family, the early sign of the second

bodhisattva ground is that the bodhisattva, the great being, sees the three thousand-fold universe of world systems as if in the palm of the hand, fully adorned with ten million times one hundred thousand billion multitudes of jewels. Child of a good family, . . . ([the same formula] is applied to the following as well).

The early sign of the third ground is to see oneself as a hero bearing weapons and solid armor and defeating all opposition.

The early sign of the fourth ground is to see various flowers manifestly strewn over the all-inclusive great earth mandala by all the wind mandalas in the four directions.

The early sign of the fifth ground is to see women adorned with all of the ornaments attaching garlands of *tsampaka* flowers[169] to their heads.

The early sign of the sixth ground is to see a bathing pond with four steps and golden sand freely flowing around, completely filled with water possessing the eight kinds of purity[170] and adorned with *kumuta* and *utpala* flowers and white lotuses, and to see oneself delightfully enjoying it.

The early sign of the seventh ground is to see sentient beings in the abyss of hell to the right and left, and to see oneself bringing them back without damage or impairment.

The early sign of the eighth ground is to see, on [one's own] two shoulders, the king of the beasts, the maned lion bearing a crown, frightening all the little wild animals.

The early sign of the ninth ground is to see the wheel-wielding universal monarch completely surrounded by ten million billion people. Looking in front, one sees them holding a white parasol hung with various jewels above his head.

The early sign of the tenth ground is to see the Body of the Tathāgata in a fathom of light of a color like gold, completely surrounded by ten million billion brahmās. Looking in front, one sees [the Tathāgata] teaching the dharma.

Those ten are the early signs of the bodhisattva grounds

> that [are experienced] by the bodhisattvas, the great beings.[171]

Thus it is taught here, and similarly in the *Sublime Golden Light.*

[157–59] As to which perfection is achieved on which ground, it further states:

> Child of a good family, a bodhisattva on the first ground achieves the perfection of generosity. In that way, the second-ground bodhisattva achieves ethical discipline, the third patience, the fourth diligence, the fifth meditative stability, the sixth wisdom, the seventh skill in methods, the eighth aspirations, the ninth power, and, child of a good family, the bodhisattva dwelling on the tenth bodhisattva ground achieves the perfection of timeless awareness.[172]

[160–65] The defining characteristics of the ten perfections are taught in the *Flower Ornament Sūtra*:

> The perfection of generosity is that while seeking the timeless awareness of buddhahood, one completely dedicates all roots of virtue to sentient beings. Ethical discipline is to thoroughly pacify all anguish of afflictive emotion. Patience is to be without malice toward sentient beings because love and compassion were initially developed. Diligence is [to promise] never to be satisfied[173] in one's quest for more and more virtuous factors. Meditative stability is to be in possession of a path with no regrets concerning the actualization of omniscient timeless awareness. Wisdom is the actualization of what is naturally unborn. Skillful method is the accomplishment of the immeasurable timeless awareness of the victors. Aspiration is to actually accomplish the timeless awareness that one has envisioned. Power is when all the opposing forces and all the evil hordes do not interfere at all with the

> path. The perfection of timeless awareness is the realization of [the genuine state of][174] all phenomena just as they are.[175]

The meditative absorptions, as stated above, are the seven branches of the bodhisattvas of the first ground, and the eightfold path of the noble ones from the second through the tenth grounds.

What is eliminated are the [previously taught] Path of Seeing eliminations and Path of Meditation eliminations.

[166–69] The obscurations of twenty [kinds of] delusion are as follows:

> Child of a good family, two kinds of delusion obscure the first ground:
> (1) Delusion of overt attachment to phenomena and individuals as bearing characteristics[176] and
> (2) delusion of the fear of the afflictive states of samsara and bad states.
> Two kinds of delusion obscure the second ground:
> (3) Delusion of confusion over subtle downfalls and
> (4) delusion of the arising of various actions and behaviors.
> Two kinds of delusion obscure the third ground:
> (5) Delusion of desiring to obtain what was not obtained and
> (6) delusion about the excellent attainment of sublime [mental] retention.
> Two kinds of delusion obscure the fourth ground:
> (7) Delusion of craving the joyful experience of equipoise and
> (8) delusion of craving the total purity of phenomena.
> Two kinds of delusion obscure the fifth ground:
> (9) Delusion of extreme weariness with samsara and
> (10) delusion of overt dedication to nirvana.
> Two kinds of delusion obscure the sixth ground:
> (11) Delusion about the manifestation of the movement of [karmic] formations and

(12) delusion about the manifestation of coarse characteristics.

Two kinds of delusion obscure the seventh ground:

(13) Delusion about the manifestation of subtle marks and

(14) delusion about the absence of mental engagement in the lack of characteristics.

Two kinds of delusion obscure the eighth ground:

(15) Delusion about purposefully seeking the absence of characteristics and

(16) delusion about attaining power over the fixation on characteristics.

Two kinds of delusion obscure the ninth ground:

(17) Delusion of not becoming skilled in the immeasurable teachings and immeasurable words and letters of any dharma and

(18) delusion of not attaining the power of confidence.

Two kinds of delusion obscure the tenth ground:

(19) Delusion of not attaining the total mastery of manifest great knowing and

(20) delusion of not becoming skilled in the subtle [meaning] of the ultimate, and so on.

Two kinds of delusion obscure the ground of buddhahood:

(1) Delusion of the cognitive obscuration about all the extremely subtle spheres of activity and

(2) delusion about taking bad states of extremely subtle afflictive states.

[170–71] Which unobscured realizations are realized on which grounds is taught in the *Sūtra of Kumarāprahba**:

> Child of a good family, one who dwells on the first ground realizes the meaning of the realm of phenomena pervading everywhere. The second ground realizes the meaning of the sublime stainlessness of the realm of phenomena. The third ground realizes that natural luminous clarity is concordant with the realm of phenomena. The fourth ground realizes

the meaning of complete lack of fixation to all phenomena. The fifth ground realizes the meaning of undifferentiated nature since all phenomena are one in the realm of phenomena. The sixth ground realizes the meaning of the lack of true existence of all afflictive states and discursive thoughts. The seventh ground realizes the meaning of no weariness with samsara and that all phenomena are without characteristics. The eighth ground realizes the meaning of pure realms and freedom from thought patterns. The ninth ground realizes the meaning of unimpeded immeasurable dharma, letters, and confidence. The tenth ground realizes the meaning of mastery over enlightened activity. The eleventh ground realizes the dharmakāya that is the thorough transformation of the all-ground, the saṃbhogakāya that is the thorough transformation of the five sense consciousnesses, the nirmāṇakāya that is the thorough transformation of mentation by various concepts of afflictive states, the excellence of their inseparability and freedom from all extremes, and the highest perfect pure meaning.

From the *Sūtra of Kumarāprahba*:

> [172] Kumarāprahba asked, "Bhagavan, what are the signs that are seen by the bodhisattvas who dwell on the grounds?"
>
> The Bhagavan replied, "Child of a good family, these are the signs of one who dwells on the first ground of a bodhisattva: The [bodhisattva] in a fraction of a second, at will can (1) attain one hundred meditative absorptions, and (2) enter into their equipoise, (3) see one hundred buddhas, (4) completely know their blessings, (5) shake one hundred world realms, (6) travel to one hundred buddha realms, (7) completely illuminate one hundred world realms, (8) fully mature one hundred sentient beings, (9) remain for one hundred eons, (10) penetrate one hundred eons of the past and one hundred eons of the future,[177] (11) open one

hundred dharma doors, and (12) fully display one hundred bodies, each body completely surrounded by an entourage of one hundred bodhisattvas who are each perfectly teaching. Having exerted diligence, they are possessed of these very qualities.

> Attaining this ground, one is free of five fears—
> lack of sustenance, death, criticism,
> bad states, and [troublesome] retinue—
> because one knows their nature.
> As soon as the ground is attained,
> one knows the feeling of crying for joy,
> and can give up one's life for the dharma;
> these arise in the intelligent.[178]

[173–74] Child of a good family, the bodhisattva who dwells on the second ground in a fraction of a second can attain one thousand absorptions and enter into their equipoise, see one thousand buddhas, completely know their blessings, shake up one thousand world realms, travel to one thousand buddha realms, completely illuminate one thousand world realms, fully mature one thousand sentient beings, remain for one thousand eons, penetrate one thousand eons of the past and one thousand eons of the future, open one thousand dharma doors, fully display one thousand bodies, each body completely surrounded by an entourage of one thousand bodhisattvas who are each perfectly teaching.

[175–76] Child of a good family, the bodhisattva who dwells on the third ground in a fraction of a second can attain one hundred thousand absorptions, see one hundred thousand buddhas, completely know their blessings, shake up one hundred thousand world realms, travel to one hundred thousand buddha realms, completely illuminate one hundred thousand world realms, fully mature one hundred thousand sentient beings, remain for one hundred thousand eons, penetrate one hundred thousand eons of the past and one hundred thousand eons of the future, open one hundred thousand dharma doors, fully display one hundred thousand bodies, each body completely surrounded by an entourage of one hundred thousand bodhisattvas who are each perfectly teaching.

[177–78] Child of a good family, the bodhisattva who dwells on the fourth ground in a fraction of a second can attain one billion absorptions and enter into their equipoise, see one billion buddhas, completely know their blessings, shake up one billion world realms, travel to one billion buddha realms, completely illuminate one billion world realms, fully mature one hundred thousand sentient beings, remain for one hundred thousand eons, penetrate one billion eons of the past and one billion eons of the future, open one billion dharma doors, fully display one billion bodies, each body completely surrounded by an entourage of one billion bodhisattvas who are each perfectly teaching.

[179–80] Child of a good family, the bodhisattva who dwells on the fifth ground in a fraction of a second can attain ten billion absorptions and enter into their equipoise, see ten billion buddhas, completely know their blessings, shake up ten billion world realms, travel to ten billion buddha realms, completely illuminate ten billion world realms, fully mature ten billion sentient beings, remain for ten billion eons, penetrate ten billion eons of the past and ten billion eons of the future, open ten billion dharma doors, fully display ten billion bodies, each body completely surrounded by an entourage of ten billion bodhisattvas who are each perfectly teaching.

[181–82] Child of a good family, the bodhisattva who dwells on the sixth ground in a fraction of a second at will can attain one trillion absorptions and enter into their equipoise, see one trillion buddhas, completely know their blessings, shake up one trillion world realms, travel to one trillion buddha realms, completely illuminate one trillion world realms, fully mature one trillion sentient beings, remain for one trillion eons, penetrate one trillion eons of the past and one trillion eons of the future, open one trillion dharma doors, fully display ten billion bodies, each body completely surrounded by an entourage of one trillion bodhisattvas who are each perfectly teaching.

[183–84] Child of a good family, the bodhisattva who dwells on the seventh ground in a fraction of a second at will can attain ten sextillion[179] absorptions and enter into their equipoise, see ten sextillion buddhas, completely know their blessings, shake up ten sextillion world realms, travel to ten sextillion buddha realms, completely illuminate ten sextillion world realms, fully mature ten sextillion sentient beings, remain for ten sextillion eons, penetrate ten sextillion eons of the past and ten sextillion eons of the future, open ten sextillion dharma doors, fully display ten sextillion bodies, each body completely surrounded by an entourage of ten sextillion bodhisattvas who are each perfectly teaching.

[185–87] Child of a good family, the bodhisattva who dwells on the eighth ground in a fraction of a second at will can attain absorptions equal to the atoms in one hundred trillion worlds[180] and enter into their equipoise, see buddhas equal to the atoms in one hundred trillion worlds, completely know their blessings, shake up world realms equal to the atoms in one hundred trillion worlds, travel to buddha realms equal to the atoms in one hundred trillion worlds, completely illuminate realms equal to the atoms in one hundred trillion worlds, fully mature sentient beings equal to the atoms in one hundred trillion worlds, remain for eons equal to the atoms in one hundred trillion worlds, penetrate eons of the past equal to the atoms in one hundred trillion worlds and eons of the future equal to the atoms in one hundred trillion worlds, open dharma doors equal to the atoms in one hundred trillion worlds, fully display bodies equal to the atoms in one hundred trillion worlds, each body completely surrounded by an entourage of bodhisattvas equal to the atoms in one hundred trillion worlds who are each perfectly teaching.

[188–90] Child of a good family, the bodhisattva who dwells on the ninth ground in a fraction of a second at will can fully attain absorptions equal to the atoms in one million infinite[181] buddha realms and enter into their equipoise, see buddhas equal to the atoms in one million infinite buddha realms, completely know their blessings, shake up world realms equal to the atoms in one million infinite worlds, travel to buddha realms equal to the atoms in one million infinite [buddha realms], completely illuminate world realms equal to the atoms in one million infinite buddha realms, fully mature sentient beings equal to the atoms in one million infinite buddha realms, remain for eons equal to the atoms in one million infinite buddha realms, penetrate eons of the past equal to the atoms in one million infinite buddha realms and eons of the future equal to the atoms in one million infinite buddha realms, open dharma doors equal to the atoms in one million infinite buddha realms, fully display bodies equal to the atoms in one million infinite buddha realms, each body completely surrounded by an entourage of bodhisattvas equal to the atoms in one million infinite buddha realms who are each perfectly teaching.

[191–96] Child of a good family, one who dwells on the tenth ground, even from a single tathāgata, in a fraction of a second accepts the great appearance of dharma, and the great light of dharma, and the immeasurable great cloud of dharma. Completely takes it, completely grasps it, and owns it. Tathāgatas from two and three up until an immeasurable [number] in a fraction of a second attain acceptance of the great appearance of dharma, and the great light of dharma, and the immeasurable great cloud of dharma. Completely take it, completely grasp it, and own it. Why is that? From the sky-like dharmakāya one is endowed with unimaginable clouds of dharma or timeless awareness, so [this ground] is called "Cloud of Dharma."

IV. The Fruition: Buddhahood

There are two manners of becoming a buddha: in the traditions of the perfections and of mantra. Then in the perfections there are two: the small vehicle and the great vehicle.

According to the small vehicle, Prince Siddhārtha[182] attained buddhahood as an ordinary [person, after traversing] the ten grounds, at Akaniṣṭha, the Unexcelled Realm, or the Vajra Seat [in Bodhgaya].

According to the great vehicle, this victorious one had reached buddhahood countless eons earlier. It says in the *White Lotus Sūtra*:

> Children of good families, I became a buddha previously many billions of eons ago.[183]

And in the *Meeting of Father and Son*:

> In ancient times, immeasurable countless eons ago, I became a buddha called "Buddha Indraketu."[184]

[197]According to the yoga tradition of secret mantra, Prince Siddhārtha went to Akaniṣṭha, and like a sesame bag bursting open, all the buddhas said, "Son of a good family, how will you attain buddhahood?" Thinking thus, he subsequently became buddha based on the outer five manifest awakenings.

[198] According to the father tantras of highest yoga tantra, in Akaniṣṭha he received empowerment from Mahāvairochana. He became a buddha there, and an emanation of that was the buddha here. From the *Secret Moon Drop*:

> Having abandoned the Pure Domains,[185]
> in the joyous Densely Arrayed Akaniṣṭha,
> he awakened to genuine perfection and became a buddha there,
> while a single emanation is the buddha here.[186]

Alternatively, it is held that that bodhisattva on the tenth ground received the conferral of empowerment by Vajradhara in the place Akaniṣṭha. [The bodhisattva] became a buddha through the bestowal of the empowerment. As stated in the *Meaningful Discipline Tantra*:

> In the excellent secret place, the sublime Akaniṣṭha,
> Chief Lord conferred empowerment
> on the bodhisattva there in the palace of dharma,
> Samantabhadra Vajradhatu conferred [empowerment],
> Vajra Bodhichitta conferred blessing, and
> suchness manifested as genuine awakening,
> becoming Supreme Essence Vajradhara;
> manifest buddha in naturally occurring great bliss.[187]

According to the mother tantras, the renowned buddha on the eleventh ground received the complete four empowerments in the Queen's infinite palace in Akaniṣṭha. He attained the state of a thirteenth-ground vajra-holder by relying on an excellent woman. As stated in the *Tantra of Total Nonabiding*:

> All the buddhas of the eleventh ground
> attain the state of vajra-holder
> by relying on the mudra of a woman.[188]

Alternatively, that tenth-ground bodhisattva in Akaniṣṭha received the complete four empowerments from the great Vajradhara in union as saṃbhogakāya and great Vajradhara as sukhakāya, the sixth family. By that, he traversed to the fourteenth ground. It says in the *Tantra of Vajra Bliss* and in the *Tantra of Timeless Awareness Drops*:

> The vase empowerment is the eleventh,
> the secret empowerment the excellent twelfth,
> the wisdom-timeless awareness the thirteenth,
> thus the tathāgata is the fourteenth.
> Each ground for each empowerment.
> These are the lords of the grounds.[189]

As to this, some [believe that] Akaniṣṭha of the Pure Domains is perishable. The Akaniṣṭha of Dense Array is not perishable. As it states in *Vajra Peak*:

> The joyous realm of Dense Akaniṣṭha,
> the pure land Dense Array, is not perishable.
> There, the dharma of the buddhas
> arises in the manner of perfect saṃbhogakāya.[190]

They hold that, "The place where the saṃbhogakāya of great Vairochana Immense Ocean dwells, surrounded by a retinue of tenth-ground bodhisattvas, is Dense Array. That does not perish. All of the lesser pure lands that exist within that are nirmāṇakāya pure lands, and therefore will perish." If that is so, and the realm of Immense Ocean does not perish, then [Pure Domains] also does not perish. The reason is that [otherwise] there would be both an explanation as a pure land and an explanation as a worldly realm. For instance, if an individual's limbs, eyes, ears, and so on are individually all impermanent, then their whole body would also be impermanent. The reason is that the general and the particular are subject to [the same] limits. Therefore, the place of Pure Domains *is* Akaniṣṭha. Akaniṣṭha as a place that has "abandoned" Pure Domains is like a hermitage is to a town. That it is imperishable is because it only appears to tenth-ground bodhisattvas. Perishability is what would appear to impure, ordinary individuals, and there are no [such] individuals [on the tenth ground]. Therefore, all scripture is scripture in accord with that.[191]

From the *Tantra of All-Victorious Nonduality*:

> The place of supreme timeless awareness,
> the fine place of excellent Pure Domains:
> here the Bhagavan dwells forever in Akaniṣṭha.
> It is the domain of Samantabhadra.[192]

Alternatively, mind itself that is coemergent with timeless awareness is Akaniṣṭha. From the *Highest Timeless Awareness Tantra*:

Mind itself is coemergent with bliss-emptiness.
This is the excellent place of Pure Akaniṣṭha.

[199] The difference between buddhas and bodhisattvas is like [the difference in] the waters of the ocean and in the hoof print of an ox. As it says in the *Flower Ornament Sūtra*:

The difference between a buddha and a bodhisattva
is similar to an ocean and an ox's hoof print.
Even the qualities of the three pure grounds
cannot be measured or evaluated.
What need to mention measures or descriptions
of the qualities of total omniscience?

[200] And from the *Sūtra of Teaching the Unimaginable*:

As the sky is to the earth,
a hair's tip can possibly be measured.
The Victorious One's ocean of qualities
cannot be described in an immeasurable eon.
It is beyond measure or evaluation:
for that reason it is unimaginable.

The commentary on the meaning of *The Stages in the Path of Illusion* was completed by the ḍākinī of timeless awareness, Niguma. It was translated by the ḍākinī of timeless awareness herself and Lotsāwa Lendarma Lodrö.

Additionally, I, Khyungpo Naljor, received it and put it into practice.

ithi mangalam

The Six Dharmas of Niguma 2

INTRODUCTION

THE *Vajra Lines of the Six Dharmas* holds a central place in the teachings of Niguma. They were given to Khyungpo Naljor a total of four times during his encounter with the ḍākinī, and by her own testament were held only by herself and her teacher Rāhula in all of India. Their practice is "the roots" of the tree of the Five Golden Dharmas of the Glorious Shangpa Kagyu, and indeed they serve that function. The teachings of the six dharmas, whether of Niguma or Nāropa, ultimately derive from the completion phase practices (*rdzogs rim*) in the major yoga tantras. These are the practices that make use of the subtle energetic currents and essences in the body ("the subtle body" or "vajra body"), using yogic exercises, breathing techniques, and visualizations to control those energies and thereby the state of the mind. These yogic practices represent the "path of means" (*thabs lam*) or techniques in training with the body as the means to change the mind. It is a central tenet of tantric teachings that the human body in this way embodies the potential for enlightenment.

Sangye Tönpa's *Collection of Necessary Oral Advice on Niguma's Six Dharmas* attempts to differentiate the tantric sources of the two systems:

> The six dharmas, according to Nāropa's position, are the collected essence of all mother tantras, and of those are considered to be from the esoteric instructions of *Hevajra.*

> According to the Niguma position, they are the essence of all the father tantras condensed in one direction. In particular, they are based on the *Jewel Ocean Tantra*. According to Rinpoche, there are many teachings on dream and lucid clarity from the fifteenth chapter (or fifteen chapters) of *Guhyasamāja*, so the primary source is said to be *Guhyasamāja*.[1]

Concerning Niguma's six dharmas, Jamgön Kongtrul connects the *Hevajra* tantra specifically with inner heat and *Guhyasamāja* with illusory body and lucid clarity, while the tantra of *Mahāmāyā* is connected with the dream yoga practice.[2] In any case, as we have seen, it is difficult to definitely cite the source and ultimately perhaps irrelevant since these teachings are cherished as the direct revelations of the Buddha Vajradhara. In his *Treasury of Knowledge*, Kongtrul elucidates three exceptional qualities of the Shangpa lineage, among which is this:

> The oral instructions are exceptional because the *Vajra Lines* that were listed by the ḍākinī of timeless awareness are unerring in meaning and uncorrupted in letter. They have not been afflicted with the compositions and alterations derived from the intellectual analyses of ordinary people.[3]

This is a very interesting statement since, at first glance, most editions of the *Vajra Lines*—and above all the one in Kongtrul's own collection—appear to be a jumble of indecipherable notes upon notes with tiny flea-tracks connecting fragments of comments to their places between words. In fact, none of the six texts that I consulted contain the actual unadorned vajra lines. Tangtong Gyalpo, who received the "direct transmission" from Niguma in vision, quotes each verse and then comments upon it, so that presumably one may use the text in his *Collection of the Essentials* to determine which parts are the "real" vajra lines. The clearest presentation I have seen is in an illuminated manuscript, written in gold, in the collected works of Lochen Gyurme Dechen.[4] There, the scribe's wise use of fonts clarifies the intent: the main vajra lines are written in large Tibetan print called "uchen" (*dbu chen*), the clarifying prose sentences after each verse are in large letters of a different script called "ume" (*dbu med*), and the comments which adorn the interspaces are in small print (*yig chung*).

But who was responsible for each of these layers? This is not easy to sort out with certainty. The "actual" (*dngos*) vajra lines are those in all editions and commentaries that one can assume are Niguma's verses as remembered by Khyungpo Naljor. The next level may also be attributed to the same source; perhaps they were not integral to the original verses, but were added as prose clarification by Khyungpo Naljor based on Niguma's teachings. According to the colophon here, they were translated by Lendarma Lodrö and "verified" or finalized by the great translator Rinchen Zangpo at Tholing monastery. This event is also alluded to in the life story of Khyungpo Naljor. Returning from India, Khyungpo befriended the translators Lendarma Lodrö and Gayādhara, and came to Tholing monastery in Ngari (mNga ris), part of the ancient Guge kingdom of western Tibet. There he encountered the great master Atisha Dīpaṃkaraśrījñāna (982–1054), who we know was in residence there for three years beginning in 1042.[5] Khyungpo Naljor felt that his texts had been corrupted and that he should return to India, but Atisha announced that "they are in accord with my Indian texts; it would be good to give them to Rinchen Zangpo to translate."[6] So it came to be, it seems, that the *Vajra Lines of the Six Dharmas* were translated by both Lendarma Lodrö and Rinchen Zangpo, the famous translator from Tholing. Tāranātha specifies that what was first translated by Lendarma was retranslated by Rinchen Zangpo and then corrected by Atisha himself.[7] The only other Niguma text that bears the latter's name is *Glorious Immortal Great Timeless Awareness*.[8]

Finally, the interlinear small print that is not included in the canon but only in later texts appears to be ultimately by Gyurme Dechen. That is how I make sense of the following additional information found in Gyurme Dechen's edition, as well as those in Kongtrul's *Treasury of Instructions* and in the *Shangpa Texts*:

> In the *Vajra Lines*, Khyungpo's notes are an integral part. Buddhaśrī distinguished the source from the notes and made some annotations. Again, the bilingual Gyurme

> Dechen examined them carefully with his great intellect, and arranged the more expanded [version]. May this be of vast benefit to the doctrine and to sentient beings.[9]

This addition is further commented upon by Jamgön Kongtrul and appears only in his edition and in the *Shangpa Texts* which were copied directly from it:

> Here, all the verses are the vajra lines themselves, while the prose in between seems to be the oral directions of the ḍākinī that have been written and arranged. This is the extensive commentary by Lochen Gyurme Dechen.

Still confused? In another text, Kongtrul recapitulates:

> This text ends, "Lotsāwa Lendarma Lodrö translated it; later, Lochen Rinchen Zangpo verified it." One with Khyungpo's notes included and one where Buddhaśrī separated the source from the notes, adding some notes, and again carefully examined by Lochen Gyurme Dechen are two different [versions]. "Clarifying Words of the Six Dharmas" with the notes is by Khyungpo.[10]

In keeping with the plan, I have translated here the text as it appears in the canon—that is, the Vajra Lines of verse and the interspersed prose. Since these were not distinguished there by the clever use of fonts, I have followed the edition in Gyurme Dechen's collected works by using italics where he has used the ume script. I have not included the notes, but have relied on them for clarification, mainly those in Gyurme Dechen's text, since they do appear to originate with him, and in any case that is the least problematic version.

These are just translation issues. In fact, these *Vajra Lines* were never intended to be understood except by those who genuinely put them into practice with the help of a qualified teacher. They were the lines that helped Khyungpo Naljor remember Niguma's indescribable teachings and that will similarly help all lineage holders to remember the personal teachings that they have received.

VAJRA LINES OF THE SIX DHARMAS[11]

Sanskrit: *Ṣaḍdharma-vajragāthā*[12]
Tibetan: *Chos drug rdo rje'i tshig rkang*

Homage to the Glorious Unity—Great bliss.
1. I heard this talk, the natural sound of the unborn great vehicle,[13]
from one who is ineffable, spontaneously present, and unconditioned;
union[14] and great bliss saṃbhogakāya, arising to tame anyone,[15]
the mighty Vajradhara of three kāyas and seven aspects:[16]

2. Matured by four empowerments, faithful, and diligent,
having first [experienced] impermanence, weariness, [and samsara's] deficiencies,
whoever strives at this sublime path
will awaken in six months, a year, or in this lifetime.[17]

The path of methods: naturally blazing bliss-warmth.
Illusory body: naturally liberated desire and anger.
Dream: naturally pure double-delusion.
Lucid clarity: naturally awakened stupidity.
Transference: buddhahood without meditation.
Intermediate state: [the victors'] saṃbhogakāya.[18]

3. One's own body is the means: three channels and four chakras.[19]
The blazing and melting of *a-ham* adorns one in moments with four joys.[20]
By uniting with the wisdom's *khagamukhā*,[21]
dissipating and nondissipating four joys arise in sequence.[22]

4. Gather the quintessence,[23] the hollow interior purifier in three vital points,[24]
and to quicken the heat,[25] the six dharmas, such as inner heat in sequence:
rabbit descending, holding, reversing, spreading, and blending with vital energy currents.[26]
Adorn oneself with nondissipating great timeless awareness.[27]

Hollow interior of fire—the vital point of the body, eating the food of inner heat, wearing the clothing, spreading the seat, receiving the empowerment of existence, naturally liberating obstructing forces, and riding the horse of energy currents.[28]

5. Unreal illusory body is for highest, medium, and lower faculties.
With constant devotion, one's body and whatever appears
is integrated as the deity's form of empty appearance free of attachment.[29]
Passion and aggression naturally liberated, the fourteenth ground will be attained.[30]

Those of highest faculties rely on the friendship of a holy guru,
the medium are guided without interruption by other words,
and the least develop meditative absorption on a single seat. [31]

6. One who has completely abandoned all concepts
should constantly maintain the vital point of intention for dreaming.
[Dream's] double delusion[32] is naturally purified and the qualities
of the path stages of illusion will naturally arise at all times of day and night.

Dreams are recognized, refined, increased, emanated, changed, and appear objectively. Excessive delusion, excessive wakefulness, excessive bliss, and excessive emptiness should be cleared up by devotion, accumulation of merit, and clearing of obstructions, and worn as ornaments.[33]

7. Lucid clarity arises through devotion to the guru, and
the great bliss of dissipating and nondissipating steady gaze
causes bliss, clarity, and nonthought inseparable to arise naturally.
Preliminary, main, and concluding practices are adorned by vital points of time.[34]

Lucid clarity is recognized, integrated, blended, and consummated.
A holy one who actualizes lucid clarity in direct experience
[introduces] the experience, enhancement and obstruction-clearing adorn it.[35]

8. Nothing transferred, no transference; that is for the very best.
Medium and least, after abandoning passion and aggression,
with joy and devotion, project upward with single-pointed visualization,
adorned by aspiration prayers.

Transference to dharmakāya suchness,
transference to unity of the yidam,
transference of the guru's blessing,
and transference to the unerring heavenly realm.[36]

Vital points of time, of body, of speech, and of substance
are trained and stabilized in the most excellent transference.[37]

9. In the intermediate state, light and so on are lucid clarity; the deity's Body,
and nirmāṇakāya to tame whomever; at intercourse, revulsion is the vital point.
Passion, aggression, and jealously are refined by the deity's Body of lucid clarity.

The two obscurations are naturally purified and three kāyas
actualized.[38]

Lucid clarity arises naturally in the first intermediate state,
middling, the victors' saṃbhogakāya arises naturally,
at the least, the nirmāṇakāya arises naturally without hindrance.
The general vital point is [three] unerring integrations on the
path.[39]

Forms, sounds, water, earth, light, increase, and so on;[40]
one should know the progression of dissolution and eighty
natures.[41]

10. In the degenerate times of strife and the disturbance of
perverse views,
genuine dharma is as rare as daytime stars and turtle fur.
In a time when perverse dharma is bartered as the milk of ethical
behavior,[42]
cherish the adornments of practice experience, scriptures, and
directories.[43]
Those who practice this sublime path
with no time intervening, or in this life, or in the intermediate
state,
after the three kāyas of inseparable bliss-emptiness arise
naturally,
will go to the actual heavenly realm of total purity.

I stamp this with the vajra seal to not spread it
beyond the one-to-one lineage for seven generations.[44]
This completes the *Vajra Lines of the Six Dharmas*.

From the mouth of the Ḍākinī of Timeless Awareness, Lotsāwa Lendarma Lodrö translated this. I, Khyungpo Naljor, offered her five hundred measures of gold and requested it, and then put it into practice. Later, at Tholing, it was verified by Lotsāwa Rinchen Zangpo.

Mahāmudrā 3

INTRODUCTION

MAHĀMUDRĀ is the main trunk of the tree of the Five Golden Dharmas of the Glorious Shangpa. In this tradition and in others, such as the Marpa Kagyu, Kadampa, and Chöd lineages, the word "mahāmudrā" connotes the highest realization and represents the most direct path of liberation (*grol lam*). Sangye Palzang's excellent commentary on the Vajra Lines gives this semantic explanation:

> Since that great seal (*phyag rgya chen po*, Skt. *mahā-mudrā*) stamps all things both animate and inanimate, anything higher than the "seal" does not exist, so it is "great." And what is that? The lucid clear dharmakāya."[1]

Khyungpo Naljor kept the teaching ever close to his heart, literally in a charm-box around his neck, and so this particular tradition is known as the "Amulet Mahāmudrā" (*phyag chen ga'u ma*) and also the mahāmudrā of "Threefold Letting-Go" (*rang babs gsum*), referring to the main instruction from Niguma. It is also sometimes called the mahāmudrā of lucid clarity (*'od gsal*). The distinctive feature is resting the mind without any mental fabrication or contrivance, from which state realization and liberation arise naturally. Jamgön Kongtrul describes it succinctly:

> The vajra lines of the instruction on the essential meaning of no mental engagement were highly valued by the scholar-adept Khyungpo, such that he rolled up the paper and inserted it into a heart-like Nepalese amulet box, which he tied it around his neck. Thus it is known as the "Amulet Mahāmudrā." In the preliminary of the threefold letting-go, one cultivates calm abiding and higher insight. In the main practice, the descent of vajra timeless awareness points out [mind's nature] in a sneaky way (the burglar method), and by means of the liberation of the four faults in their own ground, one becomes resolved about mind itself. In the concluding practice, one maintains the state of the naturally arisen three kāyas and relies on the extraordinary enhancement and obstruction-clearing practices. Thus, it is the heart of all teachings of sūtra and tantra, the pith of all esoteric instruction, and the actualization of the natural liberation of the four kāyas in mahāmudrā.[2]

The original vajra lines attributed to Niguma are, once again, overlaid with copious interlinear notes. This time, however, one can still find the unadorned lines since almost all sources present the annotated and unannotated versions separately.[3] In the Peking Tengyur, for instance, the two are not even consecutive, and the annotated version appears earlier in the volume. There is a sense that the simple beauty of the original lines are certainly worth presenting as such, but that it is quite difficult to gain even a basic understanding of their import without comment. So, as in the canon, I present here both versions, although I have chosen to put the unelaborated vajra lines first, and then follow them up by the awkward but more informative annotated version. The interlinear notes have been added in smaller font, more or less as they appear in the text (given the radically different order of English sentence structure). In trying to keep the simple vajra lines simple, my own endnotes are confined to the latter translation.

Niguma's two known teachings on mahāmudrā, the *Vajra Lines* and *Naturally Free Mahāmudrā* (which I have placed after the two versions of the first), are also included in the *Ocean of Song* (*mGur tsho*). This is a collection of the inspired spiritual poems of the Shangpa lineage masters collected by Jamgön Kongtrul that is often recited in group service as a meditation in itself. Indeed, the full title is *The Collected Dohā, Vajra Lines, and Songs of the Glorious Shangpa Kagyu: An Ocean of Blessings Meaningful to Hear*. Niguma's verses are introduced as follows:

> The Lord of all families, the sixth victor great Vajradhara, appeared naturally to the ḍākinī of timeless awareness as unborn native natural sound, which naturally revealed the abiding nature of mahāmudrā in samsara and nirvana, and she spoke these vajra lines.[4]

VAJRA LINES OF THE AMULET MAHĀMUDRĀ[5]

Sanskrit: *Mahāmudrā*
Tibetan: *Phyag rgya chen po*

Homage to Glorious Unity Mahāmudrā!
I heard this talk, the uncreated natural sound,
from great saṃbhogakāya Vajradhara:
great bliss, spontaneous presence, and unconditioned.

Emaho! Ordinary mind—amazing!
The preliminary is threefold letting-go.
The main practice is natural liberation from four faults.
The ultimate result is naturally arisen four kāyas.

In solitude, with earth-touching mudrā, four joints and four channels relaxed: the natural resting of body.
No effort of the lips, no expression or utterance: the natural resting of speech.
Mind free of the desire to meditate with gazing eyes: the natural resting of mind.

Make that itself free of four faults: mind dharmakāya is beyond inclusion or separation, yet is so close it is not recognized.
It arises to oneself, yet is so profound it is not grasped.
So easy it is not believed, divorced from nondistraction.
So excellent that it does not fit into intellect; without conviction one wanders in cyclic existence.

Ultimately, free of meditative equipoise, subsequent attainment, and mental fabrication, the natural arising of various clear appearances is nirmāṇakāya.
Nonconceptual freedom from fixation on that clarity is dharmakāya.
The arising of bliss in that very nonconceptual clarity is the saṃbhogakāya. Those three by nature inseparable is the ultimate mahāsukakāya.
The aspect of nonconceptuality in that suchness is the awareness of things as they are.
The aspect of clarity of how things are in nonconceptuality is the timeless awareness of the understanding of things in their multiplicity.
Those two by nature inseparable is called the nonduality of space and timeless awareness.

The preliminary's sacred pledge is a vajra secret.
The enhancement is supplication for compassion.
The integration on the path is that whatever appears is that suchness.
Actualization is being without meditation and without distraction.
The blending is integrating nonconceptuality on the path.
The direct gaze of lucid clarity is enhancement.
After waking, blend without fixation with the clarity.
Lucid clarity in the day, night, and intermediate state:
See the natural arising of the three kāyas inseparable.

This is the single word that will ultimately liberate
whomever does not understand the meaning that is hidden in
the mind stream.
Habituating and stabilizing nonmeditation and nondistraction,
one traverses the grounds and paths at that time.
With no mental engagement, the two obscurations are purified
on their own.
The resultant naturally arising three kāyas are spontaneously
present.
This is taught in all sūtras and tantras, but it is naturally hidden.
One should know it directly from the guru's blessing.

In the sky of dharmakāya, lightning of five poisons
comes from the clouds of thought: See great timeless awareness.
Without mental engagement, free of all hopes and fears,
I bow to you, ordinary mind.

The vajra lines of naturally arising mahāmudrā are complete.

To please the ḍākinī of timeless awareness, I [Kyungpo Naljor] offered five hundred measures of gold and requested this. Lotsāwa Lendarma Lodrö translated it. *ham*

VAJRA LINES OF THE AMULET MAHĀMUDRĀ (WITH NOTES)[6]

Sanskrit: *Mahāmudrā*
Tibetan: *Phyag rgya chen po*

Homage to Glorious Unity Mahāmudrā!
I heard this talk of uncreated natural sound
from great saṃbhogakāya Vajradhara:
great bliss, spontaneous presence, and unconditioned.

Emaho! Ordinary mind—amazing!
The preliminary is threefold letting-go.
The main practice is natural liberation from four faults.
The ultimate result is naturally arisen four kāyas.

In a solitary place, sitting cross-legged with the hands in the earth-touching mudrā,[7] the spine straight and the four joints, channels, and lips all relaxed is the effortless natural resting of the body.[8]

No effort of smiling, no opening or closing of the lips, no expression or utterance of speech, resting in that state is the effortless natural resting of speech.

Mind being free of the concept of the desire to meditate with gazing eyes is the effortless natural resting of mind.

Second, the main practice is to make that itself free of four faults: though mind-dharmakāya is beyond inclusion or separation,[9] one wanders in samsara because of the fault of being so close that it is not recognized.

Mahāmudrā arises to oneself, yet is so profound, incapable of being illustrated by examples, since in essence it is not established by color and so on, that it is not grasped.

So easy, even arising by letting go in meditation, yet it is not believed, [and one becomes] divorced from undistracted meditation.

Since it is the natural arising of the three kāyas, it is so excellent, but certainty does not arise because it does not fit into the intellect, and without conviction in dharmakāya, one's mind wanders in cyclic existence due to that fault.

Third, the natural arising of the three kāyas: Ultimately, [being] free of meditative equipoise, subsequent attainment, and mental fabrication, is the condition for the natural arising of mahāmudrā, and those various naturally arising clear appearances are nirmāṇakāya.

Nonconceptual freedom from conceptual fixation on that clarity of those various clear appearances is dharmakāya.

The arising of nondissipating bliss in that very [state of] nonconceptual clarity is the saṃbhogakāya. Those three by nature inseparable is the ultimate mahāsukakāya.
The aspect of nonconceptuality in that suchness is the awareness of the understanding of things as they are abiding.
The aspect of clarity and understanding of how the mandalas of all knowable things are in nonconceptuality is the timeless awareness of the understanding of things in their multiplicity.
Those two by nature inseparable is called the nonduality of dharma space and fourfold timeless awareness.[10]

The preliminary's sacred pledge of threefold letting-go, the burglar's pointing-out,[11] is a vajra secret.[12]
The enhancement of mahāmudrā is devotional supplication to the guru for immeasurable compassion.
The integration on the path of the times of the four daily activities such as going, moving, and so on is that whatever appears is that suchness.
Actualization of the result is being without even a speck of meditation and without even a moment of distraction.
The blending of day and night is integrating nonconceptuality of lucid clarity in sleep and between dreams on the path.
The elephant's direct gaze of lucid clarity of sleep is enhancement that takes total sleep to lucid clarity.
After waking from sleep, blend daytime and nighttime by meditating without fixation with the clarity of all the appearances.
Threefold lucid clarity in the daytime, the nighttime, and the intermediate state:
See[13] the natural arising of the three kāyas inseparable and indivisible.

This is the single word that will ultimately liberate
whomever does not understand the meaning that is hidden in the mind stream.
Habituating and stabilizing nonmeditation and nondistraction,

one traverses the grounds and paths at that time.
With no mental engagement, the two obscurations are purified
on their own.
The resultant naturally arising three kāyas are spontaneously present.
This is taught in all sūtras and tantras, but it is naturally hidden.
One should know it directly from the guru's blessing.

In the sky of dharmakāya, lightning of five poisons
comes from the clouds of thought whose nature is suchness:
See great timeless awareness.
Mahāmudrā without mental engagement, free of all hopes and
fears for samsara and nirvana,
I bow to you, ordinary mind, the state free of contrivance and
corruption.

The vajra lines of naturally arising mahāmudrā are complete.

To please the ḍākinī of timeless awareness, I [Kyungpo Naljor] offered five hundred measures of gold and requested this. Lotsāwa Lendarma Lodrö translated it.[14] *ham*

NATURALLY FREE MAHĀMUDRĀ[15]

Sanskrit: *Svayaṃmukti-mahāmudrā*
Tibetan: *Rang grol phyag rgya chen po*

Homage to dharmakāya ḍākinī of timeless awareness!
I bow to you, mind itself,
the wish-fulfilling gem.

Wishing to attain perfect awakening,
in order to purify ordinary concepts,
imagine one's own body as the deity
and be devoted with a pure, noble heart to the guru.

Without contemplating the guru and yidam,
things and no things and all of that,
without any feats in mentation whatsoever,
rest within the uncontrived native state.

One's mind without distraction is dharmakāya.
Nondistraction from that is the vital point of meditation.
Realize the great freedom from limitations.

This thought of afflicted passion or aggression
that flings one into the ocean of samsara:
sever it as intrinsically nonexistent
with the sharp weapon of the unborn.
If the tree is cut at the root
the branches will not grow.

Just as bubbles arise and dissolve
in the water of the limpid sea,
In that way conceptual thinking is nothing
other than the dharma nature.
Don't see it as a problem—relax.

Whatever arises, whatever is born, that itself
is free by itself without fixation to it.
Phenomena appearing and resounding are one's mind.
Aside from mind there are no other phenomena.
Mind is free of the elaborations of birth and cessation.

By knowing that suchness of mind,
even when engaging in the five sense desirables,
one does not move out of the nature of phenomena.

For instance, one who goes to the golden isle
cannot find dirt and stone even when sought.

In the equality of the great realm of phenomena,
there is no rejecting or accepting, no equipoise or subsequent
attainment.

At whatever time this is actualized,
at that time it becomes spontaneously present.
One becomes like a wish-fulfilling gem
who fulfills the hopes and desires of beings.

One should understand this in intellectual stages
of highest, intermediate, and lesser personal capacity.

Naturally Free Mahāmudrā by Niguma, the ḍākinī of timeless awareness, is complete.

The Three Integrations 4

INTRODUCTION

THE BRANCHES of the tree of the Five Golden Dharmas of the Glorious Shangpa are the *Three Integrations*. The term translated as "integrate" literally means "to carry on the path" (*lam du khyer ba*) and refers to a practice or attitude that one can apply during all activities, not just in formal meditation. It is an attitude of mindful awareness that, when maintained and carried throughout daily life, makes all activities into opportunities for further insight and awakening.

Tāranātha explains: "They are known as 'branches' because they are offshoots of the threefold practice of illusory body in the Six Dharmas: for lesser, medium, and greater faculties."[1] Thus they are specifically the "meditation-in-action" practices of the illusory body emphasized as a separate, effective practice. Briefly, it is to view all experience as the guru, as the yidam deity, and as illusion (corresponding to greater, medium, and lesser faculties, respectively, in illusory body practice). Each of those three practices also has a component that includes the three dimensions of awakening, or kāyas, in the realization: dharmakāya, saṃbhogakāya, and nirmāṇakāya. This is especially emphasized in the relatively few interlinear notes in the tengyur edition.

This seems to tie into another apparent text of "vajra lines" that was not included in the canon editions of Niguma's works, namely: *Integrating the Nature of Three Kāyas* (*sKu gsum rang bzhin lam khyer*) or simply *Three Kāya Integration* (*sKu gsum lam khyer*).[2] It is interesting that this work seems to have all the elements of the other vajra line texts, including the Sanskrit title, the words "I heard this talk, the uncreated natural sound, from great saṃbhogakāya Vajradhara," and the usual colophon from Khyungpo Naljor (with the difference that he states specifically practicing it for three months, and no translator is mentioned).[3] The contents, though by no means identical, are essentially similar.

Our text here, on the other hand, does not contain those elements. The fact that this colophon uses the term *mdzad pa* (created, composed) uniquely among Niguma's vajra lines is discussed by Gyurme Dechen in *Complete Explanation of the Vajra Lines of the Six Dharmas.*[4] The use of *mdzad pa* seems to "admit" that it is in fact the work of Niguma herself rather than Vajradhara. According to Gyurme Dechen, this would designate it as "treatise vajra lines" (*bstan bchos rdo rje'i tshig rkang*) rather than "buddha-word vajra lines" (*bka' rdo rje'i tshig rkang*). In any case, Gyurme Dechen has objected to the interpretation of the opening lines, "I heard this talk, . . . and so forth" in any of the vajra line texts as meaning that Niguma heard it from Vajradhara. Rather, he says, it means that Vajradhara himself heard or "understood" it, as it is commonly understood in the Rechung Hearing Lineage and other such sources. He goes on to conclude, therefore, that since it is well known in the Shangpa tradition that these teachings of the *Three Integrations* were also received by Niguma from Vajradhara, they could just as well be set up in the same [wrong] way as the others! Unfortunately he does not take into account the *Three Kāya Integration*, which would have added another interesting twist to his argument.

Aside from Tāranātha's brief comment, it is difficult to trace the sources of these teachings. The transmissions from Niguma that are listed in Khyungpo Naljor's life story mention only "vajra lines," and one must assume that all of the texts bearing that name were included. *Three Integrations* is not specifically mentioned anywhere in his life story,[5] although a teaching on integrating the three kāyas was one of many teachings that Khyungpo received from Maitrīpa.[6] It is yet another mystery why this text rather than the other was included in the canon and why it came to occupy the important position in the Five Golden Dharmas. One may rest assured, however, that the vital points of utilizing all appearances as guru, yidam, and illusion, including the recognition of the three kāyas therein, are available in these lines and in the few commentaries on them.

THREE DHARMAS TO INTEGRATE ON THE PATH [7]

(Herein is the source text of the three integrations on the path with the guiding instructions, essence of the vital points, and so on.[8])

Sanskrit: *Dhana-dharma-treya-nāma*[9]
Tibetan: *Lam khyer [kyi chos] gsum zhes bya ba*

Homage to the glorious three-kāya great bliss.

One who has attended an excellent guru and received
  empowerment,
who dwells in solitude, having mentally given up the world,
and practices this sublime path with single-pointed effort,
will attain the three spontaneities within years or months.

In this way, using the variety of appearances
as the bliss, emptiness, and clarity
of the guru, yidam, and illusion,
integration of three kāyas will occur naturally.

The intelligent practitioner, after the preliminaries
of weariness with impermanence and sublime aspiration for
  awakening,
completes the practice of guru yoga
with one's body as yidam and the guru above the head.
Then on behalf of all beings throughout space,
one prays with the motivation of compassion.
By that, devotion will arise and
all varieties of appearance
will be gradually seen as the guru.

In all four kinds of daily activity[10]
one's body is the empty appearance of the deity's form.
Once all mental concepts are completely abandoned,
integrating the ever-present guru on the path
causes whatever appears to arise as the guru.
This is the sublime integration of the guru.[11]
(4) It becomes stable in this way,
and one [contemplates that] it is this very guru
who will liberate me from this unbearable great ocean
and [so I will] obtain in this life what is not obtained in
innumerable [eons].
Pray while constantly recalling this kindness.
Do the pure sevenfold service, such as prostrations.[12]

(5) All sounds of audible emptiness are the guru's speech.
(6) Thoughts and memories are integrated as [the guru's] mind.
This is the integration of the guru's three kāyas.

(7) Thus with the specially exalted integration on the path
during all equipoise and subsequent attainment, day and night,
(8) know everything that appears as the guru
and that very guru as one's own mind.
That inseparability of mind and guru
occurs as the natural arising of great bliss,[13]
(nirmāṇakāya) clarity, and (dharmakāya) emptiness (inseparable).

* * * * *

Then the explanation of integrating the yidam:
In order to reverse attachment to the ordinary,[14]
meditate without concepts on the clarity
of one's own body as clear [but] empty illusory form.

(9) Then, attraction to the pleasant, aversion to the unpleasant, and
stupidity toward objects difficult to comprehend—
these three objects and the variety of all external appearances

will be gradually known as the deity's form.
With faith and devotion in that,
do the pure seven such as prostrations, as before.

(10) Know whatever appears as the illusion of the deity's form,
and that very deity's form as one's own mind.
The inseparability of mind and the deity's form
is great bliss, (nirmāṇakāya) clarity, and (dharmakāya) emptiness
(inseparable as the) deity's form.
That is the explanation of the three-kāya integration.

The benefits are that all concepts are completely abandoned,
and if the deity's form is constant for six months,
then in this life or in the intermediate state
one will attain the saṃbhogakāya of the victors.

(11) In that, the aspect of appearance is creation phase and
the aspect of emptiness is completion phase.
There is no dharma that is neither creation nor completion.
This is the manner of unity that is taught.[15]

(12) Having seen oneself and appearance as deity,
view the full range of all sounds as mantra.
All mantras[16] are empty sound without intrinsic nature.
Their clear resonance is timeless awareness, their emptiness is
basic space;
knowing their inseparability is liberating
and becomes the attainment of nirmāṇakāya that tames anyone.

(13) Listen to the explanation of integrating memory and
thought:
The three poisons[17] arise naturally without restriction.
Without rejection or fixation,[18] know them as the three kāyas.
The essence of desire is bliss—saṃbhogakāya, the essence of anger is clarity—
nirmāṇakāya, the essence of stupidity is [non]-thought—dharmakāya.[19]

Knowing this will undoubtedly bring liberation.

Alternatively, the steady gaze at three poisons
will [reveal] their lack of intrinsic nature and dharmakāya will be attained.

* * * * *

Then, the integration of illusion on the path:
Using the example of the variety of dreams in this way,
appearances are ascertained as mind.
Mind, in illusory dreams,
recognizes, refines, increases, emanates, and changes.
Having completely abandoned all concepts
during all daytime activities,
practicing with intention while falling sleep,
naturally arising [illusion] occurs in dream time.
The lucid clarity free of fixation on illusion[20]
will arise from the force of devotion and steady gaze.
(Saṃbhogakāya) bliss, (nirmāṇakāya) clarity, (dharmakāya) nonthought,
ineffable three kāyas inseparable: (svabhāvikakāya) great bliss
will arise naturally at all times of day and night.
This is lucid clarity mahāmudrā.[21]

(Conclusion:) In brief, with sublime devotion and
the view of one's body as empty appearance of the deity's form,
speech as empty sound of utterance and recitation,
mind as thoughts and memories with no fixation,
practicing one-pointedly in that way,
the result will be actualized in years or months.
The secret mantra path of direct actualization
is superior to all others.[22]

This concludes the especially exalted Three Integrations on the Path created by the ḍākinī of timeless awareness.

It was translated by Lotsāwa Lendarma Lodrö. I, Khyungpo Naljor, offered that ḍākinī herself five hundred measures of gold and requested it, and have put it into practice.

Immortal and Infallible

5

INTRODUCTION

THE FRUIT of the tree of the Five Golden Dharmas of the Glorious Shangpa is the teachings of immortal mind and infallible body, called simply "Immortal and Infallible" (*'chi med 'chugs med*). It is also known as "Naturally Liberated Immortality" (*'chi med rang grol*). Tāranātha describes it as the combined essence of lucid clarity, illusory body, and mahāmudrā, and so it is known as "the fruit."[1]

The two parts have different sources, although they are practiced together in the Shangpa tradition. The teachings of infallible body are based on an esoteric instruction of the *siddhācārya* Virūpa called *Spiritual Power of Immortality* (*'Chi med grub pa*). This is included in the collection of vajra lines as "the root text of immortal body." According to the colophon, it was presented to the "Cemetarian" and the Tibetan Ma Lotsāwa,[2] who translated it right there in the cemetery of Teto. This is certainly the same text found in the tengyur with the title *Spiritual Power of Amṛita* (*bDud rtsi grub pa*) by Virūpa and translated by Enadeva (or Edewa), who has the epithet "Cemetarian."[3] The text is largely similar but with enough variations to make for a fascinating comparison, though unfortunately not here. The homage in both versions to the headless ḍākinī Chinnamuṇḍā would indicate that this is not the famous mahāsiddha Virūpa known as the source of the vajra lines in the Lamdre tradition, but the junior Virūpa, or Virūpa of the East, who is connected especially with Sukhasiddhī in the Shangpa tradition and is the formulator of the practices of Varāhi with the Severed

Head.[4] The subject matter involves esoteric yogic practices that utilize the energy currents, channels, and vital drops of the subtle body to reach the realization of its infallible and deathless nature.

Niguma's teachings on immortal mind that are translated here, on the other hand, employ a creation phase/mahāmudrā approach in first visualizing a deity and then, based on that, examining the nature of mind. This involves an introduction to or a pointing-out to oneself of the nature that was always there. The two practices together, then, form a consummate whole by including both creation and completion phases, or the two approaches known as the path of liberation and the path of methods. Kongtrul describes the two together:

> Through thirty-two exercises to achieve immortality, the body enters into the path of emancipation. One's own mind that was never born is therefore deathless and attains the great natural liberation. The fully ripened body is a corporeal collection of aggregates, so it is empty of any basis on which to designate birth and death. This means that the body occurs from the mere appearance of mind, and mind is without birth and death. When this is deeply realized, the body appears as the mahāmudrā of deity's form, held in the space that is not fallible by deluded appearance. There are various instructions, but [the point is that] in this life one can discover the kāya of unity. It is said that just hearing about this will result in awakening in the intermediate state as the saṃbhogakāya of the victors, and so forth.[5]

This edition in the tengyur has interlinear notes included, which have been replicated here also in a smaller font. The edition in Bodong's collection has interlinear notes, though not always the same ones. The other editions consulted have only a few notes.

GLORIOUS IMMORTAL GREAT TIMELESS AWARENESS[6]

(The vajra lines of immortality and such concerning deathlessness.)

Sanskrit: *Śrī-amāra-jñāna-mahā-nāma*[7]
Tibetan: *dPal 'chi med ye shes chen po zhes bya ba*

Homage to the Glorious Immortal Great Timeless Awareness

I heard this talk, the natural sound of immortal timeless awareness, the activity of nirmāṇakāya,
from the victors' dharmakāya essence, saṃbhogakāya great Vajradhara.

Anyone person with faith and devotion to the guru who has received this and other empowerments and has the root and branch sacred pledges,
will realize this meaning of immortality by attending an excellent guru.
One with faith and devotion who has mentally left this life behind, in one-pointed[8] meditation, at best in seven days, at least in years, and middling in months,
will purify this body of however much afflictive emotion
and the immortal body of timeless awareness will occur in due course.

Having done the preliminaries of the four immeasurables and arousing the aspiration,
[generate], by the three rites or instantaneously,[9]
one's own body as the yidam Chakrasaṃvara masculine-feminine.
Light rays from the seeds *hūṃ* and *baṃ* in the top of their heads[10]
purify everything outside and inside the body
and refine it as empty-clarity itself.[11]
Empty-appearance is the rainbow-like form of light;

without intrinsic nature yet appearing
with color, face, hands, ornaments, and bonfire.

Look at the great nondissipating empty-bliss
of clarity without concepts.
One's body as empty appearance of the deity's form is actually one's mind.
Mind is the empty appearance of the deity's form.
Mind and the deity's form are inseparable.
(Not that the deity's form is beyond the mind once it has been discounted, or that that the mind is truly existent beyond the deity's form that has been discounted.)

Like dream objects and water moons,
by nature inseparable great unity,
in essence ineffable and beyond intellect.
Buddhas of the three times did not see that ineffable essence in the past,
will not see it in the future, and do not see it at present.

Thus, there is no cause of illness, no cause of death, no cause of wandering in cyclic existence, and the cause of awakening in nirvana is nonexistent.
Since there is freedom from all transitors and transitions,
therefore that timeless awareness is the natural liberation of immortality.[12]

The yogin who does not realize the immortal mind in that way,
will practice hardship for an immeasurable eon without reason,
and just be wasted, having entered merely a dead-end path.

Any person, even one who committed the entire five acts of immediate retribution,
at the time of the point of death or at other times,[13]
who recalls by contemplating in the mind, hears the speech, or touches physically with the body for a mere moment or a single second,

this fourfold vajra verse of immortality from the *Ocean of Timeless Awareness Tantra*[14]
will naturally purify all suffering of the interruption of life.

Then in the first intermediate state one will actually perfectly awaken as the victor saṃbhogakāya.
What need to mention those of lesser obscurations?
This is the infallible vital point.

If, somehow, under the power of conditions, the body-mind
does not become clear[15] at the point of death,
then, for instance, like a catapult mechanism,
the previous vital points[16] will produce the natural arising
as the victor saṃbhogakāya in the intermediate state.

Even with a difficult passage that agitates the mind stream,
it is like a stone thrown into a clear limpid pool:
by the previous vital points the great bliss saṃbhogakāya
will arise naturally in the intermediate state.

Even without stability or sufficient time,
it is like the moonrise at sunset on the fifteenth:
hearing or recalling now or at the point of death
will no doubt result in the saṃbhogakāya in the intermediate state.[17]

One's mind as unborn dharmakāya
unhindered arises naturally as rūpakāya
and until the ocean of samsara is emptied
is spontaneously present for the benefit of others to be tamed.

With the realization of the great unity
of essence, form, and enlightened activity,
this conceptual thought called "death"
[known as] causeless death [relates to] the highest faculty.

The instant that this meaning is realized,
one goes to the pure heavenly realm of great bliss.[18]
The victors of the three times, by realizing this,
conquered the devil, awakened, and turned the wheel.

Therefore, this heart-essence of the victorious ones,
although taught in many tantras and sūtras,
cannot be found by any other method
except the benevolence of the holy ones.

Therefore, serving an excellent guru
with respect and consideration is the vital point.
When degenerate wrong views mixes up the mind stream,
don the ornament of confidence based on scripture.

This immortal great timeless awareness
is stamped by the seal of a one-to-one lineage
from seven generations to three.[19]

This concludes one's mind naturally liberated as immortal.

This was taught by the ḍāki-ma of timeless awareness in the teakwood forest. It was translated by Lendarma Lodrö and ascertained by himself and Lotsāwa Rinchen Zangpo.[20] I, Khyungpo Naljor, offered that ḍāki-ma herself five hundred measures of gold and requested it, and I have put it into practice.

Chakrasaṃvara

6

INTRODUCTION

THE *Chakrasaṃvara Tantra* is one of the major tantras in the division of what is now called "Mother Tantras" (*ma rgyud*) or Yoginī Tantras, within the broader category of highest yoga tantra.[1] The so-called root tantra is said to be an appendix (*uttaratantra*) of a mythic root text that was an enormous work of one hundred thousand or even three hundred thousand verses, which, if true, makes the extant tantra a tiny fraction of the original. The relative brevity of this root tantra is compensated for by at least nine major explanatory tantras, further commentaries on the root text, and hundreds if not thousands of texts that instruct practitioners in the ritual components of practice, such as sādhanas, *abhiṣekavidhis*, and *maṇḍala-vidhis*, such as we have here.[2]

The colophon of the mandala ritual translated here cites a tantra called *Saṃvara Ocean Tantra* (*sDom pa rgya mtsho*) as its ultimate source. This and the *Jewel Ocean Tantra* are said to be the main sources of all of Niguma's teachings.[3] In the *Blue Annals*, Roerich suggests that this obscure title may refer to the *Ocean of Ḍākas Tantra*,[4] which is one of the major Chakrasaṃvara explanatory tantras and would make much sense, but it is not at all certain. What is recorded in the Shangpa biographies is that Niguma granted Khyungpo Naljor "the empowerment of Chakrasaṃvara mandala of sixty-two, thirteen, and five deities."[5] This seems to be exactly what we have here in *The Mandala Ritual of Chakrasaṃvara*, as the directions at the beginning of the empowerment suggest. Khyungpo received transmissions of the Chakrasaṃvara cycle from several of his gurus, but this has prominence of place in being directly from Niguma.

The yoginī tantras, and Chakrasaṃvara in particular, are associated especially with tantric sexual practices and the experiences of meditative bliss and other nonnormative Buddhist practices associated with the siddha movement.[6] The term *saṃvara*[7] was translated by Tibetans as both "union" or "binding" (*sdom pa*), and as "sublime bliss" (*bde mchog*, from *śamvara*), giving rise to the two names commonly used in Tibetan: Khorlo Dompa, "Binder of Wheels," and Khorlo Demchok "Wheels of Bliss." The interpretation of the term as bliss connotes the fruition of the practice, while "binding" refers to the process of meditation. "Wheels" (*'khor lo*) can be synonymous with "mandala" (*dkyil 'khor*) and in the tantra refers to the visualizations of the central mandala of Chakrasaṃvara and Vajrayoginī with the four direction ḍākinīs, who are further surrounded by three concentric wheels—the blue mind wheel, the red speech wheel, and the white body wheel. Chakrasaṃvara practice binds the wheels of the network of the dakinis in the triple wheel configuration. Simultaneously the pattern is mapped on to the practitioner's subtle energy body, with the wheels corresponding to the three chakras or converging hubs of the energy channels. This simultaneous macrocosm-microcosm application is a signature theory of the tantras. From this description by David Gray, it can be seen that all of these elements from the root tantra are present in Niguma's two texts as well:

> Accordingly, the Cakrasamvara adept, who is shown the maṇḍala in the context of his or her consecration, is to engage in an intensive practice of meditation which involves visualizing the maṇḍala—which is thought to pervade the triple world of ancient Indian cosmology—within his or her body. The practitioner's body is linked to the larger cosmos via the three wheels of the maṇḍala, which are correlated to the triple world cosmology—to the heavens, earth, and underworlds, respectively—and also the three bodies of a buddha, namely to the reality body (*dharmakāya*), the

> communal enjoyment body (*saṃbhogakāya*), and the manifestation body (*nirmāṇakāya*), respectively.[8]

This microcosmic or inner application to the practitioner's body is more evident in Niguma's works, which tend to emphasize the completion phase practices of subtle energy control, as in her *Six Dharmas*. The *Mandala Ritual* is of course meant to be a guide for the preceptor bestowing the empowerment or auspicious blessing for the practitioner to pursue the practice, as is clear not only from its contents but also its secondary appellation in the colophon as an empowerment into absorption (*samādhi-abhiṣheka*). In itself it would be employed only once by a practitioner.

It is the sādhana (literally "method of accomplishment") *Swift Accomplishment of Glorious Chakrasaṃvara* that would be used as the basis for regular practice. This incorporates the three-wheel visualization as a self-visualization and purification practice. The wheel imagery is extended to include the wheels as weapons, as the meditator visualizes a "slicing and dicing" effect to subdue negative forces. The results of the purification, such as the purging of toxic emotions, obscurations, disease, and so forth, are standard vajrayāna fare. There is a final section for the enactment of the four modes of tantric action—peaceful, enriching, overpowering, and wrathful—which mentions, along with other benefits of the practice, several kinds of physical ailments that are eliminated. This has prompted Miranda Shaw to label the practice as an unusual "Chakrasaṃvara Healing Mandala," contending that "Niguma is the lineage founder of a specialized meditation that is designed for the healing of illness through visualizing Vajrayoginī and Chakrasaṃvara in sacred union."[9] Though healing in its broadest sense is certainly a component, there are clearly much loftier benefits in mind, including nothing less than total awakening. It does not strike me as a specially designed medical sādhana, and it is not utilized that way in the Shangpa tradition. In fact, it is unfortunately not used much at all since simpler methods of practice composed by later holders of the lineage, such as Tāranātha, seem to be preferred. Nevertheless, it is a powerful and beautiful practice with an unbroken transmission since its mysterious beginning.

MANDALA RITUAL OF GLORIOUS CHAKRASAṂVARA[10]

Sanskrit: *Śrī-cakrasaṃvara-maṇḍala-vidhi-nāma*
Tibetan: *dPal 'khor lo sdom pa'i dkyil 'khor gyi cho ga zhes bya ba*

Homage to Glorious Chakrasaṃvara!

Whoever desires to perform the empowerment conferral of the meditative absorption should first just become well prepared in a place where the mind can engage.[11]

There set up a nice arrangement of excellent pictures, statues, and so on of the Conqueror Saṃvara. Then anoint well the ground of the mandala with the five things of a cow,[12] saffron, alcohol, and so forth. Then do the mandala[13] of sixty-two, thirteen, or five deities. Furthermore, arrange four lotus petals with heaps of flowers of the direction colors (east: blue, north: green, west: red, south: yellow) and the center, making five.[14] Generate the five deities from those. Set up extensive fivefold offerings and five *torma*, and so on. Then seat the qualified disciples in rows. If they are experienced, have them recite the hundred-syllable mantra of Heruka or the hundred-syllable mantra of Vajrasattva, whichever is appropriate. Then do the preliminary practices from death and impermanence and so on.[15]

Then engage oneself in the yoga of the creation phase. In the practitioner's own heart imagine a lotus from *paṃ*, the sun mandala from *raṃ*, and upon that a blue *hūṃ*. Imagining the seven letters circling that, recite the mantra however much is appropriate. Then light rays radiate from *hūṃ* in the center of the mandala, purifying the sins and obscurations of all sentient beings in the three realms. The light returns and dissolves into *hūṃ*. From that is generated the mandala of sixty-two, or thirteen, or five deities. The blessings of Body, Speech, and Mind of the awareness beings come to dwell there and seal the empowerment conferral, and so forth; follow the source texts.

Next, saying the mantra *oṃ hrīḥ ha ha hūṃ hūṃ phaṭ*, offer the outer offerings of the five things, the inner offering,[16] the secret offering, and the praises. Then the consecration of the alcohol: inside the *kapāla* (skull-cup), Saṃvara masculine-feminine arises instantly in the spontaneously present manner. Reciting the mantra, imagine that from the couple's place of union, vital essence bodhichitta that is the nature of elixir falls and changes the alcohol in the skull-cup to elixir. Then imagine that the couple dissolve into the essence of bliss and fill the skull-cup to the brim. Sprinkle that [elixir] on all of the assembly items and offering substances, consecrating them as elixir.

Next, on the disciples' heads a lotus arises from *paṃ*, the sun mandala from *raṃ*, and Bhairava and Kālarātri, and on that, *hūṃ*. At the throat, from *paṃ*, is a red [four-petaled] [17] lotus with a red *a*[18] swelling up in the center. At the heart also is a lotus, sun, and Bhairava and Kālarātri, upon which is *hūṃ*. At its center is a dharma-source and within that a red *baṃ*. Have them visualize this.

Then light radiates from the *hūṃ* on the crown of the head and purifies the sins and obscurations of all beings in the three realms, placing them in the state of the Conqueror Chakrasaṃvara. The light rays gather back and dissolve into *hūṃ*. That *hūṃ* completely transforms into the nondual nature of the guru and Heruka,[19] with all the attire and adornments, in the form of the masculine and feminine surrounded by the four ḍākinīs. Thus meditate.

Light rays arise from the seed-syllables in their hearts and infuse the great bliss [chakra] with light, purifying sins and obscurations of the body. Think that the vase empowerment has been received.

Then the throat chakra of enjoyment is infused with light, purifying sins and obscurations of speech. Think that the secret empowerment has been received.

Then the dharma chakra at the heart is infused with light, purifying the sins and obscurations of mind. Think that the timeless awareness through wisdom empowerment has been received.

Then the emanation chakra at the navel is infused with light, purifying the sins and obscurations of all three—body, speech, and mind. Imagining that, the fourth empowerment is obtained.

Then the *hūṃ* at the heart completely changes into the mandala of Five Deities of the Conqueror Chakrasaṃvara. Then also, the four root ḍākinīs are made to circumambulate the principal ones. Direct the attention there. From the heart of that [Chakrasaṃvara], light rays arise and strike the *baṃ* in the dharma-source. The *baṃ* completely transforms into Jetsunma [Vajrayoginī], with one face and two hands. She holds a small drum in the right hand and a skull-cup in the left. Her body is red, adorned with the bone ornaments.[20] She is wrathfully smiling and in a playful dancing pose. Direct the attention there.

Then the guru at the crown dissolves into light and melts into the Conqueror at the heart. The Conqueror dissolves into light and melts into Yoginī at the navel. From Yoginī's right nostril emerges the vowels [of the Sanskrit alphabet] and the consonants from the left. Coming together as a red *svāstika* at her mid-brow, imagine that it revolves intensely. Then Yoginī dissolves into light and melts into oneself. One's body also becomes like a body of light, empty and clear. Enter for a moment the meditation on the nature of all phenomena being like the cloud-free sky. Meditating with the mind focused on the guru at the crown in this way causes heat to rise. That is the introduction of the vase empowerment. In terms of the joys, it is the joy of experience.

At the time of directing the attention to the host of deities at the heart, bliss arises without thinking of body-mind. That is the introduction to the secret empowerment. In terms of the joys, it is the sublime joy.

At the time of directing the attention to Yoginī in the dharma-source, no thought of body-mind arises. That is the introduction of the empowerment of timeless awareness through wisdom. In terms of the joys, it is the joy that is free of joy.

The essence of the three empowerments existing as one is the introduction to the fourth empowerment. In terms of the joys, it is the coemergent joy.

Then, unborn dharmakāya, in the fashion of unimpeded saṃbhogakāya, appears as the deities' form like an illusion. Have them meditate without attachment to it since it is mere appearance with no intrinsic nature, like the reflected image in a mirror.

Offer the single set of five offerings to them. The awareness-beings above the mandala depart, and the pledge-beings dissolve into the disciples' hearts.

By these means, those who have not received this empowerment will receive it, those who have received it will revitalize it, and once all sins quickly vanish, one will actually see the form of Glorious Great Bliss.[21] Coemergent timeless awareness will be born in one's mind stream,[22] and in this very life one will attain the fourteenth ground, Great Bliss.

Then send the torma, partake of the feast, recite the hundred-syllable mantra, and do the dedication.

This completes the empowerment ritual of meditative absorption in the Five Deities of Chakrasaṃvara that was extracted from the *Saṃvara Ocean Tantra*[23] by Niguma, the ḍākinī of timeless awareness. I, Khyungpo Naljor, having pleased the ḍākinī herself, received it from her. It was translated by Lotsāwa Lendarma Lodrö. *iti*

SWIFT ACCOMPLISHMENT OF GLORIOUS CHAKRASAṂVARA[24]

Sanskrit: *Śrī-cakrasamvara-sādhana-nāma*
Tibetan: *dPal 'khor lo sdom pa myur du sgrub pa zhes bya ba'i thabs*

Homage to glorious great bliss timeless awareness.

After first giving rise to the immeasurable spirit of awakening,
meditate in the emptiness of all phenomena.
From within that emptiness oneself appears
with the white letter *bruṃ* on the crown of one's head.
It becomes a white four-spoked wheel.
On its hub is a lotus and sun and moon,
upon which a white *hūṃ* and red *baṃ* radiate light,
establishing beings of the three existences[25] in the state of white
Chakrasaṃvara.
Light rays return, becoming the white masculine and red feminine
deities.
Imagine that on the spokes of the wheel
are the four Chakrasaṃvara goddesses, white of body,
holding flaying knives in their right hands, skull-cups in the left,
and *khaṭvāṅgas*.[26]
On the tips of the wheel's spokes are four *raṃ*

blazing with the bonfire of timeless awareness.
After the secret union and suchness mahāmudrā offerings,
white bodhichitta with a reddish glow is produced
from the joining place of the feminine and masculine in union.
The stream flows to the crown of one's head.
The four surrounding goddesses unite with their khaṭvāṅgas
as the males,
and streams of bodhichitta fall from their secret places.
The streams become one as they enter one's crown.
Falling to the four places (of crown, throat, heart, and navel),
sins and obscurations are purified.
The wheel spins swiftly, slicing and dicing
all disease and spirits; they are burned by the bonfire
and scattered by the wind into nothing.
Stream, wheel, bonfire, and wind—
stay on that without distraction and repeat the secret mantra.
Focusing[27] on the visualization refines one's dreams.
Saṃbhogakāya will occur, arising naturally.
That is the wheel of the Body.

Then from the red *bruṃ* at the throat
on a red wheel and lotus-sun
the red *hūṃ* and *baṃ*
radiate light out and back as before.[28]
In the center the Chakrasaṃvara couple
are a color resembling rubies,
adorned by bones and fresh and dry skulls,
they possess the nine modes of drama.[29]
In the four directions the goddesses are red
with knives, skulls, and khaṭvāṅgas.
As before the *raṃ* on the spokes blazes
with timeless awareness, making offerings that delight.
A stream of red bodhichitta flows from the joining places
of the main couple and their entourage.
Imagine that it fills one down to the throat,[30]
purifying disease, spirits, sins, and obscurations.

Stream, red wheel, bonfire, wind, and
repetition of the heart-mantra are no different than before.
Imagine it as a red fire pit inside the torso.
This is the red wheel of Speech.

The blue wheel of one's Mind[31]
is a lapis-colored *bruṃ* at the heart.
Imagine the sharp four-spoked wheel with a lotus at the hub.
Upon sun and moon, Bhairava and Kālarātri,
*hūṃ*s and vajras radiate and return,
becoming blue Chakrasaṃvara and the red feminine,
wrathful by nature, and with entourage.
On the tips of the four spokes, dark blue bonfires blaze with roaring and banging.
Masculine and feminine unite and arouse their energy,
causing nondissipating great bliss to expand,
as their laughter of *hūṃ* and *phaṭ* resounds like a thousand claps of thunder.
Sulphate-blue bodhichitta flows from their place of union
and fills one down to the heart,
purifying disease, spirits, sins, and obscurations of mind.
In particular, the bad spirits and hatred
are diced by the wheel, burned by the fire,
and dispersed by the winds of timeless awareness.
A torrential river of bodhichitta purges sins, obscurations,
disease, and bad spirits like a waterfall hitting a mountain of ashes.

For pacifying stupidity and fevers,
the white Body wheel at the crown spins with a stream of camphor.
For the overpowering activity, desire, and chills,
the red Speech wheel at the throat spins like burning metal and molten copper.
For obstructing spirits, anger, and phlegm,
the Mind wheel at the heart spins with a blue stream blazing with blue-black fire.
For turning back evil curses,

light rays from the *hūṃ* seed form an iron hook
that snares the harm-doers, who are diced by the wheel,
burned by the fire, and scattered by the wind.
To liberate the vow-breakers,
face all the deities outward and
repeat the heart-mantra with *maraya* added to the end.
For the Body, Speech, and Mind wheels,
repetition of the mantra seven hundred thousand times for each [syllable]
shakes the earth and accomplishes peaceful, enriching, overpowering, and wrathful activities.

Exert yourself at this total practice of Saṃvara
to complete the fourteen grounds.

I entrust to you the heart life-force of the ḍākinī.[32]
Do not spread it beyond the one-to-one lineage.
In the *chitta* palace [of your heart]
hold the guru and this close practice as dear as your own life.
Meditate on me, Niguma, on the top of your head to receive my blessing.
The stages of the ten grounds and the five paths
are traversed through the power of devotion.
This is the ultimate sublime secret mantra.

The Method of Accomplishment of the Body, Speech, and Mind of the Conqueror Saṃvara by Niguma, the Ḍākinī of Timeless Awareness, is complete.

I, Khyungpo Naljor, wrote down the notes[33] on these oral instructions of the ḍākinī on palm leaves in the dense forest of teakwood, and kept them inside an amulet box that I wear always on my body.

May spontaneous, effortless vast benefit for beings be accomplished.
This is the practice of triple white, red and blue Saṃvara.[34]
iti

Hevajra 7

INTRODUCTION

THE HEVAJRA TANTRA is also usually classified as a mother tantra. In his summary of mother tantras, Panchen Sonam Dragpa generalizes that while the Chakrasaṃvara tantra emphasizes mainly the characteristics of the external karmamudra, or spiritual consort, and the skillful methods that rely upon union practice, the Hevajra stresses the special nature of coemergent bliss.[1] That may be, but the tantra does not give that impression. In any case, the two tantras contain many of the same elements. As with Chakrasaṃvara, there is a legendary enormous root tantra, from which was extracted the extant *Hevajra Tantra in Two Parts* as a root text, with several explanatory tantras and commentaries and countless practice texts. Here again is a mandala ritual for use as the initiation process into Hevajra practice, attributed to Niguma.

As discussed in the introduction, this Hevajra practice stands apart from the other texts attributed to Niguma in several ways. In the Peking Tengyur, it is in a different volume than are all of the other Niguma texts, and it is the only one of Niguma's works that is included in the Derge Tengyur. In addition, it does not seem to have any continuity of transmission within the Shangpa tradition and is not mentioned in any of the Shangpa catalogues that have been searched. There is, however, a record of Niguma's transmission of the two-part tantra and an empowerment of "Nine Emanated Deities of Hevajra" to Khyungpo Naljor in his biography, which is repeated in Tāranātha's history.[2] This is likely the source of the mandala ritual translated here, with the nine emanated deities referring to the central deity and the surrounding eight manifestations of the goddess Nairātmyā.

There is a fascinating story about Khyungpo Naljor and Hevajra told by Tāranātha in *The Seven Instruction Lineages*.[3] It concerns a master known as "Aged Kāyastha," the scribe of King Dharmapāla, who wrote a commentary to the Hevajra tantra called *Stainless Union*.[4] According to the story, Khyungpo Naljor requested this commentary directly from him, and it was translated as usual by Lendarma Lodrö, who attributed it to Kāyastha in the colophon. This, however, does not help in tracing the Niguma lineage of Hevajra.

The deity Hevajra is also important in the core Shangpa practice called *Five Tantras' Deities*, where he is visualized abiding in the south in the outer mandala and in the heart chakra in the inner mandala. Perhaps it was the popularity of this practice, which boasts of accomplishing five tantras at once, which eclipsed the separate Hevajra practice. Tāranātha developed a practice text of the five tantras that utilizes the creation phase of Hevajra as the basis for all five deities.[5] On the other hand, the lineage that he traces for the Hevajra tantra in the Shangpa's five tantras does not include Niguma.[6] So the presence of this text remains somewhat of a mystery, not surprisingly, as well as evoking a sense of loss that this intriguing practice seems not to be upheld.

MANDALA RITUAL OF GLORIOUS HEVAJRA[7]

Sanskrit: *Śrī-hevajra-maṇḍala-vidhi-nāma*
Tibetan: *dPal dgyes pa rdo rje'i dkyil 'khor gyi cho ga zhes bya ba*

Homage to Glorious Hevajra!

After finishing hundreds of thousands and tens of thousands of the recitation practice of the Conqueror Hevajra,[8] retire to a solitary place, and in order to mature those in the family, set up a mandala there [with a lotus of] eight red petals surrounded by vajras and railings. Then arrange nine bunches of red flowers. Put two ritual vases, filled with substances and adorned, in the center and in the northeast.[9] Decorate it with canopies and curtains and so forth. In the four directions of the mandala set up four sets of five offerings, five tormas, and the articles of the feast all around.

Then the vajra master does the cleansing and, on a comfortable seat, meditates on the creation and completion phases. Instantly, within the empty vase, the infinite palace arises from the letter *bhruṃ*. In the middle of that is an eight-petaled red lotus on a lotus stem arisen from *paṃ*. In the center is the sun and the corpses of four devils. Upon that create Heruka, either through the five rites, the three rites, or instantaneously. He has eight faces and sixteen arms, or one face and two arms, and is with consort. On the eight lotus petals, from *a*, create eight one-faced two-armed Nairātmyās. Then the light of one's *hūṃ* invokes the awareness beings. Do the offerings and praises, and after doing however many required recitations of the couple's four mantras, do more offerings. The deities dissolve into the elixir.

Create Amṛtakuṇḍalī[10] in the activity vase, and doing the recitation, cleanse the disciples with that. Then arrange the disciples in rows and do the refuge, arousing the spirit of awakening, supplications, granting of permission, dissolution of concepts,[11] five branches, upholding of vows, and proclamation of truth, all according to the traditional sources. Do the descent of the awareness beings.

Then the disciples supplicate to request the guru to confer the empowerment:

> Confer empowerment in Glorious Heruka,
> brilliant in order to protect beings,
> likewise perfect as the source of all qualities.
> I request to be like that now.
>
> Just as great offerings were made
> to the Buddha by Vajra Bodhi,
> I too, for the purpose of protection,
> Beseech now the vajra of the sky.[12]

Supplicating like that, goddesses carrying vases full of elixir emanate from the hearts of the deities of the mandala and the sky and confer the empowerment with the secret stream. Think that this purifies sins and obscurations of the body.

Then say:

> Bestow the great vajra empowerment conferral,
> worshipped by everyone in the three realms,
> totally arisen from the three secrets
> of all the buddhas.[13]

Saying that, think that the vase empowerment has been received. Similarly, the secret empowerment [is received] at the throat, the awareness through wisdom empowerment at the heart, and the fourth empowerment at the navel. These empowerments are exclusively for the benefit of others.

Then [there is] the explanation of the regular conferral of the four empowerments on oneself and others:

On one's head, the syllable *paṃ* changes to a lotus stem and upon that is a red eight-petaled lotus with the sun and corpses. Through the three rites or instantaneously, imagine there Hevajra without a consort. On the eight lotus petals, upon suns and corpses, imagine from *a* the eight Nairātmyās full with bliss. Then supplicate as before. Infinite light rays come from the deities on one's head and totally pervade one's body inside and out. All obscurations from karmic action and afflictive emotion are cleansed and purified. Imagine that one's body is the nature of light. By that, one becomes Hevajra without consort. That is the vase empowerment.

Then, supplicate again. The goddesses on one's head become increasingly blissful and fuse into light.[14] She embraces the male consort and masculine and feminine unite. From their place of union white and red bodhichitta blissfully trickles down and lands on one's tongue. The arousing of bliss is the secret empowerment.

Again supplicate the host of deities. A single Nairātmyā breaks off from the principal female consort. She embraces, rubs, and unites with oneself as Hevajra. Nondissipating great bliss arises in the body. This is the empowerment of awareness [through uniting with] wisdom.

Then, after making offerings to the host of deities on one's head, the deities together with their seats dissolve into the crown of one's head. Possessing the deity's form, one rests in equipoise in great bliss without fixation on the empty clarity. In short, the essence of all phenomena included in the apparent existence of samsara and nirvana is totally pure, free of all embellishment, and by nature lucid clarity mahāmudrā—rest in that alone. That is the fourth empowerment.

Then *yaṃ raṃ kaṃ*[15] thoroughly refine the various substances within [the skull-cup arisen] from *a*, into the five meats and the five elixirs. Offer to the host of deities, and then the yogins partake of it.

Cleanse the five tormas as before and satisfy the guru, Hevajra, the dharma protectors, the local spirits, and the harm-doers with the mantra of all spirits. Sing the vajra song, do the offerings and praises to the host of deities, and the confession.

Dedicate with:

> By the merit of my generosity and so forth,
> may the Conqueror Hevajra be delighted.
> Having totally completed the six perfections
> may all beings attain the vajra monarch.

Then the master and everyone together with one voice make this aspiration:

> Born into the family and holding the sacred pledge,
> a teacher of incomparable Hevajra,
> devoted to the guru and compassionate:
> may it be so lifetime after lifetime.
>
> Vajra in hand and ringing the bell,
> reading the profound dharma,

consuming the fluids of the queen:
may it be so lifetime after lifetime.[16]

Then, circumambulating the mandala, request forgiveness. Do auspicious verses, the departure of the awareness beings, dissolution of the pledge beings into one's head, and pleasing the vajra master with compensation.

This concludes the brief ritual of the empowerment conferral in Glorious Hevajra by Niguma, the ḍākinī of timeless awareness. Translated by the Vajra Ḍākinī of Timeless Awareness herself and Lotsāwa Lendarma Lodrö.

The Ḍākinī's Personal Instructions: Five Short Texts on Yogic Techniques 8

INTRODUCTION

These five brief personal or oral instructions (*zhal gdams*) that are attributed to Niguma in the Peking Tengyur may be the source of the yogic techniques that are used in conjunction with Niguma's *Six Dharmas*, and particularly that of inner heat (*gtum mo*). In most traditions of the path of methods, while the actual seated practice involves visualization and breath-control techniques, there is also a regimen of physical training (*lus sbyong*, lujong) that enhances the efficacy of the main practice. These individual exercises are known as "trulkor" (*'khrul 'khor*), a word that in other contexts means "machine" or "device" but is here translated simply as "yogic technique." The practice of these techniques involves special clothing and housing and was traditionally kept quite secret, hidden from all viewers. The tantalizing accounts in Alexandra David-Neel's travel books of her surreptitious witnessing of strange goings-on were most likely in regard to such techniques.[1] Any number of texts, commentaries, and descriptions, however, will never successfully convey the actual practice, which must be learned directly from a master who is accomplished in both the physical training and the meditation technique. These descriptions are thus "self-secret," perhaps more than any other textual accounts. They offer only some tips for those already initiated into their practice.

Niguma's instructions here are particularly cryptic, and practitioners in this tradition have long relied on other sources for clarification, which in any case are mostly used to jog one's memory of the instructor's direct demonstration. Lineage holders of the past culled from the original sources a system of eighteen or twenty-five specific techniques (though, as noted, there are some issues with enumeration). Perhaps the most central such text is, again, by the great Tāranātha: *Nigu's Yogic Exercises, Root and Commentary.* "Root" in this case refers to a section quoted by Tāranātha that appears to be the jumbled remains of what was once Niguma's outline of these practices. The commentary is Tāranātha's own attempt to make sense of them. He explains:

> Most of these yogic exercises each have vital points of visualization that should be learned from the source text. These are the personal instructions of Niguma, Ḍākinī of Timeless Awareness. They are esoteric instructions for dissolving the energy-mind in the central channel and for releasing the knots in the channels, primarily using one's own body as the method. They are the esoteric instructions for the supreme accomplishment of the path of liberation that are known as "The Eighteen Physical Trainings" (*lus sbyong bco brgyad pa*). As for the source text of this, the oral directions are somewhat arcane and have been scattered among a great many words, and there have been many that do not know how to collect them. Although it is possible that there are select collections assembled by uneducated persons, the practical application does not actually emerge clearly. Since I saw that the practice was close to disappearing, in order to save it and spread it, I, Tāranātha, having attained some degree of devotion in the glorious Shangpa Kagyu, have not kept it hidden and have laid it out clearly.[2]

The "vital points of visualization" to which Tāranātha refers are, at least partially, apparent in the collection translated here. Most of the currently available practice manuals, on the other hand, even some illustrated notebooks that have been in circulation at monasteries, do not include these essential visualizations. These five "originals," if that is what they are, as well as some others that should have been included in this set, are indeed contained within the eleven-volume *Shangpa Texts*, hidden in a collection of more than thirty brief instructions labeled with the names of only two of them.[3] This seems to represent a wholesale incorporation of an older collection into the puzzling organization of the *Shangpa Texts*. They are not mentioned individually in either of the Shangpa catalogues written by Jamgön Kongtrul to record his doxological methods.[4]

Comparing the five texts here with that collection and the commentary by Tāranātha, it appears that the exercises described here correlate loosely with the fifth through the eighteenth of Niguma's eighteen yogic exercises. In that system, the eighteenth is further subdivided into eight (or maybe nine), which leads to the alternate accounting of twenty-five exercises of Niguma. But who's counting? Perhaps initially they were meant to be one continuous, flowing yoga of body and mind, synchronized in movement and creative visualization.

ESOTERIC INSTRUCTIONS ON OPENING THE CHANNEL[5]

Nāmo Guru

These are esoteric instructions on opening the channel:

Sitting cross-legged with spine straight,
put your left clenched fist to your chest,
extend the right [arm] down vigorously.
Then do the same with your left.

After that, the four limbs
are vigorously extended for that reason.
Open your mouth and also open the eyes wide.
Then vigorously shake your four limbs.

After that, meditate on the guru's inner heat.
With your body in the seven-point posture of Vairochana,[6]

imagine the central channel remaining straight,
and imagine the root guru on your head.

After that, the fire of timeless awareness
blazes up again into the central channel
and touches the guru's feet,
causing elixir to fall—meditate in bliss.

Un-visualizing the guru, fire abides on its own.
Un-visualizing the elixir, meditate in emptiness.

This is Niguma's personal instruction. *iti*

MEDITATION ON CHANNELS, PRĀṆA, AND SUCH[7]

Nāmo Guru

In the meditation on channels, prāṇa, and such,
once bliss has arisen in the body,
if there is danger of losing the bliss externally
due to the bliss falling below,
then bringing the prāṇa into the channel entrance is crucial.

In a secluded place, on a soft seat,
stand with the two [legs] straight.
Demolish down the prāṇa wheel,[8]
extend the two hands above the head,
and join it together with the fire wheel.
Raise the heels and hit the ground.

Visualize that four fingers beneath the navel,
from the region where the three channels gather,
the fire of timeless awareness of inner heat blazes.
It moves up within the *avadhūti*[9]
and straight away reaches the top of the head.
Visualize the letter *kṣa* in the aperture of Brahmā,[10]

and the tongue of fire stretching out.
Imagine that the prāṇa that accompanies the fire
is blue in color and wafting upward,
issuing forth in the manner of smoke.

Then, just at the time of entering,
[the prāṇa] goes to that fire's place.
Imagine that the *kṣa* blocks the aperture of Brahmā.
That will draw in the vital essence.

To spread the vital essence through the body,
stand and hold the two hands in clenched fists.
Extend the right [arm] to the crook of the thigh
and hold the left one slightly bent.
With the left side [of the body],
forcefully pull toward the right seven times.[11]
Similarly with the left extended
forcefully pull toward the right seven times.
Then, with the fingers of the two hands
interlocking over the chest
and the two thumbs under the armpits,
squeeze the breasts from below.
Forcefully twist the upper torso
seven times each to the right and left.
That spreads [the vital essence] through the body.
It releases the flaws in the vital essence.

This is Niguma's personal advice.

MEDITATION ON INNER HEAT IN THE PATH OF METHODS

Nāmo Guru

Meditating on inner heat in the path of methods,
if the prāṇa-mind is not captured with precision

and the problem of bodily pain occurs,
one should go to an isolated area
and diligently practice the vajra dance.[12]

First, to insert in the central channel
there are three: guiding, heat, and gathering.
To first insert in the central channel,
on a soft seat, raise up with the hands,
line up and straighten the legs,
and extend the two clenched fists to the crooks of the thighs.
Holding prāṇa, forcefully draw up the lower prāṇa,
strike the chest three times with the heels [of the hands],
lift up [on the toes] three times and, swirling the arms
like vulture wings, shake the upper torso.

With a straight body and two clenched fists
crossed, press on the breast.
Bend the body, leaning forcefully right and left.
This is done three times; holding prāṇa is crucial.

Then, standing up, cross the two hands
and cover the upper arms,
forcefully twisting the waist right and left.

The visualization is to imagine [the syllable] *a* at the navel,
and the vital essence of all the channels gather into *a*.
Meditate on *a* as unborn emptiness.
Do this three times with everything the same.
If heart-prāṇa arises, imagine *a* within the heart
and focus the attention on its radiating light.
This will clear it up.

This instruction of the vajra dance is the instruction of the ḍākinī of timeless awareness. *iti*

YOGA OF MEDITATION IN THE PATH OF METHODS[13]

Nāmo Guru

In the yoga of meditation in the path of methods,
the diseases that are among the results
of the three poisons arising in the mind stream
are healed by the yogic exercises of physical training.

[1. Clearing up Stupidity][14]
When the force of stupidity occurs,
take the position of Vairochana,[15]
while the radiation and convergence of white light
illuminates the darkness of stupidity.
Imagine the afflictive emotion of stupidity pacified.

[2. Clearing up Agitation]
When the force of agitation makes you restless,
put your body in the vajra cross-legged position,
grasp the nape of the neck by [interlocking] ring fingers,
bend forward and forcefully twist
the right and left [arms] three times each.
Slap your palms on your head and think that it dissolves.

[3. Clearing up Fury]
When you are infuriated by the force of hungry ghosts,
take the position of Amoghasiddhi,
and satisfy the dangerous hungry ghosts
with a continuous flow of elixir.

[4. Pained by Harm-Doers]
After that, assume the vajra position
and with the "burning" mudra at the heart,
gaze with wrathful eyes in the ten directions.
As the seeds of ten directions blaze all around,

imagine that those who would harm you are expelled.
Do a bit of wrathful recitation.

[5. Clearing up Anger]
When the arising of anger in your mind stream
results in aching pain in the upper body,
assume the vajra position with intertwined fingers on your chest,
and twist your chest three times each to left and right,
looking to the right and left with wrathful eyes.

[6. Clearing up Pride]
After that, with the mudra of equipoise,[16]
hold the belly tight and strike it three times.

[7. Clearing up Desire]
When the arising of desire in your being
results in discomfort of the lower body,
stretch out prone and wave the legs,
doing the dough-kneading mudra with your hands.

For those two the visualization is the same:
In the heart center is the letter *ma*;
by the joining of the red and white vital essences,
imagine that bliss-emptiness arises in your being.

[8. Clearing up Greed, for Much Descent of Bliss]
When losing [vital essence] externally and lacking heat
internally,
body and mind are separated, and should be united.
Pure inner heat is fire;
imagine that fire as fine as a thread
reaches through the central channel from top to bottom,
and focus the mind there, meditating clearly.
When heat arises but bliss does not,
use the esoteric instruction of bringing down the vital essence:
On a seat that is big enough for three arm spans,[17]

stand up suddenly [with a hop][18] and point with outstretched
forefinger.
Twist and turn as far as possible to the front
and similarly as far as possible to the back.

[9. Threefold Shake, for Less Descent of Bliss]
After that, take the heroic sitting posture, with fingers
intertwined,
forcefully twist and rub the forearms.
Following that, shake [the body] three times.
That will cause the descent of bliss.

Whichever of those physical trainings you practice,
holding the prāṇa is most critical.

Ḍākinī Niguma's personal instruction. *iti*

CHANNEL CHAKRAS OF ONE'S BODY[19]

Nāmo Guru

The channel chakras in one's own body
that are extended should be contracted
and those that are contracted should be extended.
If one meditates without doing so,
discomfort in the channels and prāṇa will develop.

For that, in an isolated place,
to raise oneself up by the palms,
grasp a staff with two hands.[20]
Put the heel of the right [foot]
on the thigh of the left [leg],[21]
move back the right knee,
and lift up the body.
After that, strike with the left heel three times.
Similarly the right, making it straight.

After that, put the two legs together,
straight and extended,
and strike the ground forcefully
three times with the right heel.
The same for the left, three times each.
After that, set aside the staff.

Cover the chest with the fingers of both hands entwined,
with two thumbs under the armpits
and squeeze the breasts together.
Twist your upper torso forcefully
to the right and left three times.

After that, do the small child yogic exercise,[22]
[tilting] your head in four directions.
That can also be done three times each.

After that leap up and after that
hit the ground with the heels three times.[23]
It is critical not to leave the mat.

That also is the ḍākinī's personal instruction. *iti*

Niguma's Aspiration Prayer 9

ASPIRATION PRAYER OF THE SEALED WORD ("KAGYAMA")[1]

Sanskrit: *Ārya-praṇidhānarāja-nāma*
Tibetan: *'Phag pa smon lam gyi rgyal po zhes bya ba*
English (alternative title): *The Sovereign of Noble Aspirations*

Homage to all the buddhas and bodhisattvas!

May the ocean of victors in the ten directions and three times,
with their abundance of compassionate activity,
accomplish all these prayers of mine
just as they have been supplicated.

May everything in every form from now on
please the guru through immeasurable devotion,
and by offering infinite pure bodies and enjoyments,
may you ever be close and your activities flourish.

May I attain enlightenment relying on gurus in all lives
while hearing, explaining, meditating, and practicing dharma,
and not meet with bad āchāryas and bad lamas,
or bad friends and bad benefactors.[2]

May I have good family, health, eloquence, fine physique,
charisma, and power in all lives,
and with longevity, companions, and wealth
arising spontaneously, be respected by all.

May I be free of discord and harmonious with all
throughout all my lives wherever I am born,
so that beings who see, hear, recall, or touch me
perceive beauty and charm that is ever interesting.

May I become the protector, hope, and reinforcement
for all sentient beings equaling space,
their every desire and hope, whatever they are,
satisfied by me exactly as they wish.

May those friends who wish me well,
who practice the same aspirations of body, speech, and mind,
ever be close from this moment on,
and enjoy abundant happiness and pure perception.

May I become a wish-fulfilling gem wherever I'm born
and establish all beings in happiness
by raining down an immeasurable abundance
of all their desires as soon as they think of them.

May all lands and countries wherever I am
be free of disease, negative forces, strife, and poverty,
and all beings possess long life, health, wealth, and dharma,
in an abundance of auspiciousness and well-being.

May I, in this life and in all lives,
gain access to the sky-treasure of wealth
and dispense the four kinds of gifts[3] in the ten directions,
ripening and liberating all beings through the ten perfections.

May every mandala of knowledge in the three times
all become manifest in a mere instant

through the sublime knowing of all dharmas
in samsara and nirvana without attachment or obstruction.[4]

May I be indisputably adorned by the correct stainless three
  trainings,[5]
such that the world and its gods render offerings and praise,
and by placing all beings in sublime ethical discipline,
fully perfect all good qualities without exception.

May I be content in a remote hermitage with food and clothes,
perfecting ultimate realization without a moment of outer or
  inner obstacle,
ripening and liberating all beings without exception
through immeasurable enlightened activity.

May all the arrogant powerful gods and demons,
without need of a moment of exhortation or worship,
offer their life-force and obey like servants
to protect the doctrine with abundant magical power.

May I, by actualizing loving-kindness and compassion,
totally pacify destructive hostility that sentient beings have
toward each other in the three realms,
so that they dwell in the love of a mother toward her only child.

May there be no interruption in manifesting dharmakāya
when the time of my death is upon me,
so that the spontaneously present form-kāyas help others
and my remains and relics continue to influence beings.

May I make offerings, for an ocean of eons,
of Samantabhadra's offering clouds equal to space
to an ocean of buddhas as numerous as atoms in the universe
in all the pure realms of the victors.

May I manifest an ocean of totally pure buddha realms
and with immeasurable knowledge and totally pure conduct

thoroughly see the whole ocean of dharmas
and realize the whole ocean of timeless awareness.

May I actualize the melodious speech of an ocean of victors
and proclaim throughout the reaches of space with Brahmā's
voice,
teaching dharma in the languages of all people
and placing all sentient beings in the state of buddha.

May I actualize the absorption of illusion without limit,
just as in Samantabhadra's life story of illusion,
and instantly manifest buddha bodies
and every buddha field upon a single atom.

May my aspirations, absorptions, and activities
be as boundlessly deep and vast and impossible to measure
as the realms of beings and the depths and reaches of the oceans,
the limits of the sky and the immeasurable realm of reality.[6]

May I emanate as endless universal monarchs
to fulfill the hopes of beings and guard the dharma domain,
and gaining dominion over all realms equaling space,
establish all sentient beings in happiness.

May I become the sovereign of supreme healing,
to instantly soothe the pain of sentient beings
when they are worn out by the suffering
brought on by the future age of disease and weapons.

May there be a rain of five desirables in the ten directions
from thick clouds of abundance equaling the sky,
replete with a wealth of food, drink, textiles, silver, and gold
for the times of hunger and thirst during the age of famine.

May the tremendous force of my bodhisattva activity
manifest precisely in the way appropriate to transform

each and every sentient being throughout the reaches of space
until the ocean of samsara becomes empty.

May I totally subdue powerful and haughty beings
who engaged a perverse path and were not subdued
by the victors in three times and ten directions,
and establish them in buddhahood instantly.

May naturally arising effortless enlightened activity
ripen and liberate all sentient beings
with spontaneously present uninterrupted benefit
for as long as there are sentient beings in samsara.

May my enlightened activity of aspiration
be greater than the combined enlightened activity of aspirations
of the ocean of victors in the ten directions and three times
who, when they were ordinary beings and bodhisattvas,
made aspirations for generating awakening mind for countless eons,
perfected the two accumulations and actualized buddhahood,
and then through an ocean of qualities, might, and excellence,
ripened and liberated limitless sentient beings.

May all of my aspiration prayers that produce
limitless spontaneously present benefit for others
fully generate sublime awakening, interest, and faith
and be completely realized by whoever adopts them.

May all abundance of auspiciousness and happiness
in the ten directions, three times, samsara and nirvana,
flow uninterruptedly like the course of a great river
and pervade myself and others everywhere in all directions.

Thus ends the *Sovereign of Noble Aspirations* by Niguma, the ḍākinī of timeless awareness. *iti*

Appendix 1: "The Basis of Everything"

by Khyabje Kalu Rinpoche

(Copied by the translator from a scrap of paper circulating in the monastery, circa 1975)

THIS ALL-BASE, buddha nature (*sugatagarbha*), is the original great timeless awareness occurring naturally through the empty, lucid, unimpeded pristine quintessence of five elements. Not recognizing itself, it is wrapped up in the darkness of ignorance. Thus it presides pervasively as samsara's common all-base consciousness, the source of all delusion, like the basic ground or principal sovereign. Then the empty [aspect is apprehended] as "self," the clarity as "other," and attachment, aversion, stupidity, and all afflicted mentation with its associates occur from its unimpededness. Further, the natural radiance of the five [qualities of] original emptiness, clarity, movement, firm solidity, and continuous flow occur as the appearance of extremely subtle five lights: blue, red, green, yellow, and white. On that basis, then, arise the appearances of the five elements: space, fire, wind, earth, and water. The one [experiencing] these deluded appearances in that way is the aggregate of consciousness, and based on that, first a mental body arises, and then in relation to it, feeling, perception, and formation: four and a half aggregates. Mixing with external elements, such as the father's semen and the mother's blood, the coarse physical form of a fully ripened corporeal body consisting of the five elements as orifices, warmth, breath, flesh, and blood is achieved, and the six faculties of the eyes, ears, nose, tongue, body, and mind occur. Based on that, like the sovereign's heir, the unvirtuous afflicted mentation arises from the aspect of consciousness and virtuous mentation such as faith, compassion, and wisdom arise from the aspect of timeless awareness. Like their emissaries, the six kinds of consciousness arise, and the six objects of form, sound, smell, taste, touch, and [mental] phenomena [appear] to them. Then the prince-like afflicted mentation presides over the conference with the six sense faculties, six objects, and six consciousnesses, and a whole host of interdependent causes and conditions are convened. The bodies, speech, and minds of hundreds and thousands of deluded concepts are consigned into service and perform various acts. Habitual patterns, like seeds, are planted in the all-base consciousness, which is like the basic ground. For instance, to grow crops one must assemble many dependent conditions such as water, fertilizer, warmth, moisture, and the seeds to produce the cause and result. Similarly, assembling the various dependent causes and conditions for the seeds of one's previous actions will result in the higher realms and liberation from virtuous causes, and samsara and lower realms from unvirtuous causes.

Appendix 2: The Tibetan Text of *Stages in the Path of Illusion and the Commentary*[1]

༄༅། །སྒྱུ་མ་ལམ་གྱི་རིམ་པ་ཞེས་བྱ་བ།

༄༅༅། །རྒྱ་གར་སྐད་དུ། མ་ཡ་ཛྙ་ན་ཀྲ་མ་ནཱ་མ། བོད་སྐད་དུ། སྒྱུ་མ་ལམ་གྱི་རིམ་པ་ཞེས་བྱ་བ། སངས་རྒྱས་དང་བྱང་ཆུབ་སེམས་དཔའ་ཐམས་ཅད་ལ་ཕྱག་འཚལ་ལོ། །གདོད་ནས་རང་བཞིན་འོད་གསལ་བ། །དགོས་འདོད་མ་ལུས་འབྱུང་འགྱུར་ཞིང་། ཡིད་བཞིན་ནོར་བུ་ལྟ་བུ་ཡི། །སེམས་ཉིད་ཁྱོད་ལ་ཕྱག་འཚལ་ལོ། །རྒྱལ་བ་རྒྱ་མཚོའི་ཐུགས་ཀྱི་བཅུད། །བརྗོད་བྱའི་སྙིང་པོར་གྱུར་པ་ཡི། །སྒྱུ་མ་ལམ་གྱི་རིམ་པ་འདི། །གཞན་ལ་ཕན་ཕྱིར་བཤད་པར་བྱ། །སྒྱུ་མ་གདོད་ནས་མ་གྲུབ་པ། །ཐོག་མ་མེད་པའི་དབྱིངས་ཉིད་ནི། །ཆོས་རྣམས་ཀུན་གྱི་ས་བོན་ཏེ། །བདེ་གཤེགས་སྙིང་པོ་དགེ་བའང་དེ། །སྙིང་པོ་ཀུན་གཞིར་གྲགས་པའོ། །ཆོས་རྣམས་སྒྱུ་མ་ལྟ་བུ་ལ། །དད་བརྩོན་གུས་པའི་མཆོག་ལྡན་པས། །སྒྱུ་མ་ལྟ་བུར་སྒོམས་བྱས་ན། །སྒྱུ་མ་ལྟ་བུར་མངོན་སངས་རྒྱས། །དེ་ཡང་ལམ་ལྔ་ས་བཅུ་རྣམས། །ལེགས་པར་བཤད་ཀྱིས་

1. The Tibetan texts of the root and commentary are based on five editions from the Peking Tengyur, Collated Tengyur, *Shangpa Texts*, *Kinnaur Shangpa Texts*, and an Ume edition. Where there was significant variation, the translator's choices are referenced in the endnotes to the translation. The few bracketed words represent portions of quotation from scripture that were missing in all Niguma texts.

ཉན་པར་བྱོས། །བརྟན་དང་གཡོ་བ་ཇི་སྙེད་པ། །སྒོ་ལྔའི་ཡུལ་དུ་གང་སྣང་ཀུན། །ཐམས་ཅད་སྣང་སྟོང་ལྷའི་སྐུ། །ལྷ་སྐུ་མཐའ་བྲལ་སྒྱུ་མ་ཏེ། །བྱང་ཆུབ་ཕྱོགས་ཆོས་ཐམས་ཅད་དང་། །ལྷ་སྐུ་སྒྱུ་མ་དབྱེར་མེད་པར། །མཁས་པས་ཉམས་སུ་བླང་བར་བྱ། །ལམ་ལྔ་ས་བཅུའི་རིམ་པ་རྣམས། །མོས་གུས་སྟོབས་ཀྱིས་བསྒྲོད་པར་བྱེད། །བླ་མའི་སྣང་བ་མི་འབྲལ་བ། །རྒྱུད་སྡེའི་དགོངས་པ་གནད་ཀྱི་མཆོག །དེ་ལྟར་སྣང་གྲགས་ཆོས་རྣམས་ཀུན། །ལྷ་དང་བླ་མའི་རང་བཞིན་དུ། །ཉམས་སུ་ལེན་པ་ཁྱད་པར་འཕགས། །དབྱིབས་དང་ཁ་དོག་དུག་ལྔ་དང་། །ལས་རིགས་གྲུབ་པ་རིགས་ལྔ་སྟེ། །ཅིར་སྣང་སྣང་དང་སྟོང་པ་ཉིད། །བསྐྱེད་དང་རྫོགས་དང་ཟུང་འཇུག་གོ། །གང་ཞིག་དག་བྱེད་ཐུམ་པ་སྟེ། །དབྱེར་མེད་དཀར་དམར་གསང་བ་ལ། །བདེ་བའི་ཚ་ནི་གསུམ་པ་སྟེ། །བརྗོད་མེད་བཞི་པར་ཤེས་པར་བྱ། །གང་ལ་བདེ་གསལ་མི་རྟོག་པ། །དེ་ནི་སྐུ་གསུམ་རང་ཤར་ཏེ། །གསལ་ལ་མི་རྟོག་མཁྱེན་གཉིས་སོ། །དེ་ཡང་ཞི་གནས་ལྷག་མཐོང་གཉིས། །ཟུང་དུ་འབྲེལ་པའི་ཕྱིར་དང་ནི། །བླ་ན་མེད་པའི་ཕྱིར་དང་ནི། །ཕྱིན་པར་འདོད་ལས་ལམ་ཞེས་བྱ། །སྡིག་པ་ཆུང་ཡང་སྤྱོང་བྱེད་ཅིང་། །དགེ་བ་རྣམས་ནི་དང་དུ་ལེན། །ཆོས་ཉིད་སྒྱུ་མ་ཐོབ་དོན་དུ། །ཚོགས་སོགས་པས་ན་ཚོགས་ལམ་མོ། །དེ་ལ་ཆེ་འབྲིང་ཆུང་གསུམ་སྟེ། །རེ་རེ་ལ་ཡང་བཞི་བཞིར་འདོད། །དྲན་པ་བཞི་དང་སྤོང་བ་བཞི། །རྫུ་འཕྲུལ་རྐང་པ་རྣམ་བཞིའོ། །བག་མེད་དྲན་ཉམས་ལྟུང་བའི་རྒྱུ། །དེ་ཕྱིར་ཐོག་མར་དྲན་པ་བཤད། །སྙིང་པོ་མེད་ལུས་རྒྱལ་བའི་སྐུ། །སྣང་སྟོང་དབྱེར་མེད་སྒྱུ་མ་ལ། །དྲན་དང་ཤེས་བཞིན་ཉམས་སུ་ལེན། །ལུས་ཀྱི་དྲན་པ་ཉེར་གཞག་གོ། །བདེ་སྡུག་བཏང་སྙོམས་དམིགས་པ་དང་། །ཆོས་སུ་བཏགས་པ་ཐམས་ཅད་ཀྱི། །ཚོར་བ་ལ་ནི་ཚོར་བར་ཤེས། །ཚོར་བ་དྲན་པ་ཉེར་གཞག་གོ། །ཆོས་རྣམས་ཐམས་ཅད་སེམས་ཡིན་ཏེ། །སེམས་ནི་ཕྱི་ནང་ཧྲེད་མི་འགྱུར། །སེམས་གང་མ་གྲུབ་སྒྱུ་མ་སྟེ། །སེམས་ཀྱི་དྲན་པ་ཉེར་གཞག་གོ། །ཉན་ཐོས་རང་རྒྱལ་ཐམས་ཅད་ཀྱི། །ཇི་སྙེད་ཆོས་སུ་བཏགས་པ་ཡིན། །མིང་ཙམ་བཏགས་པ་བློ་བུར་སྟེ།

།ཆོས་ཀྱི་དྲན་པ་ཉེར་བཞག་གོ། །མི་དགེ་བ་ནི་སྡུག་བསྔལ་རྒྱུ། །དེ་ལས་ཐར་བར་
འདོད་པ་ཡིས། །སྡིག་རྣམས་དུག་དུ་ལྟ་བའི་ཕྱིར། །ཡང་དག་སྤོང་བ་རྣམ་བཞི་ནི།
།སྡིག་པ་མི་དགེ་བ་ཡི་ཆོས། །མ་སྐྱེད་པ་རྣམས་མི་སྐྱེད་ཕྱིར། །འདུན་པ་འབད་རྩོལ་
སེམས་འཛིན་ཅིང་། །ཡང་དག་རབ་ཏུ་འཇོག་བྱེད་དོ། །གང་ཞིག་སྡིག་པ་མི་དགེའི་
ཆོས། །སྐྱེས་པ་རྣམས་ནི་སྤོང་བའི་ཕྱིར། །འདུན་པ་བསྐྱེད་དང་འབད་ལ་སོགས།
།གོང་བཞིན་དུ་ནི་ཤེས་པར་བྱ། །དགེ་བའི་ཆོས་ནི་མ་སྐྱེས་པ། །རྣམས་ནི་བསྐྱེད་པར་
བྱ་བའི་ཕྱིར། །འདུན་པའི་སྤྲོ་བ་བསྐྱེད་པ་དང་། །འབད་པ་ལ་སོགས་གོང་བཞིན་
ནོ། །དགེ་ཆོས་སྐྱེས་རྣམས་གནས་པ་དང་། །འཕེལ་བ་ཉམས་པར་མི་འགྱུར་དང་།
།ཆུད་མི་ཟ་བར་བྱ་བའི་ཕྱིར། །འདུན་པ་བསྐྱེད་སོགས་གོང་བཞིན་ནོ། །དེ་ཡང་སྡིག་
པ་མི་དགེའི་ཆོས། །མ་སྐྱེས་པ་རྣམས་མི་བསྐྱེད་ཅིང་། །འདུན་པ་བསྐྱེད་ཅེས་བྱ་བ་ནི།
།ཚུལ་བཞིན་ཡིད་ལ་བྱེད་པ་སྟེ། །ཅིར་སྣང་སྒྱུ་མར་ཉམས་བླངས་པས། །མི་དགེའི་
ཆོས་རྣམས་འབྱུང་མི་འགྱུར། །དེ་ཡང་ཚུལ་ཁྲིམས་ཏིང་འཛིན་དང་། །ཤེས་རབ་མི་
མཐུན་ཕྱོགས་རྣམས་ནི། །སྡིག་པ་མི་དགེའི་ཆོས་ཞེས་བྱ། །ཚུལ་བཞིན་ཡིད་ལ་བྱེད་
པ་ཡིས། །མི་དགེ་དེ་དག་སྤང་བའི་ཕྱིར། །མདུན་པ་ལ་སོགས་བསྐྱེད་པ་ནི། །ཡང་
དག་སྤོང་བ་དང་པོར་འདོད། །གཞན་ཡང་མི་དགེའི་ཆོས་རྣམས་ནི། །འདོད་པས་
ཆགས་ལ་ཁོང་ཁྲོས་སྡང་། །མ་རིག་པས་ནི་གཏི་མུག་གོ། །ཚུལ་བཞིན་ཡིད་ལ་བྱེད་
པ་ནི། །མི་གཙང་འདོད་ཆགས་ཞི་བར་བྱེད། །བྱམས་པས་ཞེ་སྡང་རྟེན་འབྲེལ་གྱིས།
།གཏི་མུག་ཞི་བར་བྱེད་པས་ཏེ། །རང་བཞིན་མེད་པར་ཤེས་པ་ཡིས། །ཉོན་མོངས་ཞི་
བར་བྱེད་པ་ནི། །ཡང་དག་སྤོང་བ་གཉིས་པར་འདོད། །དགེ་ཆོས་མ་སྐྱེས་བསྐྱེད་པའི་
ཕྱིར། །འདུན་པ་བསྐྱེད་ཅིང་འབད་རྩོལ་གྱིས། །སངས་རྒྱས་བསྒྲུབ་ལ་འདུན་པ་ནི།
།དགེ་རྩ་ཀུན་གྱི་རྩ་བ་སྟེ། །སེམས་འཛིན་ཉམས་ལེན་དགེ་བའི་མཆོག །ཡང་དག་
སྤོང་བ་གསུམ་པར་འདོད། །དགེ་ཆོས་སྐྱེས་རྣམས་མི་ཉམས་དང་། །ཆུད་མི་ཟ་ཕྱིར་
འདུན་པ་བསྐྱེད། །འབད་རྩོལ་སེམས་འཛིན་ཡང་དག་འཇོག །དགེ་རྩ་སྒྱུ་མའི་

ཉམས་ལེན་ནི། །ཁམས་གསུམ་དག་ཏུ་མི་གནས་པ། །ཐམས་ཅད་མཁྱེན་པར་བསྔོས་པ་ཡིས། །མཐའ་ནི་ཟད་པར་མི་འགྱུར་བ། །ཡང་དག་སྦྱོང་བ་བཞི་པར་འདོད། །འཁོར་བ་སྡུག་བསྔལ་རྒྱ་མཚོ་ལ། །རྒལ་ནས་མྱ་ངན་འདས་པ་ཡི། །ས་ལ་ཕྱིན་པར་འདོད་རྣམས་ཀྱིས། །ཏིང་འཛིན་རྫུ་འཕྲུལ་རྣམས་བཞི་ནི། །ཆོས་རྣམས་ཐམས་ཅད་སྒྱུ་མ་ལྟར། །གང་དུ་མ་གྲུབ་མཐའ་བྲལ་བའི། །ཆོས་ལ་མི་སྐྲག་སྦྱོང་ཞིང་འདུན། །དེ་ཕྱིར་འདུན་པའི་ཏིང་འཛིན་ནོ། །འདུན་མ་སྒྱུ་མའི་ཉམས་ལེན་ཆོ། །འཇིག་རྟེན་ཞེན་པ་དོར་བྱས་ནས། །ལེ་ལོར་གྱུར་སྤྱངས་བརྩོན་འགྲུས་ལྡན། །དེ་ནས་བརྩོན་འགྲུས་ཏིང་འཛིན་ནོ། །རྒྱུན་མི་འཆད་པའི་བརྩོན་འགྲུས་དེས། །སེམས་ནི་ཕྱི་ནང་གང་དུ་ཡང་། །མི་དམིགས་འཛིན་བྲལ་སྒྱུ་མ་ལ། །རྩེ་གཅིག་སེམས་ཀྱི་ཏིང་འཛིན་ནོ། །རྩེ་གཅིག་གྱུར་པའི་ཏིང་འཛིན་གྱིས། །འགྲོ་འཆག་ཉལ་འདུག་ཐམས་ཅད་དུ། །བདེན་མེད་སྒྱུ་མའི་ལམ་འཁྱེར་གྱིས། །སྤྱོད་པའི་ཕྱིར་ན་སྤྱོད་པའོ། །སྤྱོད་པའི་ཏིང་འཛིན་ལ་སོགས་པའི། །འདུ་བྱེད་དང་ལྡན་རྫུ་འཕྲུལ་གྱི། །རྐང་པ་ཞེས་བྱ་ཀུན་ལ་སྦྱར། །ཏིང་ངེ་འཛིན་གྱི་རང་བཞིན་ནི། །རྫུ་འཕྲུལ་གྱིས་ནི་རྐང་པ་ཏེ། །འཛིན་མེད་དེ་ཡིས་ལོག་པ་ཡི། །ཆོས་རྣམས་ཡང་དག་སྤྱངས་ནས་ནི། །དགེ་དང་ཡང་དག་དགེ་བར་བྱེད། །གང་ཞིག་དགེ་བའི་ཆོས་དེ་ཡང་། །རྣམ་པར་མི་རྟོག་རྟོག་བྲལ་བྱེད། །ཏིང་འཛིན་རྫུ་འཕྲུལ་རང་བཞིན་ནོ། །ལམ་མཆོག་དྲི་མ་མེད་པས་ཏེ། །ཡང་དག་གནས་སུ་ཕྱིན་བྱེད་ཕྱིར། །རྫུ་འཕྲུལ་རྐང་པ་ཞེས་བྱའོ། །ཚོགས་ལམ་རྟགས་ནི་དད་བརྩོན་ལྡན། །ཚུལ་ཁྲིམས་དག་ཕྱིར་དབང་པོའི་སྒོ། །ཁ་ན་མ་ཐོ་ཕྲ་ལ་འཛེམ། །ཕྱི་རོལ་ཆགས་སྣང་ཡུལ་རྣམས་ཀུན། །གཞན་མིན་རང་ལ་སྐྱེ་བར་ཤེས། །སྐྱེས་པ་དེ་ཉིད་སྒྱུ་མས་ཏེ། །ཉིན་མཚན་སྤྱོད་ལམ་ཀུན་དུ་སྦྱང་། །འདུན་པ་དྲག་པོའི་བག་ཆགས་འབྱུང་། །འདི་ལྟར་སྣང་བའི་དངོས་པོ་ལ། །སྔོན་གྱི་བག་ཆགས་བཏབ་པ་ཡིས། །རྟག་ཅིང་བདེན་པར་མི་རྟོག་པ། །བདེན་མེད་ཐེ་ཚོམ་སྐྱེ་མི་འགྱུར། །རྒྱུ་ལ་ཐེ་ཚོམ་སྐྱེས་པས་ཀྱང་། །སྲིད་པའི་དྲ་བ་འཇིག་གྱུར་ན། །འདུས་བྱས་ཆོས་རྣམས་མི་རྟག་པར། །ཤེས་ཤིང་ཐག་

ཚོད་སློམས་ཅི་དགོས། །དེ་ཕྱིར་འཁོར་བ་སྡུག་བསྔལ་གྱི། །རྩ་བ་བདག་འཛིན་བཏང་བྱས་པས། །མི་དེ་བདེ་དང་ཕྲད་པར་ངེས། །མི་མ་ཡིན་མཐོང་མཆོད་བསྟོད་བྱེད། །གང་གིས་འདུན་པ་སྟོན་སོང་བའི། །སེམས་ནི་དང་པོ་བསྐྱེད་པ་ནས།།དྲོད་ཀྱི་ཡེ་ཤེས་མ་སྐྱེས་བར།།ཚོགས་ལམ་ཡིན་པར་ཤེས་པར་བྱ། །མཐོང་ལམ་མི་རྟག་སྒྱུ་མ་ལ། །སྦྱོར་བའི་ཕྱིར་ན་སྦྱོར་ལམ་མོ། །དྲོད་དང་རྩེ་མོ་ཏིང་འཛིན་ནོ། །དབང་པོ་རྣམ་པ་ལྔ་ཡིན་ཏེ། །སྲོག་ལ་བབ་ཀྱང་སྡིག་མི་བྱེད། །སྟོབས་དང་མི་འཇིགས་སྟོང་ཉིད་དང་། །སྒྱུ་མའི་དོན་ལ་དད་པས་ཏེ། །དད་པའི་དབང་པོ་ཞེས་བྱའོ། །དད་གྱུར་སྒྱུ་མའི་ཉམས་ལེན་ལ། །རྒྱུན་ཆད་མེད་པར་གོམས་གྱུར་པ། །བརྩོན་འགྲུས་དབང་པོ་བསྐྱེད་པས་ན། །བརྩོན་འགྲུས་དབང་པོ་ཞེས་བྱའོ། །བརྩོན་འགྲུས་ལས་བྱུང་སྒྱུ་མ་སྟེ། །དྲན་པས་ཆུད་ཟོས་མི་བྱེད་པར། །བདེན་ཞེན་ཐམས་ཅད་སྤངས་པས་ན། །དྲན་པའི་དབང་པོ་ཞེས་བྱའོ། །དྲན་འདུན་སྒྱུ་མའི་ཏིང་འཛིན་ལ། །མ་ཡེངས་རྩེ་གཅིག་གྱུར་པ་ནི། །ཏིང་འཛིན་རྩེ་གཅིག་བསྡུས་པའི་ཕྱིར། །ཏིང་ངེ་འཛིན་གྱི་དབང་པོ་ཡིན། །ཏིང་འཛིན་བསྡུས་པའི་སྒྱུ་མ་དེ། །ཤེས་རབ་སོ་སོར་རྟགས་བྱས་པས། །ཆོས་རྣམས་རང་བཞིན་མ་གྲུབ་པར། །ཤེས་པས་ཤེས་རབ་དབང་པོའོ། །མི་མཐུན་ཕྱོགས་ཀུན་ཟིལ་གནོན་པས། །དེ་ཕྱིར་དབང་པོ་ལྔ་ཞེས་བྱ། །དེ་ལྟར་ཉམས་སུ་བླངས་པ་ཡི། །ཉིན་པར་སྣང་གྲགས་ཆོས་རྣམས་ཀུན། །བདེན་མེད་སྒྱུ་མའི་ཉམས་མྱོང་འབྱུང་། །དུས་དང་ལུས་དང་དམིགས་པ་ཡིས། །དབེན་པའི་གནས་སུ་རྨི་ལམ་བཟུང་། །རྨི་ལམ་ཇི་སྙེད་རྨིས་གྱུར་ཀྱང་། །བག་ཆགས་བཞི་ལས་མི་འདས་ཏེ། །དགེ་དང་སྡིག་དང་ལུང་མ་བསྟན། །གོམས་ཞུགས་ཡེ་ཤེས་ཆེན་པོའོ། །དེ་ཕྱིར་བློ་དང་ལྡན་པ་ཡིས། །རྨི་ལམ་གསེར་སྣང་ལྷ་བུ་ལ། །དགེ་སྡིག་བཅས་ནས་བླང་དོར་བྱ། །རྨི་ལམ་སྒྱུ་མའི་དོན་ལ་སྦྱར། །རྨི་ལམ་ཟིན་ཙམ་དྲོད་ཡིན་ཏེ། །མི་རྟོག་སྒྱུ་མ་རང་ཤར་གྱི། །མེའི་སྔ་རྟགས་ཡིན་པར་དྲོད། །གཟུགས་སོགས་སྣང་སྟོང་དབྱེར་མེད་ཅིང་། །འཕེལ་འགྲིབ་མེད་པས་སྒྱུ་མ་སྟེ། །སྒྱུ་མ་རྨི་ལམ་རང་ཤར་དུ། །བག་ཙམ་འབྱུང་བ་རྩེ་མོའོ། །དེ་ཡང་དྲན་འདུན་མོས་

གྲུས་དང་། །བསྲེ་འཕོའི་གནད་ཀྱི་མཚམས་སྦྱར་ནས། །གཉིད་ལོག་སད་པར་གྱུར་པ་
དེ། །སྔར་གྱི་རྨི་ལམ་ཟིན་པ་དང་། །སད་པོའི་འཁྲུལ་སྣང་ཁྱད་མེད་བསྒོམ། །དེ་ཡང་
མིག་ནི་མི་འབྱེད་པར། །དྲན་སྣང་རྟོགས་པའི་རི་མོ་རྣམས། །སྒྱི་མ་རྨི་ལམ་ཐག་བཅད་
ནས། །འདུན་པ་དྲག་པོས་ཉམས་སུ་བླང་། །འཁྲུལ་སྣང་བྱུང་ན་ཡང་ཡང་སྦྱང་། །ཕྱི་
ནང་སྣོད་བཅུད་ཐམས་ཅད་ཀུན། །རྟེན་དང་བརྟེན་པར་བསྒོམ་བྱས་ནས། །དེ་ཉིད་སྒྱུ་
མ་རྨི་ལམ་དུ། །ཡང་ཡང་སྦྱངས་པ་གནད་དུ་ཆེ། །འཁོར་བ་སྙིང་མེད་དགའ་གདུང་དང་
། །སྣང་བ་བསླུ་འབྲིད་མཁན་འདི་ལ། །སྐྱོ་ཤས་དྲག་པོས་རྒྱབ་ཕྱུལ་ནས། །འདུན་མ་
དྲག་པོའི་བཅུད་ལ་བོར། །ཚེ་འདི་བློ་ཡིས་མ་ཐོངས་ན། །ཅི་བྱས་དོན་མེད་སྡུག་
བསྔལ་ཏེ། །འཁོར་གཡོག་མང་ཡང་གྲོག་ཚང་འདྲ། །ལོངས་སྤྱོད་མི་རྟག་སྤྲིན་དང་
མཚུངས། །ནགས་ཁྲོད་འདུག་ཀྱང་རི་དྭགས་ལ། །ཐ་སྙད་མཁས་ཀྱང་ནེ་ཙོ་འདྲ། །དེ་
ཕྱིར་བསམ་དང་ལྡན་པ་ཡིས། །འཇིག་རྟེན་འདི་ལ་ཆགས་མི་བྱ། །སྤྱོད་ལམ་སྣང་
གྲགས་ཐམས་ཅད་ཀུན། །གཉིད་སོང་འདུན་པས་ཉམས་སུ་བླང་། །དངོས་སུ་སྣང་
དང་རྨི་ལམ་གཉིས། །ཁྱད་པར་ཅིག་ཀྱང་ཡོད་མིན་ཏེ། །མ་རྟོགས་པ་ལ་གཉིས་སུ་སྣང་
། །དེ་ཕྱིར་དེ་ལས་གཞན་དུ་མིན། །དྲོད་རྟགས་ཕུང་པོ་ལྔ་པ་ཡིས། །བདེན་འཛིན་འདུ་
ཤེས་སྒྱུ་མས་བཟློག །ཡང་དག་ཟབ་དོན་སྒྱུ་མ་ལ། །ཐེ་ཚོམ་སོམ་ཉི་མེད་པ་དང་།
།བདག་གཞན་དགེ་བ་དག་ལ་སྦྱོར། །ལུས་སོགས་རང་བཞིན་བྱམས་སེམས་ལྡན།
།གཉིད་རྨུགས་ལ་སོགས་དབང་མི་འགྲོ། །ཉོན་མོངས་བག་ཆགས་འཇོམས་པའི་
ཕྱིར། །སྒྱུ་མའི་དྲན་དང་ཤེས་བཞིན་ལྡན། །རྩེ་མོའི་རྟགས་ནི་གོས་གདན་སོགས།
།དྲི་མ་འང་ནི་མི་འཆགས་ཤིང་། །ལུས་ཀྱི་ཕྱི་ནང་སེམས་ཅན་མེད། །སེར་སྣ་མེད་ཅིང་
ལུས་ངག་ཡིད། །གཡོ་རྒྱུ་མེད་དང་དབེན་པའི་གནས། །དགའ་ཞིང་རྟེན་པར་བྱེད་
པའོ། །བཟོད་དང་ཆོས་མཆོག་ཏིང་འཛིན་ནི། །སྟོབས་ནི་རྣམ་པ་ལྔ་ཡིན་ཏེ། །དད་
མོས་སྒྱུ་མའི་ཉམས་ལེན་ཆེ། །བདུད་ཀྱིས་སངས་རྒྱས་གཟུགས་སྤྲུལ་ནས། །དེ་ནི་
ཆོས་མིན་བཟློག་བྱ་ཞེས། །བསྒྱུར་ཀྱང་མི་འགྱུར་དད་པའི་སྟོབས། །བརྩོན་འགྲུས་

ཀྱིས་ནི་སྒྱུ་མ་ལ། །བརྟན་པའི་སྟོབས་ཀྱིས་མཐུ་སྟོབས་ཀྱང་། །མཐར་ཕྱིན་ཚེ་ན་ལྷར་བཅས་ཀྱིས། །བཟློག་པར་མི་ནུས་བརྩོན་འགྲུས་སྟོབས། །དྲན་པའི་སྟོབས་བསྐྱེད་སྒྱུ་མ་ཡི། །དོན་ལ་སེམས་ནི་མ་ཡེངས་པས། །རྟོག་པས་གཡེང་བར་མི་ནུས་ཤིང་། །ཉོན་མོངས་འཇིགས་པས་དྲན་པའི་སྟོབས། །རྟོག་བྲལ་སྒྱུ་མའི་ཏིང་འཛིན་གྱིས། །ཆགས་སྡང་ཡུལ་རྣམས་ཐམས་ཅད་ལ། །དེར་འཛིན་མེད་པས་འདུ་འཛི་ལས། །དབེན་པའི་སྟོབས་ཐོབ་ཏིང་འཛིན་སྟོབས། །ཤེས་རབ་ཀྱིས་ནི་ཆོས་རྣམས་ཀུན། །རང་བཞིན་མ་གྲུབ་སྒྱུ་མ་ཤེས། །འཇིག་རྟེན་པ་དག་སྒྲོལ་བར་བྱེད། །ཤེས་རབ་ལས་བྱུང་ཤེས་རབ་སྟོབས། །མི་མཐུན་ཕྱོགས་ཀྱིས་མི་གཡོ་བའི། །དེ་ཕྱིར་སྟོབས་ལྔ་ཞེས་བྱའོ། །སྣང་ཡང་འཛིན་མེད་སྒྱུ་མ་ཡི། །ཟབ་དོན་མི་སྐྲག་བཟོད་པ་སྟེ། །རྨི་ལམ་ཟིན་པའི་སྦྱོང་སྤེལ་གྱིས། །མི་སྐྲག་པས་ན་བཟོད་པའོ། །དེའི་རྟགས་ནི་སྤྱོད་ལམ་ཀུན། །སྒྱུ་མའི་དོན་དང་ལྡན་པ་དང་། །ཚིག་གིས་མཚོན་ལ་བཟོད་ལྡན་ཞིང་། །དོན་འགྱུར་དམྱལ་སོགས་སྐྱེ་བར་ནུས། །ལོག་པའི་ཆོས་ཀྱིས་མི་འགྱུར་ཞིང་། །ཆོས་ལྟར་བཅོས་པའི་བདུད་རྣམས་ཀྱིས། །དབང་དུ་འགྲོ་བར་མི་འགྱུར་རོ། །རྨི་ལམ་ན་ཡང་ཆོས་རྣམས་ཀུན། །རྨི་ལམ་ཉིད་དུ་ཤེས་པ་དེ། །བཟོད་པ་དག་གི་རྟགས་ཡིན་ཏེ། །ངན་སོང་གསུམ་དུ་ཡོངས་མི་ལྟུང་། །རྨི་ལམ་ཟིན་ནས་ལྷ་ཡི་སྐུ། །རང་ཤར་ཡུད་ཙམ་བྱུང་གྱུར་ན། །བར་དོ་ཟིན་པར་ཐེ་ཚོམ་མེད། །སྒྱུ་མར་གྱུར་པ་དེ་དང་མཚངས། །ཆོས་རྣམས་སྐྱེ་འགག་བྲལ་གྱུར་པ། །སྒྱུ་མར་གྱུར་པ་ཆོས་ཀྱི་མཆོག །རྨི་ལམ་ཡུལ་རྣམས་རང་སེམས་སུ། །རྟོགས་པ་འཇིག་རྟེན་ཆོས་ཀྱི་མཆོག །ཆོས་མཆོག་རྟགས་ནི་སྤྱོད་ལམ་ཀུན། །ཅི་བྱེད་སེམས་ཅན་དོན་དུ་བྱེད། །སངས་རྒྱས་དགྱེས་པའི་སྤྱོད་པས་ཏེ། །ཚེ་འདིའི་ཞེན་པས་འཁྲིས་དང་བྲལ། །ཆོས་བརྒྱད་དུག་གི་མེ་ཏོག་རྣམས། །སྒྱུ་མ་ཉིད་དུ་ཡང་དག་གྲོལ། །རྨི་ལམ་ཟིན་ནས་འོད་གསལ་རྟོགས། །དེས་ནི་བར་དོ་འཇོམས་པ་ཡིན། །དྲོད་ནས་འཇིག་རྟེན་ཆོས་མཆོག་བར། །སྦྱོར་བའི་ལམ་དུ་ཤེས་པར་བྱ། །ཆོས་མཆོག་སྐད་ཅིག་ཕྱི་མ་ལ། །མཐོང་ལམ་རྣམ་པར་མི་རྟོག་པའི། །ཡེ་

ཤེས་སྒྱུ་མ་རང་ཤར་ཉིད། །ཕྱིན་ཅི་མ་ལོག་མཚན་ཉིད་ཅན། །སྦྱར་མ་མཐོང་བ་མཐོང་བས་ན། །མཐོང་བ་ལམ་གྱི་ཡེ་ཤེས་སོ། །བྱང་ཆུབ་ཡན་ལག་རྣམས་བདུན་ནི། །མཐོང་བ་ལམ་གྱི་ཏིང་འཛིན་ཏེ། །སྒྱུ་མ་བློ་ལས་འདས་པ་ཡིས། །དྲན་པ་ཡིད་ལ་བྱར་མེད་ཕྱིར། །ཆོས་རྣམས་དངོས་པོ་མེད་མཐོང་བ། །དྲན་པ་བྱང་ཆུབ་ཡན་ལག་གོ། །སྒྱུ་མ་ལྟ་བུའི་ཆོས་རྣམས་ལ། །སྒྱུ་མ་ལྟ་བུར་ཉམས་བླངས་པས། །དགེ་དང་མི་དགེ་ལུང་མ་བསྟན། །ཆོས་རྟགས་མི་གྲུབ་མི་དམིགས་པ། །ཆོས་རྣམས་འབྱེད་པའི་ཡན་ལག་གོ། །སྒྱུ་མ་འཛིན་པ་ཀུན་འདྲ་བ། །འདུ་ཤེས་ཐམས་ཅད་བཞིག་པའི་ཕྱིར། །ཆོས་རྣམས་མི་ལེན་མི་འདོར་བ། །བརྩོན་པས་བརྩོན་འགྲུས་ཡན་ལག་གོ། །དགག་བསྒྲུབ་བྲལ་བའི་སྒྱུ་མ་ལ། །དགའ་དང་མི་དགའ་བཞིག་པའི་ཕྱིར། །འདུ་བྱེད་ཀུན་ལ་དགའ་མི་བསྐྱེད། །གདུལ་སེམས་དགའ་བ་ཡན་ལག་གོ། །སྒྱུ་མ་ངོ་བོ་མ་གྲུབ་པས། །གང་དམིགས་ཐམས་ཅད་མི་དམིགས་ཕྱིར། །ཆོས་རྣམས་ཀུན་ལ་སེམས་སྦྱངས་པས། །སེམས་སྦྱངས་བྱང་ཆུབ་ཡན་ལག་གོ། །སྒྱུ་མ་ཉིད་ཀྱང་མ་གྲུབ་པ། །ཆོས་རྣམས་བཞིག་པ་རྗེས་རྟོགས་པས། །སེམས་ནི་གང་དག་མི་དམིགས་པ། །ཏིང་འཛིན་བྱང་ཆུབ་ཡན་ལག་གོ། །སྒྱུ་མ་གང་དུའང་མི་གནས་ཤིང་། །རྗེན་དང་འཆག་དང་འཆིང་མི་བྱེད། ཆོས་རྣམས་རྗེས་སུ་མི་མཐོང་བ། །བཏང་སྙོམས་བྱང་ཆུབ་ཡན་ལག་གོ། །ཏིང་འཛིན་དེ་ལ་གོམས་བྱས་པས། །ཉིན་དང་མཚན་ཕྱེད་བར་དག་ཏུ། །སྣང་གྲགས་རྣམ་པ་ཐམས་ཅད་ཀུན། །རང་བཞིན་མ་གྲུབ་མཐའ་བྲལ་བའི། །སྣང་སྟོང་དབྱེར་མེད་སྒྱུ་མར་ཤར། །དེ་ཡང་དངས་པའི་རྒྱ་མཚོ་ལས། །ཆུ་བུར་འབྱུང་ཞིང་ཐིམ་གྱུར་པ། །དེ་བཞིན་རྣམ་རྟོག་ཆུ་བུར་ཡང་། །ཆོས་ཉིད་རྒྱ་མཚོ་མ་གཏོགས་པ། །གཞན་དུ་འགྱུར་བར་མི་སྲིད་ཀྱིས། །དགག་བསྒྲུབ་མི་བྱ་གློད་ལ་ཞོག །དེ་ཚེ་རྟོགས་ཚོགས་ན་བུན་རྣམས། །གཞི་མེད་གྱུར་པས་གཡོ་མི་ནུས། །ངེས་ཤེས་བསྐྱེད་ཅིང་ཐག་བཅད་ནས། །གསལ་གཞག་མེད་པར་གོམས་པར་བྱ། །མོས་གུས་བཟླ་བས་མཚམས་སྦྱར་ནས། །ལྷ་སྐུ་གསལ་ལ་རྟོག་པ་མེད། །བདེ་བ་འཛིན་མེད་ཞེན་བྲལ་

བའི། །རང་ཤར་རང་གྲོལ་འདུས་མ་བྱས། །རྟོག་བྲལ་ཀུན་མཁྱེན་འོད་གསལ་བ།
།གཉིད་དང་རྨི་ལམ་བར་དོ་འམ། །ཡང་ན་རྨི་ལམ་ཟིན་པ་དང་། །རང་ཤར་འབྱུང་བ་
ལོངས་སྐུ་སྟེ། །ཇི་སྲིད་མ་གཡོས་བར་དུའོ། །ཉིན་མཚན་དབྱེར་མེད་བསྲེ་བ་དང་།
ཅིར་སྣང་འཁོར་ཡུག་སུམ་ལྡན་དུ། །མ་ཡེངས་ཉམས་སུ་བླངས་བྱས་ན། །མཆོད་པ་
འབུལ་ཞིང་གསོལ་བ་གདབ། །དེ་ཡིས་རྨི་ལམ་སྤྲུལ་བསྒྱུར་བ། །བརྟན་པ་ཐོབ་པས་
སངས་རྒྱས་ནས། །འཛག་མིག་སྲིན་བུ་ཡན་ཆད་ལ། །སྒྱུ་མའི་རྒྱལ་ནི་སྦྱངས་པ་
ལས། །དམིགས་མེད་སྒྱུ་ལུས་དངོས་གྱུར་ནས། །སྒྱུ་མ་ལྷ་སྐུ་མངོན་གསལ་རྣམས།
།དབྱེར་མེད་གྱུར་པས་གསལ་སྣང་མཆེད། །ཡུལ་སྣང་ཇི་བཞིན་བསྒྲོད་གྱུར་པས།
།མཐོང་སྤྱངས་བརྒྱ་དང་བཅུ་གཉིས་སྤྱངས། །མངོན་པར་ཤེས་པར་གྱུར་ནས་ནི།
།དགའ་ཞིང་འཇིགས་པའི་སྣང་བ་འབྱུང་། །སྒྱུ་མའི་གསལ་སྣང་སྐྱེས་པའི་རྟགས།
།གཉིད་ཀྱི་དུས་སུ་གཞན་དུ་ཡང་། །སྐད་ཅིག་ཡུད་ཙམ་ཐང་ཅིག་ལ། །ཡོན་ཏན་
བརྒྱ་ཕྲག་བཅུ་གཉིས་ཏེ། །ཏིང་འཛིན་བརྒྱ་ལ་སྙོམས་འཇུག་དང་། །སངས་རྒྱས་
བརྒྱ་ཡི་ཞལ་ལྟ་དང་། །སངས་རྒྱས་བརྒྱ་ལ་ཆོས་ཉན་དང་། །འཇིག་རྟེན་ཁམས་
བརྒྱར་བསྐྱོད་པ་དང་། །སངས་རྒྱས་ཞིང་བརྒྱར་འགྲོ་བ་དང་། །ཞིང་བརྒྱར་འོད་ཀྱིས་
འགེངས་པ་དང་། །སེམས་ཅན་བརྒྱ་ནི་སྨིན་བྱེད་དང་། །ཆོས་ཀྱི་སྒོ་བརྒྱ་འབྱེད་པ་
དང་། །བསྐལ་པ་བརྒྱར་ནི་གནས་པ་དང་། །སྔོན་དང་ཕྱི་མཐའ་བརྒྱར་འཇུག་དང་།
།ལུས་ཀྱི་སྤྲུལ་བརྒྱར་འགྱེད་ནུས་དང་། །ལུས་རེ་ལ་ཡང་འཁོར་བརྒྱ་ཡིས། །ཡོངས་
སུ་བསྐོར་ནས་སྟོན་པར་བྱེད། །ཆོས་ཕྱིར་སྲོག་ཀྱང་བཏང་ནུས་ཕྱིར། །འདོད་པའི་
ཡོན་ཏན་གྲོགས་སུ་འགྱུར། །སྦྱིན་པ་རྣམ་བཞི་རྫོགས་བྱེད་ཅིང་། །ལྷག་མ་རྣམས་
ཀྱང་ཅི་ནུས་བྱེད། །ས་ཐོབ་འཇིགས་པ་ལྔ་བྲལ་ཏེ། །འཚོ་བ་མེད་དང་འཆི་བ་དང་།
།ངན་འགྲོའི་ཚིགས་བཅད་མ་ཡིན་བརྗོད། །འཁོར་གྱི་འཇིགས་བྲལ་བག་ཚ་སྤྲངས།
དེས་ནི་སྣང་གྲགས་ཐམས་ཅད་ཀུན། །བདེན་མེད་སྒྱུ་མར་རྟོགས་ལས་བྱུང་། །ཉིན་
པར་དང་ནི་རྨི་ལམ་གྱི། །འཁྲུལ་པའི་བག་ཆགས་མ་དག་ན། །ས་བརྒྱུད་ལ་ཡང་མི་

གནས་ཏེ། །པདྨ་ཅན་ལ་སློས་ཅི་དགོས། །དེ་ཕྱིར་སྣང་བ་སྣ་ཚོགས་ནི། །སྒོ་ལྔའི་རྣམ་ཤེས་བསལ་དངས་ལ། །ཡིད་ཀྱི་འཛིན་པ་མ་ཞུགས་པ། །དེ་ནི་གསལ་སྟོང་དབྱེར་མེད་དེ། །ཞེན་མེད་སྒྱུ་མ་རང་སྣང་ངོ་། རྨི་ལམ་དག་གི་ཆོས་རྣམས་ཀུན། །བདེ་ཆེན་གསལ་སྟོང་འཛིན་མེད་རྟོགས། །མཐོང་བ་ལམ་གྱི་ཡེ་ཤེས་དེ། །ཕྱིར་མི་ལྡོག་པའི་རྟོགས་སུ་བཤད། །ཆོས་མཆོག་རྗེས་ནས་ས་གཉིས་པར། །མཐོང་ལམ་ཡིན་པར་ཤེས་པར་བྱ། །སྒོམ་ལམ་མི་རྟོག་སྒྱུ་མའི་དོན། །མཐོང་བ་གོམས་ཕྱིར་སྒོམ་ལམ་མོ། །ས་ནི་གཉིས་ནས་བཅུའི་བར།།ཡིད་ལ་བྱེད་པའི་ཏིང་འཛིན་ནི། །འཕགས་ལམ་ཡན་ལག་བརྒྱད་ཡིན་ཏེ། །འཁོར་འདས་ལ་སོགས་ཆོས་རྣམས་ཀུན། །ཐམས་ཅད་སྒྱུ་མར་མཉམ་པ་སྟེ། །ལྟ་བའི་དམིགས་པ་ཀུན་བྲལ་བ། །ཡང་དག་པའི་ལྟ་བའོ། །གང་དུ་རྟོག་པ་ཐམས་ཅད་ཀུན། །སྒྱུ་མ་ཉིད་དུ་ཡང་དག་གྲོལ། །རྟོག་པ་ཐམས་ཅད་རྣམ་སྤྲངས་པ། །ཡང་དག་པའི་རྟོག་པའོ། །ཚིག་གི་བདག་གཞན་རྟོག་པ་བྲལ། །ཚོ་ག་བརྗོད་པས་ཆོས་རྣམས་ཀུན། །མཉམ་ཉིད་སྒྱུ་མར་རྟོགས་བྱེད་པ། །དེ་ནི་ཡང་དག་ངག་ཡིན་ནོ། །ལས་ཀྱི་མཐའ་ནི་ཟས་གྱུར་ཏེ། །དཀར་ནག་འདུས་བྱས་འདུས་མ་བྱས། །ཐམས་ཅད་མཐའ་དང་བྲལ་བ་ནི། །ཡང་དག་པ་ཡི་ལས་མཐའོ། །འཚོ་བ་གང་ཞིག་གནོད་འཚེ་བྲལ། །སེམས་ཅན་འཚོ་བ་དག་གྱུར་ཏེ། །བདག་གཞན་དོན་རྣམས་མཐར་ཕྱིན་པ། །ཡང་དག་པའི་འཚོ་བའོ། །ཟབ་ཅིང་སྤྲོས་བྲལ་སྒྱུ་མའི་དོན། །བསྒྲུབ་ཕྱིར་སེམས་ནི་རབ་ཏུ་འཛིན། །རྩོད་དང་མི་ཞུམ་ནན་ཏན་བྱེད། །དེ་ནི་ཡང་དག་བརྩོལ་བའོ། །གང་ཞིག་སྒྱུ་མ་རང་ཤར་ལ། །བདུད་དང་མི་དགེ་གོལ་ས་ཡིས། །བར་ཆད་སྐབས་ནི་མི་རྙེད་པས། །ཡང་དག་པའི་དྲན་པའོ། །བདག་གཞན་སྒྱུ་མར་མཉམ་པ་ཉིད། །ཆོས་རྣམས་སྒྱུ་མར་རྣམ་དག་སྟེ། །སྐད་ཅིག་ཉིད་ལ་ཐམས་ཅད་མཁྱེན། །ཐོབ་པ་ཡང་དག་ཏིང་འཛིན་ནོ། །ས་ནི་གཉིས་པ་དྲི་མེད་ནས། །བཅུ་པ་ཆོས་ཀྱི་སྤྲིན་གྱི་བར། །བསྒོམས་སྤྱངས་བཞི་བརྒྱ་བཅུ་བཞི་སྟེ། །མཐུ་དང་རྫུ་འཕྲུལ་ལྡན་ལ་སོགས། །ས་དགུའི་རྟགས་དང་ཡོན་ཏན་རྣམས། །ས་བཅུའི་སྐབས་ལས་

ཞེས་པར་བྱ། །མཐོང་ལམ་རྗེས་ལ་ཐོབ་པ་ནས། །ས་བཅུ་མན་ཆད་སྒོམ་ལམ་མོ། །སྒྲིབ་པ་ཀུན་ལས་རྣམ་གྲོལ་བའི། །སྒྱུ་མ་ཡང་དག་རྫོགས་སངས་རྒྱས། །བླ་ན་མེད་པའི་བྱང་ཆུབ་སྟེ། །མྱུར་དུ་ཐོབ་པར་བྱེད་པ་ལ། །ཆོས་གཞན་བར་ཆད་མེད་པས་ན། །བར་ཆད་མེད་པའི་ལམ་ཞེས་བྱ། །སྒོམ་ལམ་སྒྲིབ་པ་ཀུན་སྤངས་ནས། །ས་བཅུ་རྒྱུན་གྱི་ཐ་མ་ལ། །སྒྱུ་འཛིན་ཕྲ་ཞིང་ཕྲ་བ་ནི། །ཤེས་བྱའི་སྒྲིབ་པར་ཤེས་པར་བྱ། །ཡང་ན་ལྟ་བ་མཐར་ཐུག་པ། །བཟང་པོར་འདོད་པའི་སྒྲིབ་པ་ཡིན། །སྒྲིབ་པ་དེ་ཉིད་སྤོང་བ་ནི། །རྡོ་རྗེ་ལྟ་བུའི་ཏིང་འཛིན་ཏེ། །གསལ་སྟོང་འཛིན་མེད་བདེ་བ་ཆེ། །འོད་གསལ་རང་ཤར་འདུས་མ་བྱས། །བྱིན་བརླབས་སྟོབས་ཀྱིས་འབྱུང་བ་སྟེ། །མུན་ཁུང་སྒྲོན་མེ་གསེར་སྲང་ལྟར། །ཕྲ་ཞིང་ཕྲ་བའི་སྒྲིབ་པ་ནི། །ཐོགས་མེད་ནུས་པས་རང་དག་པས། །འདུས་མ་བྱས་པའི་དབྱིངས་ཉིད་དང་། །ཡེ་ཤེས་གཉིས་སུ་མེད་པ་སྟེ། །ཉོན་མོངས་ཞེས་བྱ་ཡང་དག་པའི། །ཆོས་སྐུ་དག་པ་གཉིས་ལྡན་ནོ། །སྐུ་ནི་རྟེན་དང་བསགས་པ་དང་། །ཁྱབ་དང་རང་བཞིན་གྲུབ་པ་སྟེ། །མི་འགྱུར་མ་སྐྱེས་མཚན་མེད་པའི། །སངས་རྒྱས་རྣམས་ནི་ཆོས་ཀྱི་སྐུ། །དེ་ལ་བཞེངས་བཞུགས་མི་མངའ་ཡང་། །སྔོན་གྱི་བསོད་ནམས་སེམས་བསྐྱེད་དང་། །སྨོན་ལམ་བསྐྱེད་རིམ་སྟོབས་ལས་ནི། །གཟུགས་སྐུ་རྣམ་གཉིས་རང་ཤར་ཏེ། །དེ་ཡང་འོག་མིན་ཕོ་བྲང་དུ། །ལོངས་སྐུ་སྣང་མཛད་རྡོ་རྗེ་འཆང་། །མཚན་བཟང་དཔེ་བྱད་རབ་ཏུ་ལྡན། །སྤྲོས་བྲལ་སྣང་སྟོང་དབྱེ་མེད་སྐུ། །བྱང་ཆུབ་སེམས་དཔའི་ཚོགས་དང་བཅས། །མཐའ་བྲལ་ཐེག་ཆེན་ཆོས་ཀྱི་སྒྲ། །རྒྱུན་མི་འཆད་པར་སྒྲོགས་པར་བྱེད། །སྤྲུལ་སྐུ་རང་ཤར་གང་འདུལ་ཏེ། །གནས་དུས་སྟོན་པ་ཆོས་འཁོར་སོགས། །གདུལ་བྱ་གང་ལ་གང་མོས་པ། །བཀོད་པ་བསམ་གྱིས་མི་ཁྱབ་པས། །དེ་དང་དེ་ཡི་སྐུར་བསྟན་ནས། །འཁོར་བའི་རྒྱ་མཚོ་མ་སྟོངས་བར། འདམ་གྱིས་མ་གོས་པད་མ་འདམ། །ནོར་བུ་དཔག་བསམ་ལྟ་བུ་ཡིས། །སེམས་ཅན་སྨིན་ཅིང་གྲོལ་བར་བྱེད། །ཡེ་ཤེས་ཚོགས་དང་རྫོགས་རིམ་ལས། །སྐྱེ་འགག་བྲལ་བའི་ཆོས་སྐུ་ཐོབ། །ཚོགས་གཉིས་བསྐྱེད་རྫོགས་དབྱེར་མེད་ལས། །སྐུ་གསུམ་

དབྱེར་མེད་བདེ་ཆེན་ཐོབ། །མདོར་བསྡུས་མཁའ་འདྲའི་ཆོས་སྐུ་ལས། །གཟུགས་སྐུ་
འཛའ་ཚོན་རང་ཤར་བ། །རྣམ་རྟོག་མི་མངའ་ཐམས་ཅད་མཁྱེན། །དབྱེར་མེད་རང་
གྲོལ་ལྷུན་གྲུབ་པོ། །ངོ་བོ་ཉིད་དང་ལོངས་སྤྱོད་རྫོགས། །སྤྲུལ་པ་ཆོས་སྐུ་མཛད་པར་
བཅས། །རྣམ་བཞིའི་ལེགས་བཤད་གང་ཡིན་པ། །སྤྲོས་པ་ལ་ནི་དགའ་འགྱུར་ན།
།མདོ་དང་བྱམས་མགོན་མཛད་པ་རྣམས། །གུས་པས་བླང་ཞིང་ཤེས་པར་བྱ། །འདིར་
ནི་བསྒྲུབ་པ་གཙོར་བྱེད་པ། །ཐ་སྙད་མིག་སྒྲུ་དག་དང་མཚུངས། །དེ་ཕྱིར་ཚེ་ལ་ལོང་
མེད་པས། །འཇིག་རྟེན་འདི་ནི་བློས་བཏང་སྟེ། །བླ་མ་དམ་པ་མཆོག་བརྟེན་ནས།
།རྟོགས་པ་མངོན་དུ་གྱུར་པར་བྱ། །ཚེ་འདི་ཡུན་ཐུང་ཤེས་བྱ་མང་། །ཚེ་ཡི་ཚད་ཀྱང་མ་
ངེས་པས། །ངང་པས་འོ་མ་ལེན་པ་ལྟར། །རང་གི་དགོས་པ་བླང་བར་བྱ། །ཇི་སྲིད་
འདུ་ཤེས་ཡོད་ཀྱི་བར། །ཐེག་པའི་མཐའ་ལ་ཐུག་པ་མེད། །འདུ་ཤེས་མེད་པར་གྱུར་
པ་ན། །ཐེག་པ་མེད་ཅིང་བརྗོད་དུ་མེད། །ལམ་དང་སའི་རྟགས་རྣམས་ནི། །གོམས་པ་
ཆེ་ཆུང་སྟོབས་ཁྱད་དང་། །རྒན་གཞོན་དག་གི་ཁྱད་པར་གྱིས། །ཕྱི་རོལ་ཡུལ་སྣང་
མཐོང་སྣང་དང་། །ངོ་བོ་མཐོང་དང་ཡོན་ཏན་ཐོབ། །དགྲ་བཅོམ་རྒྱན་ཅན་རྒྱན་མེད་
དང་། །རྒྱུར་ཆུ་ཆོས་སྤྱོད་ཆོས་སྐད་སོགས། །ཕྱི་རོལ་རྫུ་འཕྲུལ་རིམ་པ་རྣམས། །མདོ་
དང་རྒྱུད་ལས་ཤེས་པར་བྱ། །ས་བཅུ་རྒྱུན་གྱི་ཐ་མ་ནས། །མཁྱེན་གཉིས་སྐུ་བཞི་
མཛད་པར་བཅས། །རང་གཞན་ལྷུན་གྲུབ་པར་དག་ཏུ། །མཐར་ཕྱིན་ལམ་དུ་ཤེས་
པར་བྱ། ། དེ་ནས་བྱང་ཆུབ་སེམས་དཔའ་ཡི། །ས་བཅུ་ལེགས་པར་བཤད་ཀྱིས་ཉོན།
།འཇིག་རྟེན་འདས་པའི་ཞི་གནས་དང་། །ལྷག་མཐོང་ཟུང་དུ་འབྲེལ་པ་ནི། །འཛིན་
མེད་སྒྱུ་མ་རང་ཤར་ཏེ། །རྣམ་པར་མི་རྟོག་ཡེ་ཤེས་སོ། །ཡོན་ཏན་དག་གི་གཞི་རྟེན་
ཅིང་། །གོང་དུ་བགྲོད་པས་ས་ཞེས་བྱ། །དབྱེ་ན་རབ་དགའ་ལ་སོགས་དང་། །སྔ་
ལྟས་བཅུ་ནི་ཤེས་པར་བྱ། །དེ་ཡང་ས་བཅུའི་མཚན་ཉིད་ནི། །བློ་འདས་མཐའ་བྲལ་
སྒྱུ་མའི་དོན། །སྔར་མ་མཐོང་བ་མངོན་གྱུར་ཅིང་། །དོན་གྲུབ་གྱུར་པས་དགའ་བ་སྐྱེས།
།དེ་ཕྱིར་རབ་ཏུ་དགའ་བའོ། །ལུས་ངག་ཡིད་གསུམ་འཁྲུལ་པའི་ཚོགས། །སྐྱེ་བ་མེད་

པས་སྒྱུ་མར་རྟོགས། །ཚུལ་ཁྲིམས་དྲི་མའི་སྐྱོན་བྲལ་བས། །དྲི་མ་མེད་པ་ཞེས་བྱའོ།
།སྣང་གྲགས་ཆོས་རྣམས་ཐམས་ཅད་ཀུན། །གསལ་ལ་འཛིན་མེད་སྒྱུ་མར་ཤར། །ཡེ་
ཤེས་དབང་གིས་འོད་སྣང་བས། །དེ་ཕྱིར་འོད་བྱེད་པ་ཤེས་བྱ། །གསལ་སྣང་འཛིན་
མེད་འོད་དེ་ཡང་། །རང་བཞིན་མ་གྲུབ་སྒྱུ་མ་སྟེ། །ཉོན་མོངས་བསྲེག་བྱེད་འོད་འཕྲོ་
བས། །འོད་འཕྲོ་ཅན་ཞེས་བྱ་བའོ། །སྤྱང་བྱ་གཉེན་པོའི་བདེན་འཛིན་ཀུན། །གང་
ཡང་བདེན་མེད་སྒྱུ་མར་འགྱུར། །ཉོན་མོངས་གདུལ་དཀའ་ཐུལ་བའི་ཕྱིར། །དེ་ནི་
སྦྱངས་པ་དཀའ་ཞེས་བྱ། །འཁོར་འདས་ལ་སོགས་ཆོས་རྣམས་ཀུན། །དབྱེར་མེད་
མཐའ་བྲལ་སྒྱུ་མ་སྟེ། །རང་བཞིན་གནས་པ་མངོན་གྱུར་པས། །མངོན་དུ་གྱུར་པ་
ཞེས་བྱའོ། །ཆོས་རྣམས་སྒྱུ་མར་ཡང་དག་གྲོལ། །དམིགས་མེད་སྙིང་རྗེས་དོན་རྣམས་
བྱེད། །ཉན་ཐོས་རང་རྒྱལ་རིང་གྱུར་པས། །དེ་ཕྱིར་རིང་དུ་སོང་ཞེས་བྱ། །སྒྱུ་མ་བློ་
འདས་བསྐྱོལ་བ་མེད། །ལྷུན་གྲུབ་རང་ཤར་ཆེན་པོ་ལ། །ཉོན་མོངས་གཡོ་བར་མི་
ནུས་པས། །མི་གཡོ་བ་ཞེས་བརྗོད་པར་བྱ། །ཇི་སྲིད་ཆོས་སུ་འཛིན་པ་རྣམས། །སྒྱུ་མ་
ཉིད་དུ་གྲོལ་གྱུར་པ། །བློ་གྲོས་ཡངས་ཤིང་ཐོགས་མེད་ཕྱིར། །ལེགས་པའི་བློ་གྲོས་
ཞེས་བྱའོ། །ཚོགས་གཉིས་ཟུང་འཇུག་སྒྱུ་མ་ཡིས། །ཕྲིན་ལས་ལ་ནི་དབང་ཐོབ་ཅིང་།
།ཆོས་སྐུའི་མཁའ་ལ་ཡེ་ཤེས་སྤྲིན། །ཁྱབ་པས་ཆོས་ཀྱི་སྤྲིན་ཞེས་བྱ། །ས་བཅུ་ཕ་རོལ་
ཕྱིན་བཅུའོ། །གང་གིས་གང་ནོན་རིམ་པ་ནི། །དང་པོ་སྦྱིན་པ་གཙོ་ཞིང་རྫོགས།
།ལྷག་མ་རྣམས་ནི་ཅི་ནུས་བསྒྲུབ། །གཉིས་པ་ཚུལ་ཁྲིམས་ཕ་རོལ་ཕྱིན། །གསུམ་
པ་དག་གིས་བཟོད་པས་ཏེ། །བཞི་པ་བརྩོན་འགྲུས་ཕ་རོལ་ཕྱིན། །ལྔ་པ་ཡིས་ནི་
བསམ་གཏན་ཏེ། །དྲུག་པ་ཤེས་རབ་ཕ་རོལ་ཕྱིན། །བདུན་པ་ཡིས་ནི་ཐབས་ཡིན་ཏེ།
།བརྒྱད་པ་སྨོན་ལམ་ཕ་རོལ་ཕྱིན། །དགུ་པ་ཡིས་ནི་སྟོབས་ཡིན་ཏེ། །བཅུ་པ་ཡེ་ཤེས་
ཕ་རོལ་ཕྱིན། །དེ་ལྟར་ཕ་རོལ་ཕྱིན་བཅུ་ཡི། །མཚན་ཉིད་མ་ནོར་བཤད་པར་བྱ། །ཡེ་
ཤེས་འཚོལ་ཕྱིར་སེམས་ཅན་ལ། །དགེ་རྩ་གཏོང་བས་སྦྱིན་པ་སྟེ། །ཉོན་མོངས་
གདུང་བ་ཐམས་ཅད་ཀུན། །ཞི་བའི་ཕྱིར་ན་ཚུལ་ཁྲིམས་སོ། །བྱམས་དང་སྙིང་རྗེས་

སེམས་ཅན་ལ། །འཚིག་པ་མེད་པས་བཟོད་པ་སྟེ། །དགེ་བའི་ཆོས་རྣམས་ཚོལ་བ་
ལས། །མི་ངོམས་བརྩོན་པས་བརྩོན་འགྲུས་སོ། །མཁྱེན་པའི་ཡེ་ཤེས་མངོན་བྱེད་ལ།
།འགྱོད་མེད་སེམས་ལྡན་བསམ་གཏན་ནོ། །རང་བཞིན་གྱིས་ནི་མ་སྐྱེས་པ། །མངོན་
དུ་གྱུར་པས་ཤེས་རབ་པོ། །རྒྱལ་བའི་ཡེ་ཤེས་ཚད་མེད་པ། །སྒྲུབ་པར་བྱེད་པ་ཐབས་
ཡིན་ཏེ། །ཡེ་ཤེས་ལས་ནི་འགྱུར་བས་ན། །མངོན་པར་བསྒྲུབ་པས་སྨོན་ལམ་མོ།
།ཕས་ཀྱི་རྒོལ་དང་བདུད་ཚོགས་ཀྱིས། །ལམ་བརྒྱུད་མི་གཅོད་སྟོབས་ཡིན་ཏེ། །ཆོས་
རྣམས་ཇི་བཞིན་རྟོགས་པ་འདི། །ཡེ་ཤེས་ཕ་རོལ་ཕྱིན་པར་འདོད། །བྱང་ཆུབ་སེམས་
དཔའ་སངས་རྒྱས་ལ། །ས་ནི་བཅུ་དང་བཅུ་གཅིག་ཡིན། །རྨོངས་པ་ཉི་ཤུ་རྩ་གཉིས་
ཀྱི། །སྒྲིབ་པ་གང་ཡིན་ཤེས་པར་བྱ། །གང་གིས་རྨོངས་ན་དེར་འཛིན་རྨོངས། །དེ་ཕྱིར་
ས་ཡི་ཆོས་རྣམས་ལ། །གང་དུ་འཛིན་པ་ཡོངས་སྤངས་ནས། །འཛིན་མེད་སྒྱུ་མར་
རྟོགས་པར་བྱ། །གལ་ཏེ་སྒྱུ་མ་ཙམ་དེ་ཡང་། །འཛིན་པར་གྱུར་ན་དེ་ཡང་སྤངས། །སྒྱུ་
མ་ཡོད་མེད་ལས་འདས་ཤིང་། །སྤང་ཐོབ་དགག་སྒྲུབ་རང་སར་གྲོལ། །གང་དུ་འཛིན་
པ་ཀུན་རྫོབ་སྟེ། །འཛིན་མེད་རང་གྲོལ་བློ་ལས་འདས། །དེ་ཕྱིར་ས་ཡི་ཆོས་རྣམས་
ཀུན། །འཛིན་མེད་གོམས་བྱས་སྒྲིབ་པ་འདག རང་ཤར་རྟོགས་པའི་རིམ་པ་དང་།
།རྟགས་རྣམས་རིམ་པར་འཆར་བར་འགྱུར། །སྒྱུ་མ་རང་ཤར་དོན་རྟོགས་པས།
།འཁོར་གསུམ་ཡོངས་དག་སྤྲིན་རྩོལ་མེད། །ཉིན་དང་མཚན་མོ་དུས་ཀུན་ཏུ། །སྒྱུ་མ་
ལྟ་བུར་རང་ཤར་འབྱུང་། །དེ་ཡང་ཆོས་དབྱིངས་སྒྱུ་མ་ནི། །ཀུན་འགྲོ་ཁྱབ་པའི་དོན་དུ་
རྟོགས། །གསལ་སྣང་བརྒྱ་ཕྲག་བཅུ་གཉིས་སོ། །ཕྱི་ནང་རྟགས་ནི་གོང་བཞིན་ནོ།
།དྲི་མེད་པ་ལ་སྒྱུ་མ་དང་། །ལྷ་སྐུ་ཞེན་བྲལ་དྲི་མེད་སྐུ། །འགྲོ་འོང་ཡོད་མེད་བློ་ལས་
འདས། །དེ་ཉིད་གོམས་བརྟན་མཆོག་ཡིན་ཏེ། །ཆོས་དབྱིངས་སྒྱུ་མ་རང་ཤར་ཉིད།
།མཆོག་ཏུ་གྱུར་པའི་དོན་དུ་རྟོགས། །རྟགས་ནི་ཉིན་མཚན་གང་ལ་ཡང་། །སྐད་ཅིག་
ཡུད་ཙམ་ཐང་ཅིག་ལ། །ཏིང་འཛིན་སྟོབས་ལ་སྙོམས་འཇུག་སོགས། །སྟོང་ཕྲག་བཅུ་
གཉིས་ཤེས་པར་བྱ། །འོད་བྱེད་པ་ལ་འོད་གསལ་དང་། །ལྷ་སྐུ་བདེ་ཆེན་དབྱེར་མེད་

དོ། །གསལ་དང་རྨི་ལམ་དུས་ཉིད་དུ། །སེམས་ཅན་དཔག་མེད་འདུལ་བའི་ཕྱིར།
།བསམ་གྱིས་མི་ཁྱབ་ལྷ་ཡི་སྐུ། །རང་ཤར་ཁམས་ཁེངས་ཆོས་སྒྲ་སྒྲོགས། །ཆོས་ཀྱི་
དབྱིངས་སུ་ཆོས་རྣམས་ཀུན། །རྒྱུ་མཐུན་དག་གི་དོན་རྣམས་རྟོགས། །ཏིང་འཛིན་
བརྒྱ་སྟོང་སྙོམས་འཇུག་སོགས། །བརྒྱ་སྟོང་ཕྲག་ནི་ཤེས་པར་བྱ། །འོད་འཕྲོ་ཅན་ལ་
ལྷ་ཡི་སྐུ། །རྩོལ་མེད་གོམས་ཕྱིར་འབད་བྱས་པས། །རྩལ་བའི་དུག་ལས་གྲོལ་གྱུར་
ནས། །ཆོས་དབྱིངས་ཡོངས་སུ་འཛིན་པ་ནི། །མེད་པའིདོན་དུ་རྟོགས་པའོ། །ཏིང་
འཛིན་ཁྲག་ཁྲིག་སྙོམས་འཇུག་སོགས། །ཁྲག་ཁྲིག་ཕྲག་ནི་བཅུ་གཉིས་སོ། །སྣང་
དཀའི་ས་ལ་ཆོས་རྣམས་ཀུན། །སྐྱེ་མེད་རྟོགས་པའི་ངག་ཉིད་ནས། །འགག་མེད་
དམིགས་མེད་སྙིང་རྗེ་ཡིས། །གཞན་དོན་ལྷ་སྐུ་ཕྱུག་རྒྱ་ཆེ། །སྤྱོད་ལམ་ཀུན་དང་དབྱེར་
མེད་གྱུར། །ཆོས་ཀྱི་དབྱིངས་རྣམས་ཐམས་ཅད་ཀུན། །རྒྱུད་གཞན་ཐ་དད་མེད་པར་
རྟོགས། །སྐད་ཅིག་ཡུད་ཙམ་ཐང་ཅིག་ལ། །རིང་འཛིན་ཁྲག་ཁྲིག་སྟོང་དག་ལ།
།སྙོམས་པར་འཇུག་ལ་སོགས་པ་སྟེ། །ཁྲག་ཁྲིག་སྟོང་ཕྲག་བཅུ་གཉིས་སོ། །མངོན་
དུ་གྱུར་ལ་འཁོར་འདས་ཀྱིས། །རྒྱུ་འབྲས་ཐམས་ཅད་མངོན་གྱུར་པས། །རྟེན་ཅིང་
འབྲེལ་འབྱུང་ལྷ་ཡི་སྐུ། །གསལ་ལ་འཛིན་མེད་འོད་གསལ་འཆར། །ཆོས་དབྱིངས་
ཀུན་ནས་ཉོན་མོངས་དང་། །རྣམ་བྱང་ཐ་དད་མེད་པར་རྟོགས། །ཏིང་འཛིན་ཁྲག་ཁྲིག་
བརྒྱ་སྟོང་སོགས། །ཁྲག་ཁྲིག་བརྒྱ་སྟོང་བཅུ་གཉིས་སོ། །རིང་པོ་ས་ཡི་ཆོས་རྣམས་
ཀུན། །སྐྱེ་འགག་བྲལ་བ་སྒྱུ་མའི་སྐུ། །ཟུང་འཇུག་མཐའ་འབྲལ་བདེ་བ་ཆེ། །ཉིན་
མཚན་སྤྱོད་ལམ་ཐམས་ཅད་དུ། །ཞེན་མེད་དེ་ལ་དྲན་ཐོབ་པས། །ཕྱིར་མི་ལྡོག་པར་
ཤེས་པར་བྱ། །ཆོས་དབྱིངས་ཆོས་ཀྱི་མཚན་ཉིད་དང་། །ཐ་མི་དད་པའི་དོན་དུ་
རྟོགས། །བྱེ་བ་ཁྲག་ཁྲིག་བརྒྱ་སྟོང་ལ། །སྙོམས་པར་འཇུག་སོགས་བཅུ་གཉིས་སོ།
།མི་གཡོའི་ས་ལ་ཉིན་མཚན་ཀུན། །ལྷ་སྐུ་འོད་གསལ་རྩོལ་བ་བྲལ། །རང་ཤར་
ལོངས་སྐུའི་ཆ་འཐུན་དེ། །ཕྱོགས་བཅུ་དུས་གསུམ་སངས་རྒྱས་ཀྱི། །ཞིང་ཁམས་སྒྱུ་
མའི་བཀོད་པས་སྤྱོང་། །རྣམ་དག་ལྷུན་གྲུབ་མཁའ་བཞིན་ནོ། །ཆོས་དབྱིངས་འཕེལ་

འགྲིབ་མེད་གྱུར་ཅིང་། །ཞིང་དག་པ་ལ་དབང་ཐོབ་རྟགས། །སྐད་ཅིག་ལ་ནི་ཏིང་ངེ་འཛིན། །སྟོང་དང་སུམ་བརྒྱ་སྟོང་ཕྲག་བཅུ། །རྫུལ་ནི་ཕྲ་རབ་སྙེད་ཐོབ་པ། །ཕྲག་ནི་བཅུ་གཉིས་ཤེས་པར་བྱ། །བློ་གྲོས་ས་ལ་འོད་གསལ་ནི། །ཆོས་ནི་མཐའ་བྲལ་འདུས་མ་བྱས། །འགྲོ་འོང་སྐྱེ་ཤི་དགག་བསྒྲུབ་བྲལ། །སྒྲ་བསམ་བརྗོད་འདས་སྐྱེ་བ་བྲལ། །བསྒོམ་བྱ་བསྒོམ་བྱེད་གཉིས་མེད་ཅིང་། །སྤྲིན་མེད་དག་པའི་མཁའ་བཞིན་ནོ། །སྤྲོས་པ་ཐོགས་པ་མེད་པ་ཡིས། །ཡེ་ཤེས་དམ་པའི་དོན་དུ་རྟོགས། །སྐད་ཅིག་ལ་ནི་ཏིང་ངེ་འཛིན། །སངས་རྒྱས་ཞིང་ནི་གྲངས་མེད་པ། །བརྒྱ་སྟོང་ཕྲག་བཅུའི་རྫུལ་སྙེད་ལ། །སྙོམས་པར་འཇུག་སོགས་བཅུ་གཉིས་སོ། །ཚོགས་གཉིས་ཟུང་འཇུག་ཆོས་སྤྲིན་ལ། །མི་གནས་གནས་མེད་འོད་གསལ་ཏེ། །རང་བཞིན་རྣམ་དག་རྟོག་མེད་སྐུ། །འཛིན་པའི་རྟོག་བྲལ་ས་ལེ་མཁྱེན། །བློ་འདས་དམིགས་པའི་མཐའ་དང་བྲལ། །ནམ་མཁའ་ལྟ་བུར་སྐྱེ་འགག་མེད། །མཚན་ཉིད་ཀུན་བྲལ་མཁའ་ལྟར་དག །སྒྲ་བསམ་བརྗོད་བྲལ་བློ་ལས་འདས། །ཉིན་མཚན་དུ་རྣམས་ཐམས་ཅད་དུ། །སྣང་སྟོང་བདེ་སྟོང་དབྱེར་མེད་མཆོག །འཕེལ་འགྲིབ་མེད་པར་འཆར་བ་སྟེ། །ཕྲིན་ལས་དབང་བའི་དོན་དུ་རྟོགས། །དེ་ཡང་ས་བཅུའི་མགོན་པོ་ལ། །དབང་བསྐུར་བ་ནི་རྨད་བྱུང་ཆེ། །ཁམས་གསུམ་གྱི་ནི་ཡང་དག་ཆེ། །མི་འཇིགས་སེང་གེའི་ཁྲི་ལ་བཞག །ཕྱོགས་བཅུ་རྒྱལ་བའི་ཕྱག་དང་ནི། །འོད་ཟེར་ཆེན་པོའི་དབང་བསྐུར་བས། །སྐད་ཅིག་ཡུད་ཙམ་ཐང་ཅིག་ལ། །ཆོས་ཀྱི་སྣང་བ་ཆེན་པོ་དང་། །འོད་དང་ཆོས་སྤྲིན་ཚད་མེད་དང་། །དེ་བཞིན་གཤེགས་པ་ཚད་མེད་པའི། །ཆོས་ཀྱི་སྣང་བ་ཆོས་ཀྱི་འོད། །ཆོས་ཀྱི་སྤྲིན་ཆེན་ཚད་མེད་ཐོབ། །སྲིད་པ་ཐ་མར་གྱུར་པ་དེས། །ཤེས་བྱའི་སྒྲིབ་པ་ལེགས་སྤྱངས་ནས། །རྡོ་རྗེ་ལྟ་བུའི་ཏིང་འཛིན་རྟོགས། །ནང་ལྟར་བཅུ་གཅིག་མགོན་པོ་སྟེ། །འོག་མིན་བཙུན་མོའི་གཞལ་ཡས་སུ། །ཟག་མེད་མ་ཧཱའི་དབང་བསྐུར་བས། །འོད་གསལ་རྡོ་རྗེའི་ཏིང་འཛིན་རྟོགས། །བཅུ་གཉིས་མ་ཆགས་པདྨ་ཅན། །ཡང་དག་སངས་རྒྱས་དེར་སངས་རྒྱས། །སྤྲུལ་པ་པོ་གཅིག་འདིར་འཚང་རྒྱ། །བྱང་ཆུབ་སེམས་དཔའ་

སངས་རྒྱས་ཁྱེད། །རྒྱ་མཚོ་བ་ལང་རྨིག་རྗེས་མཚུངས། །དག་པ་ས་གསུམ་ཡོན་ཏག་ཀྱང་། །དཔག་ཅིང་གཞལ་བར་མི་ནུས་ན། །ཐམས་ཅད་མཁྱེན་པའི་ཡོན་ཏན་ནི། །བརྗོད་ཅིང་དཔག་པར་སྨོས་ཅི་དགོས། །ནམ་མཁའ་ས་གཞི་གང་ཡིན་པ། །སྒྲ་རྩེས་གཞལ་བར་ནུས་སྲིད་ཀྱིས། །རྒྱལ་བའི་ཡོན་ཏན་རྒྱ་མཚོ་ནི། །བསྐལ་པར་གྲངས་མེད་བརྗོད་མི་ནུས། །དེ་ཕྱིར་ཐམས་ཅད་མཁྱེན་པ་ཡི། །སྤྱོད་ཡུལ་བརྗོད་ལས་འདས་པའོ། །དེ་ལྟར་ས་རྣམས་བགྲོད་པ་ཡིས། །ལྷུགས་སྲེགས་བཞིན་དུ་གནས་གྱུར་ཏེ། །ཉོན་མོངས་ཡིད་ལ་མི་རྟོགས་དང་། །སྒོ་ལྔའི་རྣམ་ཤེས་ཡེ་ཤེས་ལྔ། །ཀུན་གཞི་གནས་གྱུར་མཐར་ཐུག་སྐུ། །ཟག་མེད་བདེ་ཆེན་འདུས་མ་བྱས། །དབྱིངས་དང་ཡེ་ཤེས་གཉིས་མེད་ཅིང་། །ཕྲིན་ལས་ལྷུན་གྲུབ་རྒྱུན་ཆད་མེད། །མཐའ་བྲལ་རང་ཤར་ཆེན་པོའོ། །སྒྱུ་མ་ལམ་གྱི་རིམ་པ་འདི། །ལུང་བསྟན་ཐོབ་ནས་མདོ་རྒྱུད་ནས། །ལེགས་བཏུས་ཉམས་སུ་མྱོང་བ་ལྟར། །འགལ་འཁྲུལ་མེད་པར་ཡི་གེར་བཀོད། །དགེ་བ་དྲི་མེད་རྒྱ་ཆེན་དེས། །འགྲོ་ཀུན་སྡུག་བསྔལ་གཟིར་གྱུར་རྣམས། །སྒྱུ་མའི་ལམ་ལ་རབ་སྦྱངས་ནས། །འོད་གསལ་ཆེན་པོ་ཐོབ་པར་ཤོག །

།སྒྱུ་མ་ལམ་གྱི་རིམ་པ་དྲི་མེད་སྙིང་པོ་ཞེས་བྱ་བ། །ཡེ་ཤེས་ཀྱི་མཁའ་འགྲོ་མ་ནི་གུ་མས་མཛད་པ་རྫོགས་སོ། །ཡེ་ཤེས་ཀྱི་མཁའ་འགྲོ་མ་དེ་ཉིད་དང་། ལོ་ཙཱ་བ་གླན་དར་མ་བློ་གྲོས་ཀྱིས་བསྒྱུར་བའོ། །སླད་ནས་ཁྱུང་པོ་རྣལ་འབྱོར་པས་ཞུས་ཏེ་ཉམས་སུ་མྱོང་བར་བགྱིས་པའོ།། །མངྒ་ལཾ།།

༄༅། །སྒྱུ་མ་ལམ་གྱི་རིམ་པའི་འགྲེལ་པ་ཞེས་བྱ་བ།

༄༅༅། །རྒྱ་གར་སྐད་དུ། མ་ཡ་ཛྙ་ན་ཀྲ་མ་བྲིད་ཏི་ནཱ་མ། བོད་སྐད་དུ། སྒྱུ་མ་ལམ་གྱི་རིམ་པའི་འགྲེལ་པ་ཞེས་བྱ་བ། སངས་རྒྱས་དང་བྱང་ཆུབ་སེམས་དཔའ་ཐམས་ཅད་ལ་ཕྱག་འཚལ་ལོ། །རྒྱལ་བ་རྒྱ་མཚོ་རྡོ་རྗེ་འཆང་། །ཁྱོད་ཞབས་བདག་ནི་གུས་བཏུད་ནས། །སྒྱུ་མ་ལམ་རིམ་གསལ་བྱེད་དོན། །མདོ་དང་རྒྱུད་ལས་གསུངས་བཞིན་བྲིས། །

དེང་འདིར་རྒྱལ་བའི་བཀའ་ཡང་དག་པའི་དོན་ཉེ་བར་མངོན་སུམ་དུ་གཏན་ལ་འབེབས་པའི་བསྟན་བཅོས་ཕྱིན་ཅི་མ་ལོག་པ་གང་ཞེ་ན། གང་གིས་གང་ལ་བརྟེན་གང་བརྩམས། དེའི་རྒྱུ། དགོས་པ། དོན་རབ་ཏུ་གསལ་བྱེད་དོ། །དེ་ལ་དང་པོ་གང་གིས་ན། །དག་པའི་ས་གསུམ་ལ་གནས་ཤིང་། །རྡོ་རྗེ་འཆང་གིས་རྗེས་གནང་ཐོབ་པ་བདག་གིས་སོ། །གང་ལ་བརྟེན་ན། ཉམས་མྱོང་མདོ་རྒྱུད་དུ་མ་ལས་སོ། །གང་བརྩམས་ན། སྒྱུ་མ་ལམ་གྱི་རིམ་པའོ། །རྒྱུ་ནི་འགྲོ་བ་ལ་ཕན་འདོགས་པ་དེ་ལ་སྤྲོ་བའོ། །དགོས་པ་ནི། འཁོར་འདས་ཀྱི་ཆོས་ཐམས་ཅད་ལ་འཛིན་པའི་བདུད་ཀྱིས་བཅིངས་པ་ལས་གྲོལ་བར་བྱེད་པའོ། །

དོན་གསལ་བར་བྱེད་པ་གང་ཞེ་ན། བར་ཆད་ལས་གྲོལ་བར་བྱེད་པའི་ཕྱག་དང་། མཐར་ཕྱིན་པའི་དམ་བཅའ་དང་། དོན་གསལ་བར་བྱེད་པའི་གཞུང་ངོ་། །དེ་ལ་ཐོག་མར་སེམས་ཉིད་ནོར་བུ་རིན་པོ་ཆེ་འདི་ལ། ཚོགས་གཉིས་ཀྱི་བྱི་དོར་བྱས་པས། དགོས་འདོད་ཐམས་ཅད་འབྱུང་བས་ན་ཕྱག་གི་འོས་ཏེ། བྲམ་ཟེ་ཆེན་པོས། རང་གི་སེམས་ནི་ཀུན་གྱི་ས་བོན་ཏེ། །གང་ལ་སྲིད་དང་མྱ་ངན་འདས་འཕྲོ་བ། །འདོད་པའི་འབྲས་བུ་སྟེར་བར་བྱེད་པ་ཡི། །ཡིད་བཞིན་ནོར་འདྲའི་སེམས་ལ་ཕྱག་འཚལ་ལོ། །ཡང་ན་སེམས་ལྟ་བའི་དྲ་བ་འཛིན་བྱེད་ཐམས་ཅད་བྲལ་བའི་གསལ་སྟོང་འཛིན་མེད་བདེ་བ་ཆེན་པོ་ལ་བཞུགས་པ་ནི་ཕྱག་རྣམས་ཀྱིས་ནང་ནས་མཆོག་ཏུ་གྱུར་པ་སྟེ། རྡོ་རྗེ་

ཕྲེང་བ་ལས། ཇི་ལྟར་ཆུ་ལ་ཆུ་བཞག་དང་། །ཇི་ལྟར་མར་ལ་མར་བཞག་ལྟར། །རང་གིས་རང་གི་ཡེ་ཤེས་ནི། །ལེགས་མཐོང་གང་ཡིན་འདིར་ཕྱག་འཚལ། །ཞེས་སོ། །

དམ་བཅའ་ནི། དྲང་སྲོང་རྣམས་ཁ་འོག་ཏུ་ལུས་ཚུད་པའམ། རྒྱལ་པོའི་བྱ་བ་ཁས་བླངས་པ་ལྟ་བུའོ། །དོན་རབ་ཏུ་གསལ་བར་བྱེད་པའི་གཞུང་ནི། ཡེ་ཤེས་མངོན་པར་འབྱུང་བའི་རྒྱུད་རྒྱས་པ་ལས། སྒྱུ་མ་ཆོས་དབྱིངས་ཀུན་གཞི་སྟེ། སྒྱུ་མ་ལྟ་བུའི་ཆོས་རྣམས་ལ། །སྒྱུ་མ་ལྟ་བུར་བསྒོམས་བྱས་ན། །སྒྱུ་མ་ལྟ་བུར་མངོན་སངས་རྒྱ། །ལམ་ལྔ་ས་ནི་བཅུ་གཉིས་ཏེ། །འདི་ནི་གཞན་གྱིས་རྟོགས་པ་མིན། །གཞི་དང་རང་བཞིན་འབྲས་བུའི་དོན། །ཟབ་དང་རྒྱ་ཆེར་དབྱེར་མེད་པའོ། །ཞེས་སོ། །དེའི་དོན་གང་ཞེ་ན། ཇི་ལྟར་གནས་པའི་གཞི་ཟུང་འཇུག་གཏན་ལ་དབབ། ཐབས་ཀྱི་རང་བཞིན་ལམ་ཟུང་འཇུག་ཉམས་སུ་བླངས། འབྲས་བུ་ཟུང་འཇུག་མངོན་གྱུར་རང་ཤར།

དེ་ལ་ཇི་ལྟར་གནས་པའི་གཞི་ཟུང་འཇུག་ཀུན་གཞི་དང་། དབང་བཞི་ལས། ཇི་ལྟར་གནས་པའི་གཞི་གང་ཞེ་ན། ཀུན་གཞི་རྣམ་པར་ཤེས་པ་དང་། །ཉོན་མོངས་པ་ཅན་གྱི་ཡིད་དང་། །ཡིད་ཀྱི་རྣམ་པར་ཤེས་པ་དང་། །སྒོ་ལྔའི་རྣམ་པར་ཤེས་པའོ། །

དེ་ལ་ཀུན་བཞིའི་རྣམ་པར་ཤེས་པ་ལ་དབྱེ་ན། ཀུན་གཞིའི་རིག་པ་ལུང་མ་བསྟན་དང་། ཀུན་གཞི་ཀུན་གྱི་ས་བོན་དང་། ཀུན་གཞི་ལས་བག་ཆགས་སུ་སྨིན་པ་དང་། ཀུན་གཞིའི་རྣམ་ཤེས་སུ་ཇི་ལྟར་བཞག་པའོ། །དང་པོ་ནི་རིག་པ་གསལ་སྟོང་ལུང་མ་བསྟན་ཀུན་གཞིའི་རྣམ་ཤེས་ཏེ། སྙིང་པོ་རབ་ཏུ་གསལ་བའི་མདོ་ལས། རིག་པ་གསལ་སྟོང་ཀུན་གཞི་སྟེ། །ལུང་མ་བསྟན་དུ་གྲགས་པའོ། །ཞེས་སོ། །ཀུན་གཞི་གསལ་སྟོང་དེ་གཅིག་དང་ཐ་དད་པ་མ་ཡིན་པའི་ཟུང་འཇུག་སྟེ། དྲི་མེད་སྙིང་པོའི་མདོ་ལས། ཀུན་གཞི་གསལ་སྟོང་ལུང་མ་བསྟན། །གཅིག་དང་ཐ་དད་མ་ཡིན་ཞིང་། །སྟོང་དང་སྟོང་མིན་ཟུང་དུ་འཇུག །དེ་ནི་ཆོས་རྣམས་ས་བོན་ནོ། །ཞེས་སོ། །དེ་ལས་རིག་པ་གསལ་ལ་སྟོང་དེ། ལས་ཀྱི་བག་ཆགས་ཀྱིས་གཡོགས་པས་ཟླ་བ་འགྲིབ་པ་དང་། འགྲིབ་མེད་ཀྱི་དཔེ་ལྟར། ཀུན་གཞི་སེམས་ཅན་གྱི་ཁམས་ན་འཁོར་ཡང་སྐྱེ་འགྲིབ་

མེད་པས་རང་བཞིན་གྱིས་འོད་གསལ་ཏེ། རྒྱན་སྟུག་པོ་བཀོད་པ་ལས། །ལུས་ཅན་ཀུན་གྱི་གཞི་འདི་ནི། །ལས་ཀྱི་བག་ཆགས་རྣམས་ཀྱིས་གཡོགས། །དབང་པོ་ཆེས་པའི་ཟླ་ཡོག་ལྟར། །དབྱེ་བའི་ཞིང་དུ་སྣང་བ་སྟེ། །རི་རབ་གནས་ཤིང་འཁོར་བ་ཡང་། །དངོས་པོའི་འཇིག་པ་མ་ཡིན་ནོ། །དེ་བཞིན་སེམས་དང་རྣམ་ཤེས་ཡིད། །སེམས་ཅན་ཁམས་ན་འཁོར་མོད་ཀྱི། །རྟག་ཏུ་རང་བཞིན་འོད་སྣང་བའོ། །ཅེས་གསུངས་སོ།།

ཀུན་གཞི་ཀུན་གྱི་ས་བོན་ནི། །ཀུན་གཞིའི་སྟེང་དུ་དགེ་མི་དགེ་ལུང་མ་བསྟན་གྱི་བག་ཆགས་བསགས་པས་ས་བོན་དུ་གྱུར་ཏེ། དེ་ཉིད་ལས། ཀུན་གཞི་སྣ་ཚོགས་གཟུགས་ཅན་ནི། །རྣམ་ཤེས་ཀུན་གྱི་གནས་ཡིན་ནོ། །བག་ཆགས་རྣམས་དང་ལྡན་པ་ཡི། །ཀུན་གཞི་ཀུན་གྱི་ས་བོན་ཅན། །དེ་ལས་བག་ཆགས་སྔ་མའི་ས་བོན་ལས་ཕྱི་མ་སྐྱེ། སྙིང་པོ་གསལ་བ་ལས། སྔ་མ་སྔ་མའི་བག་ཆགས་ལས། །ཕྱི་མ་སྐྱེ་ཕྱིར་ས་བོན་ནོ། །བག་ཆགས་དེ་རྣམས་ཇི་ལྟར་བསགས་ཞེ་ན། སྟུག་པོ་བཀོད་པ་ལས། བྱིས་པ་རྣམས་ཀྱིས་འཁོར་གཟུགས་རྟགས། །དེ་ཡི་དབྱིབས་ལས་ཐོག་མ་མེད། །གནས་ངན་ལེན་དང་ལས་ཀྱི་རྒྱུན། །བག་ཆགས་ཐོག་མ་མེད་པ་བསགས། །དེ་ལྟར་ཐོག་མ་མེད་པའི་ཀུན་གཞི་དང་། །བག་ཆགས་གཉིས་ཇི་ལྟར་གནས་ཞེ་ན། །སྙིང་པོ་རབ་གསལ་ལས། གསེར་དང་གཡའ་ནི་ཇི་བཞིན་དུ། །ཀུན་གཞིའི་བག་ཆགས་དེ་བཞིན་ནོ། །ཡང་ཆུ་རྡོ་དང་ཉ་ལྤིབས་ལྟ་བུ་སྟེ། །རྒྱན་ལས། ཇི་ལྟར་ཆུ་རྫིང་རྡོ་བ་དག །ཉ་ལྤིབས་དག་གིས་ཡོངས་དགྲིས་པ། །དེ་བཞིན་ཀུན་གཞིའི་རྣམ་ཤེས་ཀྱང་། །བག་ཆགས་དྲི་མ་ཅན་དུ་བྱས། །ཞེས་སོ། །

ཀུན་གཞི་ལས་བག་ཆགས་སུ་སྨིན་པ་ནི། ཀུན་གཞིའི་སྟེང་དུ་དགེ་མི་དགེ་ལུང་དུ་མ་བསྟན་གྱི་བག་ཆགས་ཕྲ་བ་ལས་རགས་པར་སྨིན་པས། རིགས་དྲུག་སོ་སོའི་རྣམ་པར་སྨིན་པའོ། །སྙིང་པོ་རབ་གསལ་ལས། དགེ་དང་མི་དགེ་བར་མ་ཡི། བག་ཆགས་སྨིན་ལས་རིགས་དྲུག་འཁོར། །ཞེས་སོ། །

ཀུན་གཞིའི་རྣམ་ཤེས་སུ་ཇི་ལྟར་བཞག་པ་ནི། ཀུན་གཞི་སྟོང་གསལ་འོད་

ཀྱི་རང་བཞིན་དུ་རྣམ་པར་ཤེས་ཤིང་། རིག་པའི་ཆ་ནས་ཀུན་གཞིའི་རྣམ་ཤེས་ཏེ།
ས་སྡེ་ལས། ཀུན་གཞིའི་རྣམ་ཤེས་གསལ་ལ་རྟོག་མེད་ཀྱི་རྣམ་པར་ཤེས་པ་རྣམ་པར་
ཤེས་ཏེ། རྣམ་པར་ཤེས་པ་ཉིད་གསལ་ལ་རྟོག་པ་མེད་པའོ། །ཞེས་པས། ཀུན་གཞིའི་
རྣམ་ཤེས་ལ་ཕྱི་རོལ་གྱི་ཡུལ་དུ་གྲུབ་པ་མ་དམིགས་པས། དམིགས་པ་བརྒྱ་ཡོངས་
སུ་ཆད་པ་མེད་དོ། །དེ་ཡང་འཁོར་འདས་ཐམས་ཅད་ཀྱི་གཞི་རྟེན་པར་གྱུར་པས་ན།
རྣམ་བྱང་དང་ཐ་དད་པ་མེད་དོ། །རྒྱན་ལས། རྣམ་པར་བྱང་དང་ཐ་དད་མེད། །ཀུན་
གཞི་ཐ་དད་གྱུར་པ་མིན། །དེ་དེ་རྣམ་བྱང་ཐ་དད་ན། །ཀུན་གཞིའི་རྟག་པ་མ་ཡིན་
འགྱུར། །སྙིང་པོ་གསལ་བ་ལས། ཀུན་གཞི་ཀུན་གྱི་གཞིར་གྱུར་ པས། །དེ་ཕྱིར་རྣམ་
བྱང་གཞི་ཡིན་ནོ། །མདོ་གཞན་ལས་ཀྱང་དེ་ལྟར་རོ། །དེ་ལས། ཐོག་མ་མེད་པའི་དུས་
ཀྱི་དབྱིངས། །གཞི་ཁམས་ཞེས་བྱ་སྟེ། །ལང་ཀར་གཤེགས་པ་ལས། ཐོག་མ་མེད་
པའི་དུས་ཀྱི་དབྱིངས། །ཆོས་རྣམས་ཀུན་གྱི་གཞི་ཡིན་ཏེ། །དེ་ཡོད་པས་ན་འགྲོ་ཀུན་
ཀྱང་། །མྱ་ངན་འདས་པ་ཐོབ་པར་འགྱུར། །ཡང་ན་ཀུན་གཞི་འམ། བདེ་གཤེགས་
སྙིང་པོ་སྟེ། རྒྱུད་བླ་མ་ལས། ཐོག་མ་མེད་ཅན་གྱི་ནི་ཁམས། །དེ་ཡོད་པས་ན་འགྲོ་
ཀུན་ཀྱང་། །མྱ་ངན་འདས་པ་འབྱུང་བར་འགྱུར། །ཡང་ན་ཀུན་གཞི་འམ། བདེ་
གཤེགས་སྙིང་པོ་སྟེ། རྒྱན་ལས། ས་རྣམས་སྣ་ཚོགས་ཀུན་གྱི་གཞི། །བདེ་གཤེགས་
སྙིང་པོ་དགེ་བའང་དེ། །སྙིང་པོ་དེ་ཡང་ཀུན་གཞིའི་སྒྲ། །དེ་བཞིན་གཤེགས་པས་སྟོན་
པར་བྱེད། །སྙིང་པོ་ཀུན་གཞི་གྲགས་པ་ཡང་། །བློ་ངན་རྣམས་ཀྱིས་མི་ཤེས་སོ།
།ཡང་ན་ལེན་པའི་རྣམ་ཤེས་ལུས་ཀྱི་གཞི། །ཀུན་གྱི་གཞི། སེམས་བརྟེན་པ་ཞེས་བྱ་
སྟེ། ས་སྡེ་ལས། རྣམ་པར་ཤེས་པ་དེས་དེ་ལྟར་ལུས་འདི་བཟུང་ཞིང་ཉེ་བར་བླངས་པ་
ནས་ལེན་པའི་རྣམ་ཤེས་ཞེས་ཀྱང་བྱའོ། །ལུས་འདིའི་གཞིར་གྱུར་པས་ན་ཀུན་གཞི་
ཞེས་བྱའོ། །ལུང་དུ་མ་བསྟན་པས་ནི་སེམས་ཅན་ཞེས་ཀྱང་བྱ་སྟེ། རྣམ་པར་ཤེས་པ་
ཐམས་ཅད་དེ་ལ་བརྟེན་ནས་འབྱུང་བའི་ཕྱིར་རོ། །ཞེས་གསུངས་སོ། །དེ་ལྟར་ཐོག་
མ་མེད་པའི་དུས། རིག་པ། དབྱིངས། ཁམས། ཀུན་གཞི། དེ་བཞིན་ཉིད། ཆོས་

དབྱིངས། སྙིང་པོ། ཆོས་སྐུ། མ་སྐྱེས་པ། ཀུན་གཞིའི་རྣམ་པར་ཤེས་པ། སེམས་ཅན་ཀུན་ཁྱབ་གཞི་རྟེན། གསལ་སྟོང་། ལུང་མ་བསྟན། རིག་པ་འོད་ཀྱི་ཁང་པ། གནས་པའི་གཞི་ལ་སོགས་པ། མདོ་ལས། རྣམ་གྲངས་དཔག་ཏུ་མེད་དོ། ། སྔགས་ནས་རྒྱུའི་རྒྱུད། གཞིའི་རྒྱུད། བཅུད་ཀྱི་རྒྱུད། བརྟེན་པའི་རྒྱུད། ཀུན་གྱི་རྒྱུད། ཐོག་མ་མེད་པའི་རྒྱུད། སྙིང་པོའི་རྒྱུད་ལ་སོགས་པ་རྣམ་གྲངས་དུ་མ་བཤད་དོ། །དེ་ལྟར་མདོ་རྒྱུད་ནས། ཀུན་གཞིའི་རྣམ་གྲངས་དཔག་ཏུ་མེད་པ་བཤད་པའི་མིང་དོན་ལ་མ་རྨོངས་པར་ཀུན་གཞི་དང་། སེམས་དང་རྣམ་པར་ཤེས་པའི་གསང་བ་ལ་མཁས་པ་ནི། སངས་རྒྱས་ཀྱི་ཆོས་ཐམས་ཅད་ལ་མ་རྨོངས་ཤིང་། །ཁོང་དུ་ཆུད་པའོ། །ཞེས་ས་སྙེའི་མདོ་ལས་གསུངས་སོ། །

ཉོན་མོངས་པ་ཅན་གྱི་ཡིད་ནི། ཀུན་གཞིའི་རྣམ་པར་ཤེས་པ་རིག་པ་གསལ་སྟོང་འོད་ཀྱི་རང་བཞིན་དེ་ལ་དམིགས་པ་མ་ཡིན་པའི་བདག་ཏུ་འཛིན་པ་ནི་ཉོན་མོངས་པ་ཅན་གྱི་ཡིད་དོ། །

ཡིད་ཀྱི་རྣམ་པར་ཤེས་པ་ནི། ཕྱི་ནང་གི་ཆོས་སམ་ཡུལ་རྣམས་འཛིན་པར་བྱེད་པས་ན་ཡིད་ཀྱི་རྣམ་པར་ཤེས་པ་སྟེ། ལང་ཀར་གཤེགས་པ་ལས། སེམས་ནི་ཀུན་གཞིའི་རྣམ་ཤེས་ཏེ། །ངར་སེམས་དེ་ནི་ཉོན་མོངས་ཡིད། །གང་གི་ཡུལ་རྣམས་འཛིན་པས་ན། །དེ་ནི་རྣམ་པར་ཤེས་པར་བརྗོད། །

སྒོ་ལྔའི་རྣམ་པར་ཤེས་པ་ནི། །མིག་གི་རྣམ་ཤེས་ཀྱིས་གཟུགས་འཛིན་པའོ། །རྣ་བས་སྒྲ། སྣས་དྲི། ལྕེས་རོ། ལུས་ཀྱིས་རེག་བྱ་འཛིན་པའོ། །དེ་ལྟར་ཡུལ་དེ་རྣམས་ཀྱི་རྣམ་པར་ཤེས་ཤིང་རིག་པས་ན་རྣམ་ཤེས་སུ་འཛིན་པའོ། །ཡང་སེམས་ཀུན་གཞི་ནི་ལུང་མ་བསྟན་ནོ། །ཉོན་མོངས་པ་ཅན་གྱི་ཡིད་ནི་མི་དགེ་བའོ། །ཡིད་ཀྱི་རྣམ་པར་ཤེས་པ་ནི་དགེ་མི་དགེ་གཉིས་སུ་འགྱུར་ཏེ། ལང་ཀར་གཤེགས་པ་ལས། སེམས་ནི་ཀུན་ཏུ་ལུང་མ་བསྟན། །ཡིད་ནི་གཉིས་ཀར་འགྱུར་བ་སྟེ། །རྣམ་པར་ཤེས་པ་འབྱུང་བ་ཡང་། །དེ་ནི་དགེ་དང་མི་དགེ་བའོ། །ཞེས་པས་ཡིད་ཀྱི་དགེ་བ་ནི་བཅུའོ།

།ཡིད་ཀྱི་མི་དགེ་བ་ནི་དྲུག་རྩ་བའི་ཉོན་མོངས་པ་ཉི་ཤུ་ཉེ་བའི་ཉོན་མོངས་པའོ། །དེས་ན་ཡིད་ནི་དགེ་མི་དགེ་གཉིས་སུ་འགྱུར་རོ། །སྒོ་ལྔའི་རྣམ་པར་ཤེས་པ་ནི་ལུང་མ་བསྟན་ནོ། །དེ་ལྟར་ཡང་། ཏིང་ངེ་འཛིན་མཆོག་གི་མདོ་ལས། །སེམས་ནི་ལུང་དུ་མ་བསྟན་པའོ། །ཉོན་མོངས་ཅན་ནི་མི་དགེའོ། །ཡིད་ནི་དགེ་སྡིག་གཉིས་ཀ་སྟེ། །སྒོ་ལྔ་ལུང་དུ་མ་བསྟན་པའོ། །ཞེས་གསུངས་སོ། །

གསང་བསྡུས་ཀྱི་གཞི་ནི་དབང་བཞི་སྟེ། ཡེ་ཤེས་མཛོད་འབྱུང་ལས། གཞི་ཡི་རྒྱུད་ནི་དབང་བཞི་སྟེ། །བསྐྱེད་རྫོགས་གཞི་རྟེན་ཡིན་ཕྱིར་རོ། །མཁའ་འགྲོ་གསང་བ་ལས། རྒྱུད་ནི་དབང་བཞིའི་ངོ་བོ་སྟེ། །བརྗོད་བྱ་རྗོད་བྱེད་རྒྱུད་དུ་འགྱུར། །ཞེས་གསུངས་སོ། །དེ་དག་གིས་ཇི་ལྟར་གནས་པའི་གཞི་བསྟན་ཏོ། །

དེ་ནས་ཐབས་ཀྱི་རང་བཞིན་ནམ། །ལམ་ཟུང་འཇུག་རྟགས་མཚུངས་ལྡན་དུ་བསྟན་པར་བྱ་སྟེ། དེ་དག་གང་ཞེ་ན། ལམ་མདོར་བསྟན་པ་དང་། རྒྱས་པར་བཤད་པའོ། །དང་པོ་བྱང་ཆུབ་ཀྱི་ཕྱོགས་ཀྱི་ཆོས་དང་། །སྒྱུ་མ་རྨི་ལམ་དབྱེར་མེད་དུ་བསྟན་པ་ནི། ཁྲི་བརྒྱད་སྟོང་པ་ལས། ལྷའི་བུ་དག་དྲན་པ་ཉེ་བར་བཞག་པ་རྣམས་ནི། རྨི་ལམ་ལྟ་བུ། སྒྱུ་མ་ལྟ་བུ། དེ་བཞིན་དུ་ཡང་དག་པར་སྤོང་བ་རྣམས་དང་། རྫུ་འཕྲུལ་གྱི་རྐང་པ་རྣམས་དང་། དབང་པོ་ རྣམས་དང་། སྟོབས་རྣམས་དང་། བྱང་ཆུབ་ཀྱི་ཡན་ལག་རྣམས་དང་། འཕགས་པའི་ཡན་ལག་བརྒྱད་པ་ཡང་རྨི་ལམ་ལྟ་བུ། སྒྱུ་མ་ལྟ་བུ་ཡིན་ནོ། །ལྷའི་བུ་དག །དེ་བཞིན་གཤེགས་པའི་སྟོབས་བཅུ་ཡང་རྨི་ལམ་ལྟ་བུ། སྒྱུ་མ་ལྟ་བུ་ཡིན་ནོ། །དེ་བཞིན་དུ་མི་འཇིགས་པ་བཞི་དང་། སོ་སོ་ཡང་དག་པར་རིག་པ་བཞི་དང་། བྱམས་པ་ཆེན་པོ་དང་། སྙིང་རྗེ་ཆེན་པོ་དང་། སངས་རྒྱས་ཀྱི་ཆོས་མ་འདྲེས་པ་བཅོ་བརྒྱད་ཀྱང་རྨི་ལམ་ལྟ་བུ། སྒྱུ་མ་ལྟ་བུ་ཡིན་ནོ། །དམ་ ཚིག་བཀོད་པའི་རྒྱུད་ཕྲེ་མ་ལས། གསང་བའི་བདག་པོ་སྒོ་ལྔའི་ཡུལ་གྱི་རྟེན་དང་། དབྱེ་བ་ཐམས་ཅད་རྟེན་གཞལ་ཡས་ཁང་དང་། བརྟེན་པ་ལྷ་སྐུ་སྒྱུ་མ་ལྟ་བུར་རྟོགས་པར་གྱིས་ཤིག །དེ་ལྟར་རྟེན་དང་བརྟེན་པ་དེ་དག་ཀྱང་། །བྱང་ཆུབ་ཀྱི་ཕྱོགས་ཀྱི་ཆོས་དང་དབྱེར་མེད་དུ

རྟོགས་པར་གྱིས་ཤིག །དེ་ལྟར་རྟེན་དང་བརྟེན་པ་དེ་དག་ཀྱང་། །སྒྱུ་མ་དང་བྱང་ཆུབ་ཀྱི་ཕྱོགས་ཀྱི་ཆོས་རྣམས་ལ་གཉིས་སུ་མེ་དེ། གཉིས་སུ་བྱར་མེད་དོ། །ཞེས་སོ། །དེ་ལས་ཀྱང་ལམ་མཆོག་ཏུ་གྱུར་པ། བླ་མའི་མོས་གུས་ལོ་ཟླས་ལམ་བགྲོད་དེ། ཡེ་ཤེས་མངོན་འབྱུང་ལས། ས་དང་ལམ་གྱི་རིམ་པ་རྣམས། །བླ་མའི་མོས་གུས་ལོ་ཟླས་བསྒྲོད། །བླ་མའི་སྣང་བ་མ་བྲལ་ན། །སངས་རྒྱས་རྣམས་དང་འབྲལ་མེད་གནས། །ཞེས་སོ། དམ་ཚིག་བཀོད་པ་ལས། གཡོ་མེད་མོས་གུས་ཟླ་དྲུག་གིས། །རྡོ་རྗེ་འཆང་གི་ས་ཐོབ་འགྱུར། །ཞེས་སོ། །རྒྱུད་སྡེ་ལྔ་བཅུ་ལས་ཀྱང་དེ་ལྟར་རོ། །དེ་ཡང་སྣང་བ་ཐམས་ཅད་རིགས་ལྔར་གནས་པ་དེ་ལམ་དུ་བླངས་ནས་བསྒོམས་པས། སྣང་བ་གཞན་གྱི་སེལ་མི་འཇུག་པ་ནི་གསང་སྔགས་ཀྱི་དམ་ཚིག་ལ་གནས་པ་སྟེ། རིགས་ལྔའི་དམ་ཚིག་བཀོད་པ་ལས། སྒྲིབ་པ་རྣམ་པར་སེལ་བ་གང་དེ་ལ་རིགས་ལྔའི་དམ་ཚིག་ལ་གནས་པར་འདོད་པས། སྣང་བའི་དབྱིབས་ཐམས་ཅད་ཕྱག་མཚན་ལྔར་ཤེས་པར་བྱའོ། །ཁ་དོག་སྣ་ཚོགས་རིགས་ལྔར་ཤེས་པར་བྱའོ། །དེ་བཞིན་དུ་འབྱུང་བ་ལྔ་དང་། ཕུང་པོ་ལྔ་དང་། ཉོན་མོངས་པ་ལྔ་དང་། སེམས་ཅན་སྣ་ཚོགས་པའང་རིགས་ལྔར་ཤེས་པར་བྱའོ། །དེ་ལྟར་དབྱིབས་དང་། ཁ་དོག་དང་། འབྱུང་བ་དང་། ཕུང་པོ་དང་། ཉོན་མོངས་པ་དང་། སེམས་ཅན་སྣ་ཚོགས་པ་དང་། རིགས་ལྔ་ལ་གཉིས་སུ་མེད་དེ་གཉིས་སུ་བྱར་མེད་དོ། །ཡང་ན་ཆོ་གས་བསྐྱེད་པའམ། རང་ཤར་ལྷ་སྐུ་དེའི་སྣང་ཆ་བསྐྱེད་རིམ། སྟོང་ཆ་རྫོགས་རིམ། རང་བཞིན་དབྱེར་མེད་ཟུང་འཇུག་སྟེ། མངོན་འབྱུང་ལས། ཐ་མལ་དག་བྱེད་ལྷའི་སྐུ། །སྣང་བའི་ཆ་ལས་བསྐྱེད་པ་དང་། །སྟོང་པའི་ཆ་ལས་རྫོགས་རིམ་སྟེ། །དབྱེར་མེད་ཚུལ་འདི་བསྟན་པའོ། །ཡང་དེ་ཉིད་ལས། དངོས་རྣམས་སྣང་སྟོང་དབྱེར་མེད་པ། །བསྐྱེད་དང་རྫོགས་དང་ཟུང་འཇུག་དང། །བསྐྱེད་རྫོགས་མ་ཡིན་ཆོས་འགག་མེད། །བྱང་ཆུབ་ཚུལ་འདི་བསྟན་པའོ། ལྷའི་སྣང་བ་གསལ་བ་སྤྲུལ་སྐུ། བདེ་བ་ལོངས་སྐུ། མི་རྟོག་པ་ཆོས་སྐུར་ལམ་དུ་བླངས་ཏེ། དམ་ཚིག་བཀོད་པ་ལས། ཆོས་རྣམས་གསལ་བ་སྤྲུལ་པའི་སྐུ། །དེ་ལ་མི་རྟོག་ཆོས་

ཀྱི་སྐུ། །རྟོག་བྲལ་དེ་ཕྱིར་ལོངས་སྤྱོད་རྫོགས། །བྱང་ཆུབ་ཚུལ་འདི་བསྟན་པའོ། །དེ་ལྟར་ཆོས་ཐམས་ཅད་གསལ་ལ་རྟོག་པ་མེད་པར་ཤེས་པ་ནི་ལམ་གྱི་ཡེ་ཤེས་ཚེས་ཅིག་གི་ཟླ་བ་ལྟ་བུ་དང་། འབྲས་བུའི་ཡེ་ཤེས་ཟླ་བ་ཉ་གང་བ་ལྟ་བུ་དང་། དྲི་མེད་པར་གྲགས་པའི་མདོ་ལས། །གང་གིས་ཏིང་འཛིན་མཆོག་ལ་གནས། །དེ་ནི་གསལ་ལ་རྟོག་མེད་དོ། །རྣམ་རྟོག་མི་མངའ་ས་ལེ་མཁྱེན། །ལམ་དང་འབྲས་བུའི་ཡེ་ཤེས་ཏེ། །ཚེས་ཅིག་དང་པོ་རྒྱས་བཞིན་ནོ། །དེ་ལྟར་སྣང་བ་དང་ལྟ་དང་བྱང་ཆུབ་ཀྱི་ཕྱོགས་ཀྱི་ཆོས་དང་། སྒྱུ་མ་རྣམ་གཉིས་སུ་མེད་པར་ལམ་དུ་སློངས་པ་ནི། རྒྱལ་བའི་མདོ་རྒྱུད་ཐམས་ཅད་ཁོང་དུ་ཆུད་པར་ཤེས་པར་བྱའོ། །

དེ་ནས་ཉམས་མྱོང་དང་། ལམ་ལྔ་ས་བཅུ་སྒྱུ་མ་དབྱེར་མེད་དུ་རྒྱས་པར་བཤད་པར་བྱ་སྟེ། དེ་ཡང་ལམ་གྱི་ངོ་བོ་ཞི་གནས་དང་། ལྷག་མཐོང་ཟུང་དུ་འབྲེལ་པའི་ལམ་མོ། །ངེས་ཚིག་ནི། བླ་ན་མེད་པའི་བྱང་ཆུབ་ལ་ཕྱིན་པར་འདོད་པས་ན་ལམ་མོ། དབྱེ་ན་ཚོགས་ལམ། སྦྱོར་ལམ། མཐོང་ལམ། བསྒོམ་ལམ། མཐར་ཕྱིན་པའི་ལམ་མོ། དེ་ལ་ཚོགས་ལམ་གྱི་ངོ་བོ་སྡིག་པ་སྤོང་ཞིང་དགེ་བ་དང་དུ་ལེན་པའོ། །ངེས་ཚིག་ནི། ཆོས་ཉིད་ཐོབ་པའི་དོན་དུ་ཚོགས་གསོག་པའོ། །དབྱེ་ན་ཚོགས་ལམ་ཆུང་དུ། འབྲིང་པོ། ཆེན་པོའོ། །

དེ་ལ་བག་མེད་པ་དྲན་པ་ཉམས་པ་ལྡང་བའི་རྒྱུ་ཡིན་ལ། ཚོགས་ལམ་ཆུང་ངུའི་ཏིང་ངེ་འཛིན་གྱི་དྲན་པ་ཉེ་བར་བཞག་པ་བཞི་འབྱུང་སྟེ། བྱང་ཆུབ་སེམས་དཔའ་བློ་གྲོས་རབ་བརྟན་གྱི་མདོ་ལས། བློ་གྲོས་རབ་བརྟན་གྱིས་གསོལ་བ། བཅོམ་ལྡན་འདས་དྲན་པ་ཉེ་བར་བཞག་པ་བཞི་ཇི་ལྟར་བསྒོམ་པར་བགྱི། བཅོམ་ལྡན་འདས་ཀྱིས་བཀའ་སྩལ་པ། བློ་གྲོས་རབ་བརྟན། གང་དེ་ལ་བྱང་ཆུབ་སེམས་དཔའ་ལུས་ལ་ལུས་ཀྱི་རྗེས་སུ་ལྟ་བའི་དྲན་པ་ཉེ་བར་བཞག་པ་གང་ཞེ་ན། ལུས་སྔོན་གྱི་མཐའ་དང་། ཕྱི་མའི་མཐའ་དང་། ད་ལྟར་བྱུང་བ་སོ་སོར་ བརྟགས་ཏེ། ཀྱེ་མ། ལུས་འདི་རྒྱུ་དང་རྐྱེན་ལ་བརྟགས་པ་མི་རྟག་ཅིང་འགྱུར་བ་སྒྱུ་མ་ལྟ་བུ་སྟེ། ལུས་འདི་ལ་ང་ཡིར་མི་བྱ་

བར། ལུས་འདི་སྙིང་པོ་མེད་པ་ལ་སྙིང་པོ་བླང་བར་བྱའོ། །སྙིང་པོ་གང་ཞེ་ན། དེ་བཞིན་བཤེགས་པའི་སྐུ་བསྒྲུབ་ཅིང་ཐོབ་པར་བྱའོ། །དེ་ནི་ལུས་ཀྱི་དྲན་པ་ཉེ་བར་བཞག་པའོ། །བློ་གྲོས་རབ་བརྟན། ཚོར་བ་ལ་ཚོར་བའི་རྗེས་སུ་ལྟ་བའི་དྲན་པ་ཉེ་བར་བཞག་པ་གང་ཞེ་ན། ཚོར་བ་གང་ཅིའང་རུང་སྟེ། བདེ་བའི་ཚོར་བ་ལ་དགའ་བར་བྱེད། སྡུག་བསྔལ་གྱི་ཚོར་བ་ལ་ཞེ་སྡང་བར་བྱེད། གཉིས་ཀ་མ་ཡིན་པ་ལ་རྨོངས་པར་བྱེད། བདག་གི་ཚོར་བ་ཐམས་ཅད་སྒྱུ་མ་ལྟ་བུར་རང་བཞིན་མེད་པར་སྤྲངས་ལ། སེམས་ཅན་ཐམས་ཅད་ཀྱི་ཚོར་བ་རྒྱུན་ཆད་པའི་ཕྱིར་ཆོས་བསྟན་པར་བྱའོ། །དེ་ཅིའི་ཕྱིར་ཞེ་ན། རྟོགས་པའི་ཚོར་བ་ནི་བདེ་བ། མ་རྟོགས་པའི་ཚོར་བ་ནི་སྡུག་བསྔལ་བར་འགྱུར་བས་ན། དམིགས་པ་དང་། ཡིད་ལ་བྱེད་པ་ཐམས་ཅད་དང་། ཇི་སྲིད་ཆོས་སུ་བརྟགས་པ་ཐམས་ཅད་ཀྱི་ཚོར་བ་ཐམས་ཅད་སྒྱུ་མ་ལྟ་བུར་ཤེས་པ་ནི་ཚོར་བ་དྲན་པ་ཉེ་བར་བཞག་གོ། །བློ་གྲོས་རབ་བརྟན། སེམས་ལ་སེམས་ཀྱིས་རྗེས་སུ་ལྟ་བའི་དྲན་པ་ཉེ་བར་བཞག་པ་གང་ཞེ་ན། སེམས་ནི་སྐྱེས་ནས་འཇིག་ཅིང་མི་གནས་པས། བདག་གིས་ཐོག་མར་སེམས་བསྐྱེད་ཅིང་། གནས་པ་དེ་ཡང་ཟད་ཅིང་། གང་ནས་ཀྱང་མི་གནས་པས། སེམས་ཀྱིས་སེམས་མི་མཐོང་ངོ་། །དེ་ལ་སེམས་ཀྱི་མཚན་ཉིད་ནི། སྒྱུ་མ་འདྲ་བ་སྟེ། མཚན་ཉིད་མེད་པས་འཛིན་པ་དང་བྲལ་བ་ལ་གནས་པར་བྱའོ། །དེ་ནི་སེམས་དྲན་པ་ཉེ་བར་གཞག་པའོ། །བློ་གྲོས་རབ་བརྟན། ཆོས་ལ་ཆོས་ཀྱི་རྗེས་སུ་ལྟ་བའི་དྲན་པ་ཉེ་བར་བཞག་པ་གང་ཞེ་ན། གང་སྟོང་པ་ཉིད་དང་། མཚན་མ་མེད་པ་དང་། སྨོན་པ་མེད་པ་མ་གཏོགས་པའི་ཆོས་སུ་གྲུབ་པའང་རྡུལ་ཙམ་མི་དམིགས་ཏེ། ཆོས་དེ་ལ་ལྟ་ཞིང་གནས་པ་ནི་ཆོས་ཉིད་ཡང་དག་པར་མཐོང་གིས། ཆོས་མ་ཡིན་པ་ལ་ཡང་དག་པར་རྗེས་སུ་མི་མཐོང་ངོ་། །དེ་ལ་དྲན་པ་ཉེ་བར་བཞག་པ་ཞེས་བྱ་བ་ནི། སངས་རྒྱས་ཀྱིས་ཆོས་ཇི་སྙེད་དུ་བཏགས་པ་ཐམས་ཅད་མིང་ཙམ་མོ། །མིང་དང་ཆོས་ཕྱི་ནང་གང་དུའང་མི་རྙེད་པས་མཐའ་མེད་ཅིང་མ་གྲུབ་པ་ནི་ཆོས་ཀྱི་དྲན་པ་ཉེ་བར་བཞག་གོ། །

དེ་ཡང་ཚོགས་ལམ་འབྲིང་པོར་སྡིག་པ་མི་དགེ་བ་སྡུག་བསྔལ་གྱི་རྒྱུ་ལ་དུག་ཏུ་བལྟས་ནས་སྤོང་བའི་ཕྱིར། ཡང་དག་པར་སྤོང་བ་བཞི་བསྒོམ་པ་སྟེ། བློ་གྲོས་རབ་བརྟན་གྱིས་གསོལ་པ། ཡང་དག་སྤོང་བ་བཞི་ཇི་ལྟར་ལྟ་བར་བགྱི། །བཅོམ་ལྡན་འདས་ཀྱིས་བཀའ་སྩལ་པ། བློ་གྲོས་རབ་བརྟན། བྱང་ཆུབ་སེམས་དཔའི་ལམ་བཞི་གང་ཞེ་ན། སྡིག་པ་མི་དགེ་བའི་ཆོས་མ་སྐྱེས་པ་རྣམས་མི་བསྐྱེད་པའི་ཕྱིར་འདུན་པ་བསྐྱེད། འབད་པ་བྱེད། བརྩོན་འགྲུས་བརྩམས། སེམས་རབ་ཏུ་འཛིན། ཡང་དག་པར་རབ་ཏུ་འཛོག་གོ། །སྡིག་པ་མི་དགེ་བའི་ཆོས་སྐྱེས་པ་རྣམས་རབ་ཏུ་སྤོང་བའི་ཕྱིར་འདུན་པ་བསྐྱེད་པ་ལ་སོགས་སྔ་མ་བཞིན་ནོ། །དགེ་བའི་ཆོས་མ་སྐྱེས་པ་རྣམས་བསྐྱེད་པའི་ཕྱིར། འདུན་པ་བསྐྱེད་པ་ལ་སོགས་པ་སྔ་མ་བཞིན་ནོ། །དགེ་བའི་ཆོས་སྐྱེས་པ་རྣམས་གནས་པ་དང་། ཕྱིར་བཞིན་འཕེལ་བ་དང་། ཉམས་པར་མི་འགྱུར་བ་དང་། ཆུད་མི་ཟ་བའི་ཕྱིར་འདུན་པ་བསྐྱེད་པ་ལ་སོགས་པ་སྔ་མ་བཞིན་ནོ། །བློ་གྲོས་རབ་བརྟན། གང་སྡིག་པ་མི་དགེ་བའི་ཆོས་རྣམས་ཞེས་བྱ་བ་ནི། ཚུལ་ཁྲིམས་དང་། ཏིང་ངེ་འཛིན་དང་། ཤེས་རབ་ཀྱི་མི་མཐུན་ཕྱོགས་སོ། །ཚུལ་ཁྲིམས་ཀྱི་མི་མཐུན་ཕྱོགས་ནི། ཚུལ་ཁྲིམས་ཉམས་པ་དང་། ཚུལ་ཁྲིམས་ཉམས་པར་འགྱུར་བའི་ཆོས་རྣམས་སོ། ཏིང་ངེ་འཛིན་གྱི་མི་མཐུན་ཕྱོགས་ནི། སེམས་གཡེང་བར་བྱེད་ཅིང་། ཏིང་ངེ་འཛིན་ཉམས་པར་བྱེད་པ་རྣམས་སོ། །ཤེས་རབ་ཀྱི་མི་མཐུན་ཕྱོགས་ནི་ལྟ་བ་ཉམས་པ་དང་། ལྟ་བ་མཆོག་འཛིན་གྱི་ཡང་དག་པར་སྒྲིབ་པའི་ཆོས་རྣམས་སོ། །ཚུལ་བཞིན་ཡིད་ལ་བྱེད་པ་ནི། མི་དགེ་བའི་ཆོས་སྤོང་བའི་ཕྱིར་འདུན་པ་བསྐྱེད། འབད་པར་བྱེད། བརྩོན་འགྲུས་རྩོམ་སེམས་རབ་ཏུ་འཛིན། ཡང་དག་པར་འཛོག་པ་ནི་ཡང་དག་པར་སྤོང་བ་དང་པོའོ། །གཞན་ཡང་མི་དགེ་བའི་ཆོས་རྣམས་ཞེས་བྱ་བ་ནི། འདོད་པས་ཆགས། ཁོང་ཁྲོས་སྡང་། མ་རིག་པས་རྨོངས་ཏེ། རྒྱུ་གང་ལས་བྱུང་ཞེས་པའོ། །ཚུལ་བཞིན་ཡིད་ལ་བྱེད་པ་ནི། མི་གཙང་བས་འདོད་ཆགས། བྱམས་པས་ཞེ་སྡང་། རྟེན་འབྲེལ་གྱིས་གཏི་མུག་ཞི་བར་བྱེད་དོ། །གང་ཉོན་མོངས་པ་དེ་དག་ཐ་དད་

དུ་བརྟགས་པས་སྦྱོང་ཞེས་བྱ་ཡིས། གང་སྦྱོང་བ་དེ་ནི་བརྟེས་པར་མི་འགྱུར་བས་ཡང་དག་པར་སྦྱོང་བ་གཉིས་པའོ། །གང་དགེ་བའི་ཆོས་མ་སྐྱེས་པ་རྣམས་བསྐྱེད་པའི་ཕྱིར། འདུན་པ་བསྐྱེད། འབད། བརྩོན། སེམས་ཡང་དག་པར་རབ་ཏུ་འཛོག་ཅེས་བྱ་བ་ནི། བསྒྲུབ་པར་བྱ་བའི་དགེ་བའི་ཆོས་ཚད་མེད་པ་ལ་འདུན་པ་དང་། སེམས་རབ་ཏུ་འཛིན་པས་ཉམས་སུ་ལེན་པར་བྱེད་པ་ནི། དགེ་བའི་རྩ་བ་ཐམས་ཅད་ཀྱི་རྩ་བ་སྟེ། ཡང་དག་པར་སྦྱོང་བ་གསུམ་པའོ། །དགེ་བའི་ཆོས་སྐྱེས་པ་གནས་པ་དང་། ཉམས་པར་མི་འགྱུར་བ་དང་། ཆུད་མི་ཟ་བར་བྱ་བའི་ཕྱིར་དགེ་བའི་རྩ་བ་ཐམས་ཅད་བྱང་ཆུབ་ཏུ་བསྔོའོ། དེ་ཅིའི་ཕྱིར་ཞེ་ན། གང་ཡང་དགེ་བའི་རྩ་བ་ཐམས་ཅད་ཁམས་གསུམ་ལ་མི་གནས་པར་ཐམས་ཅད་མཁྱེན་པར་བསྔོས་པས་དེ་ལ་ཟད་པར་འགྱུར་བ་གང་ཡང་མེད་པས་ཡང་དག་པར་སྦྱོང་བ་བཞི་པའོ། །

དེ་ནས་ཚོགས་ལམ་ཆེན་པོར་ཏིང་ངེ་འཛིན་གྱི་རང་བཞིན། རྫུ་འཕྲུལ་གྱི་རྐང་པ་བཞི་བསྒོམ་པར་བྱ་སྟེ། བློ་གྲོས་རབ་བརྟན་གྱིས་གསོལ་པ། བཅོམ་ལྡན་འདས་རྫུ་འཕྲུལ་གྱི་རྐང་པ་བཞི་ཇི་ལྟར་བལྟ་བར་བགྱི། བཅོམ་ལྡན་འདས་ཀྱིས་བཀའ་སྩལ་པ། བློ་གྲོས་རབ་བརྟན་བྱང་ཆུབ་སེམས་དཔའི་ལམ་ལ་བཞི་སྟེ། བཞི་གང་ཞེ་ན། འདུན་པའི་ཏིང་ངེ་འཛིན་སྤོང་བའི་འདུ་བྱེད་དང་ལྡན་པའི་རྫུ་འཕྲུལ་གྱི་རྐང་པ་དང་། བརྩོན་འགྲུས་ཀྱི་ཏིང་ངེ་འཛིན་སྤོང་བའི་འདུ་བྱེད་དང་ལྡན་པའི་རྫུ་འཕྲུལ་གྱི་རྐང་པ་དང་། སེམས་ཀྱི་ཏིང་ངེ་འཛིན་སྤོང་བའི་འདུ་བྱེད་དང་ལྡན་པའི་རྫུ་འཕྲུལ་གྱི་རྐང་པ་དང་། སྤྱོད་པའི་ཏིང་ངེ་འཛིན་སྤོང་བའི་འདུ་བྱེད་དང་ལྡན་པའི་རྫུ་འཕྲུལ་གྱི་རྐང་པའོ། །བློ་གྲོས་རབ་བརྟན། གང་དེ་ལ་ཆོས་ཐམས་ཅད་གང་དུའང་མ་གྲུབ་པ་སྒྱུ་མ་ལྟ་བུ་དང་། གང་དུ་ཡང་མི་དམིགས་ཤིང་འཛིན་པ་བྲལ་བའི་ཆོས་ཐམས་ཅད་ལ་མི་དངང་། དངང་བར་མི་འགྱུར་བར་དགའ་བ་དང་སྤྲོ་བ་དང་འདུན་པར་བྱེད་པ་དེ་ནི་འདུན་པའི་ཏིང་ངེ་འཛིན་ཏོ། །བློ་གྲོས་རབ་བརྟན་གང་དད་པ་རྩེ་གཅིག་དང་ལྡན་པའི་འདུན་པ་དེས་འཇིག་རྟེན་གྱི་ཆོས་ཐམས་ཅད་ཀྱི་བརྩོན་པ་འདོར་

ཞིང་། ལེ་ལོར་གྱུར་པ་ཐམས་ཅད་ཀྱིས་མི་ཚུགས་པར་བརྩོན་འགྲུས་རྒྱུན་ཆད་མེད་པ་དང་ལྡན་པ་ནི་བརྩོན་འགྲུས་ཀྱི་ཏིང་ངེ་འཛིན་ཏོ། །བློ་གྲོས་རབ་རྟན་གང་རྩོལ་བའི་རྩོལ་བ་རྒྱུན་མི་འཆད་པ་དང་ལྡན་པ་དེས་སེམས་ནི་གང་དུ་ཡང་མ་གྲུབ་ཅིང་མི་དམིགས་ཏེ། སེམས་ཀྱི་རང་བཞིན་འོད་གསལ་བ་དེ་ལ་སེམས་རྩེ་ཅིག་པ་ནི། སེམས་ཀྱི་ཏིང་ངེ་འཛིན་ཏོ། །བློ་གྲོས་རབ་བརྟན། གང་རྩེ་ཅིག་ཏུ་གྱུར་པའི་ཏིང་ངེ་འཛིན་དང་ལྡན་པ་དེས་འགྲོ་བ་དང་། འཆག་པ་དང་། འདུག་པ་དང་། ཉལ་བའི་དུས་ཐམས་ཅད་དུའང་ཏིང་ངེ་འཛིན་ལས་མི་འདའ་བར་སྤྱོད་པ་ནི་སྤྱོད་པའི་ཏིང་ངེ་འཛིན་ཏོ། །ཡང་བློ་གྲོས་རབ་བརྟན། དེ་ལ་ཅིའི་ཕྱིར་རྫུ་འཕྲུལ་གྱི་རྐང་པ་ཅེས་བྱ་ཞེ་ན། ཏིང་ངེ་འཛིན་དེས་ལོག་པར་གྱུར་པའི་ཆོས་ཐམས་ཅད་སྤོང་བར་བྱེད། ཡང་དག་པར་དགེ་བར་བྱེད་དེ། ཡང་དག་པའི་གནས་སུ་ཕྱིན་པར་བྱེད། བགྲོད་པར་བྱེད་པས་ན་ཏིང་ངེ་འཛིན་གྱི་རང་བཞིན་རྫུ་འཕྲུལ་གྱི་རྐང་པ་ཞེས་བྱའོ། །

ཚོགས་ལམ་ཆུང་ངུའི་ཐར་པའི་ཆ་མཐུན་དཀོན་མཆོག་ལ་དད་པའི་དམིགས་པ་ཁྱད་པར་ཅན་དང་། ཆོས་ཐམས་ཅད་སོ་སོར་འབྱེད་པའི་དད་པ་ཁྱད་པར་ཅན་རྒྱུད་ལ་སྐྱེས་པའོ། འབྲིང་པོའི་ཐར་པའི་ཆ་འཐུན་ནི། ཕ་རོལ་ཏུ་ཕྱིན་པ་དྲུག་ལ་དམིགས་པའི་སྤྲོ་བ་དང་བརྩོན་པ་སྐྱེ་བའོ། ཆེན་པོའི་ཐར་པའི་ཆ་མཐུན་ནི། རྣམ་པར་མི་རྟོག་པའི་ཏིང་ངེ་འཛིན་རྒྱུན་ཐུང་ལ་གྲངས་མང་བ་རྒྱུད་ལ་སྐྱེ་བའོ། །དེ་ལྟར་ཚོགས་ལམ་བཞི་གསུམ་བཅུ་གཉིས་ཀྱི་རྟགས་ནི། ཚུལ་ཁྲིམས་དག་པའི་དབང་པོའི་སྒོ་ཚུལ་བཞིན་མ་ཡིན་པ་ལས་བསྡམས་ནས། ཁ་ན་མ་ཐོ་བའི་སྡིག་པ་ཕྲ་མོ་ལ་འཛེམས་པས། ཕྱི་རོལ་ཆགས་སྡང་གི་དགྲ་ཐམས་ཅད་རང་ལས་བྱུང་བར་ཤེས་ཤིང་བདག་དང་གཞན་མེད་པར་ཤེས་པའོ། །

སྦྱང་བྱ་ནི་དུག་གསུམ་གྱིས་བསྡུས་པའི་མི་དགེ་བ་བཅུའོ། །ས་མཚམས་ནི། འདུན་པ་སྔོན་དུ་སོང་བའི་སེམས་དང་པོ་བསྐྱེད་པ་ནས་དྲོད་ཀྱི་ཡེ་ཤེས་མ་སྐྱེས་པར་དུ་ཚོགས་ལམ་མོ། །

དེ་ནས་སྦྱོར་ལམ་བཤད་པར་བྱ་སྟེ། སྦྱོར་ལམ་གྱི་ངོ་བོ་ནི། ཞི་གནས་ལྷག་མཐོང་ཟུང་འཇུག་ཏུ་གོ་བའོ། །ངེས་ཚིག་ནི། མཐོང་ལམ་ལ་སྦྱོར་བའི་ཕྱིར་ན་སྦྱོར་ལམ་མོ། །དབྱེ་བ་ལ་བཞི་སྟེ། དྲོད། རྩེ་མོ། བཟོད་པ། ཆོས་མཆོག་གོ། །

མཚན་ཉིད་ནི། མཐོང་ལམ་རྣམ་པར་མི་རྟོག་པའི་ཡེ་ཤེས་ཀྱི་མེའི་སྔ་ལྟས་ཡིན་པས་དྲོད། ཡང་ན་ཉོན་མོངས་པ་སྐྱེས་པ་རྣམས་གཞི་མེད་དམ་རང་བཞིན་མེད་པར་རྟོགས་པས་དྲོད་དེ། དགེ་བའི་རྩ་བ་རྣམས་གཡོ་བའི་ཕྱིར་རམ། རྣམ་བྱང་གི་ཆོས་རྣམས་གསལ་སྟོང་འཛིན་མེད་དུ་བག་ཙམ་རྟོགས་པས་རྩེ་མོའི་ཡེ་ཤེས་སོ། །

ཡིད་ལ་བྱེད་པའི་བསྒོམ་པ་ནི་དྲོད་དང་རྩེ་མོའི་དུས་སུ་དབང་པོ་ལྔ་བསྒོམ་པར་བྱ་སྟེ། བློ་གྲོས་རབ་བརྟན་གྱིས་གསོལ་པ། བཅོམ་ལྡན་འདས་དབང་པོ་ལྔ་གང་ལགས། བཅོམ་ལྡན་འདས་ཀྱིས་བཀའ་སྩལ་པ། བློ་གྲོས་རབ་བརྟན། བྱང་ཆུབ་སེམས་དཔའི་ལམ་ལ་ལྔ་སྟེ། ལྔ་གང་ཞེ་ན། དད་པའི་དབང་པོ་དང་། བརྩོན་འགྲུས་ཀྱི་དབང་པོ་དང་། དྲན་པའི་དབང་པོ་དང་། ཏིང་ངེ་འཛིན་གྱི་དབང་པོ་དང་། ཤེས་རབ་ཀྱི་དབང་པོའོ། །དེ་ལ་དད་པའི་དབང་པོ་གང་ཞེ་ན། འཁོར་བ་ན་སྤྱོད་པའི་འཇིག་རྟེན་པའི་ཡང་དག་པའི་ལྟ་བ་ལ་མངོན་པར་དད་དེ། ལས་ཀྱི་རྣམ་སྨིན་ལ་འཇིགས་པས། སྡིག་པ་སྲོག་གི་ཕྱིར་ཡང་མི་བྱེད་པ་དང་། བྱང་ཆུབ་སེམས་དཔའི་སྤྱོད་པ་ལ་ཞུགས་པ་དང་། སྟོང་པ་ཉིད་དང་། མཚན་མ་མེད་པ་དང་། སྟོབས་དང་། མི་འཇིགས་པ་ལ་སོགས་པ་སངས་རྒྱས་ཀྱི་ཆོས་ཐོས་ནས་ཐེ་ཚོམ་མེད་པར་དགའ་ཞིང་དད་པ་ནི་དད་པའི་དབང་པོའོ། །བརྩོན་འགྲུས་ཀྱི་དབང་པོ་གང་ཞེ་ན། ཆོས་གང་ལ་དད་པ་བརྩོན་འགྲུས་ཀྱི་དབང་པོས་བསྐྱེད་པར་བྱེད་དེ། དེ་བརྩོན་འགྲུས་ཀྱིའོ། །དྲན་པའི་དབང་པོ་གང་ཞེ་ན། ཆོས་གང་བརྩོན་འགྲུས་ཀྱིས་བསྒྲུས་པ་དེ་དག་དྲན་པའི་དབང་པོས་ཆུད་མི་ཟ་བར་བྱེད་པ་དེ་དག་ནི་དྲན་པའི་དབང་པོའོ། །ཏིང་ངེ་འཛིན་གྱི་དབང་པོ་གང་ཞེ་ན། ཆོས་གང་དྲན་པའི་དབང་པོས་ཆུད་མི་ཟ་བར་བྱེད་པའི་ཆོས་དེ་དག་ཏིང་ངེ་འཛིན་གྱི་དབང་པོས་རྩེ་གཅིག་ཏུ་མ་ཡེངས་པར་བྱེད་པ་དེ་ནི་ཏིང་ངེ་འཛིན་གྱི་དབང་

པོའོ། །ཤེས་རབ་ཀྱི་དབང་པོ་གང་ཞེ་ན། ཆོས་གང་ཏིང་ངེ་འཛིན་གྱིས་རྩེ་གཅིག་ཏུ་བྱེད་པ་དེ་དག་ཤེས་རབ་ཀྱི་དབང་པོས་བརྟགས་པས་ཆོས་ཐམས་ཅད་སྒྱུ་མ་ལྟར་ཡོངས་སུ་མ་གྲུབ་པར་ཤེས་པ་ནི་ཤེས་རབ་ཀྱི་དབང་པོའོ། །

དེ་ལ་སྤྱིར་སྦྱོར་ལམ་བཞི་ལ་གནས་པའི་རྟགས་ཉི་ཤུ་ལས། དང་པོ་དྲོད་རྟགས་བཅུ་ནི། བྱམས་མགོན་གྱིས་གཟུགས་སོགས་འདུ་ཤེས་ལྡོག་པ་དང་། །ཐེ་ཚོམ་མི་དལ་ཟད་པ་དང་། །བདག་ཉིད་དགེ་ལ་གནས་པ་དང་། །གཞན་ཡང་དེ་ལ་འགོད་པ་དང་། །གཞན་གྱི་རྟེན་སོགས་སྦྱིན་པ་དང་། །ཟབ་མོའི་དོན་ལ་སོམ་ཉི་མེད། །བྱམས་སེམས་ལུས་སོགས་སྒྲིབ་པ་ནི། །རྣམ་པ་ལྔ་དང་མི་འགྲོགས་དང་། །བག་ལ་ཉལ་ཀུན་འཛོམས་པ་དང་། །དྲན་པ་དང་ནི་ཤེས་བཞིན་ནོ། །ཞེས་སོ། །ཡེ་ཤེས་མངོན་འབྱུང་ལས། སྒྱུ་མ་ལྟ་བུའི་ཉམས་མྱོང་ནི། །ཅུང་ཟད་དྲོད་ཀྱི་ཡེ་ཤེས་ཏེ། རེས་འགའ་སྐྱོད་པའི་ཡེ་ཤེས་བསྐྱེད། །དེ་ཡིས་ཉམས་མྱོང་འཕེལ་བར་བྱེད། །ཅེས་སོ། །རྩེ་མོའི་རྟགས་བཞི་ནི། བྱམས་པས། གོས་ལ་སོགས་པ་གཙང་མ་དང་། །ལུས་ལ་སྲིན་བུ་རྣམས་མི་འབྱུང་། །གྱ་གྱུ་མེད་སེམས་སྦྱངས་པས་ནི། །ལེན་དང་སེར་སྣ་མེད་སོགས་དང་། །རྨི་ལམ་ན་ཡང་ཆོས་རྣམས་ཀུན། །རྨི་ལམ་ལྟ་བུར་ལྟ་ལ་སོགས། །རྩེ་མོར་ཕྱིན་པ་སྦྱོར་བའི་རྟགས། །རྣམ་པ་བཅུ་གཉིས་དག་ཏུ་བཞེད། །རྒྱ་མཚོའི་རྒྱུད་ཕྱི་མ་ལས། །རྨི་ལམ་ནུབ་གཅིག་ཟིན་གྱུར་ན། རྣལ་འབྱོར་ཟླ་ཕྱེད་བར་དུ་བདེ། །ལྷ་ཀླུ་དྲི་ཟས་མཆོད་ཅིང་བསྟོད། །དཔའ་བོ་མཁའ་འགྲོ་དངོས་སུ་འདུ། །ངན་སོང་མཚོ་ལས་སྒྲོལ་བའི་གྲུ། །ཞེས་སོ། །

དེ་ནས་སྟོབས་ལྔ་བཟོད་པ་དང་ཆོས་མཆོག་ཏུ་བསྒོམ་པར་བྱ་སྟེ། བློ་གྲོས་རབ་བརྟན་གྱིས་གསོལ་པ། བཅོམ་ལྡན་འདས་སྟོབས་ལྔ་གང་ལགས། བཅོམ་ལྡན་འདས་ཀྱིས་བཀའ་སྩལ་པ། བློ་གྲོས་རབ་བརྟན། བྱང་ཆུབ་སེམས་དཔའི་ལམ་ལ་ལྔ་སྟེ། ལྔ་གང་ཞེ་ན། དད་པའི་སྟོབས་དང་། བརྩོན་འགྲུས་ཀྱི་སྟོབས་དང་། དྲན་པའི་སྟོབས་དང་། ཏིང་ངེ་འཛིན་གྱི་སྟོབས་དང་། ཤེས་རབ་ཀྱི་སྟོབས་སོ། །དེ་ལ་དད་པའི་

སྟོབས་གང་ཞེ་ན། གང་ལ་དད་ཅིང་མོས་པ་རྩེ་གཅིག་པ་དེ་ལ་གང་གིས་ཀྱང་མི་བརྫི་བ་སྟེ། དེའི་དྲུང་དུ་བདུད་ཀྱིས་སངས་རྒྱས་སུ་བསྒྱུར་ནས་འོང་སྟེ། ཁྱོད་ཀྱི་དེ་ནི་ཆོས་མ་ཡིན་ནོ་ཞེས་བསྒྱུར་བར་བྱེད་དོ། བཟློག་པར་བྱེད་ཀྱང་། དེ་ནི་འབྲལ་བར་མི་བྱེད་འབྱེར་བར་མི་བྱེད་དོ། དེ་ཡང་འབྱུང་བ་ཆེན་པོ་བཞི་ནི་འགྱུར་སྲིད་ཀྱི། དད་པའི་སྟོབས་ལ་མོས་པ་དེ་ནི། སྟོབས་དེ་ལས་འབྲལ་བར་མི་ནུས་པས་ན་དད་པའི་སྟོབས་སོ། །བརྩོན་འགྲུས་ཀྱི་སྟོབས་གང་ཞེ་ན། གང་བརྩོན་འགྲུས་རྩོམ་ཞིང་དགེ་བའི་ཆོས་གང་དང་གང་ལ་བརྟན་པའི་སྟོབས་ཀྱི་མཐུ་སྟོབས་ཀྱང་གནས་དེར་མ་ཕྱིན་བར་ལ་བརྩོན་པའི་སྟོབས་དེ་སུས་ཀྱང་བཟློག་པར་མི་ནུས་པ་དེ་ནི་བརྩོན་འགྲུས་ཀྱི་སྟོབས་སོ། །དྲན་པའི་སྟོབས་གང་ཞེ་ན། ཆོས་གང་དང་གང་ལ་དྲན་པ་ཉེ་བར་བཞག་པས་སེམས་མི་གཡེངས་ཏེ། དེ་ལ་ཉོན་མོངས་པ་གང་གིས་ཀྱང་བརྫི་བར་མི་ནུས་པ་དྲན་པའི་སྟོབས་ཏེ། ཉོན་མོངས་པས་དྲན་པ་དེ་མི་ཚོམས་པས་ན་དྲན་པའི་སྟོབས་ཞེས་བྱའོ། །ཏིང་ངེ་འཛིན་གྱི་སྟོབས་གང་ཞེ་ན། དྲན་པ་བག་ཡོད་ཉོན་མོངས་པས་མི་བརྫི་བ་དེ་གང་དུ་གནས་ཀྱང་འདུ་འཛི་ལས་དབེན་པ་སྟེ། གཟུགས་ལ་སོགས་པ་ཆགས་སྡང་གི་ཡུལ་ཐམས་ཅད་ལ་དེར་འཛིན་གྱི་འདུ་ཤེས་མ་ཞུགས་པར་ཆོས་གང་ལ་ཡང་རྣམ་པར་མི་རྟོག་པ་ནི་འདུ་འཛི་ལས་དབེན་པའི་སྟོབས་ཐོབ་པ་སྟེ། ཏིང་ངེ་འཛིན་གྱི་སྟོབས་ཞེས་བྱའོ། །ཤེས་རབ་ཀྱི་སྟོབས་གང་ཞེ་ན། འཇིག་རྟེན་དང་འཇིག་རྟེན་ལས་འདས་པའི་ཆོས་ཐམས་ཅད་ཤེས་རབ་ཀྱི་སྟོབས་དེས་ཡོངས་སུ་ཤེས་ནས། འཇིག་རྟེན་པ་རྣམས་འཁོར་བ་ལས་སྒྲོལ་བར་བྱེད་པ་དེ་ནི་ཤེས་རབ་དང་ཡེ་ཤེས་ཀྱི་སྟོབས་ལས་བྱུང་བ་ན་ཤེས་རབ་ཀྱི་སྟོབས་ཞེས་བྱའོ། །

དེ་ལ་ཅིའི་ཕྱིར་སྟོབས་ལྔ་ཞེས་བྱ་ཞེ་ན་དབང་པོ་ལྔ་བརྟན་ཞིང་། དེའི་སྟོབས་རྒྱས་པས་ན་སྟོབས་ལྔ་ཞེས་བྱ་སྟེ། དེ་ལ་བཟོད་པའི་རྟགས་ནི། བྱམས་པས། ཆོས་ཉིད་ལྡན་པར་འགྲོ་བ་དང་། སེམས་ཅན་དོན་དུ་དམྱལ་ཚོལ་དང་། གཞན་གྱིས་བཀྲི་བར་མི་ནུས་དང་། །ལམ་གཞན་ཉེ་བར་སྟོན་བདུད་དང་། །བདུད་ཅེས་བྱ་བར་རྟོགས་

པ་དང་། །ཞེས་དང་བུ་མོ་བཞིས་ཞུས་པ་ལས། ནགས་ཁྲོད་གཅིག་ཕུར་གནས་བཅས་ནས། །ཆོས་རྣམས་སྐྱུར་མར་ཉམས་བླངས་པས། །རྨི་ལམ་སྣ་ཚོགས་རྨི་ལམ་ཤེས། །བཟོད་པ་ལ་གནས་ངན་སོང་བྲལ། ཅེས་སོ། །ཆོས་མཆོག་རྟགས་ནི་གཅིག་པ་སྟེ། །སངས་རྒྱས་དགྱེས་པའི་སྤྱོད་པའོ། །རྟགས་ནི་ཉི་ཤུ་དེ་དག་གིས། །དྲོད་དང་རྩེ་མོ་བཟོད་བཅས་དང་། །ཆོས་མཆོག་རྣམས་ལ་གནས་པ་ནི། །རྫོགས་པའི་བྱང་ཆུབ་ལས་མི་ལྡོག ཅེས་སོ། །ཁྲིའུ་རབ་སྣང་ལས། འཇིག་རྟེན་ཞེན་པ་ཀུན་བྲལ་ནས། །ཕན་པའི་སེམས་དང་གང་ལྡན་པ། །རྒྱལ་བ་མཉེས་པར་བྱེད་པ་ཡི། །ཆོས་གཞན་ཡོད་པ་མ་ཡིན་ནོ། །སྐྱང་བྱ་ནི་གོང་བཞིན་ནོ། །ས་འཚམས་ནི་དྲོད་ཀྱི་ཡེ་ཤེས་ནས་འཇིག་རྟེན་ཆོས་མཆོག་གི་བར་རོ། །

དེ་ནས་མཐོང་ལམ་བཤད་པར་བྱ་སྟེ། མཐོང་ལམ་གྱི་ངོ་བོ་ནི། བདེན་བཞི་དོན་དམིགས་མེད་དོ། །ངེས་ཚིག་ནི་སྔར་མ་མཐོང་བའི་ཆོས་ཉིད་མངོན་སུམ་དུ་མཐོང་བས་མཐོང་ལམ་མོ། །

དབྱེ་ན་བཞི་སྟེ། སྡུག་བསྔལ། ཀུན་འབྱུང་། འགོག་པ། ལམ་མོ། །དབྱེ་བའི་མཚན་ཉིད་ནི། སྡུག་བསྔལ་ལ་སོགས་པའི་བདེན་བཞི་སྟོང་པ་ཉིད་དུ་མཐོང་བ་ནི། ཆོས་ཤེས་པའི་བཟོད་པ། དེའི་སྟེང་དུ་སྐད་ཅིག་ཕྱི་མའི་ཤེས་པ་སྟོང་ཉིད་དེ་རྒྱ་ཆེར་མཐོང་བ་ནི། མཐོང་ལམ་གྱི་ཆོས་ཉིད་མཐོང་བའོ། །བཟོད་པ་དང་ཆོས་ཤེས་པ་གཉིས་བྱང་ཆུབ་ཐོབ་པའི་རྒྱུ་ཕྱིན་ཅི་མ་ལོག་པར་འདུག་སྙམ་དུ་རྟོགས་པ་དེ། བདེན་པ་བཞི་ལ་རྗེས་སུ་ཤེས་པའི་བཟོད་པའོ། །དེ་ལྟར་རྟོགས་པ་དེ་མ་ནོར་ཐག་ཆོད་ངེས་ཤེས་སྐྱེས་པ་ནི་བདེན་པ་བཞི་ལ་རྗེས་སུ་ཆོས་ཤེས་པའི་བཟོད་པའོ། །དེ་ནི་མཐོང་ལམ་གྱི་ཡེ་ཤེས་ཀྱི་མཐོང་བའོ། །དེ་རྣམས་ནི་ཆོས་ཉིད་རྒྱ་ཆུང་བ་ཆེ་བ་དེ་བས་ཆེ་བ་དང་། ཤིན་ཏུ་ཆེ་བ་དང་བཞི་སྟེ། ཁྱབ་ཆེ་ཆུང་གི་ཁྱད་པར་དུ་བྱས་པའོ། །ཡིད་ལ་བྱེད་པའི་ཏིང་ངེ་འཛིན་ནི། བྱང་ཆུབ་ཀྱི་ཡན་ལག་བདུན་ཏེ། བྱང་ཆུབ་སེམས་དཔའ་བློ་གྲོས་འབྱུང་གནས་ཀྱིས་ཞུས་པའི་མདོ་ལས། བློ་གྲོས་འབྱུང་གནས་ཀྱིས་གསོལ་པ།

བཅོམ་ལྡན་འདས་བྱང་ཆུབ་ཀྱི་ཡན་ལག་བདུན་ཇི་ལྟར་བལྟ་བར་བགྱི། བཅོམ་ལྡན་འདས་ཀྱིས་བཀའ་སྩལ་པ། བློ་གྲོས་འབྱུང་གནས། གང་དྲན་པ་མེད་ཅིང་ཡིད་ལ་བྱར་མེད་པའི་ཕྱིར། ཆོས་ཐམས་ཅད་རང་གི་མཚན་ཉིད་ཀྱིས་སྟོང་པ་སྟེ། གང་དེ་ལ་ཆོས་ཐམས་ཅད་ངོ་བོ་མ་གྲུབ་པར་མཐོང་བ་དེ་ནི་དྲན་པ་ཡང་དག་བྱང་ཆུབ་ཀྱི་ཡན་ལག་གོ། །བློ་གྲོས་འབྱུང་གནས་གང་གིས་དགེ་བ་དང་མི་དགེ་བ་དང་། ལུང་དུ་མ་བསྟན་པ་ཡང་མ་གྲུབ་པའི་ཕྱིར་རོ། །ཆོས་སུ་བཏགས་པ་ཐམས་ཅད་གང་དུ་མི་དམིགས་པ་སྒྱུ་མ་ལྟ་བུ་ནི། ཆོས་རྣམ་པར་འབྱེད་པ་བྱང་ཆུབ་ཀྱི་ཡན་ལག་གོ། །བློ་གྲོས་འབྱུང་གནས། གང་གི་ཆོས་ཐམས་ཅད་ཀྱི་འདུ་ཤེས་ཤིན་ཏུ་བཤིག་པའི་ཕྱིར་ཁམས་གསུམ་དང་མྱ་ངན་ལས་འདས་པའི་ཆོས་ཐམས་ཅད་མི་ལེན་མི་འདོར་བར། ལམ་གྱི་མངོན་པར་རྟོགས་པ་འཛིན་པ་དང་བྲལ་བ་ལ། སྤྲོ་བ་དང་། མི་རྟོག་པའི་མོས་པ་དང་། བརྩོན་པ་མི་འདོར་བ་འདི་ནི། བརྩོན་འགྲུས་ཡང་དག་བྱང་ཆུབ་ཀྱི་ཡན་ལག་གོ། །བློ་གྲོས་འབྱུང་གནས། གང་གིས་དགའ་བ་དང་། མི་དགའ་བ་ཐམས་ཅད་རྣམ་པར་བཤིག་པའི་ཕྱིར་འདུ་བྱེད་ཀྱི་ཆོས་ཐམས་ཅད་ལ་དགའ་བ་མི་བསྐྱེད་པར། ཀུན་ནས་ཉོན་མོངས་པ་སེལ་བ་འདི་ནི་དགའ་བ་ཡང་དག་བྱང་ཆུབ་ཀྱི་ཡན་ལག་གོ། །བློ་གྲོས་འབྱུང་གནས་གང་གི་དམིགས་པར་འགྱུར་བའི་ཆོས་རྡུལ་ཙམ་ཡང་མི་དམིགས་པའི་ཕྱིར། ཆོས་ཐམས་ཅད་ལུས་ཤིན་ཏུ་སྦྱངས་པ་དང། སེམས་ཤིན་ཏུ་སྦྱངས་པས་སྒྲིབ་པ་མེད་པ་དང་། དམིགས་པ་མེད་པའི་ཏིང་ངེ་འཛིན་ལ་སེམས་གནས་པ་ནི། སེམས་ཤིན་ཏུ་སྦྱངས་པ་ཡང་དག་བྱང་ཆུབ་ཀྱི་ཡན་ལག་གོ། །བློ་གྲོས་འབྱུང་གནས། གང་གིས་ཆོས་ཐམས་ཅད་ཀྱི་འཛིན་པ་རྣམ་པར་བཤིག་པའི་ཕྱིར་རམ། རྟོགས་པའི་ཕྱིར་སེམས་ནི་གང་ལ་ཡང་མི་དམིགས་ཏེ། གང་ལ་སེམས་མཉམ་པར་བཞག་ཅིང་ཆོས་རྣམས་རྟོགས་པར་འགྱུར་གྱི། སེམས་མཉམ་པར་མ་བཞག་པས་མ་ཡིན་པ་དང་། སེམས་མཉམ་པར་བཞག་པས་སངས་རྒྱ་ཡི། མཉམ་པར་མ་བཞག་པས་མ་ཡིན་ནོ། །དེ་ལྟར་འཛིན་པ་དང་བྲལ་བར་མཉམ་པར་འཇོག་པ་དེ་ནི་ཏིང་ངེ་འཛིན་ཡང་དག་བྱང་

ཆུབ་ཀྱི་ཡན་ལག་གོ། །བློ་གྲོས་འབྱུང་གནས། གང་གིས་ཆོས་ཐམས་ཅད་གང་ལའང་གནས་པར་མི་བྱེད། བསྟེན་པར་མི་བྱེད། ཆགས་པར་མི་བྱེད། འཆིང་བར་མི་བྱེད། གང་ཡང་ཡིད་བདེ་སྡུག་བར་མ་ལ་སོགས་པའི་ཆོས་ཐམས་ཅད་ལ་སེམས་མི་འཛིན་ཏེ། འཇིག་རྟེན་གྱི་ཆོས་ཐམས་ཅད་ཀྱིས་མི་འཕྲོག་ཤིང་། དེས་ཆོས་ཐམས་ཅད་ཡང་དག་པར་རྗེས་སུ་མི་མཐོང་བའི་བཏང་སྙོམས་ཅན་དུ་གྱུར་ནས། དགའ་བ་ཐོབ་པ་འདི་ནི་བཏང་སྙོམས་ཡང་དག་བྱང་ཆུབ་ཀྱི་ཡན་ལག་གོ། །བློ་གྲོས་འབྱུང་གནས་བྱང་ཆུབ་ཀྱི་ཡན་ལག་བདུན་དེ་ལྟར་དུ་བལྟ་བར་བྱའོ། །དེ་ལྟར་ཏིང་ངེ་འཛིན་དེ་སྟོབས་ཀྱིས། ཆོས་ཉིད་མངོན་སུམ་མཐོང་བ་དང་། །མངོན་ཤེས་དག་དང་ལྡན་དུས་སུ། །དགའ་ལ་དུ་བྲོའི་ཤེས་པ་དང་། །རྟག་ཏུ་ཚངས་པར་སྤྱོད་པ་དང་། །སེམས་ཕྱིར་ལུས་འདི་བསྒྱུར་བཏུབ་དང་། །ཆོས་ཕྱིར་སྲོག་ནི་གཏོང་ཡོད་དང་། །བློ་ལྡན་མཐོང་བའི་ལམ་ལ་སྐྱེ། །ཕྱིར་མི་ལྡོག་པའི་རྟགས་སུ་བཤད། །དེ་མ་ཡིན་པའི་ཡོན་ཏན་ནི། །བརྒྱ་ཕྲག་བཅུ་གཉིས་འབྱུང་བར་འགྱུར། །ཕལ་པོ་ཆེ་ལས། ས་ཐོབ་གྱུར་མ་ཐག་ཏུ་འཇིགས་པ་ལྔ་དང་བྲལ། །འཚོ་བ་མེད་དང་འཆི་དང་མི་བསྔགས་ངན་འགྲོ་དང་། །འཁོར་གྱི་འཇིགས་བྲལ་དེ་ལ་བག་ཚའི་རྣམ་པ་མེད། །ཅིའི་ཕྱིར་ཞེ་ན་དེ་ལ་བདག་གི་གནས་མེད་དོ། །ཞེས་པས་འཇིགས་པ་ལྔ་བྲལ་དུ་ཤེས་པར་བྱའོ། །

དེ་ལས་དང་པོའི་མཐོང་སྤངས་བརྒྱ་རྩ་བཅུ་གཉིས་ནི། །ཀུན་བརྟགས་ཀྱི་ཉོན་མོངས་པ་དྲུག་གི་བྱེ་བྲག་སྟེ། དྲུག་གང་ཞེ་ན། མ་རིག་པ། འདོད་ཆགས། ང་རྒྱལ། ཁོང་ཁྲོ། ཐེ་ཚོམ་ལྟ་བའོ། །ལྟ་བ་ལ་ལྔ་སྟེ། འཇིག་ཚོགས་ཀྱི་ལྟ་བ། མཐར་འཛིན། ལོག་ལྟ། ཚུལ་ཁྲིམས། བརྟུལ་ཞུགས་ཀྱི་ལྟ་བ་མཆོག་ཏུ་འཛིན་པའོ། །དེ་ལ་ལྟ་བ་ལྔ་དང་། མ་རིག་པ་ལ་སོགས་ལྟ་བ་མ་ཡིན་པ་ལྔ་སྟེ་བས་པས་ཉོན་མོངས་པ་བཅུ། དེ་ལྟར་ལྟ་བའི་ཉོན་མོངས་པ་བཅུ་པོ་དེ། འདོད་ཁམས་ན་བདེན་པ་བཞི་པོ་རེ་རེ་ལ་ཕྲག་བཅུ་བཅུ་འབྱུང་བས་བཞི་བཅུའོ། །ཁམས་གོང་མ་གཟུགས་ཁམས་དང་། གཟུགས་མེད་ཀྱི་ཁམས་གཉིས་ན། ཁོང་ཁྲོ་མ་གཏོགས་པའི་དགུ་པོ་དེ་བདེན་པ་བཞི་

ལ་དགུ་དགུ་སྦྱར་བས། གཟུགས་ཁམས་ལ་དགུ་བཞི་སུམ་ཅུ་སོ་དྲུག །གཟུགས་མེད་ན་དགུ་བཞི་སུམ་ཅུ་སོ་དྲུག་སོ་དྲུག་དེའི་སྟེང་དུ་འདོད་ཁམས་ཀྱི་བཞི་བཅུ་བསྣན་པས་མཐོང་སྤང་བརྒྱ་དང་ལྔ་བཅུ་རྩ་གཉིས་ཟེར་བ་དོན་ཐོག་ཏུ་དགོས་སམ་སྙམ་པ་དེ་དག་ཡིན་ན་གོང་དུ་མཐོང་སྤང་བརྒྱ་དང་ལྔ་བཅུ་རྩ་གཉིས་ཟེར་བའང་དགོས་སྟེ། བདུན་ཅུ་དོན་གཉིས། དེའི་སྟེང་དུ་འདོད་ཁམས་ཀྱི་བཞི་བཅུ་མནན་པས་མཐོང་སྤང་བརྒྱ་དང་བཅུ་གཉིས་སོ། །

དེ་ཡང་སྤོང་ཚུལ་ནི། མཐོང་སྤངས་ཀྱིས་ཉོན་མོངས་པ་ཆེན་པོའི་ཆེན་པོ་མུན་ནག་ལྟ་བུ་སྟེ། ཡེ་ཤེས་ཆུང་དུས་ཏེ། མར་མེ་ལྟ་བུས་སྤོང་ངོ་། །དེ་ཡང་གོང་བཞིན་བདེན་པ་བཞིས་སྤོང་བ་དང་། བདག་མེད་རྟོགས་པས་ཅིག་ཆར་དུ་སྤོང་བའོ། །

དེ་ཡང་བསྡུགས་ཀྱི་བདེན་པ་མཐོང་ཚུལ་ནི། ཡེ་ཤེས་མངོན་འབྱུང་ལས། བདེ་ཆེན་ལས་ཀྱི་ཕྱག་རྒྱ་ཡིས། །ཉིན་པར་བདེན་འཛིན་རྩ་མདུད་གྲོལ། །མཚན་མོ་འཁྲུལ་པའི་རྩ་མདུད་གྲོལ། །བྱང་ཆུབ་ཚུལ་འདི་བསྟན་པའོ། །དེ་ཉིད་ལས། ཕྱག་རྒྱའི་བདེ་བ་བདེ་བ་ཆེ། །བླ་མའི་དྲིན་ལས་བྱུང་བ་ཡི། །ཆོས་ཉིད་དངོས་སུ་མཐོང་བ་སྟེ། །དང་པོའི་བདེན་པ་ཞེས་སུ་གྲགས། །དམ་ཚིག་བཀོད་པ་ལས། །ཉིན་པར་སྣང་སྟོང་སྒྱུ་མ་དང་། །མཚན་མོ་རྨི་ལམ་ལྷའི་སྐུ། །རང་ཤར་དེ་ལས་མ་གཡོས་ཚེ། །དེ་ནི་རྒྱལ་བ་ལོངས་སྤྱོད་རྫོགས། །སྐད་ཅིག་བར་དོར་མྱ་ངན་འདས། །རྒྱུན་ལ་གནས་ན་སྒོམས་ཅི་དགོས། །སྒྱུ་མ་འོད་གསལ་དེ་བཞིན་ནོ། །འདི་ནི་གཞན་དུ་བརྗོད་མི་བྱ། །ཡེ་ཤེས་གསལ་བའི་རྒྱུད་ཕྱི་མ་ལས། །ཕྱོགས་བཅུའི་ཞིང་ཁམས་གང་ཡིན་པ། །རྨི་ལམ་ལུས་ཀྱི་བཀོད་པས་སྦྱངས། །དང་པོ་ས་ཡི་ཡོན་ཏན་རྣམས། །དེ་ནས་བྱུང་གིས་གཞན་དུ་མིན། །དེ་ཉིད་ལས། ཉིན་པར་དང་ནི་རྨི་ལམ་གྱི། །འཁྲུལ་པའི་བག་ཆགས་མ་དག་པར། །ས་བརྒྱད་ལ་ཡང་མི་གནས་ན། །པདྨ་ཅན་ལ་སྒོམས་ཅི་དགོས། །ཚངས་པ་ཀུན་དགའི་མདོ་ལས། ས་དང་ལམ་གྱི་ཡོན་ཏན་རྣམས། །རྨི་ལམ་སྐབས་ལས་རྟོགས་པར་བྱ། །ས་འཚམས་ནི། ཆོས་མཆོག་ནས་མཐོང་ལམ་གྱི་བར་རོ། །

དེ་ནས་བསྒོམ་ལམ་བཤད་པར་བྱ་སྟེ། ངོ་བོ་ནི་རྣམ་པར་མི་རྟོག་པའི་ཡེ་ཤེས་སོ། །ངེས་ཚིག་ནི་ཆོས་ཉིད་བདེན་པ་མཐོང་ཟིན་གོམས་པར་བྱ་བའི་ཕྱིར་བསྒོམ་ལམ་མོ། །དབྱེ་ན་བསྒོམ་ལམ་ལ་ས་དགུ་སྟེ། དྲི་མ་མེད་པའི་ས་ལ་སོགས་པའོ། །

ཡིད་ལ་བྱེད་པའི་ཏིང་ངེ་འཛིན་ནི། འཕགས་པའི་ལམ་ཡན་ལག་བརྒྱད་དེ། བློ་གྲོས་འབྱུང་གནས་ཀྱིས་གསོལ་པ། བཅོམ་ལྡན་འདས་བྱང་ཆུབ་སེམས་དཔའི་འཕགས་ལམ་ཡན་ལག་བརྒྱད་ཇི་ལྟར་བལྟ་བར་བགྱི། བཅོམ་ལྡན་འདས་ཀྱིས་བཀའ་སྩལ་པ། བློ་གྲོས་འབྱུང་གནས། དེ་ལ་ཆོས་ཐམས་ཅད་མཉམ་པ་ཉིད་ནི། ཡང་དག་པའི་ལྟ་བ་སྟེ། དེ་ལ་བདག་ཏུ་བལྟ་བ་དང་། གང་ཟག་དང་། སེམས་ཅན་དང་། སྲོག་དང་། སྟོང་ཉིད་དུ་ལྟ་བ་ཡང་དག་པར་མི་བྱེད་དོ། །དེ་ལ་ལྟ་བའི་དམིགས་པ་ཆུང་ངུ་ནས་མྱ་ངན་ལས་འདས་པའི་བར་དང་། གང་ཡང་རབ་འབྲིང་ཐ་མའི་ལྟ་བར་གྱུར་པ་ཐམས་ཅད་དང་བྲལ་བ་ནི་ཡང་དག་པའི་ལྟ་བའོ། །

བློ་གྲོས་འབྱུང་གནས་དེ་ལ་རྟོག་པ་གང་གིས་རྟོག་པ་སྤྱོང་བར་འགྱུར་བའོ། །དེ་ཡང་ཞི་གནས་ཀྱིས་བསྐྱུས་པའི་ལྷག་མཐོང་ལ་མཁས་པ་སྟེ། དེ་ལ་ཆོས་བཟང་ངན་དུ་རྟོགས་པ་དང་། ཡོངས་སུ་རྟོག་པ་དང་། རྣམ་པར་རྟོག་པ་ཐམས་ཅད་སྤངས་ཏེ། ཅིར་ཡང་མི་རྟོག །རྣམ་པར་མི་རྟོག །ཡང་དག་པར་ཡང་མི་རྟོག་པ་འདི་ནི་ཡང་དག་པའི་རྟོག་པའོ། །

བློ་གྲོས་འབྱུང་གནས། དེ་ལ་ཚིག་གང་གིས་བདག་གཞན་ཐམས་ཅད་ལ་མི་གནོད་པ་སྟེ། དེ་ལ་བདག་ཀྱང་ཉོན་མོངས་པར་མི་བྱེད། གཞན་ཡང་ཉོན་མོངས་པར་མི་བྱེད་པར། ཚིག་གང་གིས་ཆོས་ཐམས་ཅད་མཉམ་པ་ཉིད་དུ་ངེས་པར་རྟོག་པར་བྱེད་པ་འདི་ནི་ཡང་དག་པའི་ངག་གོ། །

བློ་གྲོས་འབྱུང་གནས། དེ་ལ་ལས་གང་ཟད་ཅིང་མ་གྲུབ་པ་ནི་ལས་ཀྱི་མཐའོ། །དེ་ལ་ལས་ཉོན་མོངས་པ་ཞི་བར་འགྱུར་གྱི། ཉོན་མོངས་པ་འབར་བའི་ཕྱིར་

མ་ཡིན་པ་དང་། ལས་གང་ཉོན་མོངས་པ་དང་བྲལ་བར་འགྱུར་གྱི། ཉོན་མོངས་པ་སྐྱེ་བའི་ཕྱིར་མ་ཡིན་པ་དང་། དཀར་བ་དང་། གནག་པ་དང་། འདྲེས་པའི་ལས་ཀྱི་མཐའ་ཐམས་ཅད་དང་བྲལ་ཞིང་མ་གྲུབ་པ་ནི་ཡང་དག་པའི་ལས་མཐའོ། །

བློ་གྲོས་འབྱུང་གནས། དེ་ལ་ཉོན་མོངས་པ་མི་སོག་པ་ནི་ཡང་དག་པའི་འཚོ་བ་སྟེ། དེ་ལ་འཚོ་བ་གང་བདག་ལ་ཡང་མི་གནོད་པར་གཞན་ལ་ཡང་མི་གནོད་དེ། ཆོས་ཀྱི་དོན་རྫོགས་པར་འགྱུར་བ་འདི་ནི་ཡང་དག་པའི་འཚོ་བའོ། །བློ་གྲོས་འབྱུང་གནས། དེ་ལ་ཟབ་ཅིང་སྤྲོས་པ་དང་བྲལ་བ་འདུས་མ་བྱས་པའི་ཆོས་བསྒྲུབ་པ་ལ་རྩོལ་བ་སྟེ། དེའི་ཕྱིར་སེམས་རབ་ཏུ་འཛིན་པ་དང་། འདུན་པ་དང་། བརྩོན་པ་དང་། མི་ཞུམ་པར་ཡང་དག་པའི་ནན་ཏན་མངོན་སུམ་དུ་བྱེད་པ་འདི་ནི་ཡང་དག་པའི་རྩོལ་བའོ། །

བློ་གྲོས་འབྱུང་གནས། དེ་ལ་དྲན་པ་གང་གིས་ཉོན་མོངས་པ་ཐམས་ཅད་ཀྱི་སྐབས་མི་སྐྱེད་པའོ། །དེ་ལ་བྱང་ཆུབ་ཀྱི་ཡན་ལག་སེམས་དང་། ཚད་མེད་པ་དང་། ཕ་རོལ་ཏུ་ཕྱིན་པ་དྲུག་གི་དྲན་པ་སྟེ། དྲན་པ་གང་གིས་བདུད་ཀྱི་སྐབས་མི་སྐྱེད་པ་དང་། དྲན་པ་གང་གིས་ལམ་ལོག་པར་མི་འགྱུར་བ་དང་། དྲན་པ་སྒོ་བ་ལྟ་བུས་སེམས་དང་སེམས་བྱུང་གི་ཆོས་མི་དགེ་བ་ཐམས་ཅད་ཀྱི་སྐབས་མི་སྐྱེད་པ་འདི་ནི་ཡང་དག་པའི་དྲན་པའོ། །

བློ་གྲོས་འབྱུང་གནས། བདག་མཉམ་པ་ཉིད་ལས་ཆོས་ཐམས་ཅད་མཉམ་པ་ཉིད་དང་། བདག་རྣམ་པར་དག་པས་ཆོས་ཐམས་ཅད་རྣམ་པར་དག་པ་དང་། བདག་སྟོང་པ་ཉིད་ལས་ཆོས་ཐམས་ཅད་སྟོང་པ་ཉིད་དུ་ཡང་དག་པར་སྙོམས་པར་འཇུག་ལ། ཡང་དག་པའི་ཏིང་ངེ་འཛིན་གང་གིས་སེམས་སྐད་ཅིག་དང་ལྡན་པའི་ཤེས་རབ་ཀྱིས་ཐམས་ཅད་མཁྱེན་པ་དང་། ཐམས་ཅད་མཁྱེན་པའི་ཡེ་ཤེས་ཀྱིས་མངོན་པར་སངས་རྒྱས་པ་འདི་ནི་ཡང་དག་པའི་ཏིང་ངེ་འཛིན་ཏོ། །བློ་གྲོས་འབྱུང་གནས། བྱང་ཆུབ་སེམས་དཔའི་འཕགས་པའི་ལམ་ཡན་ལག་བརྒྱད་དེ་ལྟར་བལྟ་བར་བྱའོ། །

།དེའི་རྟགས་ནི། ཟབ་མོའི་དོན་ཁོང་དུ་ཆུད་ནས། གོམས་ཞིང་བརྟན་པར་འགྱུར་བས། མཐུ་དང་རྫུ་འཕྲུལ་དང་ལྡན་པར་འགྱུར་ཏེ། ས་གཉིས་པ་ནས་བཅུ་པའི་བར་དུ། ཡོན་ཏན་བརྒྱ་ཕྲག་བཅུ་གཉིས་བསམ་གྱིས་མི་ཁྱབ་པར་འབྱུང་བར་འགྱུར་རོ། །དེ་ཡང་སྒོམ་སྤྱངས་ཀྱི་ཉོན་མོངས་པ་བག་ལ་ཉལ་བའི་ལྷན་སྐྱེས་ལས་ཕྱེ་བ་དྲུག་སྟེ། དྲུག་གང་ཞེ་ན། མ་རིག་པ་དང་། འདོད་ཆགས། ཁོང་ཁྲོ། ང་རྒྱལ། འཇིག་ཚོགས་སུ་ལྟ་བ། མཐར་འཛིན་གྱི་ལྟ་བའོ། །འདོད་ཁམས་ན་ཉོན་མོངས་པ་དྲུག་པོ་རེ་རེ་ལ་ཆེ་འབྲིང་དགུ་དགུར་ཕྱེ་ནས། །དེ་ལ་ཡེ་ཤེས་ཀྱང་ཆེ་འབྲིང་དགུ་དགུར་ཕྱེ་ནས་སྤོང་སྟེ། དགུ་པ་དྲུག་ལ་ལྔ་བཅུ་རྩ་བཞི། གཟུགས་ཁམས་ནས་ཁོང་ཁྲོ་བོར་བའི་ལྔ་པོ་ལ། བསམ་གཏན་དང་པོའི་ཉོན་མོངས་པ་ལྔ་པོ་ལ་ཆེ་འབྲིང་དགུ་དགུར་ཕྱེ་ནས་དེ་ཡིས་ཤེས་ཆེ་འབྲིང་དགུས་སྤོང་ངོ་། །དགུ་པ་ལྔ་ལ་བཞི་བཅུ་ཞེ་ལྔ། གཉིས་པ་དང་། གསུམ་པ་དང་། བཞི་པ་རྣམས་ལ་ཞེ་ལྔ་ལྔ་སྟེ། བརྒྱ་བརྒྱད་བཅུ། གཟུགས་མེད་ལ་ཡང་། ནམ་མཁའ་མཐའ་ཡས་སྐྱེ་མཆེད་ལ་བཞི་བཅུ་ཞེ་ལྔ། དེ་བཞིན་དུ་རྣམ་ཤེས་མཐའ་ཡས་དང་། ཡོད་མིན་མེད་མིན་དང་། ཅི་ཡང་མེད་པའི་སྐྱེ་མཆེད་གསུམ་པོ་ལ་ཞེ་ལྔ་ལྔ་སྟེ། བརྒྱ་དང་བརྒྱད་བཅུ། དེ་ལྟར་བརྒྱ་བརྒྱད་བཅུ་གཉིས་ལ་གསུམ་བརྒྱ་དྲུག་བཅུ། དེའི་སྟེང་དུ་འདོད་ཁམས་ཀྱི་ལྔ་བཅུ་རྩ་བཞི་མནན་པས་སྒོམ་སྤྱང་བཞི་བརྒྱ་དང་བཅུ་བཞིའོ། །

དེ་ནས་མཐར་ཕྱིན་པའི་ལམ་བཤད་དེ། བསམ་གྱིས་མི་ཁྱབ་པ་བསྟན་པའི་མདོ་ལས། དེ་ལ་རིགས་ཀྱི་བུ། མཐར་ཕྱིན་པའི་ལམ་གང་ཞེ་ན། བླ་ན་མེད་པའི་བྱང་ཆུབ་མྱུར་དུ་ཐོབ་པར་བྱེད་པ་ལ་ཆོས་བཞན་གྱིས་བར་ཆད་མེད་པས་ན་བར་ཆད་མེད་པའི་ལམ་ཞེས་བྱ། གང་དེ་ལ་རིགས་ཀྱི་བུ། བསྒོམ་པར་བྱ་བའི་ལམ་གྱིས་སྒྲིབ་པ་ཀུན་སྤྱངས་ནས། ས་བཅུ་རྒྱུན་གྱི་ཐ་མ་ལ་སྒྲིབ་པ་ཕྲ་ཞིང་ཕྲ་བ་དེ་ཉིད་རྡོ་རྗེ་ལྟ་བུའི་ཏིང་ངེ་འཛིན་ནུས་པ་ཐོགས་མེད་དང་ལྡན་པ་དེས་འཇོམས་པར་འགྱུར་རོ། །དགོངས་པ་བླ་ན་མེད་པའི་རྒྱུད་ལས། གསལ་སྟོང་འཛིན་མེད་བདེ་བ་ཆེ། །འོད་གསལ་རང་

ཤར་འདུས་མ་བྱས། །ཀེ་སར་གསང་བའི་བདེ་བ་དང་། །བྱིན་བརླབས་སྟོབས་ལས་འབྱུང་བ་སྟེ། །སྨུན་ཁུང་སྒྲོན་མེ་གསེར་གསལ་ལྟར། །ཕྲ་ཞིང་ཕྲ་བའི་སྒྲིབ་པ་དེ། །རང་དག་རང་གྲོལ་སྟོབས་ཀྱིས་འཇོམས། །འདི་ནི་གསང་བའི་སྤྱོད་ཡུལ་ལོ། །

དེ་ལྟར་ཤེས་བྱའི་སྒྲིབ་པ་དག་པའི་སངས་རྒྱས་དེ་ཇི་ལྟ་བུ་ཞེ་ན། ཡེ་ཤེས་བླ་ན་མེད་པའི་རྒྱུད་ལས། འདུས་མ་བྱས་པའི་དབྱིངས་ཉིད་དང་། །ཡེ་ཤེས་གཉིས་སུ་མེད་པ་སྟེ། །ཉོན་མོངས་ཤེས་བྱ་ཡོངས་དག་པའི། །ཆོས་སྐུ་དག་པ་གཉིས་ལྡན་ཏེ། །མི་འགྱུར་མ་སྐྱེས་མཚན་མེད་པའི། །སངས་རྒྱས་རྣམས་ནི་ཆོས་ཀྱི་སྐུ། །དེ་ལ་བཞེངས་བཞུགས་མི་མངའ་ཡང་། །སྔོན་གྱི་སེམས་བསྐྱེད་བསོད་ནམས་ཚོགས། །སྨོན་ལམ་བསྐྱེད་རིམ་རྒྱུ་རྐྱེན་ལས། །གཟུགས་སྐུ་གཉིས་ནི་རང་ཤར་འབྱུང་། །དེ་ཡང་འོག་མིན་པོ་བྲང་དུ། །སྣང་མཛད་ལོངས་སྐུ་རྡོ་རྗེ་འཆང་། །མཚན་བཟང་དཔེ་བྱད་རབ་ཏུ་ལྡན། །དཔེ་བྲལ་སྣང་སྟོང་དྲི་མེད་སྐུ། །ཞེན་བྲལ་བདེ་སྟོང་དབྱེར་མེད་རྫོགས། །སངས་རྒྱས་བྱང་ཆུབ་སེམས་དཔས་བསྐོར། །མཐའ་བྲལ་བདེ་སྟོང་དབྱེར་མེད་ཆོས། །སྐྱེ་མེད་རང་སྒྲ་སྒྲོགས་པར་བྱེད། །གནས་དུས་སྟོན་པ་འཁོར་ལ་སོགས། །སྤྲུལ་སྐུ་གང་འདུལ་རང་ཤར་གྱིས། །གདུལ་བྱ་གང་འདུལ་སྐུར་གྱུར་ནས། །སྐྱོན་བྲལ་པད་ལྟར་སྨིན་གྲོལ་བྱེད། །ཡང་ན་ནོར་བུ་དཔག་བསམ་ལྟར། །ཡང་དགོངས་པ་བླ་ན་མེད་པ་ལས། །བསྐྱེད་རིམ་བདེ་བའི་མཚན་ཉིད་ཅན། །དེ་ལ་སྐུ་གཉིས་འབྱུང་འགྱུར་ཏེ། །རྫོགས་རིམ་ལས་ནི་ཆོས་ཀྱི་སྐུ། །དབྱེར་མེད་ཚུལ་འདི་བསྟན་པའོ། །

དེ་ཡང་ཆོས་སྐུ་ལས་ལོངས་སྐུ། །ལོངས་སྐུ་ལས་སྤྲུལ་སྐུ་འབྱུང་བའམ་འཆར་ཏེ། གསེར་འོད་དམ་པ་ལས། དཔེར་ན་ནམ་མཁའ་སྟོང་པ་ལ་བརྟེན་ནས་གློག་འབྱུང་ངོ་། [།གློག་ལ་བརྟེན་ཏེ་འོད་སྣང་ངོ་།] །དེ་བཞིན་དུ་ཆོས་སྐུ་ལ་བརྟེན་ཏེ། །བསོད་ནམས་ཀྱི་སྐུ་སྣང་ངོ་། །བསོད་ནམས་ཀྱི་སྐུ་ལ་བརྟེན་ཏེ་སྤྲུལ་སྐུ་སྣང་ངོ་། །སྐུ་གསུམ་དུ་བགྲང་དུ་ཡོད་ཀྱི། ངོ་བོས་ནི་གསུམ་དུ་མེད་དོ། །མདོར་ན་ཆོས་སྐུ་ནམ་མཁའ་ལྟ་བུ་ལ། གཟུགས་སྐུ་འཇའ་ཚོན་ལྟ་བུ་འབྱུང་ཞིང་། རྟོག་བྲལ་ཤེས་བྱ་ཐམས་

ཅན་མ་ལུས་པ་ཇི་ལྟ་བ་བཞིན་མཁྱེན་ཏེ། རྣམ་རྟོག་མི་མངའ་ཅིར་ཡང་ས་ལེ་མཁྱེན། །ཆོས་སྐུ་མཁའ་འདྲ་གཟུགས་སྐུ་མཛེས་སྐུ་ལྡན། །ཅེས་སོ།

དེ་ལ་ཆོས་སྐུའི་ངོ་བོ་གསུམ་སྟེ། འདུས་མ་བྱས་པ་ལྷུན་གྱིས་གྲུབ་སྟེ། དེ་ལ་རྐྱེན་གཞན་གྱིས་བསྒྱུར་བར་མི་ནུས་པའོ། །གཟུགས་སྐུའི་ངོ་བོ་ལ་ཡང་གསུམ་ཏེ། མཁྱེན་པ་དང་བརྩེ་བ་དང་། ནུས་པར་ལྡན་པའོ། །དེ་ལྟར་ཡང་བྱམས་པས། ལྷུན་གྱིས་གྲུབ་ཅིང་འདུས་མ་བྱས། །གཞན་གྱི་རྐྱེན་གྱིས་རྟོགས་མིན་པས། །མཁྱེན་དང་བརྩེ་དང་ནུས་པར་ལྡན། །དེ་ཡང་ཡེ་ཤེས་ལྔ་ལས་སྐུ་བཞི་གྲུབ་ཚུལ་དང་། བསྐྱེད་རྫོགས་དང་། ཚོགས་གཉིས་ལས་སྐུ་བཞི་དང་། དབང་བཞི་ལས་སྐུ་བཞི་འགྲུབ་ཚུལ་ལ་སོགས་པ་སྤྲོས་པ་ལས་དགའ་བར་གྱུར་ན་མདོ་རྒྱུད་དུ་མ་ལས་ཤེས་པར་བྱའོ། །འདི་ནི་རྩེ་གཅིག་ཏུ་སྒྲུབ་པའི་ཉམས་མྱོང་དང་། མདོ་རྒྱུད་ཀྱི་དགོངས་པ་མི་འགལ་བར་མདོར་བསྡུས་ནས་བསྟན་པ་ཡིན་གྱི། ཤེས་བྱ་དང་ཐེག་པ་མ་ལུས་པ་ཤེས་པར་བྱ་བའི་ལོང་མེད་ཅིང་ཐུག་མཐའ་མེད་དེ། ལང་ཀར་གཤེགས་པ་ལས། ཇི་སྲིད་འདུ་ཤེས་ཡོད་ཀྱི་བར། །ཐེག་པའི་མཐའ་ལ་ཐུག་པ་མེད། །འདུ་ཤེས་མེད་པར་གྱུར་པ་ན། །ཐེག་པ་མེད་ཅིང་བརྗོད་དུ་མེད། །ཅེས་གསུངས་སོ། །ས་འཚམས་ནི། ས་བཅུ་རྒྱུན་གྱི་ཐ་མ་ནས་སྐུ་བཞི་འཕྲིན་ལས་དང་བཅས་པའི་བར་ལ་མཐར་ཕྱིན་པའི་ལམ་དུ་ཤེས་པར་བྱའོ། །

དེ་ནས་སའི་རིམ་པ་བཤད་པར་བྱ་སྟེ། སའི་ངོ་བོ་ནི། འཇིག་རྟེན་ལས་འདས་པའི་ལྷག་མཐོང་གཉིས་བྲལ་ལོ། །ངེས་ཚིག་ནི། ཡོན་ཏན་ཐམས་ཅད་ཀྱི་རྟེན་ནམ་གོང་དུ་བགྲོད་པའི་གཞི་ཡིན་པས་ན་ས་ཞེས་བྱ་སྟེ། མདོ་སྡེ་རྒྱན་ལས། འབྱུང་པོ་དཔག་མེད་འཇིག་མེད་ཕྱིར། །དཔག་ཏུ་མེད་པ་དེ་དག་ལ། །ཕྱི་ཕྱིར་གོང་དུ་འགྲོ་ལྡན་ཕྱིར། །དེ་དག་ཉིད་ནི་སར་འདོད་དོ། །ཅེས་སོ། །དབྱེ་བ་ནི་རབ་ཏུ་དགའ་བ་ལ་སོགས་ས་བཅུའོ།

ས་བཅུ་སོ་སོའི་མཚན་ཉིད་ནི། གསེར་འོད་དམ་པ་ལས། དེ་ལ་རིགས་ཀྱི་བུ་

ཅིའི་ཕྱིར་ན། ས་དང་པོ་རབ་ཏུ་དགའ་བ་ཞེས་བྱ་ཞེ་ན། དེ་ནི་ཐོག་མར་འཇིག་རྟེན་
ལས་འདས་པའི་སེམས་སྐྱོན་མ་མཐོང་བ་དེ་མངོན་དུ་གྱུར་ཏེ། དོན་ཆེན་པོའི་བསམ་
པ་ཕུན་སུམ་ཚོགས་པ་ཐོབ་པའི་ཕྱིར། [རབ་ཏུ་དགའ་བ་ཆེན་པོ་སྐྱེ་བས་]ས་དང་པོ་
རབ་ཏུ་དགའ་བ་ཞེས་བྱའོ། །ལྷུང་བ་ཕྲ་མོའི་དྲི་མ་དང་། ཚུལ་ཁྲིམས་ཀྱི་ཉེས་སྐྱོན་
ཐམས་ཅད་རྣམ་པར་དག་པའི་ཕྱིར། ས་གཉིས་པ་དྲི་མ་མེད་པ་ཞེས་བྱའོ། །མཚན་མ་
མེད་པ་ཡིད་ལ་བྱེད་པ་མེད་པའི་ཚད་མེད་པའི་ཡེ་ཤེས་དང་། ཏིང་ངེ་འཛིན་གྱི་ཡེ་ཤེས་
ཀྱི་འོད་སྣང་བ་དེ་བསྐྱོད་པར་མི་ནུས་ཤིང་གང་གིས་ཀྱང་ཟིལ་གྱིས་མི་ནོན་པ་དང་།
ཐོས་པ་འཛིན་པའི་གཟུངས་ལ་གནས་པའི་ཕྱིར་ས་གསུམ་པ་འོད་བྱེད་པ་ཞེས་བྱའོ།
།ཡེ་ཤེས་ཀྱི་མེ་དེས་ཉོན་མོངས་པ་ཐམས་ཅད་བསྲེག་ཅིང་། བྱང་ཆུབ་ཀྱི་ཕྱོགས་ཀྱི་
ཆོས་བསྒོམས་པའི་མེའི་འོད་འཕྲོ་བ་[ཆེན་གྱུར་པས་]ཕྱིར་འབྱུང་བས་ན། ས་བཞི་པ་
འོད་འཕྲོ་བ་ཞེས་བྱའོ། །དེ་བསྒོམས་པའི་ཐབས་དང་། མཆོག་གི་ཡེ་ཤེས་ལ་དབང་
བསྒྱུར་དཀའ་བ་དང་། མཐོང་སྤྲང་དང་། བསྒོམ་སྤྲང་གི་ཉོན་མོངས་པ་ཐུལ་བར་
དཀའ་བ་ཐུལ་བའི་ཕྱིར་ས་ལྔ་པ་སྦྱང་དཀའ་བ་ཞེས་བྱའོ། །འདུ་བྱེད་ཀྱིས་ཆོས་
ཐམསས་ཅད་བར་ཆད་མེད་པར་མངོན་དུ་གྱུར་ཏེ། མཚན་མ་མེད་པ་ཡིད་ལ་བྱེད་པ་
ཐམས་ཅད་མངོན་དུ་བྱེད་པས། །ས་དྲུག་པ་མངོན་དུ་གྱུར་པ་ཞེས་བྱའོ། །ཟག་པ་མེད་
པའི་ཆོས་རྣམས་ལ་བར་ཆད་མེད་ཅིང་མཚན་མ་མེད་པ་ཡིད་ལ་བྱེད་པས་རྣམ་པར་
གྲོལ་བའི་ཏིང་ངེ་འཛིན་ཡུན་རིང་དུ་བསྒོམས་པས་དེ་རྣམ་པར་དག་ཅིང་ཐོགས་པ་མེད་
པ་དང་། ཉན་ཐོས་དང་རང་རྒྱལ་ལས་རིང་དུ་སོང་བའི་ཕྱིར། ས་བདུན་པ་རིང་དུ་
སོང་བ་ཞེས་བྱའོ། །མཚན་མ་མེད་པ་ཡིད་ལ་བྱེད་པ་བསྒོམ་པ་ལ་དབང་ཐོབ་སྟེ།
ཉོན་མོངས་པ་རྣམས་ཀྱིས་གཡོ་བར་མི་ནུས་པས་ན་ས་བརྒྱད་པ་མི་གཡོ་བ་ཞེས་
བྱའོ། །རྣམ་པ་ཐམས་ཅད་ལ་ཆོས་སྟོན་པ་ལ་དབང་དུ་གྱུར་པ་དང་། ཁ་ན་མ་ཐོ་བ་
མེད་ཅིང་བློ་གྲོས་ཤིན་ཏུ་ཡངས་པ་ཐོགས་པ་མེད་པ་ཐོབ་པའི་ཕྱིར། ས་དགུ་པ་
ལེགས་པའི་བློ་གྲོས་ཞེས་བྱའོ། །ཆོས་ཀྱི་སྐུ་ནམ་མཁའ་ལྟ་བུ་ལ་ཡེ་ཤེས་ཆེན་པོ་སྤྲིན་

ལྷ་བུས་ཁྱབ་པར་འགྲེམས་པའི་ཕྱིར་ས་བཅུ་པ་ཆོས་ཀྱི་སྤྲིན་ཞེས་བྱའོ། །ཞེས་གསུངས་སོ། །

ས་བཅུ་པའི་སྔ་ལྟས་ནི། བསམ་གྱིས་མི་ཁྱབ་པ་བསྟན་པའི་མདོ་ལས། རིགས་ཀྱི་བུ་དེ་ལ་བྱང་ཆུབ་སེམས་དཔའ་སེམས་དཔའ་ཆེན་པོའི། བྱང་ཆུབ་སེམས་དཔའ་ས་དང་པོའི་སྔ་ལྟས་ནི། སྟོང་གསུམ་གྱི་སྟོང་ཆེན་པོའི་འཇིག་རྟེན་གྱི་ཁམས་གཏེར་བྱེ་བ་ཁྲག་ཁྲིག་བརྒྱ་སྟོང་གིས་ཡོངས་སུ་གང་བ་མཐོང་། རིགས་ཀྱི་བུ་དེ་ལ་བྱང་ཆུབ་སེམས་དཔའ་སེམས་དཔའ་ཆེན་པོའོ། །བྱང་ཆུབ་སེམས་དཔའི་ས་གཉིས་པའི་སྔ་ལྟས་ནི། སྟོང་གསུམ་གྱི་སྟོང་ཆེན་པོའི་འཇིག་རྟེན་གྱི་ཁམས་ལག་མཐིལ་ལྟ་བུར་གྱུར་པ་ལ། རིན་པོ་ཆེ་བྱེ་བ་ཁྲག་ཁྲིག་བརྒྱ་སྟོང་དུ་མས་རབ་ཏུ་བརྒྱན་པར་མཐོང་ངོ་། །རིགས་ཀྱི་བུ་ཞེས་འོག་མ་རྣམས་ལའང་སྦྱར་རོ། །ས་གསུམ་པའི་སྔ་ལྟས་ནི། བདག་ཉིད་དཔའ་ཞིང་ལག་ཆ་དང་གོ་ཆ་སྲ་བ་ཐོགས་ནས་ཕས་ཀྱི་རྒོལ་བ་ཐམས་ཅད་འདུལ་བར་མཐོང་ངོ་། །ས་བཞི་པའི་སྔ་ལྟས་ནི། ཕྱོགས་བཞི་ན་རླུང་གི་དཀྱིལ་འཁོར་[བཞིས]ཐམས་ཅད་དང་ལྡན་པའི་སའི་དཀྱིལ་འཁོར་ཆེན་པོ་ལ། མེ་ཏོག་སྣ་ཚོགས་ཀྱིས་མཛེས་པར་མཐོར་བ་མཐོང་། །ས་ལྔ་པའི་སྔ་ལྟས་ནི། རྒྱན་ཐམས་ཅད་ཀྱིས་བརྒྱན་པའི་བུད་མེད་ཀྱིས་དབུ་ལ་མེ་ཏོག་ཙམ་པ་ཀའི་ཕྲེང་བ་འདོགས་པར་མཐོང་ངོ་། །ས་དྲུག་པའི་སྔ་ལྟས་ནི། རྫིང་ཐེམ་སྐས་བཞི་དང་ལྡན་པ་གསེར་གྱི་བྱེ་མ་བརྡལ་བ་རྙོག་པ་མེད་ཅིང་དང་བ་ལ་ཡན་ལག་བརྒྱད་དང་ལྡན་པའི་ཆུས་ཡོངས་སུ་གང་བ། མེ་ཏོག་ཨུད་པ་ལ་དང་། ཀུ་མུ་ད་དང་། པདྨ་དཀར་པོས་བརྒྱན་པའི་ཆུར་མཐོང་སྟེ། དེ་ལ་བདག་ཉིད་རྩེ་དགའ་ཞིང་ལོངས་སུ་སྤྱོད་པར་མཐོང་ངོ་། །ས་བདུན་པའི་སྔ་ལྟས་ནི། ཕྱོགས་གཡས་གཡོན་གཉིས་ན་སེམས་ཅན་དམྱལ་བའི་གཡང་ས་མཐོང་སྟེ། དེ་ནས་བདག་ཉིད་མ་གནོད་མ་ཉམས་པར་སླར་ལྡོག་པར་མཐོང་ངོ་། །ས་བརྒྱད་པའི་སྔ་ལྟས་ནི། ཕྲག་པ་གཉིས་ན་རི་དྭགས་ཀྱི་རྒྱལ་པོ་སེང་གེ་རལ་པ་ཅན་ཅོད་པན་ཐོགས་པ་གཙན་ཟན་ཕྲ་མོ་ཐམས་ཅད་སྐྲག་པར་བྱེད་ཅིང་འདུག་པར་

མཐོང་ངོ་། །ས་དགུ་པའི་སྨོན་ལམ་ནི། འཁོར་ལོས་བསྒྱུར་བའི་རྒྱལ་པོར་མཐོང་སྟེ། སྐྱེ་བོ་ཁྲག་ཁྲིག་བརྒྱ་སྟོང་ཕྲག་དུ་མས་ཡོངས་སུ་བསྐོར་ཞིང་། མདུན་གྱིས་བལྟས་ལ། མགོ་བོའི་སྟེང་ན་རིན་པོ་ཆེ་སྣ་ཚོགས་ཀྱིས་སྤྲས་པའི་གདུགས་དཀར་པོ་འཛིན་པར་མཐོང་། །ས་བཅུ་པའི་སྨོན་ལམ་ནི། དེ་བཞིན་གཤེགས་པའི་སྐུ་མཐོང་སྟེ། ཁ་དོག་གསེར་ལྟ་བུའི་ འོད་འདོམ་གང་བ། ཚངས་པ་བྱེ་བ་ཁྲག་ཁྲིག་བརྒྱ་སྟོང་ཕྲག་དུ་མས་ཡོངས་སུ་བསྐོར་ཞིང་མདུན་གྱིས་ལྟས་ན་ཆོས་སྟོན་པ་མཐོང་སྟེ། བཅུ་པོ་དེ་དག་ནི་བྱང་ཆུབ་སེམས་དཔའ་སེམས་དཔའ་ཆེན་པོ་རྣམས་ཀྱི་བྱང་ཆུབ་སེམས་དཔའི་ས་བཅུའི་སྨོན་ལམ་ཡིན་ནོ་ཞེས་གསུངས་སོ། གསེར་འོད་དམ་པ་ལས་ཀྱང་དེ་ལྟར་རོ། །

ས་གང་གིས་ཕ་རོལ་ཏུ་ཕྱིན་པ་གང་ནོན་པ་ནི། རིགས་ཀྱི་བུ། དེ་ལ་ས་དང་པོའི་བྱང་ཆུབ་སེམས་དཔའ་ནི་སྦྱིན་པའི་ཕ་རོལ་ཏུ་ཕྱིན་པ་གནོན་ཏོ། །དེ་བཞིན་དུ་ས་གཉིས་པས་ཚུལ་ཁྲིམས་སོ། །ས་གསུམ་པས་བཟོད་པ། ས་བཞི་པས་བརྩོན་འགྲུས། ས་ལྔ་པས་བསམ་གཏན། ས་དྲུག་པས་ཤེས་རབ། ས་བདུན་པས་ཐབས་ལ་མཁས་པའི། ས་བརྒྱད་པས་སྨོན་ལམ། ས་དགུ་པས་སྟོབས། རིགས་ཀྱི་བུ་དེ་ལ་བྱང་ཆུབ་སེམས་དཔའ་ས་བཅུ་པ་ལ་གནས་པའི་བྱང་ཆུབ་སེམས་དཔའ་ནི། ཡེ་ཤེས་ཀྱི་ཕ་རོལ་ཏུ་ཕྱིན་པ་གནོན་ཏོ། །

ཕ་རོལ་ཏུ་ཕྱིན་པ་བཅུའི་མཚན་ཉིད་ནི། ཕལ་ཆེན་ལས། དེ་ལ་སངས་རྒྱས་ཀྱི་ཡེ་ཤེས་ཚོལ་ཞིང་། སེམས་ཅན་རྣམས་ལ་དགེ་བའི་རྩ་བ་ཐམས་ཅད་ཡོངས་སུ་གཏོང་བ་ནི་སྦྱིན་པའི་ཕ་རོལ་ཏུ་ཕྱིན་པའོ། །ཉོན་མོངས་པའི་གདུང་བ་ཐམས་ཅད་རབ་ཏུ་ཞི་བ་ནི་ཚུལ་ཁྲིམས་སོ། །བྱམས་པ་དང་སྙིང་རྗེ་སྔོན་དུ་འགྲོ་བས་སེམས་ཅན་ལ་འཚིག་པ་མེད་པ་ནི་བཟོད་པའོ། །གོང་ནས་གོང་དུ་དགེ་བའི་ཆོས་ཚོལ་བས་མི་ངོམས་པར་[དམ་འཆའ་བ་]འདི་ནི་བརྩོན་འགྲུས་སོ། །ཐམས་ཅད་མཁྱེན་པའི་ཡེ་ཤེས་མངོན་དུ་བྱ་བ་ལ་འགྱོད་པ་མེད་པའི་ལམ་དང་ལྡན་པ་འདི་ནི་ བསམ་གཏན་ནོ། །རང་བཞིན་གྱིས་མ་སྐྱེས་པ་མངོན་དུ་གྱུར་པ་འདི་ནི་ཤེས་རབ་བོ། །རྒྱལ་བའི་ཡེ་

ཤེས་ཚད་མེད་པ་བསྒྲུབ་པ་འདི་ནི་ཐབས་སོ། །ཡེ་ཤེས་དེ་ལ་དམིགས་ཤིང་དེ་ཉིད་མངོན་པར་བསྒྲུབ་པ་འདི་ནི་སྨོན་ལམ་མོ། །ཕས་ཀྱི་རྒོལ་བ་ཐམས་ཅད་དང་བདུད་ཀྱི་ཚོགས་ཐམས་ཅད་ཀྱིས་ལམ་རྒྱུད་ཡོངས་སུ་མི་གཅོད་པ་འདི་ནི་སྟོབས་སོ། །ཆོས་ཐམས་ཅད་[ལ་ཡང་དག་པ་]ཇི་ལྟ་བ་བཞིན་དུ་རྟོགས་པ་འདི་ནི་ཡེ་ཤེས་ཀྱི་ཕ་རོལ་ཏུ་ཕྱིན་པ་དང་བཅུའོ། །

ཏིང་ངེ་འཛིན་གོང་བཞིན་དུ་ས་དང་པོའི་བྱང་ཆུབ་ཀྱི་སེམས་ཡན་ལག་བདུན་དང་། ས་གཉིས་པ་ནས་ས་བཅུ་པའི་བར་གྱི་འཕགས་པའི་ལམ་བརྒྱད་དོ། །སྤང་བྱ་ནི་མཐོང་སྤང་དང་བསྒོམ་སྤང་ངོ་། །

སྦྱོངས་པ་ཉི་ཤུའི་སྦྲིབ་པ་ནི། དེ་ལ་རིགས་ཀྱི་བུ་ཆོས་དང་གང་ཟག་ལ་མཚན་མ་ཅན་དུ་ཞེན་པའི་སྦྱོངས་པ་དང་། འཁོར་བ་དང་ངན་སོང་གི་ཉོན་མོངས་པས་འཇིགས་པའི་སྦྱོངས་པ་དང་། སྦྱོངས་པ་འདི་གཉིས་ཀྱི་ས་དང་པོ་ལ་སྦྲིབ་པའོ། །ལྷུང་བ་ཕྲ་མོའི་འཁྲུལ་པ་ལ་སྦྱོངས་པ་དང་། ལས་དང་སྤྱོད་པ་སྣ་ཚོགས་སྐྱེ་བ་ལ་སྦྱོངས་པ་དང་། སྦྱོངས་པ་འདི་གཉིས་ཀྱིས་ས་གཉིས་པ་ལ་སྦྲིབ་པོ། །མ་ཐོབ་པ་ཐོབ་པར་འདོད་པའི་སྦྱོངས་པ་དང་གཟུངས་དམ་པའི་མཆོག་ཐོབ་པ་ལ་སྦྱོངས་པ་དང་། སྦྱོངས་པ་འདི་གཉིས་ཀྱིས་ས་གསུམ་པ་ལ་སྦྲིབ་པོ། །མཉམ་པར་བཞག་པའི་དེའི་དགའ་བ་ལ་སྲེད་པའི་སྦྱོངས་པ་དང་ཆོས་རྣམ་པར་དག་པའི་སྲེད་པ་ལ་སྦྱོངས་པ་དང་། སྦྱོངས་པ་འདི་གཉིས་ཀྱིས་ས་བཞི་པ་ལ་སྦྲིབ་པོ། འཁོར་བ་ལ་ཤིན་ཏུ་སྐྱོ་བའི་སྦྱོངས་པ་དང་། མྱ་ངན་ལས་འདས་པ་ལ་མངོན་པར་གཞོལ་བ་ལ་སྦྱོངས་པ་དང་། སྦྱོངས་པ་འདི་གཉིས་ཀྱིས་ས་ལྔ་པ་ལ་སྦྲིབ་པོ། །འདུ་བྱེད་ཀྱི་རྒྱུ་བ་མངན་དུ་གྱུར་པའི་སྦྱོངས་པ་དང་། མཚན་མ་སྦྲོམ་པོའི་མངོན་དུ་གྱུར་པའི་སྦྱོངས་པ་དང་། སྦྱོངས་པ་འདི་གཉིས་ཀྱིས་ས་དྲུག་པ་ལ་སྦྲིབ་པོ། །མཚན་མ་ཕྲ་མོ་མངོན་དུ་གྱུར་པའི་སྦྱོངས་པ་དང་། མཚན་མ་མེད་པ་ཡིད་ལ་བྱེད་པ་མེད་པའི་སྦྱོངས་པ་དང་། སྦྱོངས་པ་འདི་གཉིས་ཀྱིས་ས་བདུན་པ་ལ་སྦྲིབ་པོ། །མཚན་མ་མེད་པ་ལ་ཆེད་དུ་རྩོལ་བའི་སྦྱོངས་པ་དང་། མཚན་མར་

འཛིན་པ་ལ་དབང་ཐོབ་པའི་རྨོངས་པ་དང་། རྨོངས་པ་འདི་གཉིས་ཀྱིས་ས་བརྒྱད་པ་ལ་སྒྲིབ་པོ། །གང་ཆོས་སྟོན་པ་ལ་ཚད་མེད་པ་དང་། ཚིག་དང་ཡི་གེ་ཚད་མེད་པ་ལ་མཁས་པར་མ་གྱུར་པའི་རྨོངས་པ་དང་། སྤོབས་པ་ལ་དབང་མ་ཐོབ་པའི་རྨོངས་པ་དང་། རྨོངས་པ་འདི་གཉིས་ཀྱིས་ས་དགུ་པ་ལ་སྒྲིབ་པོ། །མངོན་པར་ཤེས་པ་ཆེན་པོ་ལ་དབང་བསྒྱུར་བ་མ་ཐོབ་པའི་རྨོངས་པ་དང་། དོན་དམ་ལ་སོགས་པའི་ཕྲ་མོ་ལ་མཁས་པར་མ་གྱུར་པའི་རྨོངས་པ་དང་། རྨོངས་པ་འདི་གཉིས་ཀྱིས་ས་བཅུ་པ་ལ་སྒྲིབ་པོ། །སྤྱོད་ཡུལ་ཤིན་ཏུ་ཕྲ་བ་ཐམས་ཅད་ལ་ཤེས་བྱའི་སྒྲིབ་པའི་རྨོངས་པ་དང་། ཉོན་མོངས་པ་ཤིན་ཏུ་ཕྲ་བའི་གནས་ངན་ལེན་ལ་རྨོངས་པ་དང་། རྨོངས་པ་འདི་གཉིས་ཀྱིས་སངས་རྒྱས་ཀྱི་ས་ལ་སྒྲིབ་པོ། །

སྒྲིབ་པ་དང་བྲལ་བའི་རྟོགས་པ་ས་གང་གིས་གང་རྟོགས་པ་ནི། ཕྲེང་རབ་སྣང་གི་མདོ་ལས། རིགས་ཀྱི་བུ་གང་དེ་ལ་ས་དང་པོ་ནི། ཆོས་ཀྱི་དབྱིངས་ཀྱིས་ཀུན་ཏུ་ཁྱབ་པའི་དོན་དུ་རྟོགས་སོ། །ས་གཉིས་པ་ཆོས་ཀྱི་དབྱིངས་དྲི་མ་དང་བྲལ་བ་མཆོག་གི་དོན་དུ་རྟོགས་སོ། །ས་གསུམ་པ་ཆོས་ཀྱི་དབྱིངས་སུ་མཐུན་པ་རང་བཞིན་འོད་གསལ་བར་རྟོགས་སོ། །ས་བཞི་པ་ཆོས་ཐམས་ཅད་ཡོངས་སུ་འཛིན་པ་མེད་པའི་དོན་དུ་རྟོགས་སོ། །ས་ལྔ་པ་ཆོས་ཐམས་ཅད་ཆོས་ཀྱི་དབྱིངས་སུ་གཅིག་པས་རྒྱུད་ཐ་དད་མེད་པའི་དོན་དུ་རྟོགས་སོ། །ས་དྲུག་པ་ཉོན་མོངས་པ་དང་རྣམ་པར་རྟོགས་པ་ཐམས་ཅད་མ་གྲུབ་པའི་དོན་དུ་རྟོགས་སོ། །ས་བདུན་པ་འཁོར་བ་ལ་མི་སྐྱེ་བ་དང་། ཆོས་ཐམས་ཅད་མཚན་མ་མེད་པའི་དོན་དུ་རྟོགས་སོ། །ས་བརྒྱད་པ་ཞིང་དག་པ་དང་། རྟོག་པའི་ཚོགས་དང་བྲལ་བའི་དོན་དུ་རྟོགས་སོ། །ས་དགུ་པ་ཆོས་དང་ཡི་གེ་ཚད་མེད་པ་དང་སྤོབས་པ་ཐོགས་པ་མེད་པའི་དོན་དུ་རྟོགས་སོ། །ས་བཅུ་པ་འཕྲིན་ལས་དབང་བསྒྱུར་བའི་དོན་དུ་རྟོགས་སོ། །ས་བཅུ་གཅིག་པས་ནི་ཀུན་གཞི་གནས་འགྱུར་བའི་ཆོས་ཀྱི་སྐུ་དང་། སྒོ་ལྔའི་རྣམ་ཤེས་གནས་འགྱུར་བའི་ལོངས་སྐུ་དང་། ཉོན་མོངས་པའི་རྟོག་པ་སྣ་ཚོགས་ཀྱིས་ཡིད་གནས་འགྱུར་བའི་སྤྲུལ་སྐུ་དང་། དབྱེར་མེད་

ཅིང་མཐའ་ཐམས་ཅད་དང་བྲལ་བ་མཆོག་ཏུ་གྱུར་པ་དང་། གོང་ན་མེད་པ་ཡང་དག་པའི་དོན་དུ་རྟོགས་སོ། །

ཁྱེའུ་རབ་སྣང་གི་མདོ་ལས། ཁྱེའུ་རབ་སྣང་གིས་གསོལ་པ། བཅོམ་ལྡན་འདས་ས་ལ་གནས་པའི་བྱང་ཆུབ་སེམས་དཔའ་རྣམས་ཀྱི་རྟགས་ཇི་ལྟར་བལྟ་བར་བགྱི། བཅོམ་ལྡན་འདས་ཀྱིས་བཀའ་སྩལ་པ། རིགས་ཀྱི་བུ། དེ་ལ་བྱང་ཆུབ་སེམས་དཔའི་ས་དང་པོ་ལ་གནས་པའི་རྟགས་ནི། འདོད་ན་སྐད་ཅིག་ཡུད་ཙམ་ཐང་ཅིག་ལ་ཏིང་ངེ་འཛིན་བརྒྱ་རབ་ཏུ་ཐོབ་ཅིང་སྙོམས་པར་འཇུག་པ་དང་། སངས་རྒྱས་བརྒྱ་མཐོང་བ་དང་། དེ་དག་གིས་བྱིན་གྱིས་བརླབས་ཡང་དག་པར་ཤེས་པ་དང་། འཇིག་རྟེན་གྱི་ཁམས་བརྒྱར་བསྒྲོད་པ་དང་། སངས་རྒྱས་ཀྱི་ཞིང་བརྒྱར་འགྲོ་བ་དང་། འཇིག་རྟེན་གྱི་ཁམས་བརྒྱ་ཡང་དག་པར་སྣང་བར་བྱེད་པ་དང་། སེམས་ཅན་བརྒྱ་ཡོངས་སུ་སྨིན་པར་བྱ་བ་དང་། བསྐལ་པ་བརྒྱར་གནས་པར་བྱ་བ་དང་། སྔོན་གྱི་མཐའི་བསྐལ་པ་བརྒྱ་དང་། ཕྱི་མའི་མཐའི་བསྐལ་པ་བརྒྱ་ལ་འཇུག་པ་དང་། ཆོས་ཀྱི་སྒོ་བརྒྱ་རྣམ་པར་འབྱེད་པ་དང་། ལུས་བརྒྱ་ཡོངས་སུ་སྟོན་པ་དང་། ལུས་རེ་རེ་ལ་ཡང་བྱང་ཆུབ་སེམས་དཔའ་འཁོར་བརྒྱ་བརྒྱ་ཡང་དག་པར་སྟོན་པའི་བརྩོན་འགྲུས་རྩོམ་ཞིང་ཡོན་ཏན་དེ་ཉིད་དང་ལྡན་པའོ། །ས་ཐོབ་འཇིག་པ་ལྔ་དང་བྲལ། །འཆི་མེད་འཆི་དང་མི་བསྡུགས་དང་། །ངན་འགྲོ་འཁོར་གྱི་འཇིགས་བྲལ་བ། །ཅི་ཕྱིར་རང་བཞིན་ཤེས་ཕྱིར་རོ། །ས་ཐོབ་གྱུར་མ་ཐག་ཏུ་ནི། །དགའ་ལ་དུ་བྲོའི་ཤེས་པ་དང་། །ཆོས་ཕྱིར་སྲོག་ནི་འདོར་ནུས་པ། །བློ་ལྡན་དེ་ལ་སྐྱེ་བར་འགྱུར། །

རིགས་ཀྱི་བུ་ས་གཉིས་པ་ལ་གནས་པ་ནི། སྐད་ཅིག་ཡུད་ཙམ་ཐང་ཅིག་ལ་ཏིང་ངེ་འཛིན་སྟོང་ཐོབ་ཅིང་སྙོམས་པར་འཇུག་པ་དང་། སངས་རྒྱས་སྟོང་མཐོང་བ་དང་། དེ་དག་གི་བྱིན་བརླབས་ཡང་དག་པར་རབ་ཏུ་ཤེས་པ་དང་། འཇིག་རྟེན་གྱི་ཁམས་སྟོང་བསྒྲོད་པ་དང་། སངས་རྒྱས་ཀྱི་ཞིང་སྟོང་དུ་འགྲོ་བ་དང་། འཇིག་རྟེན་གྱི་ཁམས་སྟོང་དུ་སྣང་བར་བྱ་བ་དང་། སེམས་ཅན་སྟོང་ཡོངས་སུ་སྨིན་པར་བྱ་བ་དང་།

བསྐལ་པ་སྟོང་དུ་གནས་པར་བྱ་བ་དང་། སྔོན་གྱི་མཐའི་བསྐལ་པ་སྟོང་དང་། ཕྱི་མའི་མཐའི་བསྐལ་པ་སྟོང་ལ་འཇུག་པ་དང་། ཆོས་ཀྱི་སྒོ་སྟོང་འབྱེད་པ་དང་། ལུས་སྟོང་ཡོངས་སུ་སྟོན་པ་དང་། ལུས་རེ་རེ་ལ་ཡང་བྱང་ཆུབ་སེམས་དཔའི་འཁོར་སྟོང་སྟོང་རབ་ཏུ་སྟོན་ཏོ། །

རིགས་ཀྱི་བུ་ས་གསུམ་པ་ལ་གནས་པ་ནི་སྐད་ཅིག་ཡུད་ཙམ་ཐང་ཅིག་ལ་ཏིང་ངེ་འཛིན་བརྒྱ་སྟོང་རབ་ཏུ་ཐོབ་བོ། །སངས་རྒྱས་བརྒྱ་སྟོང་མཐོང་བ་དང་། དེ་དག་གི་བྱིན་བརླབས་ཡང་དག་པར་ཤེས་པ་དང་། འཇིག་རྟེན་གྱི་ཁམས་བརྒྱ་སྟོང་རབ་ཏུ་བསྒྱོད་པ་དང་། སངས་རྒྱས་ཀྱི་ཞིང་བརྒྱ་སྟོང་དུ་འགྲོ་བ་དང་། འཇིགས་རྟེན་གྱི་ཁམས་བརྒྱ་སྟོང་སྣང་བར་བྱ་བ་དང་། སེམས་ཅན་བརྒྱ་སྟོང་ཡོངས་སུ་སྨིན་པར་བྱ་བ་དང་། བསྐལ་པ་བརྒྱ་སྟོང་དུ་གནས་པར་བྱ་བ་དང་། སྔོན་གྱི་མཐའི་བསྐལ་པ་བརྒྱ་སྟོང་དང་། ཕྱི་མའི་མཐའི་བསྐལ་པ་བརྒྱ་སྟོང་ལ་སྙོམས་པར་འཇུག་པ་དང་། ཆོས་ཀྱི་སྒོ་བརྒྱ་སྟོང་འབྱེད་པ་དང་། ལུས་བརྒྱ་སྟོང་ཡོངས་སུ་སྟོན་པ་དང་། ལུས་རེ་རེ་ལ་ཡང་བྱང་ཆུབ་སེམས་དཔའི་འཁོར་བརྒྱ་སྟོང་བརྒྱ་ཡང་དག་པར་རབ་ཏུ་སྟོན་ཏོ། །

རིགས་ཀྱི་བུ་ས་བཞི་པ་ལ་གནས་པས་སྐད་ཅིག་ཡུད་ཙམ་ཐང་ཅིག་ལ་ཏིང་ངེ་འཛིན་ཁྲག་ཁྲིག་ཐོབ་ཅིང་སྙོམས་པར་འཇུག་པ་དང་། སངས་རྒྱས་ཁྲག་ཁྲིག་མཐོང་བ་དང་། དེ་དག་གི་བྱིན་བརླབས་ཡང་དག་པར་རབ་ཏུ་ཤེས་པ་དང་། འཇིག་རྟེན་གྱི་ཁམས་ཁྲག་ཁྲིག་བསྒྱོད་པ་དང་། སངས་རྒྱས་ཀྱི་ཞིང་ཁྲག་ཁྲིག་ཏུ་འགྲོ་བ་དང་། འཇིག་རྟེན་གྱི་ཁམས་ཁྲག་ཁྲིག་སྣང་བར་བྱ་བ་དང་། སེམས་ཅན་ཁྲག་ཁྲིག་ཡོངས་སུ་སྨིན་པར་བྱ་བ་དང་། བསྐལ་པ་ཁྲག་ཁྲིག་ཏུ་གནས་པར་བྱ་བ་དང་། སྔོན་གྱི་མཐའི་བསྐལ་པ་ཁྲག་ཁྲིག་ཏུ་གནས་པ་དང་། ཕྱི་མའི་མཐའི་བསྐལ་པ་ཁྲག་ཁྲིག་ལ་འཇུག་པ་དང་། ཆོས་ཀྱི་སྒོ་ཁྲག་ཁྲིག་འབྱེད་པ་དང་། ལུས་ཁྲག་ཁྲིག་ཡོངས་སུ་སྟོན་པ་དང་། ལུས་རེ་རེ་ལ་ཡང་བྱང་ཆུབ་སེམས་དཔའི་འཁོར་ཁྲག་ཁྲིག་ཡང་དག་པར་རབ་ཏུ་སྟོན་ཏོ། །

རིགས་ཀྱི་བུ་ས་ལྔ་པ་གནས་པས་སྐད་ཅིག་ཐང་ཅིག་ཡུད་ཙམ་ལ་ཏིང་ངེ་འཛིན་ཁྲག་ཁྲིག་སྟོང་ཐོབ་ཅིང་། དེ་དག་ལ་སྙོམས་པར་འཇུག་པ་དང་། སངས་རྒྱས་ཁྲག་ཁྲིག་སྟོང་མཐོང་བ་དང་། དེ་དག་གི་བྱིན་བརླབས་ཡང་དག་པར་རབ་ཏུ་ཤེས་པ་དང་། འཇིག་རྟེན་གྱི་ཁམས་ཁྲག་ཁྲིག་སྟོང་བསྒྱོད་པ་དང་། སངས་རྒྱས་ཀྱི་ཞིང་ཁམས་ཁྲག་ཁྲིག་སྟོང་དུ་འགྲོ་བ་དང་། འཇིག་རྟེན་གྱི་ཁམས་ཁྲག་ཁྲིག་སྟོང་སྣང་བར་བྱེད་པ་དང་། སེམས་ཅན་ཁྲག་ཁྲིག་སྟོང་ཡོངས་སུ་སྨིན་པར་བྱེད་པ་དང་། བསྐལ་པ་ཁྲག་ཁྲིག་སྟོང་དུ་གནས་པར་བྱ་བ་དང་། སྔོན་གྱི་མཐའི་བསྐལ་པ་ཁྲག་ཁྲིག་སྟོང་དང་། ཕྱི་མའི་མཐའི་བསྐལ་པ་ཁྲག་ཁྲིག་སྟོང་དུ་འཇུག་པ་དང་། ཆོས་ཀྱི་སྒོ་ཁྲག་ཁྲིག་སྟོང་འབྱེད་པ་དང་། ལུས་ཁྲག་ཁྲིག་སྟོང་ཡོངས་སུ་སྟོན་པ་དང་། ལུས་རེ་རེ་ལ་ཡང་བྱང་ཆུབ་སེམས་དཔའི་འཁོར་ཁྲག་ཁྲིག་སྟོང་ཡང་དག་པར་རབ་ཏུ་སྟོན་ཏོ། །

རིགས་ཀྱི་བུ་ས་དྲུག་པ་ལ་གནས་པས། འདོད་ན་སྐད་ཅིག་ཡུད་ཙམ་ཐང་ཅིག་ལ་ཏིང་ངེ་འཛིན་ཁྲག་ཁྲིག་བརྒྱ་སྟོང་ཐོབ་ཅིང་། དེ་དག་ལ་སྙོམས་པར་འཇུག་པ་དང་། སངས་རྒྱས་ཁྲག་ཁྲིག་བརྒྱ་སྟོང་མཐོང་བ་དང་། དེ་དག་གི་བྱིན་བརླབས་ཡང་དག་པར་རབ་ཏུ་ཤེས་པ་དང་། འཇིག་རྟེན་གྱི་ཁམས་ཁྲག་ཁྲིག་བརྒྱ་སྟོང་བསྒྱོད་པ་དང་། སངས་རྒྱས་ཀྱི་ཞིང་ཁྲག་ཁྲིག་བརྒྱ་སྟོང་དུ་འགྲོ་བ་དང་། འཇིག་རྟེན་གྱི་ཁམས་ཁྲག་ཁྲིག་བརྒྱ་སྟོང་སྣང་བར་བྱ་བ་དང་། སེམས་ཅན་ཁྲག་ཁྲིག་བརྒྱ་སྟོང་ཡོངས་སུ་སྨིན་པར་བྱ་བ་དང་། བསྐལ་པ་ཁྲག་ཁྲིག་བརྒྱ་སྟོང་གནས་པར་བྱ་བ་དང་། སྔོན་གྱི་མཐའི་བསྐལ་པ་ཁྲག་ཁྲིག་བརྒྱ་སྟོང་དང་། ཕྱི་མའི་མཐའ་བསྐལ་པ་ཁྲག་ཁྲིག་བརྒྱ་སྟོང་དུ་འཇུག་པ་དང་། ཆོས་ཀྱི་སྒོ་ཁྲག་ཁྲིག་བརྒྱ་སྟོང་འབྱེད་པ་དང་། ལུས་ཁྲག་ཁྲིག་བརྒྱ་སྟོང་ཡོངས་སུ་སྟོན་པ་དང་། ལུས་རེ་རེ་ལ་ཡང་བྱང་ཆུབ་སེམས་དཔའི་འཁོར་ཁྲག་ཁྲིག་བརྒྱ་སྟོང་ཡང་དག་པར་སྟོན་ཏོ། །

རིགས་ཀྱི་བུ་ས་བདུན་པ་ལ་གནས་པས། འདོད་ན་སྐད་ཅིག་ཡུད་ཙམ་ཐང་ཅིག་ལ་ཏིང་ངེ་འཛིན་བྱེ་བ་ཁྲག་ཁྲིག་བརྒྱ་སྟོང་ཐོབ་ཅིང་། དེ་དག་ལ་སྙོམས་པར་

འཇུག་པ་དང་། སངས་རྒྱས་བྱེ་བ་ཁྲག་ཁྲིག་བརྒྱ་སྟོང་མཐོང་བ་དང་། དེ་དག་གིས་བྱིན་གྱིས་བརླབས་པ་ཡང་དག་པར་རབ་ཏུ་ཤེས་པ་དང་། འཇིག་རྟེན་གྱི་ཁམས་བྱེ་བ་ཁྲག་ཁྲིག་བརྒྱ་སྟོང་བསྐྱོད་པ་དང་། སངས་རྒྱས་ཀྱི་ཞིང་ཁམས་བྱེ་བ་ཁྲག་ཁྲིག་བརྒྱ་སྟོང་དུ་འགྲོ་བ་དང་། འཇིག་རྟེན་གྱི་ཁམས་བྱེ་བ་ཁྲག་ཁྲིག་བརྒྱ་སྟོང་སྣང་བར་བྱ་བ་དང་། སེམས་ཅན་བྱེ་བ་ཁྲག་ཁྲིག་བརྒྱ་སྟོང་ཡོངས་སུ་སྨིན་པར་བྱ་བ་དང་། བསྐལ་པ་བྱེ་བ་ཁྲག་ཁྲིག་བརྒྱ་སྟོང་དུ་གནས་པར་བྱ་བ་དང་། སྔོན་གྱི་མཐའི་བསྐལ་པ་བྱེ་བ་ཁྲག་ཁྲིག་བརྒྱ་སྟོང་དང་། ཕྱི་མའི་མཐའི་བསྐལ་པ་བྱེ་བ་ཁྲག་ཁྲིག་བརྒྱ་སྟོང་དུ་འཇུག་པ་དང་། ཆོས་ཀྱི་སྒོ་བྱེ་བ་ཁྲག་ཁྲིག་བརྒྱ་སྟོང་འབྱེད་པ་དང་། ལུས་བྱེ་བ་ཁྲག་ཁྲིག་བརྒྱ་སྟོང་ཡོངས་སུ་སྟོན་པ་དང་། ལུས་རེ་རེ་ལ་ཡང་བྱང་ཆུབ་སེམས་དཔའི་འཁོར་བྱེ་བ་ཁྲག་ཁྲིག་བརྒྱ་སྟོང་ཡང་དག་པར་རབ་ཏུ་སྟོན་ཏོ། །

རིགས་ཀྱི་བུ་ས་བརྒྱད་པ་ལ་གནས་པས་འདོད་ན་སྐད་ཅིག་ཡུད་ཙམ་ཐང་ཅིག་ལ། ཏིང་ངེ་འཛིན་སུམ་སྟོང་སུམ་བརྒྱ་སྟོང་ཕྲག་བཅུའི་རྡུལ་ཕྲ་རབ་སྙེད་ཐོབ་ཅིང་། དེ་དག་ལ་སྙོམས་པར་འཇུག་པ་དང་། སངས་རྒྱས་སྟོང་སུམ་བརྒྱ་སྟོང་ཕྲག་བཅུའི་རྡུལ་ཕྲ་རབ་སྙེད་མཐོང་བ་དང་། དེ་དག་གི་བྱིན་གྱིས་བརླབས་ཡང་དག་པར་རབ་ཏུ་ཤེས་པ་དང་། འཇིག་རྟེན་གྱི་ཁམས་སྟོང་སུམ་བརྒྱ་སྟོང་ཕྲག་བཅུའི་རྡུལ་ཕྲ་རབ་སྙེད་དུ་བསྐྱོད་པ་དང་། སངས་རྒྱས་ཀྱི་ཞིང་ཁམས་སྟོང་སུམ་བརྒྱ་སྟོང་ཕྲག་བཅུའི་རྡུལ་ཕྲ་རབ་སྙེད་དུ་འགྲོ་བ་དང་། འཇིག་རྟེན་གྱི་ཁམས་སྟོང་སུམ་བརྒྱ་སྟོང་ཕྲག་བཅུའི་རྡུལ་ཕྲ་རབ་སྙེད་དུ་སྣང་བར་བྱ་བ་དང་། སེམས་ཅན་སྟོང་གསུམ་བརྒྱ་སྟོང་ཕྲག་བཅིུ་རྡུལ་ཕྲ་རབ་ཡོངས་སུ་སྨིན་པར་བྱ་བ་དང་། བསྐལ་པ་སྟོང་སུམ་བརྒྱ་སྟོང་ཕྲག་བཅུའི་རྡུལ་ཕྲ་རབ་སྙེད་དུ་གནས་པར་བྱ་བ་དང་། སྔོན་གྱི་མཐའི་བསྐལ་པ་སྟོང་སུམ་བརྒྱ་སྟོང་ཕྲག་བཅུའི་རྡུལ་ཕྲ་རབ་སྙེད་ལ་འཇུག་པ་དང་། ཕྱི་མའི་མཐའི་བསྐལ་པ་སྟོང་སུམ་བརྒྱ་སྟོང་ཕྲག་བཅུའི་རྡུལ་ཕྲ་རབ་སྙེད་ལ་འཇུག་པ་དང་། ཆོས་ཀྱི་སྒོ་སྟོང་སུམ་བརྒྱ་སྟོང་ཕྲག་བཅུའི་རྡུལ་ཕྲ་རབ་སྙེད་རྣམ་པར་འབྱེད་པ་དང་། ལུས་སྟོང་སུམ་བརྒྱ་སྟོང་

ཕྲག་བཅུའི་རྡུལ་ཕྲ་རབ་སྙེད་ཡོངས་སུ་སྟོན་པ་དང་། ལུས་རེ་རེ་ལ་ཡང་བྱང་ཆུབ་སེམས་དཔའི་འཁོར་སྟོང་སུམ་བརྒྱ་སྟོང་ཕྲག་བཅུའི་རྡུལ་ཕྲ་རབ་སྙེད་པ་ཡང་དག་པར་རབ་ཏུ་སྟོན་ཏོ། །

རིགས་ཀྱི་བུ་ས་དགུ་པ་ལ་གནས་པས། འདོད་ན་སྐད་ཅིག་ཡུད་ཙམ་ཐང་ཅིག་ལ། ཏིང་ངེ་འཛིན་སངས་རྒྱས་ཀྱི་ཞིང་ཁམས་གྲངས་མེད་པ་བརྒྱ་སྟོང་ཕྲག་བཅུ་ཚང་བའི་རྡུལ་ཕྲ་རབ་སྙེད་རབ་ཏུ་ཐོབ་ཅིང་། དེ་དག་ལ་སྙོམས་པར་འཇུག་པ་དང་། སངས་རྒྱས་གྲངས་མེད་པ་བརྒྱ་སྟོང་ཕྲག་བཅུ་ཚང་བའི་རྡུལ་ཕྲ་རབ་སྙེད་མཐོང་བ་དང་། དེ་དག་གི་བྱིན་གྱིས་བརླབས་ཡང་དག་པར་རབ་ཏུ་ཤེས་པ་དང་། འཇིག་རྟེན་གྱི་ཁམས་གྲངས་མེད་པ་བརྒྱ་སྟོང་ཕྲག་བཅུ་ཚང་བའི་རྡུལ་ཕྲ་རབ་སྙེད་དུ་བསྐྱོད་པ་དང་། སངས་རྒྱས་ཀྱི་ཞིང་ཁམས་གྲངས་མེད་པ་བརྒྱ་སྟོང་ཕྲག་བཅུ་ཚང་བའི་རྡུལ་ཕྲ་རབ་སྙེད་དུ་འགྲོ་བ་དང་འཇིག་རྟེན་གྱི་ཁམས་གྲངས་མེད་པ་བརྒྱ་སྟོང་ཕྲག་བཅུ་ཚང་བའི་རྡུལ་ཕྲ་རབ་སྙེད་དུ་འགྲོ་བར་བྱ་བ་དང་། སེམས་ཅན་གྲངས་མེད་པ་བརྒྱ་སྟོང་ཕྲག་བཅུ་ཚང་བའི་རྡུལ་ཕྲ་རབ་སྙེད་ཡོངས་སུ་སྨིན་པར་བྱ་བ་དང་། བསྐལ་པ་གྲངས་མེད་པ་བརྒྱ་སྟོང་ཕྲག་བཅུ་ཚང་བའི་རྡུལ་ཕྲ་རབ་སྙེད་དུ་འཇུག་པ་དང་། སྔོན་གྱི་མཐའི་བསྐལ་པ་གྲངས་མེད་པ་བརྒྱ་སྟོང་ཕྲག་བཅུ་ཚང་བའི་རྡུལ་ཕྲ་རབ་སྙེད་དང་། ཕྱི་མའི་མཐའི་བསྐལ་པ་གྲངས་མེད་པ་བརྒྱ་སྟོང་ཕྲག་བཅུ་ཚང་བའི་རྡུལ་ཕྲ་རབ་སྙེད་དུ་འཇུག་པ་དང་། ཆོས་ཀྱི་སྒོ་གྲངས་མེད་པ་བརྒྱ་སྟོང་ཕྲག་བཅུ་ཚང་བའི་རྡུལ་ཕྲ་རབ་སྙེད་རྣམ་པར་འབྱེད་པ་དང་། ལུས་གྲངས་མེད་པ་བརྒྱ་སྟོང་ཕྲག་བཅུ་ཚང་བའི་རྡུལ་ཕྲ་རབ་སྙེད་ཡང་དག་པར་སྟོན་པ་དང་། །ལུས་རེ་རེ་ལ་ཡང་བྱང་ཆུབ་སེམས་དཔའི་འཁོར་གྲངས་མེད་པ་བརྒྱ་སྟོང་ཕྲག་བཅུ་ཚང་བའི་རྡུལ་ཕྲ་རབ་སྙེད་ཡང་དག་པར་སྟོན་ཏོ།།

རིགས་ཀྱི་བུ་ས་བཅུ་པ་ལ་གནས་པས། དེ་བཞིན་གཤེགས་པ་གཅིག་ལས་ཀྱང་། སྐད་ཅིག་ཡུད་ཙམ་ཐང་ཅིག་ལ་ཆོས་ཀྱི་སྣང་བ་ཆེན་པོ་དང་། ཆོས་ཀྱི་འོད་ཆེན་པོ་དང་། ཆོས་ཀྱི་སྤྲིན་ཆེན་པོ་ཚད་མེད་པ་རྣམས་བཟོད་དོ། །ཡང་དག་པར་ལེན་ཏོ།

།ཡང་དག་པར་འཛིན་ཏོ། །བདག་གིར་བྱེད་དོ། །དེ་བཞིན་གཤེགས་པ་གཉིས་དང་གསུམ་ནས་ཚད་མེད་པའི་བར་དག་ཀྱང་། སྐད་ཅིག་ཡུད་ཙམ་ཐང་ཅིག་ལ་ཆོས་ཀྱི་སྣང་བ་ཆེན་པོ་དང་། ཆོས་ཀྱི་འོད་ཆེན་པོ་དང་། ཆོས་ཀྱི་སྤྲིན་ཆེན་པོ་ཚད་མེད་པའི་བཟོད་པ་ཐོབ་པོ། །ཡང་དག་པར་འཛིན་ཏོ། །ཡང་དག་པར་ལེན་ཏོ། །བདག་གིར་བྱེད་དོ། །དེ་ཅིའི་ཕྱིར་ཞེ་ན། འདི་ཡང་ནམ་མཁའ་ལྟ་བུའི་ཆོས་སྐུ་ལས། ཡེ་ཤེས་སེམས་ཆོས་ཀྱི་སྤྲིན་བསམ་གྱིས་མི་ཁྱབ་པ་དང་ལྡན་པས་ཆོས་ཀྱི་སྤྲིན་ཞེས་བྱའོ། །

སངས་རྒྱས་ཚུལ་ནི་ཕར་ཕྱིན་དང་སྔགས་ཀྱི་ལུགས་སོ། །དེ་ཡང་ཕ་རོལ་ཏུ་ཕྱིན་པ་ལ་ཐེག་ཆུང་དང་། ཐེག་ཆེན་གཉིས་སོ། །དེ་ལ་ཐེག་པ་ཆུང་བ་ནི། རྒྱལ་བུ་དོན་ཐམས་ཅད་འགྲུབ་པ་དེས། ས་བཅུ་རང་རྒྱུད་པ་གཅིག་འོག་མིན་ནམ། །རྡོ་རྗེ་གདན་དུ་སངས་རྒྱས་པར་འདོད་དོ། །

ཐེག་ཆེན་པོ་ནི། རྒྱལ་བ་འདིས་བསྐལ་པ་གྲངས་མེད་པའི་སྔོན་དུ་སངས་རྒྱས་ཟིན་པར་འདོད་དོ། །མདོ་སྡེ་པདྨ་དཀར་པོ་ལས། རིགས་ཀྱི་བུ་ང་ནི་བསྐལ་པ་བྱེ་བ་ཁྲག་ཁྲིག་མང་པོ་འདས་པའི་སྔོན་རོལ་ཏུ་སངས་རྒྱས་སོ། ཞེས་པ་དང་། ཡབ་སྲས་མཇལ་བ་ལས། ང་ནི་འདས་པའི་དུས་ན་བསྐལ་པ་དཔག་ཏུ་མེད་པ་གྲངས་མེད་པ་འདས་པའི་དུས་ན། སངས་རྒྱས་དབང་པོའི་ཏོག་ཅེས་བྱ་བར་སངས་རྒྱས་སོ་ཞེས་སོ། །

གསང་སྔགས་རྣལ་འབྱོར་གྱི་ལུགས་ཀྱིས་རྒྱལ་བུ་དོན་གྲུབ་འོགམིན་དུ་བྱོན་པ་དང་། ཏིལ་གྱི་གང་བུ་ཁ་ཕྱེ་བ་ལྟ་བུའི་སངས་རྒྱས་རྣམས་ཀྱིས། རིགས་ཀྱི་བུ་ཁྱོད་ཇི་ལྟར་སངས་རྒྱ་བར་བྱ་སྙམ་པའི་རྗེས་ལ། ཕྱིའི་མངོན་བྱང་ལྔ་ལ་བསྟེན་ནས་སངས་རྒྱས་པར་འདོད་དོ། །

རྣལ་འབྱོར་བླ་ན་མེད་པ་རྒྱུད་ནི། འོག་མིན་དུ་རྣམ་པར་སྣང་མཛད་ཆེན་པོ་ལ་དབང་བསྐུར་ཞུས་ནས། དེར་སངས་རྒྱས་ལ། དེའི་སྤྲུལ་པ་འདིར་སངས་རྒྱས་པར་འདོད་དེ། ཟླ་གསང་ཐིག་ལེ་ལས། གཙང་མའི་རིགས་དག་སྤྱངས་ནས་ནི།

།འོག་མིན་སྟུག་པོ་ཉམས་དགའ་བར། །ཡང་དག་རྫོགས་སངས་དེར་སངས་རྒྱས། །སྤྲུལ་པ་པོ་གཅིག་འདིར་སངས་རྒྱས། །ཞེས་སོ། །ཡང་ན་ས་བཅུའི་བྱང་ཆུབ་སེམས་དཔའ་དེ་འོག་མིན་གྱི་གནས་སུ་རྡོ་རྗེ་འཆང་ལ་དབང་བསྐུར་ཞུས་པས། དེ་ཉིད་ཀྱིས་དབང་བསྐུར་དེས་སངས་རྒྱས་པར་འདོད་དེ། འདུལ་བ་དོན་ཡོད་པའི་རྒྱུད་ལས། གསང་བའི་གནས་མཆོག་འོག་མིན་དམ་པར་ནི། །བྱང་ཆུབ་སེམས་དཔའ་གཙོ་ཆེན་དབང་ཕྱུག་དེས། །ཆོས་ཀྱི་ཕོ་བྲང་དེར་ནི་དབང་བསྐུར་བ། །ཀུན་ཏུ་བཟང་པོ་རྡོ་རྗེ་དབྱིངས་ཀྱི་བསྐུར། །བྱང་ཆུབ་སེམས་ཀྱི་རྡོ་རྗེས་བྱིན་བརླབས་པས། །དེ་ཉིད་དུ་ནི་མངོན་པར་ཡང་དག་བྱང་ཆུབ་པས། །བླ་མེད་སྙིང་པོ་རྡོ་རྗེ་འཆང་དུ་གྱུར། །རང་བྱུང་བདེ་བ་ཆེན་པོར་མངོན་སངས་རྒྱས། །ཞེས་སོ། །

མ་རྒྱུད་པ་ནི། གྲགས་ཆེན་གྱི་སངས་རྒྱས་ས་བཅུ་གཅིག་པ་དེ། འོག་མིན་བཙུན་མོའི་གཞལ་ཡས་ཁང་དུ་དབང་བཞི་རྫོགས་པར་ཞུས་པས། བུད་མེད་མཆོག་ལ་བསྟེན་ནས། ས་བཅུ་གསུམ་རྡོ་རྗེ་འཛིན་པ་ཐོབ་སྟེ། རབ་ཏུ་མི་གནས་པའི་རྒྱུད་ལས། བཅུ་གཅིག་སངས་རྒྱས་རྣམས་ཀྱིས་ཀྱང་། །བུད་མེད་ཕྱག་རྒྱ་བསྟེན་བྱས་ནས། །རྡོ་རྗེ་འཛིན་པའི་ས་ཐོབ་འགྱུར། །ཞེས་སོ། །ཡང་ན་ས་བཅུ་པའི་བྱང་ཆུབ་སེམས་དཔའ་དེས་འོག་མིན་དུ་ལོངས་སྐུ་རྡོ་རྗེ་འཆང་ཆེན་པོ་ཞལ་སྦྱོར་བདེ་བ་ཆེན་པོའི་སྐུ་དྲུག་པ་རྡོ་རྗེ་འཆང་ཆེན་པོ་དེ་ལ་དབང་བཞི་རྫོགས་ཞུས་པས། ས་བཅུ་བཞི་བགྲོད་དོ། །རྡོ་རྗེ་བདེ་བའི་རྒྱུད་དང་། ཡེ་ཤེས་ཐིག་ལེའི་རྒྱུད་ལས། བུམ་པའི་དབང་ནི་བཅུ་གཅིག་སྟེ། །གསང་བའི་དབང་ནི་བཅུ་གཉིས་མཆོག །ཤེས་རབ་ཡེ་ཤེས་བཅུ་གསུམ་པ། །དེ་ལྟར་དེ་བཞིན་བཅུ་བཞི་པ། །དབང་རེ་ལ་ནི་ས་རེ་སྟེ། །འདི་རྣམས་ས་ཡི་དབང་ཕྱུག་བདག །ཅེས་སོ། །དེ་ལ་འགའ་ཞིག་ནི། གཙང་མའི་རིགས་ཀྱི་འོག་མིན་ནི་འཇིག་པ་ཡིན་ལ། འོག་མིན་སྟུག་པོ་བཀོད་པ་ནི་མི་འཇིག་སྟེ། རྡོ་རྗེ་རྩེ་མོ་ལས། འོག་མིན་བསྟུག་པོ་ཉམས་དགའ་ཞིང་། །སྟུག་པོ་ཞིང་ཁམས་འཇིག་མེད་པར། །དེ་ན་སངས་རྒྱས་རྣམས་ཀྱི་ཆོས། །རྫོགས་པར་ལོངས་སྤྱོད་ཚུལ་འདི་འབྱུང་། །ཞེས་

པས། རྣམ་སྣང་གངས་ཆེན་མཚོ་ཆེན་པོ་ལོངས་སྤྱོད་རྫོགས་པའི་སྐུ་དེ་ལ་འཁོར་ས་བཅུ་པས་བསྐོར་ནས་བཞུགས་པའི་གནས་ནི་སྟུག་པོ་བཀོད་པ་ཡིན་ནོ། །དེ་ནི་མི་འཇིག་ལ། དེའི་ནང་ན་གནས་པའི་ཞིང་ཁམས་ཆུང་ངུ་ཐམས་ཅད་ནི་སྤྲུལ་སྐུའི་ཞིང་ཁམས་ཡིན་པས་འཇིག་པའོ། །ཞེས་འདོད་དེ། དེ་ལྟར་ན་གངས་ཆེན་མཚོའི་ཞིང་མི་འཇིག་ན། འདི་ཡང་མི་འཇིག་སྟེ། འདི་ཡང་དེའི་ཞིང་ཁམས་སུ་བཤད་པ་དང་། གཉིས་ཀ་ལ་འཇིག་རྟེན་གྱི་ཁམས་སུ་བཤད་པའི་ཕྱིར་རོ། །དེ་ལ་དཔེར་ན། སྐྱེས་བུའི་ཡན་ལག་དང་། མིག་དང་རྣ་བ་ལ་སོགས་པའི་བྱེ་བྲག་ཐམས་ཅད་ལ་མི་རྟག་ན། ཕྱི་ལུས་ཀྱང་མི་རྟག་སྟེ། སྤྱི་དང་བྱེ་བྲག་གི་མཐའ་ཅན་ཡིན་པའི་ཕྱིར་རོ། །དེས་ན་གཙང་མ་རིགས་ཀྱི་གནས་ནི་འོག་མིན་ཡིན་ལ། གཙང་མའི་རིགས་དག་སྤྲངས་པའི་གནས་འོག་མིན་ནི་གྲོང་ལས་དགོན་པ་ལྟ་བུ་སྟེ། དེ་ནི་མི་འཇིག་སྟེ་ས་བཅུ་འབའ་ཞིག་གི་སྣང་ངོ་ཡིན་པའི་ཕྱིར་རོ། །འཇིག་པ་ནི་མ་དག་པ་སོ་སོ་སྐྱེ་བོའི་སྣང་ངོ་ཡིན་ཏེ། དེ་ན་སོ་སོ་སྐྱེ་བོ་མེད་པའི་ཕྱིར་རོ། །དེས་ན་ལུང་ཐམས་ཅད་དེ་ཉིད་ཀྱི་ལུང་སྟེ། གཉིས་མེད་རྣམ་པར་རྒྱལ་བའི་རྒྱུད་ལས། ཡེ་ཤེས་བླ་ན་མེད་པའི་གནས། །གཙང་མའི་གནས་མཆོག་ལེགས་གནས་པ། །བཅོམ་ལྡན་འོག་མིན་འདིར་རྟག་བཞུགས། །ཀུན་ཏུ་བཟང་པོའི་ས་ཕྱོགས་སོ། །ཞེས་སོ། །ཡང་ན་སེམས་ཉིད་ལྷན་ཅིག་སྐྱེས་པའི་ཡེ་ཤེས་འོག་མིན་ཏེ། ཡེ་ཤེས་བླ་ན་མེད་པའི་རྒྱུད་ལས། སེམས་ཉིད་བདེ་སྟོང་ལྷན་ཅིག་སྐྱེས། །འོག་མིན་གཙང་མའི་གནས་མཆོག་གོ། །ཞེས་སོ། །

དེ་ལ་བྱང་ཆུབ་སེམས་དཔའ་དང་། །སངས་རྒྱས་ཀྱི་ཁྱད་པར་ནི་རྒྱ་མཚོ་དང་བ་ལང་གི་རྨིག་རྗེས་ཀྱི་ཆུ་ལྟ་བུ་སྟེ། ཕལ་པོ་ཆེའི་མདོ་ལས། །བྱང་ཆུབ་སེམས་དང་སངས་རྒྱས་ཁྱད། །རྒྱ་མཚོ་བ་ལང་རྨིག་རྗེས་མཚུངས། །དག་པ་ས་གསུམ་ཡོན་ཏན་ཀྱང་། །དཔག་ཅིང་གཞལ་བར་མི་ནུས་ན། །ཐམས་ཅད་མཁྱེན་པའི་ཡོན་ཏན་ནི། །བརྗོད་ཅིང་དཔག་པར་སྨོས་ཅི་དགོས། །ཞེས་པ་དང་། བསམ་མི་ཁྱབ་བསྟན་པའི་མདོ་ལས། ནམ་མཁའ་ས་གཞི་གང་ཡིན་པ། །སྐྲ་རྩེས་གཞལ་བར་ནུས་སྲིད་ཀྱིས།

།རྒྱལ་བའི་ཡོན་ཏན་རྒྱ་མཚོ་ནི། །བསྐལ་པ་གྲངས་མེད་བརྗོད་མི་ནུས། །དཔག་ཅིང་བརྗོད་པའི་ཡུལ་ལས་འདས། །དེ་ཕྱིར་བསམ་གྱིས་མི་ཁྱབ་པོ། །ཞེས་སོ། །སྒྱུ་མ་ལམ་རིམ་གསལ་བྱེད་པའི། །འགྲེལ་པ་འདི་ནི་བདག་གིས་བྱས། །དགེ་དེས་འཛིན་བྱེད་བདུད་བཅོམ་ནས། །དབྱེར་མེད་སྐུ་བཞི་ཐོབ་པར་ཤོག །སྒྱུ་མ་ལམ་གྱི་རིམ་པའི་དོན་འགྲེལ། ཡེ་ཤེས་ཀྱི་མཁའ་འགྲོ་མ་ནི་གུ་མས་མཛད་པ་རྫོགས་སོ།། །།

ཡེ་ཤེས་ཀྱི་མཁའ་འགྲོ་མ་དེ་ཉིད་དང་། ལོ་ཙྪ་བ་གླན་དར་མ་བློ་གྲོས་ཀྱིས་བསྒྱུར་བའོ། །སླད་ནས་བདག་ཁྱུང་པོ་རྣལ་འབྱོར་པས་ཞུས་ཏེ་ཉམས་སུ་མྱོང་བར་བྱས་པའོ།། །།མངྒ་ལཾ།།

Notes

Notes to Introduction

1 The so-called Eight Great Chariots of the Practice Lineages (*sgrub brgyud shing rta chen po brgyad*) is a system of identifying the streams of esoteric instructions (*man ngag*) that came into Tibet from India. Based on an initial listing by Prajñāraśmi (1517–1584), it was developed primarily by the great Tibetan savant Jamgön Kongtrul Lodrö Tayé (1813–1900) as a doxographical tool in his great efforts to preserve the histories and teachings of all those lineages by collecting and printing them in the large compendiums known as his Five Great Treasuries. He enumerates these eight chariots as (1) Nyingma, (2) Kadam, (3) Lamdre, (4) Marpa Kagyu, (5) Shangpa Kagyu, (6) Zhijé and its branch of Chöd, (7) Dorje Naljor Druk (or Jordruk), and (8) Dorje Sumgyi Nyendrup. See Jamgön Kongtrul, *The Treasury of Knowledge: Book Eight, Part Four: Esoteric Instructions.*

2 Jamgön Kongtrul mentions the existence of another life story written as a praise authored by Nyukla Paṇchen (sMyug la Paṇ chen Ngag dbang grags pa, 1458–1515), but this text has not come to light. See n. 62.

3 *'Chi med rang grol.* This is really more of a subject name. The actual title is *Glorious Immortal Great Timeless Awareness* (*dPal 'chi med ye shes chen po*).

4 *dPal 'khor lo sdom pa myur du sgrub pa* and *dPal 'khor lo sdom pa'i dkyil 'khor gyi cho ga.*

5 *dPal dgyes pa rdo rje'i dkyil 'khor gyi cho ga.*

6 *Clearing up Darkness of the Mind, T-CW*, vol. 17, 459 (f. 22a1–4). Tāranātha (1575–1635) gives his full name as Kunga Nyingpo Tashi Gyaltsen Palzangpo (Kun dga' snying po bKra shis rgyal mtshan dPal bzang po). He used the Sanskrit translation of his title Drolwai Gonpo (sGrol ba'i mgon po) as his name to show his close connection with the Indian tradition, as he studied directly with Indian teachers in Tibet. Tāranātha was an incredible master, historian, and philosopher, whose prolific writings encompass nearly every aspect of knowledge in Tibet, with his collected works numbering twenty-three volumes. He is remembered particularly in connection with the Jonang school, as his most common epithet "Jonang Tāranātha" or "Jonang Jetsun" clearly indicates, but his influence is much broader.

7 Janet Gyatso, *Apparitions of the Self*, 115: "Even Indian Buddhist hagiographical narratives are scarce and are limited to idealized renderings of the life of the Buddha and a few other works."

8 *The Life Story of the Supreme Learned Nāro Paṇchen* (*mKhas mchog nā ro paṇ chen gyi rnam thar*) by Sangye Bum, in the *Rwalung Kagyu Golden Rosary*, vol. 1, 87–129, a collection of biographies of the Middle Drukpa masters in Rwalung, compiled 1799–1803.

9 Advaitavadini Kaul mentions a monastery in the town of Anupamapurā (*grong khyer dpe med*) in connection with Guṇakaraśhrībhadra. *Buddhist Savants of Kashmir*, 49.

10 See, for example, the recounting of this tale by Bu-ston, translated by Obermiller in *The History of Buddhism in India and Tibet*, 89–91. One of a group of Ānanda's disciples called Madhyāntika is prophesied by Ānanda to be the future settler of Kashmir, "the place suitable for mystic absorption and the best resting-place." In fulfillment of that prophecy, the events of the story unfold more or less as related here. In terms of the drastic environmental change in the geography of Kashmir that resulted, the time of the previous buddha might be more appropriate. See also n. 65.

11 Nāropa's dates are given as fire-dragon to iron-dragon year, which would be 956–1040. Atīsha's departure for Tibet is reliably dated to 1040, and he brought relics from the cremation of Nāropa with him. The stūpa in which they are enshrined still survives in Nethang Dolma Lhakang temple, founded by Atīsha. According to Peter Roberts's introduction in *Mahāmudrā and Related Instructions*, the common erroneous dates of 1016–1100 (such as in Guenther, *The Life and Teaching of Nāropa*) were the result of taking literally an episode in Tsangnyön Heruka's version of the life of Marpa in which he visits Nāropa. However it turns out that the visit and Naropa's song are derived from one of Tsangnyön's *visions* and are without historical basis.

12 See Guenther, *The Life and Teaching of Nāropa*, xi–xii, which has the following information: born into the Shākya clan, brahmin caste, his father was named Zhi ba go cha (Shāntivarman) and mother dPal gyi blo gros (Shrīmatī), who was the daughter of the great king sKal ldan grags pa. They had only one daughter, the princess dPal gyi ye shes (Shrījñāna). Nāropa's wife was Dri med pa (Vimalā), whose mother was the Brahminī Nigu. (Note that the Sanskrit names are reconstructions from the Tibetan.) These names accord with those given in the biography by Karmapa Rangjung Dorje (1284–1339). However in *The Life Story of the Supreme Learned Nāro Paṇchen* by Sangye Bum, the father's name is given as the brahmin dGe ba bzang po, and his mother's name as the brahminī dPal gyi ye shes (89–90; f. 2a6–b1), which in other places is actually the daughter's name.

13 The earliest biographies of Nāropa, such as that of Gampopa (1079–1153) and Lama Zhang (1123–1193), do not name a specific birthplace other than simply "the west." All accounts of Nāropa include the story of a ḍākinī appearing to him and telling him to "go east" to find his guru Tilopa, which really only makes sense if he is somewhere in the west. In *The Life Story of the Supreme Learned Nāro Paṇchen*, which claims to have compared five different biographies, Sangye Bum (88) gives Nāropa's birthplace as the "land of Moslems" (*kha che'i yul*), which is almost universally interpreted to mean Kashmir. (Recall that Moslems gained control of Kashmir in the fourteenth century.) In case this is not clear, Karmapa Rangjung Dorje (1284–1339) specifies "ka smi ra," transcribing the Indian "Kashmir" as nearly as is possible in Tibetan in his version of the life story in the *Kagyu Golden Rosary*, f. 26a2. Khachö Wangpo (1350–1405) is

even more specific, saying: "In the east of India, the town of Jammu ('Dzam bu) in Srinagar (Sri na ga ra), a district of Bha ga la." *Earring of Accomplishment*, f. 1b1. Srinagar and Jammu are easily identified in the southeastern part of the Kashmir valley. In the Tibetan dictionary, Bangala is identified as an early Tibetan name for Zahor (usually located in northwest India), which, it says, is currently called "Ca la." *BD*, vol. 2, 2444. The biography by Lhatsun Rinchen Namgyal (1473–1557), called *The Amazing, Wonderful Life of Nāropa*, which was translated by Herbert Guenther in *The Life and Teaching of Nāropa*, is a verbatim copy of Khachö Wangpo's, a very common practice in Tibetan literature, where plagiarism is truly the highest form of flattery. Dorje Dze-ö's biography of Naropa, translated by Khenpo Könchog Gyaltsen in *The Great Kagyu Masters*, has the same information. It seems that it is only because of the inexplicable identification of the Tibetan transliteration "Bha-ga-la" as "Bengal" in these two translations (despite the obvious reference to Srinigar and Jammu) that Nāropa has been widely viewed in the Western world as Bengali. Later Tibetan authors such as Tāranātha have upheld Kashmir as his birthplace. One last twist to this research is that Sangye Bum's description of "the land of Moslems," identical to the one in Niguma's life story, adds that it is also called "Kosala"! *Rwalung Kagyu Golden Rosary*, 89 (f. 2a6). This ancient kingdom where the Buddha Shākyamuni spent most of his teaching life is nowhere near Kashmir or Bengal, but somewhere in the middle. This seems to come out of nowhere, and I have no explanation for it. On Nāropa's birthplace see also Jo nang Tāranātha, *The Seven Instruction Lineages*, 46 and 115, n. 157.

14 For example, in his translation of the *Blue Annals*, George Roerich notes that modern Tibetan pilgrims believe the location of Pullahari (alternately called Puṣhpahari) to be in Kashmir near Srinagar (400). And more interestingly, the colophon to Tilopa's *Esoteric Instructions on the Six Yogas* (*Chos drug gi man ngag*) states that it was translated by Nāropa and Marpa in Puṣhpahari in the place of the Moslems (*kha che'i gnas*), again referring to Kashmir (Toh. 2330, f. 271a2–3).

15 Guenther, "Introduction," *The Life and Teaching of Nāropa*, xi–xii.

16 "*Nā ro pa'i lcam mo.*" Gö Lotsāwa, *The Blue Annals*, vol. 2, 854 and again on 855; Roerich, *The Blue Annals*, vol. 2, 730.

17 Losang Chökyi Nyima, *Collected Works of bLo bzang chos-kyi nyi-ma*, vol. 2, f. 3a1.

18 Jamgön Kongtrul, *Increasing Enlightened Activity: The Feast Offering and Concluding Rites of White and Red Kecharī in the Shangpa Tradition*, *ST*, vol. 3, 300 (f. 2b5–6).

19 *BD*, vol. 1, 765.

20 Roerich, *BA*, 390.

21 *rus pa'i rgyan can:* The actual description is "the ḍākinī of timeless awareness with whom it is meaningful to be connected [and who] has bone ornaments" (*ye shes kyi mkha' 'gro ma 'brel tshad don ldan rus pa'i rgyan dang ldan pa*). Tsangnyön Heruka, *The Life of Marpa the Translator*, 38. Fun fact: Tsangnyön Heruka was also called "Adorned with Bone Ornaments" (gTshang smyon he ru ka Rus pa'i rgyan can).

22 Ibid., 32 and 80, respectively. The *Four Seats Tantra* (*Catuḥpīṭha*; *gDan bzhi*) is a mother tantra of Highest Yoga Tantra. In Sangye Bum's *Biography of Marpa* in the *Rwalung Kagyu Golden Rosary*, Marpa receives this from 'Phags pa rang byung. Vol. 1, 136. Khyungpo Naljor did not receive this tantra from Niguma either; it did not seem to be in her repertoire.

23 *grong khyer der che ba'i paṇḍita nāro ta pa dang/ rin chen rdo rje gnyis bzhugs so. ST*, vol. 1, 40 (f. 2b4).

24 *The Blue Annals* (*Deb ster ngon po*) by Gö Lotsāwa Zhonnu Pal (1392–1481): *chos drug gi gdams pa 'di rnams shes pa nga dang lwa ba pa ma gtogs med*. Vol. 2, 856. In the translation, Roerich inserts "Kambalapāda" as another name for Lavāpa, though this identity is not certain. The statement in Khyungpo Naljor's life story is in *ST*, vol. 1, 92 (f. 17b4).

25 Jo nang Tāranātha, *The Seven Instruction Lineages*, 33–36; and Tāranātha, *Tāranātha's History of Buddhism in India*, 241–45. The supplementary notes in the back of the latter (408) reveal that the translators also identify him with Kambhala, as in the *Blue Annals*, although the author Gö Lotsāwa did not make that identity explicit.

26 Jamgön Kongtrul, *TOK*, vol. 1, 526; *The Treasury of Knowledge: Book Eight, Part Four: Esoteric Instructions*, 137. Ācārya Lavāpa is also mentioned often in the various biographies of Tilopa. By some accounts, it was lucid clarity that Tilopa received from him, and Tāranātha seems to corroborate this, although there are many versions. For a discussion of this issue, see Mar-pa Chos-kyi bLo-gros, *The Life of the Mahāsiddha Tilopa*, 69–70, n. 31.

27 Templeman, *Tāranātha's Life of Kṛṣṇācārya/Kāṇha*, 82.

28 *A Supplement to the History of the Lineages*, *DZ*, vol. 18, 102–3 (ff. 2b6–3a3). For a brief and confusing discussion of Lavāpa's identities and dates, see Jo nang Tāranātha, *The Origin of Tara Tantra*, 60, n. 173. Also see some stories about this siddha in Dudjom Rinpoche's *The Nyingma School of Tibetan Buddhism*, vol. 1, 485–87. Here he is identified with Indrabhūti the Younger, son of King Ja, as his teacher, whereas Tāranātha associates him with Indrabhūti the Middle. In fact much of this confusion may arise from the multiple Indrabhūtis.

29 Padmasambhava and Jamgön Kongtrül, *The Light of Wisdom: Vol. 1*, 37.

30 Gyatso, *Apparitions of the Self*, 251.

31 Jamgön Kongtrul, *TOK*, vol. 3, 489.

32 *ST*, vol. 1, 736–37 (ff. 2b4–5a1).

33 Ibid., 731 (f. 14a4–5). Verse 195 in the translation.

34 *Stages in the Path of Illusion: The Commentary*, *ST*, vol. 1, 796 (f. 31b3), referencing the *Avataṃsaka Sūtra*, in the commentary to verse 199.

35 One good attempt to cover a broad spectrum on the subject is *The Presence of Light*, edited by Matthew Kapstein, and particularly his own contribution therein.

36 "*phung po 'od skur grol ba*," in *BD*, vol. 1, 892.

37 Lama Gyaltsen, oral communication to the translator. There are many accounts in recent as well as ancient history. See Tulku Urgyen Rinpoche, *Rainbow Painting*, for a particularly interesting account of a woman who was observed in the process. For instance: "From the ends of the bones, swirls of rainbow light were coiling out as the body continued to fall apart" (182).

38 Namkhai Norbu, *The Crystal and the Way of Light*, 128.

39 Jamgön Kongtrul, *TOK*, vol. 3, 521.

40 Ibid., vol. 3, 346; *The Treasury of Knowledge: Book Eight, Part Four: Esoteric Instructions*, 173.

41 *'ja' lus 'chi ba med pa'i sku can ma*, in *Transference of White Khecharī* (*mKha' spyod dkar mo'i 'pho ba*) by Gyurme Dechen, *ST*, vol. 3, 317 (f. 2a4).

42 Namkhai Norbu, *The Crystal and the Way of Light*, 129.

43 On the reticence of Indian Buddhists to reify the light imagery, see Kapstein, "The Strange Death of Pema the Demon Tamer," 123–24.

44 "Then, due to the yoga of karmamudra, one's impure physical body is transformed into a more subtle and refined state. Once this has merged in one's experience with the enlightened embodiment that is simply the unity of subtle energy and mind, this is termed 'the vajra embodiment of the rainbow body', or 'master of awareness'. This is not considered to be a body within any of the three realms. However, since one lacks direct experience of the actual nature of phenomena, one is not yet considered a master of awareness who has transcended the ordinary world. And even though the enlightened embodiment that is simply the unity of subtle energy and mind may have been achieved, if the gross physical body has not yet been transformed, it is not considered the enlightened embodiment of a master of awareness. But once what is termed 'the enlightened embodiment of nondual timeless awareness' has been achieved, it is impossible for the gross physical body not to be transformed; and so the enlightened embodiment of primordial unity constitutes that of a master of awareness who has transcended the ordinary world." Jamgön Kongtrul, *TOK*, vol. 3, 514. This and the following two citations from this source are translated by Richard Barron in Jamgön Kongtrul, *The Treasury of Knowledge: Books Nine and Ten: Journey and Goal.*

45 "Thus, when the experiences of ordinary body, speech, and mind that pertain to samsara are eliminated, all the other aspects of the mind-body aggregates are transformed. Under those circumstances, the expression 'the accomplishment of the vajrakāya, the rainbow body' is used, since the impure experience of ordinary body has been transformed; as well, the expression 'the accomplishment of the enlightened embodiment of nondual timeless awareness' is used, since what has been gained is the experience of the 'equal taste' of the four vajras." Jamgön Kongtrul, *TOK*, vol. 3, 521.

46 "When even the most subtle aspects of the subtle channels, energies, and bindu have been refined so that they are free of obscuration, one is purified of the ordinary experience of the body and abides on the thirteenth level. This is the actual accomplishment of the state of Vajradhara, that is, the enlightened embodiment of timeless awareness, the rainbow body of the consummate path of no more training." Ibid., 526.

47 "The attainment of the thirteenth bhūmi, which is the path of the ultimate conclusion, is when the subtlest aspects of the nāḍīs, vāyus and bindus are clear and free of obscuration, the ordinary body is purified, and the rainbow wisdom body is attained." Dagpo Tashi Namgyal (1512–1587), *Rays of Light from the Jewel of the Excellent Teaching.*

48 Jamgön Kongtrul, *TOK*, vol. 3, 643.

49 *The Life Story of Buddha Vajradhara* (*Sangs rgyas rdo rje 'chang gi rnam par thar pa*) by Mokchokpa (either the first incarnation, Rin chen brtson grus, or the second incarnation, Kun dga' 'od), in *Golden Rosary of Shangpa Biographies*, *ST*, vol. 1, 1–36. This whole text was also copied verbatim in the Vajradhara biography by Lhatsun Rinchen Namgyal (1473–1557), who also reproduced the life story of Nāropa that was translated into English by Herbert Guenther.

50 Ibid., 3–4 (f. 2a3–b2).

51 Ibid., 4 (f. 2b2).

52 Ibid., 16–17 (ff. 8b5–9a1). Also see Hanson and Hanson, "The Mediating Buddha," where the same conclusion is approached from a different perspective.

53 Niguma, *Stages in the Path of Illusion: The Commentary*, *ST*, vol. 6, 778 (f. 22b5–6).

54 Mokchokpa, *The Life Story of Buddha Vajradhara*, *ST*, vol. 1, 11 (f. 6a4–5).

55 Campbell, *Traveller in Space*, 139.

56 See, for instance, David Gray's discussion in *The Cakrasamvara Tantra*, 77–103, where ḍākinīs "were initially considered to be a class of nonhuman beings, akin to the rākṣasī demonesses, who were notable for their carnivorous appetite" (84).

57 This story of the guru throwing away the precious offering of the disciple appears again and again in Tibetan narratives. Nāropa thus disposes of all of Marpa's gold (Roerich, *BA*, 401), and even the epitome of all gurus, Guru Rinpoche Padmasambhava, throws it around and displays his ambivalence. Yeshe Tsogyal, *The Lotus-Born*, 60–61.

58 Tib. *Mi che ba*, "Not Great," the name of the first of five Pure Domains (*gTsang ma'i gnas*) of the form realms.

59 This reading from Tāranātha's Shangpa history (*Clearing Up Darkness of the Mind*, 457; f. 21a4) and elsewhere of *'khor ba'i rgya mtshor bskyur byed pa'i/ chags sdang rtogs pa sna tshogs 'di* is preferable to *bskyur ba yi* in the Shangpa Text version (vol. 1, 90–91; ff. 16b6–17a2), which would literally read, "This variety of desirous and hateful thoughts of stranding in the ocean of cyclic existence." I must confess confusion about the translation of *bskyur ba* as "stirring" (Kapstein) or "whirling" (Riggs). I find only meanings concerning "leaving behind" or "throwing out," as in the famous *zan bskyur* of the gCod practice: throwing out (the body) as food.

60 The following list of instructions received is from Khyungpo's life story (*ST*, vol. 1, 91; f. 17a5–b4) and is checked against Tāranātha's *Clearing Up Darkness of the Mind* (*T-CW*, vol. 17, 458; f. 21b1–6): *Vajra Lines*; *Stages in the Path of Illusion*; *Five Tantric Deities*: empowerment, sādhana, and instructions; empowerments of *Nine Emanated Deities of Hevajra* and *Thirteen Deities of the Armored One*; *Two Part [Hevajra]* and *[Vajra] Tent [Tantra]*; *Sampuṭa [Tantra]* with its sādhana; extensive, [medium], and brief creation phase of the *Armored One*; instructions of the *Fourfold Suchness*; empowerment into *Chakrasaṃvara* mandala of sixty-two, thirteen, and five deities, and teachings of many tantras and sādhanas (in Tāranātha only); *White and Red Khecharī*; obscuration-purification of *Four Tantra Classes*; completion phase of *Chakrasaṃvara Five Families* (Tāranātha has *rim lnga*, "five stages" rather than *rigs lnga*); completion phase of *Vital Essence*; and ascertainment and teaching of all yogic applications (*las tshogs*) of *Vajraḍākinī Tantras*; (or, according to Tāranātha, of all Dharma Cycles of *Jñānaḍākinī Tantras*).

61 *Nāda* in Sanskrit means sound or vibration and here indicates that the instruction was not written. According to Lochen Gyurme Dechen, Tangtong Gyalpo wrote down only the two illustrations but not the oral instructions, so they did not become well known. However, Gyurme Dechen himself received the practical instructions on these two illustrations from Kunga Drolchok (Kun dga' grol mchog) and wrote them down in the text called *Transference in White Khecharī* (*mKha' spyod dkar mo'i 'pho ba*), which is in *ST*, vol. 3, 315–23.

62 Jamgön Kongtrul, *The Beryl Key Catalogue*: "*rmog lchog pa phyi ma kun dga' 'od kyis mdzad pa.*" *GK*, vol. 10, 473 (f. 8a5). Then again, more thoroughly, in *Shangpa Catalogue*, it states: "The Vajradhara and Niguma life stories and Niguma's Praises incorporating the thirty-seven [factors of] enlightenment were all three written by the latter Mokchokpa, Kunga Ö. Both the Vajradhara [life story] and Niguma's Praises are not always reliable, so do not cling overly much to trusting in the words. There is no exaggeration or depreciation in *The Life Story of Niguma*. Nevertheless, the line of the reading transmission is presented here. Do not confuse [the author with] Mok-

chokpa Rinchen Tsöndru. There is also Niguma's *Life Story Praises* written by Nyukla Paṇchen." *ST*, vol. 9, 50 (f. 4b2–6).

I have not located this other life story of Niguma by Nyukla Paṇchen Ngawang Drakpa (sMyug la Paṇ chen Ngag dbang grags pa, 1458–1515), though he also wrote a biography of the madman of Central Tibet (dBu myon) that is available. Niguma's Praises incorporating the thirty-seven factors of enlightenment (*byang phyogs bstod pa*) follows directly on her *Life Story* in the *Shangpa Texts*. Upon comparison to the edition in the *Kinnaur Shangpa Texts*, it certainly does appear corrupt, leading one to believe that either the Kinnaur text was revised or that it comes from a separate source not available to Kongtrul.

63 Oral communication to Christian Charrier, October 15, 2008, who kindly pursued this question with Mokchokpa Rinpoche in France on my behalf. I have not been able to locate the succession of Mokchok incarnations to verify the names.

64 *Ye shes kyi dāki ma ni gu ma'i rnam thar*, in *ST*, vol. 1, 37–48. Also consulted were the *Life Story* from the *Kinnaur Shangpa Texts*, vol. 1, 529–35 and *The Life Story of the Supreme Learned Nāro Paṇchen* by Sangye Bum (Sangs rgyas 'bum), where the first section on the tale of Kashmir is found nearly verbatim. Significant variations have been noted.

65 Nyi ma'i gung pa: a group of Ānanda's followers, and their foremost leader, who attained the state of foe-destroyer (*arhant*) at midday. Another accounting of his name reports that Ananda went to pass away on an island in the Ganges midway between two groups who wanted his remains. A *ṛṣi* (sage) with five hundred disciples came and requested to enter the order. At midday in the middle island he attained arhant, so he was named Madhyāntika. See Cook, *Light of Liberation*, 170. Madhyāntika is credited with the introduction of Buddhism to Kashmir in the third century BCE. A good account of this legend can be found in Obermiller's translation of Bu-ston's *The History of Buddhism in India and Tibet*, 89–91. There is also a short account in Tāranātha, *Tāranātha's History of Buddhism in India*, 29–33, and another in Roerich, *BA*, 23 that Gö Lotsāwa translated from "a stray page from an Indian text on the hierarchy of the Doctrine." Jamgön Kongtrul praises Niguma as "emanated from Madhyāntika's blessing." *Garland of Udumbara*, 3b1.

66 Nāga are said to be subterranean beings. Also of note, one of the three tribes said to inhabit the area were the nāga tribe. The Chinese pilgrim and historian Hsuan-tsang relates that the land was protected by a dragon, possibly the same species as nāga. Cook, *Light of Liberation*, 269.

67 *bdud rtsi gam ga la* (for "Amṛtabhāvana") in this text (*ST*, vol. 1, 40; f. 2b) is likely a mistake for *bdud rtsi 'byung ba* ("arisen from elixir") as this expression is found in the same tale in Sangye Bum's Nāropa biography. Also see Cook, *Light of Liberation*, 272, concerning a vihāra called Amṛtabhāvana built by the queen Amṛtaprabhā.

68 lTa na sdug pa, literally "Pleasing to Behold," the principal city of the god Indra on top of Mount Meru, according to ancient Indian cosmology. The whole city is made of gold and filled with special medicinal herbs. See Jamgön Kongtrul, *The Treasury of Knowledge: Book One: Myriad Worlds*, 116–18, for a description.

69 *ST*, vol. 1, 40 (f. 2b3–4). Sangye Bum's *The Life Story of the Supreme Learned Nāro Paṇchen* (where the story of Kashmir is otherwise nearly identical) varies only slightly in stating "It is a city exclusively of beer maids, there being thirty-six hundred thousand." 89 (f. 2a6). From this point on, the two texts diverge into their respective sto-

ries of Niguma and Nāropa. I am not quite sure what to say about the beer maids. Certainly thirty-six hundred thousand beer maids would make any place special. Keep in mind that one classic place to find ḍākinīs is in the bar, serving alcohol.

70 Nāroṭapa is a variant of Nāropa. Ratnavajra (Rin chen rdo rje) was another master associated with Kashmir, a disciple of Ḍombīheruka. There are many works attributed to him in the Tengyur. In Kashmir he composed a Chakrasaṃvara sādhana that was given to Nāropa. Templeman, *Tāranathā's Life of Kṛṣṇācārya/Kāṇha*, 94. He is also listed as one of the six doorkeepers at Vikramashīla monastery: he was at the center while Nāropa was at the northern gate. Roerich, *BA*, 206.

71 The mother's name is added from the edition of the *Life Story* in the *Kinnaur Shangpa Texts*. Also see Zangpo, *Timeless Rapture*, 229 and n. 28, as well as Guenther, *The Life and Teaching of Nāropa*, 8.

72 At this point (p. 4; f. 3b5), there is the supplication prayer or praise, presumably by the same author, Mokchokpa, that incorporates the thirty-seven factors of enlightenment, which I have not included (see n. 62). This story of Niguma's life is retold by Kalu Rinpoche in *The Dharma That Illuminates All Beings Impartially like the Light of the Sun and the Moon*, 98–100.

73 *Ku su lu* in the Shangpa Text edition and *nyul pa* in the Kinnaur edition. Both mean about the same thing. It is a common show of modesty (false or not) to sign off in such a way.

74 Though not mentioned here, we know from the colophon to the Vajradhara life story, also signed by the vagabond Mokchokpa, that it was written at the behest of a Lama Kunsö, a short name for Kunga Sonam (Kun dga' gsod nams). *ST*, vol. 1, 36 (f. 18b1).

75 The first edition of the kangyur and tengyur prepared in Derge in Kham was done under the direction of the eighth Situ, Tenpai Nyinje (bsTan-pa'i Nyin-byed), also named Chökyi Jungne (Chos-kyi 'byung-gnas, 1700–1774). He also established Palpung Monastery near Derge in Eastern Tibet.

76 *dGyes rdor sprul pa'i lha dgu*, mentioned in Khyungpo Naljor's biography, *ST*, vol. 1, 91 (f. 17a6).

77 On the subject of rescuing teaching lineages, see my introduction to Jamgön Kongtrul, *The Treasury of Knowledge: Book Eight, Part Four: Esoteric Instructions*, 31–42 and for the Shangpa, specifically, 233–36.

78 For a useful chart of the possible sources and relationships of the tengyurs, see Schoening, *The Śālistamba Sūtra and Its Indian Commentaries*, vol. 1, 133.

79 "The profound long-life empowerment of Ni and Dhi (Niguma and Sukhasiddhī) was bestowed by the two ḍākinīs of timeless awareness on Bo dong 'Jigs med grags pa at the age of sixteen." Jamgön Kongtrul, *Catalogue of the Treasury of Precious Key Instructions, DZ*, vol. 18, 512 (f. 66b1).

80 Bodong Paṇchen Chokley Namgyal (Bo dong paṇ chen Phyogs las rnam rgyal), also known as Jigme Dragpa ('Jigs med grags pa) was one of the greatest minds to appear in Tibet. His four Denyi Dupa (*De nyid 'dus pa*) (*The Compendium of Suchness*) collections are magnificent compendia of the state of tantric knowledge as it existed in the first half of the fifteenth century. In a way, the Denyi Dupa Gyepa, which makes up the majority of these 137 volumes, is an early tengyur prototype, with writings by Tibetan authors. The scanning of these volumes of the Denyi Dupa collections was undertaken under a cooperative agreement with Ven. Doboom Rinpoche of

Tibet House New Delhi, the original publisher. Tibet House hopes to reprint the Bodong texts in a new reorganized edition. This project is still in process (TBRC). The Shangpa-related texts can be found in vols. 57, 93, and 103.

81 For a discussion of the history of the Bodong tradition and specifically its literary output, see Chok Tenzin Monlam, "The Life and Works of Bodong Chokley Namgyal." For recent attempts to reinvigorate this tradition, visit the web site of the Bodong Tradition, www.bodong.org.

82 *Kinnaur Shangpa Texts*, published under the title *Śaṅs-pa Bka'-brgyud-pa Texts.* It contains the collected biographies and teachings of the Shangpa Kagyu tradition, reproduced from an ancient manuscript from Himachal Pradesh, from the monastery of gSang sngags chos gling.

83 The following texts from the present book can be found in vol. 1 of the Kinnaur two-volume collection: *Stages in the Path of Illusion* and its *Commentary*, *Vajra Lines of the Six Dharmas*, *Aspiration Prayer of the Sealed Word*, *Glorious Immortal Great Timeless Awareness*, *Three Dharmas to Integrate on the Path*, and *Niguma's Life Story*.

84 Tsondru Zangpo (brTson 'grus bzang po) was the name of the great adept known as Tangtong Gyalpo (Thang stong rgyal po), the "King of the Empty Plain," but he liked to call himself the "Madman of the Empty Valley" (Lung stong smyon pa). His teachings are important in many lineages, and he is remembered for his miraculous construction of iron suspension bridges throughout the Himalaya. For his fascinating story, see Stearns, *King of the Empty Plain*.

85 *Collection of the Essentials* (*sNying po kun 'dus*) contains Tangtong Gyalpo's texts on the Niguma teachings, found in *Supplemental Texts to the Collected Works of Thang-stong-rgyal-po Series* (*Grub chen thang stong bka' 'bum gyi rgyab chos*), vol. 1, 241–386, and in Jamgön Kongtrul, *The Treasury of Precious Instructions* (*gDams ngag rin po che'i mdzod*), vol. 8, 147–205. These works are signed "Madman of the Empty Valley" (Lung stong smyon pa), one of the names the ḍākinīs gave Tangtong Gyalpo. Also see Gyatso, "The Literary Traditions of Thang-stong rGyal-po," 186–202, for more information about Tangtong Gyalpo's Niguma texts and his role in the Shangpa tradition.

86 Jamgön Kongtrul, *TOK*, vol. 1, 536, or my translation in Jamgön Kongtrul, *The Treasury of Knowledge: Book Eight, Part Four: Esoteric Instructions*, 235.

87 Kunga Drolchok, *Hundred Guides of Jonang* (*Jo nang khrid brgya*) is a collection of texts containing the explanations of the guiding instructions (*khrid*) for 108 special precepts of Buddhist practice whose transmissions converged and were collected in the Jonangpa tradition. They are found in *DZ*, vol. 18, 1–380, including a supplement by Tāranātha. Kunga Drolchok (Kun dga' 'grol mchog) was one of the principal masters of the Jonangpa school, founded in the eleventh century by Yumo Mikyo Dorje (Yu mo Mi bskyod rdo rje) and named after its principal seat in the Jomonang valley in the Lhatse country of Tsang. The school is known as the locus for the philosophical tenet called "other-emptiness" (*gzhan stong*).

88 Tāranātha is counted as one of the lineage holders in the Shangpa tradition. He reported receiving all relevant transmissions and realizations before the age of twenty. *Clearing Up Darkness of the Mind*, 511–12 (f. 48a6–b1). His teachings in that tradition are found primarily in vols. 14, 15, 17 and 20 of the Dzamthang edition of his *Collected Works* (*T-CW*).

89 *dPal ldan shangs pa'i chos 'khor gser chos rnam lnga'i rgya zhung*, referred to throughout as *Shangpa Texts* or *ST*.

90 For the story of this retreat, see Zangpo, *Sacred Ground.*

91 Other relevant articles include Kapstein, "The Journey to the Golden Mountain," "The Illusion of Spiritual Progress," "Chronological Conundrums in the Life of Khyung po rnal 'byor," and "The Strange Death of Pema the Demon Tamer."

92 Partly reprinted in Mullin, *The Dalai Lamas on Tantra.*

93 Forthcoming from Snow Lion Publications, translated by Ngawang Zangpo. This material on the Shangpa has been translated by Matthew Kapstein in "Kong-sprul Rin-po-che on the Shangs-pa bKa'-brgyud."

94 Khyung po rnal 'byor, from *Brief Life Story of Lama Khyungpo Naljor* in *Golden Rosary of the Shangpa Biographies, ST,* vol. 1, 59–143. In this biography, "Tsultrim Gonpo" (Tshul khrims mgon po) is the name given to him by his primary teacher, Dorje Denpa (rDo rje gdan pa). 72 (f. 7b2). Tāranātha also gives the name "Shangpa Dubupa Minyam Dorje," (Shangs pa bsdu bu pa Mi nyams rdo rje, Incomparable Vajra, Collector of Shangpa) and gives his birthplace as Nyemo Ramang (sNye mo ra mangs). *Clearing Up Darkness of the Mind,* f. 18a6. The life story is translated in Riggs, *Like an Illusion,* 44–92. For a short account, see below or Tāranātha, *Tāranātha's History of Buddhism in India,* 438–39.

95 See Matthew Kapstein's attempt to sort it all out in "Chronological Conundrums in the Life of Khyung po rnal 'byor: Hagiography and Historical Time." Kapstein suggests roughly 1050–1140 as plausible dates, but then admits of some troublesome inconsistencies, such as Khyunpo's early meeting with Atisha. Dudjom's *The Nyingma School of Tibetan Buddhism,* vol. 1, 950 and other traditional sources posit 978 or sometimes 990 as his birth year.

96 Jamgön Kongtrul, *TOK,* vol. 1, 533–34.

97 Ibid., 535.

98 This was probably established in the last years of the eleventh century. Khyungpo Naljor is said to have founded 108 religious establishments in the area over a period of three years. In present-day China, Zhangs zhongs is Nanmuling xian (Namling County), just east of the county seat, along the Shangs chu river. The nearest big town is Shigatze. It is 8,113 kilometers from Lhasa in Ho-tsang (U-tsang) in the Tibetan Autonomous Region. Brief mention is made of the monastery sites of Khyungpo Naljor and the nearby seat of Mokchokpa in Ferrari, *Guide to the Holy Places of Central Tibet,* 27 for the transliterated Tibetan and 69 in English.

99 In Tibetan the number is *khri phrag bco brgyad.* This number has also been interpreted as one hundred eighty thousand (Ringu Tulku, *The Ri-me Philosophy of Jamgon Kongtrul the Great,* 144) and eighty thousand (Tulku Thondup, *Buddhist Civilization in Tibet,* 48).

100 Jamgön Kongtrul, *TOK,* vol. 1, 536. Jambudvīpa generally refers to the whole known world in Indian cosmology, but specifically includes India, Tibet, Khotan, China, Shambhala, and the Himalaya. See Jamgön Kongtrul, *The Treasury of Knowledge: Book One: Myriad Worlds,* 151–53. The "great translator" (*lo chen*) Gyurme Dechen ('Gyur med bde chen, 1540–1615) brought this idea of the seven jewels in the one-to-one lineage under scrutiny since it seems to leave out the important figures of Lavāpa and Atisha. His concerns are expressed in his *[Questions concerning] the Instructions of Glorious Niguma, Mighty Kecharī.* See the introduction to the *Vajra Lines of the Six Dharmas* for more on this.

101 The complexities of the later lineages may be found elsewhere, such as *Catalogue,*

413–15 (ff. 17a5–18a4); Smith, *Among Tibetan Texts*, 53–57; Kapstein, "The Shangs-pa bKa'-brgyud," 141–42.

102 *Them[s] yig*, a short summary of topics that were taught by Niguma in *Vajra Lines of the Six Dharmas*, *ST*, vol. 7, 525–43.

103 *Supplement to the Lineage Stories of One Hundred Guidances*, *DZ*, vol. 18, 104 (f. 3a7–b2). *Saṃvara Ocean* (*sDom pa rgya mtsho*) is identified by Roerich (*BA*, 390) as *Śrī-Ḍakārṇavamahāyoginītantrarāja*, Dg.K. rGyud 'bum Kha 137a1–264b7 (Toh. 372), although this is by no means certain. It is said to be the source of *The Mandala Ritual of Chakrasaṃvara*, translated later in this book. *Jewel Ocean* (*Rin chen rgya mtsho*), though mentioned often, has not been found. Also see n. 124.

104 Niguma's teachings are collected in the extensive version of *Fifteen Specially Exalted Instructions of the Indian Ḍākinī* (*rGya gar mkha' 'gro'i khyad 'phags kyi gdams pa bco lnga*), the abbreviated version called *Instructions of Three Bodies* (*Lus gsum gyi gdams pa*) and the very abbreviated version that is contained in *The Natural Liberation of Deathless Mind* (*Sems 'chi med rang grol*). *Catalogue*, 432 (f. 26b4–5), and Jamgön Kongtrul, *TOK*, vol. 3, 404–7. See Jamgön Kongtrul, *The Treasury of Knowledge: Book Eight, Part Four: Esoteric Instructions*, 250–53, for a brief description of these other systems.

105 Jamgön Kongtrul, *TOK*, vol. 3, 395.

106 "Matured by four empowerments, faithful and diligent, having first [understood] impermanence, weariness [and] deficiencies, whoever strives at this sublime path will awaken in six months, a year, or in this lifetime." Verse 2 in the English translation of *Vajra Lines of the Six Dharmas*, provided in this volume.

107 Kongtrul recommends empowerment from the Five Tantras' Deities as found in the great tantra called *Jewel Ocean* (see note 123), or the particular empowerment in the Chakrasaṃvara mandala. *Catalogue*, 433 (f. 27a1).

108 *Dag byed a'i stong ra:* hollow or empty interior practice is characterized in Khyungpo Naljor's *Fifteen Especially Exalted Instructions of the Indian Ḍākinī*, *ST*, vol. 7, 539 and described in a few lines in his *Testimonial*. *ST*, vol. 7, 533. The standard explanation is in Tāranātha's *Profound Meaning Expanded* ("*Tangdalma*"). *ST*, vol. 3, 341–46. Brief descriptions in English can be found in Jamgön Kongtrul, *The Treasury of Knowledge: Book Eight, Part Four: Esoteric Instructions*, 238–40, and in Mullin, *The Dalai Lamas on Tantra*, 104–5.

109 As the preliminary practice of inner heat, it is called "the hollow interior of fire [as] the body's vital point" (*lus gnad me'i stong ra*). As the general preliminary, it has three parts: *dag byed stong ra, stong ra nad gdon sel byed*, and *rtags gsum stong ra'i khyad par*. See Tangtong Gyalpo, *Collection of the Essentials*, *TTG-S*, vol. 1, 250 (f. 5b2–3) and Dharma Mati, *Extensive Outline of the Vajra Lines of the Six Dharmas*, *ST*, vol. 7, 723–24.

110 See *Vajra Lines of the Six Dharmas* in chapter 2.

111 *Supplement to the Lineage Stories of One Hundred Guidances*, *DZ*, vol. 18, 104.

112 Maitrīpa (mNga' bdag me, 1007/1012–1085), also known as Advayavajra (Nyi su med pa'i rdo rje), according to Roerich, *BA*, 731, was a Brahmin scholar from Nepal who became a Buddhist when he met Nāropa. He became a monk at Vikramashīla Monastery, where he received the ordination name of Maitrīpagupta and studied with Shāntipa and others. He was evicted from the monastery on the grounds of having been seen drinking beer in the company of a woman. Later he became a student

of the yogin Shavari. See Jamgön Kongtrul, *TOK*, vol. 2, 527. Maitrīpa is particularly linked with the transmission of mahāmudrā. His students include Sahajavajra, Śunyatāsamādhi, Vajrapāṇi, Rāmapala, and the Tibetan Marpa, as well as Khyungpo Naljor.

113 See Jamgön Kongtrul, *Catalogue*, 433 (f. 27a4–6) and Tāranātha, *Supplement to the Lineage Stories of One Hundred Guidances*, *DZ*, vol. 18, 104 (f. 3b2–7).

114 Jamgön Kongtrul, *Catalogue*, 433 (f. 27a6–7).

115 Jamgön Kongtrul, *Releasing the Central Knots*, *ST*, vol. 3, 192 (ff. 1b4–2a2); and *ST*, vol. 6, 204 (f. 22b6) in the colophon to the actual *Vajra Lines*. Dipaṃkara Śhrījñāna is of course the famous Atīsha (982–1054), the "chief lord" (*jo bo rje*), whose move to Tibet in 1042 is often cited as marking the beginning of the second spreading of Buddhism from India. Khyungpo Naljor reports encountering him in Thöling monastery, where Atīsha verified some of Khyungpo's texts.

116 Jamgön Kongtrul, *Releasing the Central Knots*, *ST*, vol. 3, 192 (ff. 1b4–2a2) and *ST*, vol. 6, 210 (f. 25b3–4). The instructions themselves are known as "Vital Essence Transference: the Purification of the Five Birth Places All at Once" (*sKye gnas lnga gcig car du dag pa thig le'i 'pho ba*). Though not identified by name in Khyungpo's biography, a mysterious adept miraculously visits Khyungpo Naljor at his monastery in Tibet, arriving from India in less than a day. Khyungpo received almost every transmission that he had received in India again from this yogin in Tibet. He is identified in the *Blue Annals* as Rāhulaguptavajra (Gö Lotsāwa, vol. 1, 858; Roerich, 732) and is also called "the yogin of the black mountain" (*ri nag*), which may refer to Krishnāgiri in South India. He was also a teacher of Atīsha (Chattopadhyaya, *Atīsha and Tibet*, 72) and a disciple of Maitrīpa (*Biographical Dictionary*, vol. 1, 781, cited in Martin, *Tibskrit*). As quoted above, Kongtrul refers to Lama Rāhula as one of the five main sources of Khyungpo Naljor's doctrine. See Zangpo, *Timeless Rapture*, 245–48, for a brief story and a supplication to him by Kongtrul.

117 *Catalogue*, 433–34 (f. 27a7–b1). "Engage in the Space" is *mkha' la spyod pa*, a literal rendering of the name "Khechara," the realm or "heavenly abode" of those ḍākinīs, the place of "engagement" or "activity" (*spyod pa*) in "space" (*mkha' la*). Space is also a relevant metaphor for vagina, and "great unity" refers to the union of that space (of emptiness) and bliss. The description references the specific transference practice (*'pho ba*) whereby the consciousness is visualized as moving up through each of the four chakras until its final exit into Kecharī.

118 The Virūpa connected with Sukhasiddhī is apparently a different one than the Indian mahāsiddha of the same name associated with the Lamdre (*lam 'bras*) lineage. *The Story of Sukhasiddhī* can be found in *ST*, vol. 1, 49–58, with English translation in Riggs, *Like an Illusion*, 40–43.

119 Or Vairochanavajra, the Indian master active around 1150. Not to be confused with the Tibetan of the same name who brought the dzogchen teachings to Tibet (circa 800).

120 Mokchokpa et al., *Brief Life Story of Lama Khyungpo Naljor*, *ST*, vol. 1, 72 (f. 7b5–8a3); Riggs, *Like an Illusion*, 51. Vajrāsana or Dorje Denpa (rDo rje gdan pa) in Tibetan can be translated as "The One at the Vajra Seat," referring to Bodhgaya in India. There were at least four successors to that title: (1) Puṇyākaragupta, (2) Ratnākaragupta, (3) Abhayākaragupta, and (4) Tsa mi Lo tsā ba. There is much confusion around this, and both Tibetan and Western writers have avoided it by simply

calling him/them Vajrāsana or Dorje Denpa. One Tibetan author, Katok Rikdzin Tsewang Norbu (1698–1755), who tried to sort it all out, posits Puṇyākaragupta as Khyungpo Naljor's guru. See his *Biographies of Some Holy Ones* in his Selected Writings, vol. 1, ff. 669–705. (Thanks to Cyrus Stearns for providing his translation of the relevant section.) In Jamgön Kongtrul's lineage supplication, two Vajrāsanas are praised: the one called Great Dorje Denpa is presumably Puṇyākaragupta and in the next supplication Abhayākaragupta is named specifically. Jamgön Kongtrul, *Garland of Udumbara*, *DZ*, vol. 12, 398 and 400. Thus it seems that Khyungpo Naljor had a connection with two different masters who might be called Vajrāsana, a fact both helpful and frustrating.

121 Mokchokpa et al., *Brief Life Story of Lama Khyungpo Naljor*, *ST*, vol. 1, 72, 91, and 109; Riggs, *Like an Illusion*, 63 and 71. A text entitled *Lama Rāhula's Oral Instructions on Five Tantras* can be found in the *Kinnaur Shangpa Texts*, vol. 1, 352–55.

122 *dPal rgyud sde lnga'i rgya gzhung* or *dPal rgyud sde lnga'i sgrub thabs* by Loppön Dorje Denpa, translated by the Indian paṇḍita Vairochanarakṣhita and the Tibetan Lendarma Lodrö and edited by the great translator Lotsāwa Rinchen Zangpo, *ST*, vol. 9, 543–49.

123 Khyungpo's biography states that this practice was given according to the root and explanatory tantras of *Jewel Ocean* as found in the library at Srī-dhanyakataka, a stūpa in south India associated with Kālachakra and other very early teachings: "*de ni rin chen rgya mthso'i rtsa rgyud bshad brgyud dang/ dpal ldan 'bras phungs kyi bre'i nang na ji ltar bzhugs pa bzhin no.*" *ST*, vol. 1, 73 (f. 8a3–4). This tantra has not been located and may not now be extant. In the beginning lines of Kongtrul's recitation manual for this practice, *Essence of Profound Meaning*, he mentions that it was disseminated by Bodhisattva Ratnamati (Byang chub sems dpa' bLo gros rin chen) based on *Jewel Ocean* . See *GK*, vol. 8, 434. Ratnamati was a monk from central India who did translations into Chinese in the sixth century, though this may not be the same person. Also see Jamgön Kongtrul, *The Treasury of Knowledge: Book Eight, Part Four: Esoteric Instructions*, 249; *TOK*, vol. 3, 403.

124 *Nigu's Condensed Guidance Manual* (*Ni gu'i 'khrid chos drug yig bsdus pa*), *T-CW*, vol. 12, 958.

125 Jamgön Kongtrul, *TOK*, vol. 1, 534; *The Treasury of Knowledge: Book Eight, Part Four: Esoteric Instructions*, 233.

126 Mokchokpa et al., *Brief Life Story of Khyungpo Naljor*, *ST*, vol. 1, 92 (f. 17b6) and Gö Lotsāwa, *BA*, vol. 2, 857; Roerich, *BA*, 731. The Hidden Yogin (sBas pa'i rnal 'byor) is sometimes associated with Rāhulagupta or with Maitrīpagupta. In Riggs, *Like an Illusion*, for instance, the translator simply substitutes "Maitrīpa" for sBas pa'i rnal 'byor without comment. I have not found this identity explicitly stated in any records. Venerable Tenga Rinpoche states that the Hidden Yogin is a different person than either of the two masters, and that he is an incarnation of the Buddha's son Rāhula. E-mail communication through his translator Thomas Roth, Feb. 22, 2009.

127 Kalu Rinpoche, *The Sādhana of the Five Deities of Chakrasaṃvara in the Shangpa Tradition*.

128 *Catalogue*, 513 (f. 67a7) and Jamgön Kongtrul, *Five Ḍākinīs' Method of Accomplishment and Empowerment Blessing*, *ST*, vol. 2, 764. Tāranātha, *Mine of Jewels* (*Rin chen 'byung gnas*), *T-CW*, vol. 5.

129 Shavari or Shavari-pa (Sha ba ri pa, aka Ri khrod zhabs) was a great Indian master

of tantra and the guru of Saraha. He is especially associated with the mahāmudrā teachings, the *dohā* tradition, and the practice of the Six-Branch yoga of Kālachakra. For the story of his life according to the Six-Branch yoga tradition (*saḍaṅgayoga*), see Stearns, "The Life and Tibetan Legacy of the Indian Mahāpaṇḍita Vibhūticandra," 139–41.

130 Blessing of Constant Four Deities (*Byin rlabs lha bzhi 'bral ba med*) is mentioned in Jamgön Kongtrul, *Radiant Light of Timeless Awareness*. Also see *Catalogue*, 434 (f. 27b5).

131 *Catalogue*, 514 (f. 67b4); Roerich, *BA*, 730. Atayavajra is sometimes said to be Advayavajra, who in turn is identified with Maitrīpa, but that would make Kongtrul's lineage statement a rather strange redundancy.

132 The practice text called *Guru Yoga in Connection with Six-Armed Protector Dwelling in the Heart* (*mGon po phyag drug pa snying bzhugs dang 'brel pa'i bla ma'i rnal 'byor*) or Secret Precept (*mka' rgya ma*) was arranged by Khyentse Wangpo (mKhyen rtse'i dbang po; 1820–1892) at Tashi Lhunpo, based on instructions from Kachen Lozang Gelek (dKa' chen bLo bzang dge legs), although in the index the famous Chankya Rolpai Dorje (lCang skya Rol pa'i rdo rje) is also mentioned. It can be found in *DZ*, vol. 12, 747–57.

133 *Elixir Rain of Spiritual Powers*, *ST*, vol. 1, 748. See Riggs, *Like an Illusion*, 263–77, although the author is misidentified there.

134 For Kalu Rinpoche's "plan" in spreading the dharma in North America, see his *The Dharma That Illuminates All Beings Impartially like the Light of the Sun and the Moon*, 7–12.

Notes to Chapter 1, Stages in the Path of Illusion

1 The eight similes (*sgyu ma dpe brgyad*) in Tibetan are 1) *rmi lam*, 2) *sgyu ma*, 3) *mig thor* or *mig yor*, 4) *smig rgyu*, 5) *chu'i zla ba*, 6) *brag ca*, 7) *dri za'i grong khyer*, and 8) *sprul pa*. The list varies and the order varies as well. This order follows Longchenpa in *The Great Completion Natural Ease in Illusion*. The list of twelve (*sgyu ma dpe bcu gnyis*) adds to those eight: 9) *chu bur*, 10) *glog*, 11) *gzugs brnyan*, and 12) *'ja' tshon*.

2 *Diamond Sūtra*: *skar ma rab rib mar me dang/sgyu ma zil ba chu bur dang/ rmi lam klog dang sprin lta bu/ 'du byas de ltar blta bar bya*.

3 Buddhaghosa, *The Path of Purification: Visuddhimagga*, book 3, paragraph 95 (p. 106) and book 7, paragraph 59 (p. 206).

4 In *The Life of the Buddha*, Edward J. Thomas says, "Māyā has also troubled the mythologists, and the attempt has been made to connect her with the Māyā-doctrine of Vedānta. But the sense of Māyā as cosmic illusion does not exist either in Pāli or Sanskrit in the works that record her name. Māyā is magic power, deception. The idea of the magic power of beauty is often expressed in a woman's name" (25, n. 2).

5 *Sūtra of the Vast Display*, translated in Bays, *The Voice of the Buddha*, vol. 1, 47.

6 *Sūtra That Unravels the Intent*, translated in Powers, *Wisdom of Buddha*, 15–21.

7 *Analysis of the Stages of Self-Consecration* (Toh. 1805), vol. Ngi, f. 112a7, cited in Jamgön Kongtrul, *Treasury of Knowledge: Book Eight, Part Three: Elements of Tantric Practice*, 199. Āryadeva was the foremost disciple of the great philosopher Nāgārjuna in the 3rd century CE and cofounder of the madhyamaka philosophy.

8 Jamgön Kongtrul, *The Treasury of Knowledge: Book Eight, Part Three: The Elements of Tantric Practice*, 198–206.

9 Longchenpa Drimey Özer, *An Excellent Chariot*, vol. Tha, 52 (f. 3b3–6).

10 Longchenpa Drimey Özer, *Trilogy on Natural Ease* (*Ngal gso skor gsum*), translated by Herbert Guenther in *Kindly Bent to Ease Us*.

11 Nāgārjuna, *Root Verses of the Middle called Wisdom*. That verse reads:

I prostrate to the one
Who teaches that whatever is dependently arisen
Does not arise, does not cease,
Is not permanent, is not extinct,
Does not come, does not go,
And is neither one thing nor different things.
I prostrate to the perfect Buddha, the supreme of all who speak,
Who completely dissolves all fabrications and teaches peace.

Translation by Ari Goldfield, in Khenpo Tsültrim Gyamtso, *The Sun of Wisdom*, 1.

12 There are many instances of the term "bodhisattva" first used in the *nikāyas* to describe the Buddha's life immediately preceding the one where he became Buddha. See also Dayal, *The Bodhisattva Doctrine in Buddhist Sanskrit Literature*, 43; and Huntington, *The Emptiness of Emptiness*, 19–20.

13 Lopez, "Paths Terminable and Interminable," 147.

14 Karl Brunnhölz has translated the all-important *Ornament of Clear Realization* by Maitreya and other commentaries on it as *Gone Beyond*, in three volumes, and Richard Barron has translated Jamgön Kongtrul's section on the subject in books 9 and 10 as *Treasury of Knowledge: Books Nine and Ten: Journey and Goal*.

15 For example, in Vasubandhu's *Abhidharmakosha*, they are defined in verse 6.67 (*byang chub de dang mthun nyid phyir/ sum cu rtsa bdun de'i phyogs mthun*). In Buddhagosha's *Visuddhimagga*, they are described in chap. 22, 33–38. They can also be translated as "states sharing in enlightenment."

16 Jamgön Kongtrul, *TOK*, vol. 3, 465.

17 Monier-Williams, *A Sanskrit-English Dictionary*, 812.

18 Jamgön Kongtrul, *TOK*, vol. 3, 464–65.

19 Niguma, *Stages in the Path of Illusion*, *ST*, vol. 6, 708 (f. 2b4–5). English translation in this book, verse 13.

20 Niguma, *Stages in the Path of Illusion: The Commentary*, *ST*, vol. 6, 748 (f. 7b5–6). English translation in this book.

21 For instance, six or nine grounds are mentioned in the *Abhidharmakosha* of Vasubandhu, 5.15.

22 This is a Sanskrit text considered part of the Vinaya, primarily concerning the life of the Buddha (and not translated into Tibetan). The ten levels (*daśa-bhūmi*) occur in the context of the Buddha's previous life as the bodhisattva, as does the original concept of the bodhisattva: "The word *bodhisatta* is very old and occurs in the Pāli *nikāyas*. Gautama Buddha speaks of himself as a *bodhisatta*, when he refers to the time before the attainment of Enlightenment. This seems to be the earliest signification of the word." Dayal, *The Bodhisattva Doctrine in Buddhist Sanskrit Literature* , 43.

23 *Sūtra on the Ten Grounds*, Toh. 44. This is chap. 31 of the *Flower Ornament Sūtra*.

24 *Bodhisattva Grounds*, a section of the massive work by Asaṅga called *Yogāchārabhūmi*.

25 Rahula, *A Critical Study of the Mahāvastu*, 62, citing Dutt, *Buddhist Sects in India*, citing the *Madhyamakāvatāra*. For a review of the ten grounds and ten perfections according to Chandrakīrti, see Huntington, *The Emptiness of Emptiness*, 20–23, and the translation of the relevant text on 149–96. See also Padmakara Translation Group, *Introduction to the Middle Way*.
26 Maitreya, *Ornament of Clear Realization*, Toh. 3786.
27 See note 163 below.
28 Niguma, *Stages in the Path of Illusion*, *ST*, vol. 6, 725 (f. 11a2–3), vv. 145–46 and in *Stages in the Path of Illusion: The Commentary*, *ST*, vol. 6, 774–75 (ff. 20b6–21a1).
29 Dutt, *Buddhist Sects in India*, 219 and 251.
30 The ten *pāramī* in Pāli from the *Buddhavamsa* (chap. 2) are generosity (*dāna*), ethical discipline (*sīla*), renunciation (*nekkhamma*), wisdom (*paññā*), diligence (*vīrya*), patience (*khanti*), honesty (*sacca*), determination (*adhiṭṭāna*), love (*mettā*), and equanimity (*upekkhā*).
31 Dayal, *The Bodhisattva Doctrine in Buddhist Sanskrit Literature*, 168.
32 See, for example, the extensive discussion of the term in ibid. 165–67.
33 Jamgön Kongtrul, *Treasury of Knowledge: Book Eight, Part Four: Frameworks of Buddhist Philosophy*, 184. See that and 242 for more on the relationship of grounds and perfections.
34 Williams, *Mahāyāna Buddhism*, 207. Har Dayal, *The Bodhisattva Doctrine in Buddhist Sanskrit Literature*, 167, takes it one remarkable step further: "The *[Daśabhūmika]* definitely increases the number of the *pāramitās* to ten, as it teaches that a *bodhisattva* practices one of the *pāramitās* in each of the ten *bhūmis* (stages) of his career. This alteration may have been due to the rivalry with the Hīnayānists, who had devised the Pāli formula of the ten *pāramīs* . . . . But it is more probably that the number of the *pāramitās* (and the *bhūmis*) was raised to ten as a consequence of the invention of the decimal system of computation in the science of arithmetic in the third or fourth century A.D." and "Many old formulae of Indian philosophy and religion were recast according to the decimal system on account of the enthusiasm evoked by this epoch-making invention."
35 Chart by David Picariello. Thank you Dave!
36 In his introduction to *Gone Beyond*, Karl Brunnhölzl suggests, "So, if one cannot or does not want to prepare for the 'higher teachings', it seems better to study some 'lighter' Buddhist reading, since frustration is almost guaranteed."
37 In "Paths Terminable and Interminable," Donald S. Lopez suggests another point of view: "A historicist might argue that the persistence of this complex of defilements as an essential component of the vocabulary of Buddhist scholasticism only testifies to the inability of Buddhist practitioners to become enlightened: there must be such obstructions because, despite the earnest efforts of meditators, no one seemed to be arriving at the further shore. This very argument was put forth in China to prove the presence of the degenerate age" (154).
38 Buswell and Gimello, *Paths to Liberation*, 11.
39 *Perfection of Wisdom in Eight Thousand Lines*, Dg.K. Shes byin, vol. Ka. 45 (f. 23a1–3) (Toh. 12).
40 Also entitled *sGyu ma lam rim dri med snying po* (*The Essential Stainless Stages on the Path of Illusion*), the descriptive title used in the colophon. This title is also used in Jamgön Kongtrul, *The Beryl Key Catalogue* , *GK*, vol. 10, 480 (f. 11b6). Five editions were consulted for this translation and are listed in the bibliography.

41 *sku*, Skt. *kāya*, is a difficult concept to translate. I have used "kāya" when in the context of the three kāyas and "Body" (as distinguished from "body," *lus*) when in the context of the appearance of the deity's Body. Another word for body is *gzugs*, generally translated here as "form," such as in the "form kāyas" (*gzugs kyi sku*; Skt. *rūpakāya*).

42 *las rigs grub pa*: The five enlightened activities (*phrin las lnga*) of pacification, enrichment, overpowering, wrathful activity, and spontaneous accomplishment (*zhi ba, rgyas pa, dbang ba, drag po, lhun gyis grub pa*).

43 The Shangpa edition (*ST*) has *dam pa* (sublime) here, but I've preferred *bum pa* (vase) from the other editions since it is obviously a reference to the first part of an empowerment, called "the vase empowerment."

44 *spyod pa* (conduct) in all copies. However one usually finds its homonym *dpyod pa* (examination, revelation) in its place in commentaries on the subject.

45 Taking *brgya la* (in a hundred) in most texts for *rgya la* (even if).

46 These two lines have a number of variable spellings. I have used: *dus dang lus dang dmigs pa yis/ dben pa'i gnas su rmi lam bzung*. *ST* has *yul* for *lus*, *yin* for *yis*, and *bden pa'i gnas* (true place) for *dben pa'i gnas*, which would hardly make sense. According to Tāranātha, "time, body, and mental images" refer to enhancement techniques called "nine unfailing vital points (*gnad 'chugs med dgu*) for recognizing dreams: three times of day, three physical postures, and three visualization practices. *Profound Meaning Expanded*, *ST*, vol. 3, 414 (f. 40b1–3).

47 *bag chags bzhi*: The four types of habitual patterns: habitual patterns which become the basis of attached conceptualization (*mngon brjod kyi bag chags*), habitual patterns of the self-concept (*bdag lta'i bag chags*), habitual patterns of the factors of existence (*srid pa'i yan lag gi bag chags*), and concordant habitual patterns (*rigs mthun pa'i bag chags*).

48 The unusual term in all texts is *dge sdig bcas nas*, but ATG thinks this could be a mistake for its homonym *dge sdig dpyad nas* (examining virtue and nonvirtue). In any case, the sense is that dreams offer the golden opportunity to practice virtue and reject nonvirtue while comprehending the nature of illusion.

49 *drod* in the Ume and Kinnaur texts seems correct, rather than *don* in the others.

50 *bsre 'pho'i gnad*: There are various meanings given for "blending and transferring," such as that it is the blending of mind and prāṇa along with the ejection of consciousness, or the blending of basic space and awareness with the transference into the lucid clarity of dharmatā (*BD*, vol. 2, 3054). See also Jamgön Kongtrul, *The Treasury of Knowledge: Book Eight, Part Four: Esoteric Instructions* , 250–51 and *The Treasury of Knowledge: Book Eight, Part Three: The Elements of Tantric Practice* , 162–63 for the use of this term in the Kagyu traditions. Tāranātha distinguishes the Shangpa use of the term in *Profound Meaning Expanded*: "As to 'blending and transferring', all of the individual instructions of Lord Marpa the Translator display many different layouts of 'blending', but that is not explained here. In this instruction tradition itself, there are four blendings, such as blending clarity and emptiness, [equipoise and subsequent attainment, day and night, and bliss and emptiness] that were explained, and in addition the three or four wisdoms of blending and transference." *ST*, vol. 3, 481. This last refers to the sixth of *Fifteen Especially Exalted Instructions* in Niguma's extensive path. In Khyungpo Naljor's text of that name, it says "Illusion in dream (sleep) and lucid clarity, (these two) are mixed. That is the defining characteristic of blending and transference." *ST*, vol. 6, 188 (f. 14a4–5). P and CT mistakenly have *gnas* rather than *gnad*.

51 There are various versions of this phrase: *khor ba skye med* (unborn cyclic existence), *ST*; *khor ba skyed med* (useless . . .), P; *khor ba skyid med* (unhappy . . .), Kinnaur.

52 Again there are several versions here: "Leave behind" (*rgyab phul*) in the tengyur, Ume, and Kinnaur editions, but *rgyud khul* in *ST*, which might be a misspelling of *rgyud skul*, "to inspire" or "prompt one's being." These are more or less the same meaning. The last line is more problematic: *ST* and Kinnaur editions have *bdun pa drag pos bcud la bor*, which I have attempted to interpret here, although the phrase *bcud la bor* (literally "discard in/to the essence") is very unusual. The tengyurs have *mdun ma drag po'i bcud la bor*. *Mdun ma* or *'dun ma* (rather than *'dun pa*) means "concerns," "goals," or "desired results," giving a meaning that one should "abandon the essence of one's intense goals." This interpretation was favored by ATG.

53 *ST* has "four joys" (*dga' bzhi*), but I have used the reading in all other copies: *dga' zhing* (or *shing*) *brten par byed pa'o*.

54 The reading of *bral ba* here in the tengyur, as against *'dra ba* of the other texts, is consistent with the commentary, where it is given as *'dzin pa dang bral ba* . *ST*, vol. 6, 763 (f. 15a1).

55 Of the various versions (*gtags*, *rtogs*, *rtog*), I have chosen *gtogs* (except). *ST*, vol. 6, 718 (f. 7b6).

56 *'khor yug sum ldan*, in all copies except Ume, which shows abbreviated style for *'khor lo gsum ldan* (three wheels). I could not find a definitive explanation of this term. Most likely it is a reference to the other three of the four "blendings" discussed above in note 50. Or it may refer to the three times of sleep, dream, and intermediate state mentioned above, where this vision of saṃbhogakāya occurs (this according to Lama Tharchin Rinpoche), or to the immediately following mention of "illusion, deity's Bodies, and manifest clarity." In Tāranātha's teachings on blending day and night, there are three times of dawn, dusk, and evening to train one's intention, and there are also three applications of the blending: to dreams, to illusory body, and to lucid clarity. *Profound Meaning Expanded*, 468–69. Finally, if it is a mistake for "three wheels," it might be *khor lo rnam gsum*: three ways a monk practices: 1) the wheel of study through reading, listening, and thinking (*lgog pa thos bsam gyi 'khor lo*), (2) the wheel of abandonment through meditative stability (*spong ba bsam gtan gyi 'khor lo*), and (3) the wheel of service through activities (*bya ba las kyi 'khor lo*).

57 *yul snang ji bzhin* (*'phrul snang*, "deluded appearance," in Kinnaur carries the same meaning): The dream yoga sequential practices are to recognize, refine, increase, emanate, and transform dreams and to ascertain objective appearance as similarly illusion. See *Vajra Lines of the Six Dharmas* in chapter 2 of this book; *ST*, vol. 6, 167; and the relevant teachings in Tāranātha, *Profound Meaning Expanded*, 408 on.

58 *byin pa rnam bzhi*: the four kinds of generosity are to give material goods (*zang zing*), teachings (*chos*), comfort from fear (*mi 'jigs pa*), and love (*byams*).

59 *yang na lta ba mthar thug pa/ bzang por 'dod pa'i sgrib pa yin*. This is similar to afflictive states of views, where one holds one's own view as paramount (ATG). There is no clarification of this in the commentary.

60 Verses 129–34 are quoted and commented upon in Gyurme Dechen's *Complete Explanation of the Vajra Lines of the Six Dharmas* , 486–89 and are used as the take-off point for an extensive discussion of exactly who proclaims the "sounds of the mahāyāna dharma" and to whom.

61 The reference seems to be to a verse by Maitreya in *Ornament of Clear Realization* that

is famously disputed as to whether it is positing four kāyas (in the original Sanskrit: svabhavikakāya, saṃbhogikakāya, nairmanikakāya, and dharmakāya) or whether the first three are just different aspects of the dharmakāya. The verse reads "Essence [kāya], complete enjoyment [kāya] and similarly the emanation [kāya] for others are the activity of dharmakāya. Thus four are correctly named." (*ngo bo nyid longs rdzogs bcas dang/ de bzhin gzhan pa'i sprul sku ni/ chos sku mdzad pa dang bcas pa/ rnam pa bzhir ni yang dag brjod*). If you would like more elaborations, see Makransky, *Buddhahood Embodied.*

62 The metaphor refers to the myth that geese (sometimes translated as "swan," though they did not exist in India) can drink diluted milk while extracting only the milk from the water. The line in some texts, (such as *ST* and the tengyurs) reads "like a goose in a lake" (*ngang pas mtsho la 'o ma len pa ltar*), but since this breaks the meter by two syllables, it appears to be a later insertion.

63 "Arhats with or without adornments" means with or without clairvoyance (*mngon shes*). As defined by Kongtrul, they "possess dissipating miraculous abilities of their own ground, such as clairvoyance" (*rang sa'i zag bcas kyi rdzu 'phrul gyi mngon shes sogs dang ldan pa*) (RY). The translation "in the early or later part of life, and so on" sidesteps a term in the Tibetan, *rgur chu* (or *sgur chu*), for which I have no information. The line reads: *rgur chu tshes* (or *tshe*) *stod tshes smad sogs.*

64 There is some debate over this point since there is sometimes said to be no more afflictive emotion at this stage, but others say not until the eighth ground.

65 *mang* in *ST* should be *med* as in the others. Here, "generosity" also implies the other perfections.

66 Described in the Path of Seeing, verses 101–4.

67 *rgyu gzhan tha dad med pa* (with *rgyu* here referring to "stuff" or nature, according to ATG). In the commentary, however, it reads *rgyud tha dad med pa* ("undifferentiated from [others'] minds or beings"), as in the Kinnaur edition.

68 The Kinnaur edition alone has *chos nyid* (nature of phenomena) rather than *chos ni* here.

69 *zag med mahā'i dbang bskur bas*: The Tibetan retains the Sanskrit for "great" empowerment and may be a reference to receiving the empowerment from Mahāvairochana or Vajradhara, as explained in the commentary.

70 These are generic requisites for all traditional treatises (*btsan bcos*, Skt. *śastra*), although the list sometimes varies slightly. See, for example, the "five essential observations" in Jamgön Kongtrul's introduction to his great *Treasury of Knowledge* in the first volume, *Treasury of Knowledge: Book One: Myriad Worlds*, 81–82.

71 This oft-quoted verse is from the *Song of Dohā Treasury*, f. 72b5 (Toh. 2224), also known as "People's Dohā" in Saraha's dohā trilogy. In the tengyur, the first line reads instead "Mind itself alone is the seed of everything" (*sem nyid gcig pu kun gyi sa bon te*). For translations, see Snellgrove, "Saraha's Treasury of Songs," Guenther, *Ecstatic Spontaneity*, and Jackson, *Tantric Treasures.*

72 *Vajra Garland Tantra* (Toh. 445), the explanatory tantra (*bshad rgyud*) of Guhyasamāja. The quotation is not found there, but is quoted in Nāgārjuna's commentary on the Guhyasamāja called *The Five Stages*, vol. Ngi, chap. 2, v. 2, f. 48a4–5 (Toh. 1802). The original Sanskrit reads:

yathā jalaṃ jale nyastaṃ ghṛtaṃ caiva yathā ghṛte/
svakīyaṃ ca svayaṃ paśyet jñanaṃ yatreha vandanā/

Web site of the Centre for Tantric Studies at the Asia-Africa Institute of the University of Hamburg, www.tantric-studies.org/2007/08/06/pancakrama-e-text-added.

73 *Drang srong rnams kha 'og tu lus tsud pa* (should be *chud pa*).

74 *Ye shes mngon par 'byung ba'i rgyud rgyas pa*, Skt. *Jñānābhyudaya*, not located and possibly not extant. However it is confirmed in the lineage by the record of its transmission by Khyungpo Naljor, who received it from the Ḍākinī Kanakashrī of Devīkoṭī, along with the *Sampuṭa Tantra* (Toh. 381), *Completion Phase Suchness*, *Shrīparamādya Ocean of Sacred Oaths* (*dPal mchog dra ba [dang po?] sdom pa rgya mtsho*), *Ocean of Timeless Awareness*, and *Array of Sacred Oaths*, the last two also quoted in this commentary but not located. See Tāranātha, *Clearing Up Darkness of the Mind*, *T-CW*, vol. 17, 454, and Mokchokpa et al., *Brief Life Story of Lama Khyungpo Naljor*, *ST*, vol. 1, 79 (f. 11a1–2). This same quote can be found in Longchenpa, *An Excellent Chariot* (f. 43a3) with the last two lines reading, instead: *gzhan dang rang bzhin 'bras bu'i don/ zab dang rgya che dbyer me pa'o.*

75 *sNying po rab tu gsal ba'i mdo*. Not located.

76 *Dri med snying po'i mdo.* Not located.

77 *Dense Array of Adornments Sūtra* (Toh. 110), f. 36b3–4, where there is considerable difference worth noting: The first line in fact concludes a previous point, while the second line is entirely absent. The third line reads "like the countenance of the new moon" (*dang po tshes pa'i zla mdog ltar*) rather than full moon (*dbang po tshes pa*). The rest is consistent, although the important ninth line is not in our Niguma text and has been added here from the sūtra. Of note also is the possible connection with the similar metaphor from the *Mahāyāna Highest Continuum*, where buddha nature is compared to the indestructibility of space, while consciousness and defilements are compared to the destructibility of the other elements that go to make up the Supreme Mountain and the rest of the phenomenal world (ATG).

78 *sna tshogs gzugs can*: that is, it carries the potential or seeds of all of our perceptions.

79 *Dense Array of Adornments Sūtra* (Toh. 110). The first two lines are on 91 (f. 46a6) and the second two are on 98 (f. 49b4).

80 *sNying po gsal ba*, the same as *The Fully Illuminated Essence Sūtra.*

81 *Dense Array of Adornments Sūtra* (Toh. 110), 73 (f. 37a3). Line 2 (*de yi dbyings las thog ma med*) appears also as *de yi dbyibs la thog ma med* (whose shapes are without beginning). "Negative tendencies" (*gnas ngan len*) is equivalent in meaning to "afflictive states" (*nyon mong pa*) (ATG).

82 *Dense Array of Adornments Sūtra* (Toh. 110), 88 (f. 44b1–2).

83 *rig pa*, which is here equivalent to clarity (*gsal ba*).

84 *Sa sde* is usually short for *Sa sde lnga* (*Five Sections on Grounds*), the five sections in Asaṅga's huge *Yogāchārabhūmi* (Toh. 4035–43), which would make perfect sense as a source for Niguma's work. However, the quotations attributed to it are not found there, and a later reference to it as a sūtra (*sa sde'i mdo*) seems to indicate a different source.

85 A subtle explanation using the same phrase (*rnam par shes pa*) as both a verb and a noun to explain itself. In Tibetan: *kun gzhi'i rnam shes gsal la rtog med kyi rnam par shes pa rnam par shes te/ rnam par shes pa nyid gsal la rtog pa med pa'o.*

86 *Dense Array of Adornments Sūtra* (Toh. 110), 109 (f. 55a5–6).

87 *Journey to Lanka Sūtra* (Toh. 107). The quotation does not appear to be in this sūtra. However, in Asaṅga's *Compendium of the Mahāyāna* (Toh 4048), it is quoted as

a verse from the *Abhidharma Sūtra*, which is not extant: "*bcom ldan 'das kyis chos mngon pa'i mdo las tshigs su bcad*" (f. 3a6–7).

88 *Mahāyāna Highest Continuum* (Toh. 4024). This exact quote does not appear in the text, although there are many similar ones, especially in the fourth chapter on the buddha nature constituent.

89 *Dense Array of Adornments Sūtra* (Toh. 110), 110 (f. 55b1–2). The quote in the sūtra has "feeble-minded" (*blo zhan*) rather than "bad-minded" (*blo ngan*), as in the Niguma texts.

90 *len pa'i rnam shes*, also called "appropriating or acquiring consciousness." It is the consciousness that results in taking on the five aggregates of existence in a body. It is the basic consciousness that continually identifies with the physical body, as well as with objects of perception (RY).

91 *Sa sde*: See note 84. A very similar quotation with the first lines nearly identical is found in Powers, *Wisdom of Buddha: The Saṁdhinirmocana Mahāyāna Sūtra*, 70-71.

92 *Sa sde'i mdo* (see note 84 above). This line is missing in the Kinnaur edition. Again, there is a very similar statement in ibid. 74–76.

93 *nyon mongs pa can gyi yid*: There is a further twofold division of the seventh consciousness, mentation with afflictive states, posited by Karmapa Rangjung Dorje and later scholars: afflictive mentation (*nyon yid*) and instantaneous mentation (*de ma thag pa'i yid*). See Jamgön Kongtrul, *Creation and Completion*, 51–59 for more on this.

94 *Journey to Lanka Sūtra* (Toh. 107), vol. Ca, 324 (f. 162b7). In the early sūtras attributed to the Third Turning of the Wheel of Dharma, such as the *Journey to Lanka* and *Sūtra That Unravels the Intent*, the teachings on consciousness divided consciousness into three groups: 1) mind (*sems*) which is equivalent to all-ground (*kun gzhi*), (2) mentation (*yid*) which is equivalent to the afflicted mentation (*nyon yid*), and (3) consciousness (*rnam shes*) which consists of six perceptions (*tshogs drug*). The language of the "eight consciousness groups" (*rnam shes tshogs brgyad*) developed in the later sūtras of the third turning (ATG, September 13, 2007).

95 According to ATG, consciousness here refers to all six consciousnesses (*tshogs drug*).

96 *Journey to Lanka Sūtra* (Toh. 107), vol. Ca, 324–25 (ff. 162b7–163a1).

97 The six primary afflictive states (*rtsa nyon*) are: desire (*'dod chags*), anger (*khong khro*), pride (*nga rgyal*), unawareness (*ma rig pa*), doubt (*the tshom*), and [afflicted] view (*lta ba*). The twenty secondary afflictions (*nye nyon*) are: wrath (*khro ba*), resentment (*'khon du 'dzin pa*), concealment (*'chab pa*), spite (*'tshig pa*), envy (*phrag dog*), avarice (*ser sna*), deceit (*sgyu*), hypocrisy (*g.yo*), self-satisfaction (*rgyags pa*), violence (*rnam par 'tshe ba*), lack of shame (*ngo mtshar med pa*), lack of embarrassment (*khrel med pa*), lethargy (*rmugs pa*), agitation (*rgod pa*), lack of confidence (*ma dad pa*), laziness (*le lo*), lack of conscientiousness (*bag med pa*), forgetfulness (*brjed nges pa*), distraction (*rnam par g.yeng ba*), and lack of awareness (*shes bzhin ma yin pa*). These are from the list of fifty-one mental events (*sems byung*) in the *Abhidharmasamuccaya*.

98 *Sublime Absorption Sūtra* (Toh. 137). But the quotation was not found in that sūtra nor in the *King of Absorption Sūtra* (Toh. 127).

99 *Ye shes mngon 'byung*, Skt. *Jñānābhyudaya**, probably the same as *Ye shes mngon par 'byung ba'i rgyud rgyas pa*. Not located, and possibly not extant (see note 74).

100 *Secret Ḍākinī Tantra* (Toh. 408), f. 246b1. An important difference in the second line

in the tantra reads *brjod bya rjod byed brgyad du bshad* (rather than *rgyud du 'gyur*), so that the quote would read, "Tantra is the essence of the four empowerments, [both] the contents and the medium, thus eight [tantras] are explained." The eight tantras, or continuums, then, would be the subject or contents and its medium, the words of the tantra, for each of the four empowerments. This is supported by the rest of this short tantra, really a chapter in the set known as the "Complete Thirty-two Ralis" (*Ra li so gnyis yongs rdzogs*), all found together in the kangyur (Toh. 383–414). *Secret Ḍākinī* is #26 of the thirty-two Ralis.

101 *Lam zung 'jug*: the unity of calm abiding and higher insight. ATG, September 20, 2007.

102 *Perfection of Wisdom in Eighteen Thousand Lines* (Toh. 10). This quote was found in the *Perfection of Wisdom in Eight Thousand Lines* (Toh. 12), f. 255a6–7, but without the lines concerning love and compassion. Without that line, this can be regarded as a list of the thirty-seven factors leading to enlightenment, that is, the path. It is also quoted in Longchenpa, *An Excellent Chariot*, 112 (f. 28a4–b1).

103 *Dam tshig bkod pa'i rgyud phyi ma*. Not located. Probably the same as or an addition to *Array of Sacred Oaths* (*Dam tshig bkod pa*), which was bestowed on Khyungpo Naljor by the Ḍākinī Kanakashrī of Devīkoṭi. See Tāranātha, *Clearing Up Darkness of the Mind*, *T-CW*, vol. 17, 454, and Mokchokpa et al., *Brief Life Story of Lama Khyungpo Naljor*, *ST*, vol. 1, 79 (f. 11a1–2). The quotes from this tantra were not found in *Dam tshig gsum bkod pa* (Toh. 502).

104 As a note of interest, this quote and several others are given in Longchenpa, *An Excellent Chariot*, as evidence that in the practice of guru yoga (*bla ma'i rnal 'byor*) one absolutely must visualize the guru as himself or herself rather than as the yidam. He says that not to do so is not guru yoga at all and is said to be an egregious fault (*nyes pa shin tu che*) (f. 40b3–41b1).

105 *Dam tshig bkod pa*.

106 *Rgyud sde lnga bcu*. In Longchenpa, *An Excellent Chariot* (f. 41a4), the quote is identified only as being from this text (fifty sections of tantra), if it is a single text. *Array of Sacred Oaths* (*Dam thsig bkod pa*) is not mentioned.

107 *Rigs lnga'i dam tshig bkod pa*, probably the same as *Array of Sacred Oaths* and *Array of Sacred Oaths Latter Tantra*. Nirvirana Vishkambin (sGrib pa rnam par sel ba) was one of the eight bodhisattvas who received teachings directly from the Buddha.

108 *Dri ma med par grags pa'i mdo*. This should be the famous *Vimalakīrti Sūtra* (Toh. 176), but the quote is not found there.

109 *dran pa nye bar bzhag pa bzhi*; Skt. *catvāri smṛyupasthāna*.

110 *Byang chub sems dbang blo gros rab brtan gyi mdo*: not located. The Sanskrit name has been reconstructed from the Tibetan, as indicated by the asterisk. The same quotes are found in Longchenpa, *An Excellent Chariot* beginning on 88 (f.21b5). Different quotes from the same sūtra are found as interlinear notes in Khungpo Naljor, *Natural Liberation through Grasping Illusory Body and Sixfold Illusory Body* , *ST*, vol. 8, 617–33, so it was clearly available.

111 *stong pa nyid, mtshan ma med pa, smon pa med pa*: These are called the three gates or approaches to total freedom (*rnam thar sgo gsum*).

112 *yang dag spong ba bzhi*, Skt. *catvāri saṃyakprahāṇa*: "four correct abandonments," "four perfect eliminations." Also see Gampopa, *Ornament of Precious Liberation*, f. 150b.

113 *rdzu 'phrul [gyi] rkang pa bzhi*, Skt. *catvāri ṛiddhipāda*: "Four 'feet' or 'limbs' of

miraculous action: they are the meditative absorptions of *'dun pa, brtson 'grus, bsam pa* or *sems*, and *dpyod pa* or *spyod pa*. These four factors are called "supports" or "feet" because they serve as causes for the attainment of five supernormal states of perception (the "miraculous powers"): clairvoyance, clairaudience, recall of past lifetimes, telepathy, and special powers (such as flying, passing through solid matter, and creating emanations).

114 *spyod pa* in all versions of the Niguma texts, both in the root verses and commentary. However, in most instances of this list it is *dpyod pa*, "direct revelation," "analysis," or "discernment." See, for example, Gampopa, *Ornament of Precious Liberation*, f. 150b. I have left it as *spyod pa* ("conduct") since the commentary in the sūtra seems to support that reading.

115 *mi dmigs*: The Ume edition has *mi gnas pa* ("not abiding"), which also works.

116 In the opinion of Ācaryā Lama Tenpa, *'byed pa* does not mean "distinguish" or "analyze" but rather "to reveal," equivalent in meaning to *shes rab*. It is the defining characteristic (*mtshan nyid*) of wisdom (*shes rab*); wisdom develops through clear or distinct knowing.

117 *drod, rtse mo, bzod pa, chos mchog.*

118 *dbang po lnga*; Skt. *pañcendriya*. As long as they can still be overcome by their respective discordant factors (such as the lack of faith or laziness), they are called faculties, and when they are not affected any more by these factors, the same five are called powers (*stobs lnga*; Skt. *pañcabala*).

119 There are numerous discrepancies in the wording in the quotations from *Ornament of Clear Realization*, and I have translated with reference to the original and its commentaries, rather than the Niguma texts. Here, for instance, the Niguma texts say "countering the notion of form" (*gzugs sogs 'du shes ldog pa dang*), but this exact phrasing actually does not occur in the *Ornament* until the discussion of the signs on the Path of Seeing. Here it should just be *gzugs la sogs las ldog pa dang*. It is possible that there were variant translations of the Sanskrit.

120 *the tshom mi dal zad pa dang* as in the Ume and Kinnaur editions and in *Ornament of Clear Realization* (rather than *the tshom yid la zad pa dang* in the canons and *ST*) refers to both the elimination of doubts concerning the ultimate meaning being in fact the ultimate meaning, and to the expiration of any rebirth in bad existences without freedom or leisure. Mikyö Dorje, *Noble One's Resting at Ease*, vol. 2, 147.

121 According to Mikyö Dorje, *Noble One's Resting at Ease*, vol. 2, 150, the five obscurations (*sgrib pa lnga*) are: (1) sense desire (*'dod 'dun*), (2) ill-will (*gnod sems*), (3) sleep and torpor (*gnyid dang rmugs pa*), (4) agitation and guilt (*rgod pa dang rgyod pa*), and (5) doubt (*the tshom*).

122 Maitreya, *Ornament of Clear Realization* (Toh. 3786), f. 8a7–b1 (chap. 4, vv. 40–42ab). According to the commentaries, these are the signs of irreversibility on the level of warmth (the signs of culmination are different and dealt with in chapter 5 of *Ornament*), and usually there are eleven (including "clean clothing" in the next quote from *Ornament*). Thanks to Karl Brunnhölzl for his input on this and all quotations from the *Ornament of Clear Realization*.

123 Ibid. The first verse is on f. 8b1–2 (chap. 4, vv. 42cd–43ab), continuous with the last quote from *Ornament*.

124 In this enumeration it seems that a) the mind free of deception and b) assuming abstinence (*sbyong ba ni len pa*) are counted as one. In the original, this list is continuous with the preceding list. Mikyo Dorje's commentary counts "clean clothing" as the

eleventh sign of warmth, while there are six signs of peak, beginning with no parasites.

125 This verse is not connected with the former verse in the original, and is from the fifth chapter of *Ornament* (chap. 5.1, f. 9a7) on the "culminating training," rather than "peak of application" (both translating *rtse mor phyin pa'i sbyor ba* in different contexts). It describes the twelve signs of the ground of warmth (not peak). The twelve signs were taught in the prajñāpāramitā sūtras and apply either to dreams or waking states, depending on the commentator. The last line (*rnam pa bcu gnyis dag tu bzhed*) is not included in the Kinnaur edition.

126 *rGya mtsho'i rgyud phyi ma*. This text has not been positively identified but is probably the same as or an appendix to *Ocean of Timeless Awareness* (*Ye shes rgya mtsho'i rgyud*) often referenced in Shangpa literature, as for instance in *Glorious Deathless Great Timeless Awareness* in this volume. It was received by Khyungpo Naljor from the Ḍākinī Kanakashrī of Devīkoṭi.

127 Maitreya, *Ornament of Clear Realization* (Toh. 3786), f. 8b2 (chap. 4, vv. 43cd–44ac). According to the commentaries, the first two lines are the last two of the six signs of peak, while the last three lines represent the two signs of acceptance. Signs of acceptance (*bzod pa'i rtags*) is mistakenly written as *bzod pa'i stobs* in most editions except for the Kinnaur edition. Also in that edition, *bkri bar* (to guide) accords with the original in *Ornament*, rather than *sgrib pa* (to obscure) in the third line.

128 *Bu mo bzhis zhus pa*. Not located. The quotation was not found in the similarly titled *Questions of Four Goddesses* (*Caturdevī-paripṛcchā*; *Lha mo bzhis yongs su zhus pa*).

129 Maitreya, *Ornament of Clear Realization* (Toh. 3786), f. 8b2–3 (chap. 4, vv. 44d–45). This quotation closes the section in the *Ornament of Clear Realization* concerning the twenty signs on the Path of Application. In that text they are simply listed, though it seems that various commentators have divided them differently, including apparently Niguma, which explains why the quotation is divided up and interspersed with other quotations. For clarification, the list of the twenty follows, with divisions according to Mikyö Dorje's commentary in brackets.

> [The Eleven Signs of Warmth]
>
> (1) countering form and so on,
> (2) the expiration of doubts,
> (3) nonleisure,
> (4) dwelling in virtue oneself,
> (5) establishing others in it also,
> (6) generosity and so on as support for others,
> (7) no hesitation about the profound meaning,
> (8) loving [actions] of the body and so on not accompanied
> by the five obscurations,
> (9) all latent tendencies conquered,
> (10) mindfulness and awareness,
> (11) clean clothing and such.
>
> [The Six Signs of Peak:]
>
> (12) parasites and such not occurring on the body,
> (13) mind free of deception,

(14) assuming abstinence,
(15) eliminating avarice,
(16) proceeding by possessing the nature of phenomena,
(17) seeking hell for the sake of sentient beings.

[The Two Signs of Acceptance:]

(18) impervious to others' misguidance,
(19) realizing that devils who expound alien paths are "devils."

[The One Sign of Supreme Dharma:]

(20) Activity that pleases the Buddha.

130 *Khye'u rab snang [gi mdo]*, not located. (The quote is not found in the similarly named sutra at Toh. 103.) Tangtong Gyalpo (15th C.) also quotes from this sūtra, calling it *"The Questions of Kumāraprabha Sūtra"* in *Collection of the Essentials: Words on the Vital Points of the Hearing Lineage of Niguma, the Ḍākinī of Timeless Awareness* (*TTG-S*, vol. 1, 276–77). The quote there is germane: "It is said 'all phenomena are illusions, dreams'. If you recall these spoken words, you will be released from the bonds of existence and definitely awaken in this very life."

131 *chos shes pa'i bzod pa*. The knowledge or knowing of phenomena, or "dharma cognition" (*chos shes pa*) is one of the ten or eleven types of wisdom. "Acceptance of the knowing of phenomena" can also be translated as "patience acceptance producing knowledge of a phenomena."

132 Another way of explanation by Longchenpa is clarifying: 1) "Knowing phenomena" (*chos shes pa*) is to see the specifically characterized (*rang mtshan*) subject (*chos can*) of each of the four truths. (2) "Acceptance of knowing phenomena" (*chos shes pa la bzod pa*) is to be unafraid when seeing the specific characteristics. (3) "Subsequent knowing" (*rjes su shes pa*) is to see the emptiness of the specifically characterized nature of phenomena (*chos nyid*) of each of the four truths. (4) "Acceptance of subsequent knowing" (*rjes su shes pa'i bzod pa*) is to be unafraid of seeing the sky. *An Excellent Chariot*, 103 (f. 29a3–4).

133 *byang chub kyi yan lag bdun*: seven factors or branches of enlightenment: (1) *dran pa yang dag*, (2) *chos rab du rnam par 'byed pa yang dag*, (3) *brtson 'grus yang dag*, (4) *dga' ba yang dag*, (5) *shin tu sbyangs pa yang dag*, (6) *ting nge 'dzin yang dag*, and (7) *btang snyoms yang dag*.

134 *bLo gros 'byung gnas kyis zhus pa'i mdo* (called *bLo gros rab gnas kyis zhus pa'i mdo* in the Kinnaur edition). Not located. The same quotes are used by Longchenpa in *An Excellent Chariot*, beginning on 97 (f. 26a1).

135 Though this line in all texts besides the Kinnaur edition, and in Longchenpa (f. 26b), reads *sems mnyam par bzhag pa ma yin pa*, ATG feels that it simply does not make any sense unless there is a negation. Thus we are reading: *sems mnyam par <u>ma</u> bzhag pa ma yin pa*, which is also confirmed by the Kinnaur text, 181 (f. 21a3).

136 The "fear of retinue" in this quotation is simply *'khor gyi 'jigs pa*, and is often understood by Tibetans as referring to the fear of the loss or lack of retinue or support. However in Gampopa's *Ornament of Precious Liberation, a Wish-Fulfilling Gem* (156a3), also quoting from the *Ten Grounds Sūtra*, it says specifically "the fear of trouble among the retinue" (*'khor gyi nang du bag tsha ba'i 'jigs pa*). Compare to the third line here (*'khor gyi 'jigs bral de la bag tsha'i rnam pa med*), where it appears

that "trouble" refers to the lack of anxiety regarding all five fears. Note also that in Guenther's translation, sGam.po.pa, *The Jewel Ornament of Liberation*, 241, he mistakes *'khor* for *'khor ba* and mistranslates as "subjection to anxiety while in this world (Saṃsāra)."

137 *Flower Ornament Sūtra* (Toh. 44), f. 186a5–6. Titles of this sūtra are also *Great Bounteousness of the Buddhas*," and "*Sūtra of Universal Interpenetration*" (*Sangs rgyas rmad ga cad*), in addition to the name in which it appears in its English translation from Chinese, *Flower Ornament Sūtra*. This quotation is from the chapter entitled "Ten Grounds" (*sa bcu pa'i le'u*), which in some canons stands alone as the *Sūtra on the Ten Grounds*.

138 *de las dang po'i mthong spangs*: "First" here refers to the fact that this is the first noble (*'phags pa*) or exalted of the five paths (ATG, December 6, 2007).

139 *kun brtags kyi nyon mongs pa drug*: "Due to the corrupting influence of bad tenet systems, mentally imputed perverse concepts concerning the genuine truth cause extremely unpeaceful views with afflictive states and so on (*grub mtha' ngan pas blo bsgyur ba'i dbang gis yang dag pa'i don la phyin ci log gi rtog pas kun tu brtags pa'i sems rab tu ma zhi bar byed pa'i lta ba nyon mongs can la sogs pa'o*) (RY). The six acquired afflictive states are in distinction from the six innate afflictive states (*lhan skyes*) mentioned in the Path of Meditation.

140 The list in the tengyurs and Ume differ from this: they read "unawareness, desire, pride, *jealousy*, anger, and doubt, and views, making seven." The *ST* and Kinnaur editions correspond to the *Abhidharma*, which does not include jealousy.

141 These five are subdivisions of mistaken views. The views about the transitory collection is to regard the five aggregates (*phung po*; Skt. *skandha*) as an autonomous self, clinging either to "me" or "mine." The fixation on extremes refers to clinging to a personal identity as permanent and durable, or as something that is annihilated at death. Perverse views means to deny the existence of things that exist, such as karmic causes and results or future lives. Holding views as paramount means to cling to any of the wrong views of non-Buddhists as the best. Holding one's ethical discipline and deliberate conduct as paramount means to cling to them as being pure, excellent, and the path of liberation from suffering.

142 The above list of six afflictive states becomes five since the last one, "views," has itself been subdivided into five.

143 There is an interlinear note (*mchan*) inserted here in the tengyurs and *ST* editions that is not found in other copies. Apparently it concerns a debate about the number of factors to be eliminated. Numbers other than 112 are refuted in the *Ornament of Clear Realization* (Jamgön Kongtrul, "The Presentation of Grounds, Paths, and Results in the Causal Vehicle of Characteristics," 24, n. 42). The note here, which is not entirely clear to me, reads: "By adding the forty of the desire realm to that thirty-six, if one thinks or needs [to arrive at] the hundred and fifty-two [factors to be] eliminated on the [Path of] Seeing that is [sometimes] mentioned, if that is so, then one must [accept] the above [as] one hundred and fifty-two factors to be eliminated on the Path of Seeing."

144 *Ye shes gsal ba'i rgyud phyi ma*, but in Longchenpa, *An Excellent Chariot*, f. 42b6, the same quotation is attributed to *Ye shes gsang ba'i rgyud phyi ma* (*Secret Timeless Awareness Latter Tantra*). Alas, neither title has yielded positive identification.

145 Lotus-Endowed (Pad ma can) is one of the buddha realms of the ten directions

(*phyogs bcu'i zhing khams*), being the one in the lower direction (*'og phyogs*). In the tantric teachings, it is one of the three grounds of awakening (*sangs rgyas sa gsum*), or the twelfth bhūmi.

146 *Tshangs pa kun dga'i mdo*, also appears as *Tshangs pa kun dge'i mdo*, neither one located. This quote also appears in Longchenpa's *An Excellent Chariot* as an example of "some who say that these qualities of the path concern only the increase and transformations in dream and not daytime experiences." However, Longchenpa goes on to refute this by explaining that the dream is used as the special example of any stage of the path, not that these qualities do not arise in "real" life (33b2–3).

147 This contextual etymology reflects the connection between these two terms which are spelled differently but sound the same: *goms* means to become familiar or habituated to something, and *sgom* is the word commonly translated as "meditation," meaning to make a habit of mental focus.

148 The first ground Very Joyful was attained on the Path of Seeing, the remaining nine on the Path of Meditation. See the detailed discussion in the section on the ten grounds.

149 *rtog* is used in all copies of the commentary, but in the corresponding root text (721; f. 9a4), the word *rtogs* (realization) was used, which is correct (ATG). In Longchenpa, *An Excellent Chariot*, 100 (f. 27b1), the line reads *nges par ston par byed pa* (that cause the certain teaching . . .).

150 Reading *nyon mongs pa bag la nyal ba'i lhan skyes las phye ba drug* as in the Ume edition, rather than *phyi nang drug* (inner and outer six) from the others. Longchenpa, *An Excellent Chariot*, 104 (f. 29b5) has *phyi na drug*, apparently a mistake. *Lhan skyes*, usually translated as coemergent, is here more literally rendered as "born with" since these are not beginningless afflictions (ATG). It is distinguished from the acquired afflictive states mentioned in the Path of Seeing.

151 I am following the Kinnaur edition and Longchenpa, rather than the other editions of the commentary that list the six as ignorance, desire, anger, *doubt*, pride, and the view of the transitory collection [as a self]. This accords with *TOK*, (according to ATG), where the afflictive states here are four nonviews and two views.

152 The added clarification here is based on Longchenpa, *An Excellent Chariot*, 104 (f. 29b6).

153 The four meditative equilibriums or fields of perception (*skye mched mu bzhi*) of the formless god realm, in their more usual order, are Infinite Space (*nam mkha' mtha' yas*), Infinite Consciousness (*rnam shes mtha' yas*), Nothing Whatsoever (*ci yang med pa*), and Neither Presence nor Absence [of Perception] (*yod min med min te*) (RY).

154 The Path of Consummation (*thar phyin pa'i lam*) is also sometimes called the "Path of No More Learning" (*mi slob pa'i lam*). This indicates that all action or training is perfected, rather than that one cannot train or learn anything.

155 *bSam gyis mi khyab pa bstan pa'i mdo.* There are many sūtras in the canon that include this phrase, but the quote was not found in any of them.

156 This line of the quotation is not found in the root text, which is otherwise nearly verbatim. See verse 127.

157 *dGongs pa bla na med pa'i rgyud.* Not located.

158 *Ye shes bla na med pa'i rgyud.* Not located. The first section of the quote is found in Longchenpa, *An Excellent Chariot*, 33b6–34a2, but not the second part.

159 *gsod nams kyi sku*, the "merit kāya" is an archaic name for the saṃbhogakāya since it

is the result of perfecting the accumulation of merit. The original quote, in fact, uses saṃbhogakāya (*longs spyod rdzogs pa'i sku*). The bracketed line also appears in the sūtra, but not in the Niguma texts.

160 *Sublime Golden Light Sūtra* (Toh. 556), f. 169b2. Of the three versions of this sūtra in the canon, this is the middle one.

161 *Mahāyāna Highest Continuum* (Toh. 4024), f. 55a1. The treatise is attributed to Asaṅga, based on the teachings of Maitreya. These lines are explained immediately afterward in the treatise and can be found in the many available translations and commentaries.

162 *Journey to Lanka Sūtra* (Toh. 107), 217 (f. 109a2–3). The quote as found in the sūtra and also as cited in Longchenpa, *An Excellent Chariot*, 154 (f. 54b1–2) uses "mind" or "thought" (*sems*) instead of "ideas" (*'du shes*). The whole quote from the sūtra as follows is actually a discussion of approaches or vehicles (*theg pa, yāna*):

> For as long as mind exists,
> there is no reaching the end of vehicles.
> When mind is eradicated,
> there is no vehicle, and no going either.
> Although there is no presentation of vehicles,
> in order to guide sentient beings,
> I explain different vehicles,
> I teach that the vehicles are one.

163 Maitreya, *Ornament of the [Mahāyāna] Sūtras* (Toh. 4020), f. 38a1. There is a mistake in quoting this important verse (except in the Kinnaur edition), so I have changed to the original. Where it says *'byung po dpag med 'jigs med phyir* (since measureless elementals are fearless), the Niguma texts mistakenly have *'byung po dpag med 'jig byed phyir* (since measureless elementals are destroyed).

The meaning of this line is not immediately apparent, so a look at various commentaries was helpful. It is important to remember the bivalent meaning of "sa" (Skt. *bhūmi*) as both "level" and literally as "ground" or "earth." An early commentary by Vasubandhu, *Explanation of the Ornament of the Sūtras* (Toh. 4026), 255b7–256a2 glosses as follows:

> Since [the ground] makes measureless elementals fearless, [and] since for those measureless ones [the grounds] are endowed with progress while going higher, therefore those dwelling places are called "grounds." It says "since [the grounds] make measureless elementals fearless" because the fear of measureless elementals is eliminated. It says "those measureless ones" because each [of those] is also immeasurable. It says "are endowed with progress while going higher" because [they are] endowed with [the potential of] going to the higher grounds.

But this is still not entirely clear until we read Mipam's commentary in the *Complete Explanation of the Intended Meaning of "Ornament of the Mahāyāna Sūtras*:"

> Why are they called grounds? The term *bhūmi* [in Sanskrit connotes] that since in the world [the ground] is the support for measureless elemental sentient beings, as well as grasses and trees and forests and so on, and since they rely on that [ground], they have no fear of falling. And just as [the ground] becomes the foundation of journeying to other places and countries and domains, the bodhisattva grounds are the support and dwelling

> places of measureless elemental beings who are to be tamed and therefore [those grounds are] the dwelling places that cause them to be without fear. The higher and higher grounds are the places of measureless qualities, [and] since those situations have [the potential] to become the support for journeying or going progressively higher and higher, they are the dwelling places of bodhisattvas. Therefore they are held to be "grounds." (*Collected Works*, vol. 2, 745–46; f. 374a6–b3)

Finally, in the *Treasury of Knowledge*, vol. 3, 496, Jamgön Kongtrul adds some more description, which would lend itself to an interpretation of the first line as a list of possible word derivations:

> The Sanskrit equivalent is *bhūmi*. One arrives at the general hermeneutical etymologies of "ground" through the certainties that derive from deleting or adding [certain] syllables. *Bhū* derives from *bhūta* (Tib. *'byung po*, that is., elements or the beings composed of elements) for, like the great elements, these grounds serve as supports for the amassing of positive qualities. *Mi* derives from *amita*, meaning "measureless" (*dpag med*) since they are attained through measureless hardships. Alternatively, *bhu* derives from *abhaya*, meaning "fearless" (*'jigs med*), since once one has attained these grounds, one has eliminated the five fears, and so on. Or, *bhū* derives from *bhūya[s]* which means "progress" (*phyi phyir*), since one progresses by journeying higher and higher based on what preceded. So the term "ground" implies something that serves as a support. In brief, then, the general derivation of the term "ground" comes from using this word as a referent, since these grounds, similar to the earth as a foundation, serve as supports for positive qualities.

164 This line in the sūtra (*rab tu dga' ba chen po skye bas*) is not in the Niguma texts and has been added here.

165 This phrase (*mtshan ma med pa yid la byed pa med pa'i*), on the other hand, is not found in the edition of the sūtra that was consulted, or in the Kinnaur edition, which in general seems to be closer to the the sūtras.

166 The sūtra has *shes rab* (wisdom) here rather than *ye shes* (timeless awareness), but I have kept *ye shes* since it was developed on the previous ground. Also "and grows" has been added from the sutra.

167 This line (*nyan thos dang rang rgyal las ring du song ba'i phyir*) is not in the edition of the sūtra that was consulted.

168 *Sublime Golden Light Sūtra* (Toh. 556), f. 194a5–b4. The same quote is also found in *Questions of Akṣayamati Sūtra*.

169 *me tog tsam pa ka*: These are actually the seed pods of the tsampaka, which are often used in Buddhist rituals and strung into garlands to wear. Because of the abundance of seeds in one plant, they are considered to contain the essence of all flowers, and hence all beauty.

170 *yan lag brgyad ldan gyi chu*: 1) coolness (*bsil ba*), 2) sweetness (*zhim pa*), 3) lightness (*yang pa*), 4) softness (*'jam pa*), 5) clearness (*dvangs pa*), 6) free of impurities (*dri ma med pa*), 7) drinking soothes the stomach (*'thung na lto par 'jam pa*), and 8) clears and comforts the throat (*mgrin pa sang sang bde ba*).

171 This quote was found in neither the *Sūtra of Teaching the Unimaginable Secrets of the Tathāgatas* (Toh. 47) nor in the *Sūtra of Teaching the Unimaginable Buddha Realms*

(Toh. 79) but in another sūtra of the same collection (*Ratnakuta*; *dKon brtsegs*) called *Questions of Akṣayamati Sūtra* (Toh. 89), ff. 180a6–181a3. It is also in *Sublime Golden Light Sūtra* (Toh. 556), f. 193b1–194a5. The phrase "Child of a good family, the early sign of the . . . bodhisattva ground is that the bodhisattva, the great being, . . ." repeats at each of the ten grounds in the sūtras, but is left out in the Niguma texts.

172 Again, found in *Questions of Akṣayamati Sūtra* (Toh. 89), f. 181a3–6, and in an expanded version in *Sublime Golden Light Sūtra* (Toh. 556), f. 195a6–b1.

173 "Promise" (*mi ngoms par dam 'cha' ba*) is added from the sūtra, f. 230b5.

174 "Genuine state" (*yang dag pa*) is also added from the sūtra, f. 131a1.

175 *Flower Ornament Sūtra* (Toh. 44), ff. 230b3–231a1.

176 *mtshan ma* (characteristic, mark, name, or sign) translates *nimitta*, as distinguished from *mtshan nyid*, which translates *lakṣhaṇa* and is usually translated as "defining characteristic." The clinging to marks or characteristics is a perception (*msthan mar 'dzin pa 'du shes yin*) that is one of the fifty or so mental events (*sems byung*), and as such it can be conceptual or nonconceptual. It is more subtle than clinging to defining characteristics (ATG).

177 *sngon kyi mtha'i bskal pa brgya dang/ phyi ma'i mtha'i bskal pa*: This sign of the first ground, repeated in the all the grounds with progressively greater numbers, is interpreted in a variety of ways: The bodhisattva "penetrates a hundred eons past and future" (*Sūtra on the Ten Grounds*, 710–11); "is aware of one hundred previous and future lives" (Jamgön Kongtrul, *The Treasury of Knowledge: Books Nine and Ten: Journey and Goal*); "lives for a hundred eons and engages in them from beginning to end" (Jamgön Kongtrul, "The Presentation of Grounds, Paths, and Results in the Causal Vehicle of Characteristics"); and "to know one hundred kalpas into the past and future" (Dzogchen Ponlop, "The Ten Bodhisattva Bhumis," 73).

178 This verse is not included in the quotation in Longchenpa, *An Excellent Chariot*, ff. 30a5–33b2 and may be from a different source.

179 *bye ba khrag khrig brgya stong.* Other interpretations of this number are "one hundred quintillion" (in Jamgön Kongtrul, *The Treasury of Knowledge: Books Nine and Ten: Journey and Goal*), "ten sextillion" (Brunnhölzl, *Gone Beyond*), "ten-million times ten billion: 10,000,000,000,000,000,000,000" (Dzogchen Ponlop, "The Ten Bodhisattva Bhumis"), and "one hundred thousand million ten-million" (in sGam.po.pa, *The Jewel Ornament of Liberation*).

180 *sum stong sum brgya stong phrag bcu*, (but in Ume: *sum brgya stong phrag bcu*). Alternately: "one hundred thousand times one billion" (Dzogchen Ponlop, "The Ten Bodhisattva Bhumis"), "one hundred thousand three-thousandfold universes" (Jamgön Kongtrul, *The Treasury of Knowledge: Books Nine and Ten: Journey and Goal*).

181 *grangs med*, literally "without count," is also said to indicate the number ten to the fiftieth or sixtieth power (novemdecillion). Still less than a googol!

182 rGyal bu Don 'grub is the more usual rendition of the name (Ume, Kinnaur), but in *ST* and the tengyurs it is written out as rGyal bu Don thams cad 'grub pa (Prince Who Accomplishes All Purposes).

183 *mDo sde pad ma dkar po*, for *White Lotus of Great Compassion Sūtra*, *'Phags pa snying rje chen po'i pad ma dkar po*; Skt. *Ārya-mahākaruṇāpuṇḍarīka*, (Toh. 111), f. 118b1.

184 *Meeting of Father and Son* (Toh. 60), f. 30a3–5. Sangs rgyas dbang po tog, or dBang

po'i tog gi rgyal mtshan gyi rgyal po (Indraketudhvajarāja), literally Buddha of the Pinnacle of Sensory Powers, counted as one of the thirty-five tathāgatas.

185 *gTshang ma'i ri[g]s*, or *Tsangs ma'i gnas* (Skt. Śuddhanivāsa/Śuddhagasakayika), also called the Heaven of Pure Reaches.

186 *Zla gsang thig le*: one of the texts in the mahāyoga section of the rNying ma rgyud 'bum, said to be translated by Padmasambhava and Paltsek (see Roerich, *BA*, 102). See rNying ma rgyud 'bum (Collected Tantras of the Ancients), mTshams brag, vol. 18 (Tsha), 557.1–548.7 (Tb 406) (THDL). The quote was not found in the similarly titled tantra in the canon translated by Rinchen Zangpo, *Secret Moon Drop Tantra* (Toh. 477).

187 *'Dul ba don yod pa'i rgyud* (*'Dus pa don yod pa* in Longchenpa, *An Excellent Chariot*, 34b3–5). Not located.

188 *Rab tu mi gnas pa'i rgyud*. Not located. Up to this point, both the quotes and the commentary in Longchenpa's *An Excellent Chariot* are nearly identical. Hereafter, Longchenpa concludes that while this is just a brief exposition of each vehicle, the final say seems to be from the nondual tantra, the great *Net of Magical Manifestation* (*sGyu 'phrul dra ba chen po*) and he adds several quotes from that, rather than the two tantras that follow here. Longchenpa, *An Excellent Chariot*, 115 (f. 35a1–3).

189 *rDo rje bde ba'i rgyud* and *Ye shes thig le'i rgyud*. The latter would seem to be *Drop of Timeless Awareness* (Toh. 422), but this quotation is not found there.

190 *Vajra Peak Tantra* (Toh. 480), f. 152b5. This is an explanatory tantra of the Yoga Tantras. In the tantra, this verse answers the question "Where does this secret arise?" (*gsang ba 'di ni gang du byung*), and in fact the word for imperishable (*'jig med pa*) is perhaps misspelled there as "fearless" (*'jigs med pa*).

191 This discussion attempts to resolve the apparent contradiction in the statement (above from the *Secret Moon Drop Tantra*) that the Buddha abandons the Pure Domains (Tsangs pa'i gnas) before attaining the state of a buddha in Akaniṣṭha ('Og min). It would seem to indicate that the Pure Domains are actually impure and separable from Akaniṣṭha, which is pure or permanent. Here it is maintained that Akaniṣṭha is the highest or best part of the Pure Domains (actually the fifth of five grounds), and thus both are imperishable and pure from the pure perspective.

Longchenpa discusses this in *An Excellent Chariot*, 35a4–36a2, before presenting this quote. There, he presents a different view that almost seems like a response: "In any case, what is this Akaniṣṭha of buddhahood? Some believe that this is the Akaniṣṭha of the Pure Domains, but that does not make sense, because [it says that] the Pure Domains are abandoned. Some say that it is [a distance] from the Akaniṣṭha of the Pure Domains [as] a hermitage is just a distance away from the town, but that does not make sense because it is described as "without direction or extent." Here [in the *Net of Magical Manifestation*] it is explained that the primordial Buddha's natural pure manifestation is the Akaniṣṭha of pure awareness, so one finds the kāyas and timeless awareness as one in basic space."

It may be helpful to think of three kinds of Akaniṣṭha: (1) the ultimate Akaniṣṭha, that is, the formless state of the dharmakāya, (2) the Densely Arrayed Akaniṣṭha (Tib. 'Og min rgyan stug po bkod pa; Skt. Ghandavyūhākaniṣṭha), where the saṃbhogakāya manifests, and (3) the highest pure level of the form realm, which is a natural sphere of nirmāṇakāya.

192 *gNyis med rnam par rgyal ba'i rgyud*, not located.

Notes to Chapter 2, The Six Dharmas of Niguma

1 *ST*, vol. 8, 312. "Rinpoche" may refer to Shangs Rinpoche, a title for Khyungpo Naljor. However it may refer to one of Sangye Tönpa's own teachers. Drogön Sangye Tönpa was the so-called "seventh jewel," the seventh and last lineage holder in the one-to-one lineage. He was also, according to Jamgön Kongtrul, the first to actually write down the oral instructions from the root hearing lineages of the two ḍākinīs (*Beryl Key*, 72). The *Jewel Ocean Tantra (Rin chen rgya mtsho'i rgyud)*, which is often mentioned as a major source of much of the tradition, has not been located. See note 123 in the introduction.

2 Jamgön Kongtrul, *TOK*, vol. 1, 533; *The Treasury of Knowledge: Book Eight, Part Four: Esoteric Instructions*, 233.

3 Jamgön Kongtrul, *TOK*, vol. 1, 537; *The Treasury of Knowledge: Book Eight, Part Four: Esoteric Instructions*, 235. This may be a direct reference to the *Directory* (*Thems yig*) attributed to Niguma, however, and not to the *Vajra Lines* as such. A similar statement by Tāranātha on the purity of the tradition was quoted earlier, in the main introduction.

4 Lochen Gyurme Dechen (1540–1615) was recognized as an emanation of Maitrīpa and was considered the lineage holder of the vajra lines after Kunga Drolchok (1507–1566). *Catalogue*, 506 (f. 64b6). In his many works he signed himself as the "speaker of two languages (*skad gnyis rma ba*) and gained the name Lochen, "great translator," based on his excellent understanding of Sanskrit. His personal focus was on the Kālachakra practices and the teachings of the Shangpa Kagyu. While he studied with many teachers of different traditions, he received the instructions of Niguma from Kunga Drolchok. His most enduring work is the definitive biography of Tangtong Gyalpo, which is translated in Stearns, *King of the Empty Plain*. See that book for more on him, especially 8–11. Also see Zangpo, *Timeless Rapture*, 168–69, for Gyurme Dechen's beautiful supplication to Niguma.

5 Atisha's sojourn there before proceeding to Central Tibet is well known. It was at Tholing (*Tho ling*, but more properly *mtho gding*, as in Roerich, *BA*, 248, or Tāranātha's unusual *mton mting* in *Clearing Up Darkness of the Mind*, 463; f. 24a2), the residence of Rinchen Zangpo, that he composed his famous *Lamp for the Path to Enlightenment*, the prototype for the many later works of this "path-stages" genre (*lam rim*) composed by Tibetan authors. Considering the story here in Khyungpo Naljor's biography, it is interesting to speculate as to whether Atisha also had access to an even earlier prototype, namely, *Stages in the Path of Illusion*, either his own copy or that of Khyungpo, who would certainly have carried it with the *Vajra Lines* that he had received at the same time from Niguma. Unfortunately, the biography does not tell us which texts exactly were at issue. Matthew Kapstein, it should be noted, is not buying any of it and states, "That event, however, may best be read as a fiction inserted into the hagiography for apologetical reasons." "Chronological Conundrums," 8.

6 *Brief Life Story of Lama Khyungpo Naljor*, *ST*, vol. 1, 104–5/ff. 23b6–24a2.

7 *Clearing Up Darkness of the Mind*, 463/f. 24a3–4.

8 See chapter 5. There is another text of Indian origin, attributed to the Great Āchārya Vajrāsana (sLob dpon chen po rDo rje gdan pa) that bears a similar colophon and must have been included in the texts that Khyungpo Naljor showed to Atisha and Rinchen Zangpo. It is called *Indian Source Text of the Glorious Five Tantras Method*

of Accomplishment. The colophon reads: "In the presence of the Indian paṇḍita Vairochanarakṣita and the Tibetan Lotsāwa Lendarma Lodrö it was translated. Later, Lotsāwa Rinchen Zangpo verified and corrected it at the Golden Shrine Room of Tholing." *ST*, vol. 9, 549.

9 *ST*, vol. 6, 172–73. I am not sure of the identity of this Buddhaśrī. It may refer to the Mahāsiddha Buddhaśrī from Nepal—said to have been invited to Tibet in 1198 (Tāranātha, *Tāranātha's History of Buddhism in India*, 317)—although this would place him later than the dates for Khyungpo Naljor. He is mentioned several times in *BA* (Roerich, 1033, 1055, and 1065), where each invitation seems to come from a different translator. Alternatively, it might refer to Sangye Palzang (Buddhaśrī could be translated into Tibetan as Sangye Pal), the author of *Releasing the Knots of the Vajra Lines*, written in the Shangpa monastery of Kuklung (lKugs lung).

10 *Beryl Key*, *ST*, vol. 6, 83 (f. 17a1–4); *GK*, vol. 10, 477 (f. 10a4–5).

11 Niguma, *Vajra Lines of the Six Dharmas* (P 4633), ff. 142b6–144a2. Four other editions were also used: CT, vol. 42, 842–45 (2514); *ST*, vol. 6, 161–73; *DZ*, vol. 11, 1–27; and GD-CW, vol. 2 (ha). Tangtong Gyalpo's *Collection of the Essentials*, *TTG-S*, vol. 1, 241–336, where the vajra lines are quoted within the commentary, was also consulted.

12 The Sanskrit that is transliterated into Tibetan reads *Dharma shad badzra gatha nama* (clearly mistaken in CT (842) as "*dharma shat vajra yo ge tha na ma*").

13 *theg chen skye med rang sgra 'di skad thos.* Gyurme Dechen had a great deal to say about this initial verse in his *Complete Explanation of the Vajra Lines of the Six Dharmas*. According to him, it is here a misreading of the exact same phrase that appears in other source materials such as Nāropa, *Vajra Lines of the Hearing Lineage* (Toh. 2338), f. 302b6. There, it is understood to mean that Vajradhara himself heard this talk and that "heard" really means "to understand" (*mkhyen pa*) or "to realize" (*rtogs pa*). The compilers of the Shangpa texts then rendered it to mean that Niguma heard it from Vajradhara as a way to verify the Shangpa story line. Gyurme Dechen says, "Therefore, the explanation that someone 'heard this talk; the unborn natural sound of the great vehicle' means that Niguma heard [it from] Vajradhara should be understood as a sign of fabrication" (*ST*, 8, 489). He then goes on to present his reasoning in hair-splitting detail that will be of considerable interest to determined scholars. This and the many other questions that Gyurme Dechen raises concerning the Shangpa texts—all gathered in his *[Questions concerning] the Instructions of Glorious Niguma, Mighty Kecharī*, and again in *Complete Explanation of the Vajra Lines of the Six Dharmas*—in no way seemed to dampen his own faith in the lineage. I suspect that it was this seeming skepticism that made his work "meet with an ambivalent response in the Shangpa Tradition," rather than his "wordy presentation of the path," as Ngawang Zangpo suggests in *Timeless Rapture*, 344.

14 *kha 'byor* is glossed in the interlinear note as the joining of bliss-emptiness or appearance-emptiness, indicating the dharmakāya.

15 All three kāyas are presented in these first lines; "arising to tame anyone" indicates nirmāṇakāya.

16 The note says "possessed of seven branches" (*yan lag bdun dang ldan pa*). If these are the seven branches of enlightenment contained in the thirty-seven factors, then they are mindfulness, revealing phenomena, diligence, joy, agility, absorption, and equanimity (see the comments on verses 84–91 in *Stages in the Path of Illusion: The*

Commentary). More commonly, Vajradhara is described as having seven aspects of union (*kha sbyor bdun ldan*): (1) complete enjoyment (*longs spyod rdzogs pa*), (2) union (*kha sbyor*), (3) great bliss (*bde ba chen po*), (4) no intrinsic nature (*rang bzhin med pa*), (5) completely filled with compassion (*snying rjes yongs su gang ba*), (6) uninterrupted (*rgyun mi chad pa*), and (7) unceasing (*'gog pa med pa*). See Mokchokpa, *The Life Story of Buddha Vajradhara*, 13–14 (f. 7a5–b1).

17 These three time frames apply to those of excellent (*rab*), medium (*'bring*), and lesser (*smad*) caliber, respectively.

18 This formulation of the six dharmas of Niguma is quoted extensively in nearly all commentaries. "The victors'" (*rgyal ba'i*) is missing in the tengyurs but appears in all other editions.

19 With notes inserted, this line reads: "One's own body is the means *in the practice of the secret empowerment: the right, left, and central* three channels [and] four chakras *at the navel, heart, throat, and head*." "One's own body is the means" (*rang lus thabs ldan*) refers to the practice of inner heat based only on visualizations in one's own body, as distinguished from the practice of uniting with another's body (*gzhan lus shes rab kyi gtum mo*),which is suggested in the last two lines of the verse. It is this practice based on one's own body that is the main practice in the Shangpa tradition. This is made clear in Tāranātha, *Profound Meaning Expanded*, *ST*, vol. 3, 384 (f. 25b1–5) and other commentaries. In *Selected Works of the Dalai Lama 2*, 112, Glen Mullin's translation of *rang lus thabs ldan* as "sitting in correct posture" is one of many interpretations that were not fully informed by the teachings in this lineage.

20 With notes inserted this reads: "*From* the blazing and melting of the a-*stroke below the navel* and the ham *letter in the crown of the head*, one is adorned in *four* moments *(various form, matured form, form itself, and free of defining characteristics)* with four [degrees of] joy: *joy, sublime joy, special joy, and coemergent joy.*"

21 This refers to the practice of the third empowerment, the awareness-wisdom empowerment, and wisdom refers to one's partner in practice (*shes rab ma*). *Khagamukhā*, literally "bird face," refers to the particular energy channel (*rtsa*), here referenced as "ḍākinī-faced one" in the notes. See Gray, *The Cakrasamvara Tantra*, 113. Also see Jamgön Kongtrul, *Treasury of Knowledge: Book Eight, Part Four: Esoteric Instructions*, 252.

22 The descending sequence of four joys is dissipating or defiled (*zag bcas*), while the ascending sequence is undefiled (*zag med*). Tangtong Gyalpo also describes the sequence of experience as first heat, then bliss, then the absorption of bliss-emptiness. *Collection of the Essentials*, *TTG-S*, vol. 1, 260 (f. 10b4).

23 That is, gathering of the quintessence of the blessings through the preliminary practice of guru yoga. However, Gendun Gyatso (the 2nd Dalai Lama) comments that this indicates that the syllable "*a*" is the quintessence and shortest version of the prājñapāramitā sūtras. Mullin, *The Dalai Lamas on Tantra*, 105.

24 *stong ra:* the hollow interior. The interlinear note here reads "such as clearing away sickness and bad spirits with '*a*'" (*a'i nad gdon sel byed sogs*), indicating the purification practice in the Shangpa tradition in which the verbalized letter "*a*" is imagined as elixir cleansing out the interior of the channels in the body. The three vital points or stages of this practice are: "purifier hollow interior of 'a'" (*dag byed a'i stong ra*), "hollow interior clearing away disease and bad spirits" (*stong ra nad gdon sel byed*), and "special hollow interior of three signs" (*rtags gsum stong ra'i khyad par*). Tangtong

Gyalpo, *Collection of the Essentials, TTG-S,* vol. 1, 250 (f. 5b2–3). In English, there is a short summary in Jamgön Kongtrul, *Treasury of Knowledge, Book Eight, Part Four: Esoteric Instructions,* 240–41; and a longer description in Mullin, *The Dalai Lamas on Tantra,* 105–8. Also see the introduction to this book.

25 The notes elaborate: "*the methods of increasing the bliss*-heat." Instead of *drod myur,* Tangtong Gyalpo has *bgrod myur* (quicken the journey). *Collection of the Essentials, TTG-S,* vol. 1, 268 (f. 14b4).

26 The rabbit (*ri bong*) is a symbol for the moon, which is a symbol for the *bodhichitta* (*byang sems*) or seminal vital energy substance that descends in the central channel as a result of the blazing and melting. The rabbit represents the moon since one can see the form of a rabbit in the moon, and the white bodhichitta is associated with the moon. One practices control of this bodhichitta through descending, holding, and so on, finally blending it with the energy currents (*lung,* Skt. *prāṇa*).

27 Nondissipating (*zag med*) is here specified as "free of thought" and great timeless awareness (*ye shes chen po*) as "intrinsically fully known." Instead of *zag med,* Tangtong Gyalpo's commentary gives *gnyis med,* "nondual." Ibid., 268 (f. 14b5).

28 These are the names of the sequence of practice of inner heat, beginning with the special preliminary practice of the hollow interior of fire, which is the vital point for the body (*lus gnad me'i stong ra*). See Tāranātha, *Profound Meaning Expanded, ST,* vol. 3, 358–63 (ff. 12b1–15a4). (This first line is missing in the tengyur editions but present in all others.) Tāranātha considers "Eating the Food" (*zas su za ba*) as the main practice, with the next two as branches, and the empowerment and liberation of obstructers as concluding practices.

29 *zhen bral* (free of attachment) in most copies, rather than *bden bral* (free of true existence) in CT. The notes clarify that devotion is the practice for those of highest faculties, and one's body and all appearance arising as the deity's form is for those of medium faculties. One's body and all appearance arising as the deity's form are two separate phases in the practice.

30 By way of explanation, the notes in the GD-CW edition quote from the *Drop of Timeless Awareness*: "The vase empowerment is the eleventh ground, the secret empowerment is the sublime twelfth, awareness-wisdom is the thirteenth, and in the same way [the fourth empowerment] is the fourteenth; thus each ground at each empowerment." f. 3a2. All of these are progressive grounds of buddhahood in the system of vajrayāna, beyond the tenth ground where it is traditionally said to be achieved in the mahāyāna tradition. See the comments to verses 197–200 in *Stages in the Path of Illusion: The Commentary* in this volume

31 Tangtong Gyalpo explains that those of medium faculty should regard all appearing phenomena "without any interruption from any other words, such as idle chatter and so on, verbally repeating 'it is illusion, it is dream', and in mind also maintaining mindfulness and determination of illusion and dream without slacking off." *Collection of the Essentials,* 276 (f. 18b2–4). "The single seat" means that those of lower faculties can do the entire practice by visualizing all the realms of sentient beings as illusory, without ever letting their meditation cushion even cool off (*mal gyi drod ma yal ba*). Ibid., 277–78 (f. 19a3–b3).

32 "Double delusion" or the delusion of delusion (*nying 'khrul*) refers to the fact that nighttime dreaming is even more of a delusion than ordinary waking appearances.

33 This is treated as commentary in *ST, DZ,* and *TTG-S,* while in GD-CW, which is

usually the most reliable in distinguishing the sections, it is presented as the actual vajra lines, the way it appears in the tengyur. I think, however, that this is a mistake since it is clearly prose and not verse.

The dream yoga sequential practices are to recognize, refine, increase, emanate, and change dreams and to ascertain objective appearance [as also illusion] (*bzung ba, sbyang ba, spel ba, sprul pa, bsgyur ba, yul snang gtan la dbab pa*). See Tāranātha, *Profound Meaning Explained*, *ST*, vol. 3, 408–50.

The notes explain excessive delusion (*'khrul 'byams*) as not recognizing that one is dreaming, excessive wakefulness (*sad 'byams*, missing from CT) as waking up again and again, excessive bliss (*bde 'byams*) as losing the seminal bodhichitta, and excessive emptiness (*stong 'byams*) as not desiring dream and (in GD-CW only) the certainty of nihilism.

34 With the interlinear notes, this verse reads something like: "Lucid clarity *is caused to* arise through *the vital point of* devotion and *supplication* to the guru. The great bliss, *the cause* (*rgyu*, not *sku* as in *DZ* and *ST*) *of attaining the unity of no [more] training, [is] the practice of the* dissipating and nondissipating *four joys in descending* (in GD-CW only) *and ascending order, and the cause for those to arise, which is the vital points of the body* and steady gazes, causes bliss *and* clarity *and* nonthought, *those three as an* inseparable *unity,* to arise naturally. The preliminary *and* main *and* concluding practices [are] adorned by the vital points of time."

35 Again it is not clear whether it is part of the original vajra lines. In commentaries, such as those by Tangtong Gyalpo and Gendun Gyatso (Mullin, *The Dalai Lamas on Tantra*, 143–46), it is not part of the vajra lines. In GD-CW, *DZ*, and *ST*, the first line "lucid clarity is recognized . . . consummated" appears as commentary. The last two lines are in regular letter size with their own interlinear notes, as follows: "A holy *guru* who has actualized in direct experience the lucid clarity *that abides since forever*, introduces the experience (*'char sgo*) *of the disciple's* lucid clarity, and it is adorned by enhancement *and* clearing away obstacles."

36 These are the names of the different types of transference in the tradition of Niguma, described individually in Tāranātha, *Profound Meaning Expanded*, *ST*, vol. 3, 484–89. As he mentions, however, the transference most commonly practiced in the tradition is called "skylight of timeless awareness" (*ye shes skar khung ma*).

37 These two lines also appear as part of the verses, though, as before, they are not quoted in the commentaries. With the interlinear notes, they read: "The vital point of *certain* time *is the arising of the signs of death*; the vital points of the body *are cross-legged, squatting, etc.*; the vital point of speech *is to train in blending transference by, as is said, 'the intense shout of two and a half letters'* [that is, *phat*] *along with the sound of hik*; the vital point of substance *is to anoint the crown of the head with red and white bodhichitta, salt, and human brains.*"

This last rather interesting note reads *byang sems dkar dmar 'tshal la mi'i glad pa rnams sbyi bor byugs pa*. GD-CW, f. 4a2. The version in *DZ* and *ST* seems to have been corrupted: *tsha ba gsum mi klad rnam kyis spyi bor byug la*. However I'm using *tsha ba* here for "salt" (rather than *'tshal la*, which is unclear to me) based on the following comment by Gendun Gyatso, as translated in Glenn Mullin, *The Dalai Lamas on Tantra*, 146: "This is described in the oral tradition as follows: 'One's own and a female's fluids/ Lead energy and mind upward./ Salt opens the mouth of the channel/ And brain guards against hindrances.'" I cannot follow up as the source verse is not cited and Gendun Gyatso's text on Niguma does not appear in his collected works.

38 It is not readily apparent how this verse is arranged. According to the notes, those of highest acumen can be liberated in the first intermediate state after the three stages of light or appearance, the spreading of it, and the culmination of it (*snang mched thob gsum*), when lucid clarity is recognized. Those of medium capacity recognize the deity's body of saṃbhogakāya in the second intermediate state. Those of the least capacity should try to block rebirth by repulsion for the samsaric process, so that attraction and aversion and jealousy toward one's future parents during intercourse is refined away by the transformations of the lucid clarity as deities' bodies.

39 According to Tangtong Gyalpo, *Collection of the Essentials*, 332, weariness or revulsion with samsara is the vital point for all three kinds of best, medium, and least practitioners for the intermediate state after death, so one should apply the three integrations of practicing all phenomena as the guru, the yidam, and as illusion. See chapter 4 of this volume for the English translation of the *Three Integrations.*

40 Here *snang byed* should be *snang mched* (as in *ST*, 170; f. 5b4), again referring to the three lights or three "appearances" or "experiences" (*snang ba gsum*) at the time of death that begin after the dissolution of the senses (forms, sounds, and so on) and elements (water, earth, and so forth). In progressive or arising order they are light (*snang ba*), increase of the light (*snang ba mched pa*), and culmination of light (*snang ba thob pa*). When the true nature of mind as lucid clarity is not recognized, it shifts to three coarser phases of appearance in reverse order: culmination, increase, and light. See Jamgön Kongtrul's extensive discussion of the three lights in *TOK*, 2, 689–707 or *The Treasury of Knowledge: Book Six, Part Four: Systems of Buddhist Tantra*, 251–72.

41 *rang bzhin brgyad bcu'i rtog pa:* The three lights become subject to and veiled by eighty conceptions or "natures" (*rang bzhin*, Skt. *prakṛti*). They are called "natures" because they are the nature or obscuring transformations of the three lights. As mentioned in the interlinear notes, they are the seven conceptions of delusion indicative of the culmination of light, the forty of desire indicative of the increase of light, and the thirty-three of aversion indicative of light. In the final stages of the death process, or in the yogic realization of reversing the three lights, the eighty conceptions dissolve. They are listed and discussed extensively in relation to the three lights in Kongtrul, *TOK*, 2, 689–707 or *The Treasury of Knowledge: Book Six, Part Four: Systems of Buddhist Tantra*, 251–72. Tangtong Gyalpo also offers an excellent description in *Collection of Essentials*, 317–25 (ff. 39a5–43b1).

42 A reference to the common unethical behavior of selling watered-down milk. Tangtong Gyalpo says: "those bloated dharma practitioners who mostly are like merchants that sell milk polluted with water." *Collection of Essentials*, 334 (f. 47a4).

43 The notes elaborate that personal practice experience, the scriptures of the Victor's authentic word that have five aspects or branches, and the directories (*them yig*) are to be cherished. This last is likely a reference to the directory attributed to Niguma that Khyungpo Naljor assembled, called *Directory of the Vajra Lines of the Six Dharmas*, which clearly lists the sequence of practice of these teachings.

44 Here is the famous injunction of Niguma's to keep the teachings secret for "seven generations." This would actually be just four more after Khyungpo Naljor, ending with Drogön Sangye Tönpa. Again, Gyurme Dechen takes issue with this countdown, wondering what happened to the crucial figure of Niguma's teacher Lavāpa, and the fact that Atisha apparently was "in" on the secret. In any case, it was Sangye Tönpa

who did in fact spread the teachings widely. The seven-generation injunction is also found in Niguma, *Glorious Immortal Deathless Great Timeless Awareness* and in many other places, such as the life stories.

Notes to Chapter 3, Mahāmudrā

1 *Releasing the Knots of the Vajra Lines*, *ST*, vol. 9, 101–2 (f. 2a4–b1).

2 *Catalogue*, 433 (f. 27a4–6).

3 An exception is the edition in *DZ* (vol. 11, 13–15), where Jamgön Kongtrul seems to incorporate some of what are, in other editions, the notes into the main text and present them all in the same size lettering. Furthermore, his version in *Ocean of Song*, *DZ*, vol. 12, 467–68, is highly edited and reorganized into metered verse, presumably to make it fit for chanting.

4 Jamgön Kongtrul, *Ocean of Song*, *DZ*, vol. 12, 467 (f. 3a6–7). The *Vajra Lines* are on 467–68 (f. 3a7–b5), and *Naturally Free Mahāmudrā* is on 468–69 (ff. 3b5–4a6). Some of this *Ocean of Song* has been translated by Ngawang Zangpo in *Timeless Rapture*.

5 Niguma, *Vajra Lines of the Amulet Mahāmudrā*. In these canons, the text is presented as "*Vajra Lines of the Amulet Mahāmudrā and Clear Words*" (*Phyag rgya chen po ga'u ma'i rdo rje'i tshig rkang dang/ tshig gsal bzhugs so*), but "Clear Words" refers to a different text that is not contained here. The *Vajra Lines* are also in *DZ*, vol. 11, 13–15 (ff. 7a5–8a2) and *ST*, vol. 6, 192–96 (ff. 16a3–18b5) as *The Trunk, Amulet Mahāmudrā Vajra Lines* (*sDong po phyag rgya chen po ga'u ma rdo rje tshig rkang*), included in the set called *Vajra Lines of the Six Dharmas of the Ḍākinī of Timeless Awareness* (*Ye shes mkha' 'gro ni gu ma'i chos drug rdo rje'i tshig rkang*). It appears again it in *ST*, vol. 8, 785–88, followed by *Clear Words*.

6 Niguma, *Vajra Lines of the Amulet Mahāmudrā (with Notes)*. This version with the interlinear notes is in P, CT, and *ST*, vol. 8, 799–803, with only slight variations.

7 Described in the commentaries as putting the two palms so they cover the knees. Sangye Palzang, *Releasing the Knots of the Vajra Lines*, *ST*, vol. 9, 119. Elsewhere, the mudrā of meditative equipoise is recommended, such as in Tangtong Gyalpo's *Guiding Instructions on Nigu's Branch Practice, Amulet Mahāmudrā*, *ST*, vol. 3, 686.

8 Here for simplicity I have interpreted the line based on the edition in Jamgön Kongtrul, which reads: *tshigs bzhi dang rtsa dang mchu klod pa ni lus rang babs so*. *DZ*, vol. 11, 13 (f. 7a7). The versions in P, CT, and *ST* are problematic: *tshigs bzhi dang rtsa dang chu bsdus (or bsdud) pa thams cad lhod kyis glod pa ni/ lus rang babs so/*. Aside from the obvious difference in *chu* (water) rather than *mchu* (lips), there is the verb *bsdus pa* (to gather) or *bsdud pa* (dissolve). Although this version is not clear, it is possible that these were special instructions pertaining to the body, since *rtsa chu* can refer to the pulse and the urine or, alternatively, to feces and urine. That *chu* (water) is not a mistake for *mchu* (lips) here is also perhaps supported by the fact that "lips" is not misspelled in the very next line of any version (except in CT, where it is *ma*). However, there is no commentary to clarify this. (If I were giving advice on the natural resting of the body, I would say that there's no chance of relaxation if you have to go to the bathroom!)

9 The tengyurs (both P and CT) here have *sems chos sku 'du bral med*, but all other copies do not have *sems* (mind). Sangye Palzang's commentary says, "calm abiding [with] the mind free of thoughts and higher insight become a unity; the uncompounded

dharmakāya that was introduced before is not contained or separated for even an instant, it being so very close, and yet without the previous nonconceptual wisdom there is the fault of not seeing the meaning of the nature of phenomena, causing one to wander in samsara." *Releasing the Knots of the Vajra Lines, ST*, vol. 9, 152–53 (f. 27a4–b1).

10 The note states here that "four" (*bzhi*) refers to the four kāyas mentioned before and the timeless awareness associated with each: dharmakāya, dharmadhatu awareness; nirmāṇakāya, mirror-like awareness; saṃbhogakāya, discriminating awareness; and mahāsukakāya, equanimity awareness. Then the spontaneous enlightened activity arising from all four is said to be the fifth awareness, that of being all-accomplished. Sangye Palzang, *Releasing the Knots of the Vajra Lines, ST*, vol. 9, 158–59, quoting from *Clear Words*.

11 *rkun bur ngo sprad*: the visualization for this practice is described under the heading "The Burglar's Pointing-Out through Blessings" in Tāranātha's *The Amulet Mahāmudrā or Threefold Letting-Go Guidance Manual, ST*, vol. 3, 667–71 (ff. 7a1–9a5).

12 Sangye Palzang comments: "'The preliminary sacred pledge is a secret vajra' [means that] first those in whom experience has arisen are carefully questioned, and if the pointing-out that it is like that has not taken, then it is a vajra secret." *Releasing the Knots of the Vajra Lines, ST*, vol. 9, 160 (f. 31b1).

13 The imperative sense (*ltos shig*) is taken from ibid., 168 (f. 35b6).

14 Sangye Palzang adds: "To Niguma, ḍākinī of timeless awareness, the adept Kyungpo Naljor offered five measures of gold and requested it. He pleased her with devotion and practice. Then she and Lotsāwa Landarma Lodrö translated it. It was brought to Tibet, where the word lineage (*tshig brgyud*) and the instructions were given to the fortunate disciple, the incomparable Mokchokpa the Great." Ibid., 172–73 (ff. 37b6–38a2).

15 Niguma, *Naturally Free Mahāmudrā*. Also translated in Zangpo, *Timeless Rapture*, 47–48

Notes to Chapter 4, The Three Integrations

1 Tāranātha, *Supplement to the Lineage Stories of One Hundred Guides, DZ*, vol. 18, 104–5 (ff. 3b6–4a1).

2 This text is found in *ST*, vol. 10, 277–81, along with an explanatory text and lineage supplication, together entitled *Three Kāya Integration and Three Kāya Abiding Nature*.

3 Ibid., 281 (f. 3a2).

4 *ST*, vol. 8, 491–95 (ff. 12a4–14a2). For more details on Gyurme Dechen's argument, see note 13 in chapter 2, *Vajra Lines of the Six Dharmas*.

5 The statement in the translation of Khyungpo Naljor's life that Niguma bestowed "the Vajra Verses on the Three Ways of Integrating the Path" seems to be an addition by the translator since it does not appear in the Tibetan of any of my editions. Riggs, *Like an Illusion*, 63.

6 Mokchokpa et al., *Brief Life Story of Lama Khyungpo Naljor, ST*, vol. 1, 82 (f. 12b3).

7 Niguma, *Three Dharmas to Integrate on the Path*, based on editions in P, CT, *DZ*, and *ST*.

8 This line, present only in the tengyur editions and not in *DZ* or *ST*, seems to indicate

that there is more here than just the vajra lines, even another text possibly named "Essence of the Vital Points" (*gnad kyi snying po*). However it may just refer to the few interlinear notes that are included in this version and that are absent in the other editions.

9 This reconstructed Sanskrit title is quite different in *DZ*, vol. 11, 15 and in *ST*, where it appears as *Mārgga karya tridharma nāma*, a much more likely name.

10 *spyod lam rnam bzhi*: The four activities are going, walking, lying down, and staying (*'gro 'chag nyal 'dug*). Gyaltsen Bum, *Guidance Manual of Infallible Three Integrations*, *ST*, vol. 7, 304.

11 Numbering in small letters starting with "four" begins the next section, which brings up the question of what the first three were. In Tāranātha's *Ḍākinī's Personal Instructions That Clarify the Three Integrations on the Path*, *ST*, vol. 10, 396, the first of the three integrations on the path, that is, the guru—is divided into three as follows: (1) integrating the guru on the spiritual path based on appearances, (2) integrating devotion on the path based on the guru, and (3) integrating the three kāyas on the path based on devotion. These seem to match up loosely with the foregoing.

12 *bdun po rnam dag*, more familiar as *yan lag bdun*, "seven branch" practice of prostrating to the Three Jewels, confessing negative actions, making offerings, rejoicing in the virtue of others, requesting the turning of the dharma-wheel, beseeching to not pass into nirvana, and dedicating the merit to the enlightenment of all beings.

13 Great bliss in all cases is the saṃbhogakāya aspect, according to Gyaltsen Bum, *Guidance Manual of Infallible Three Integrations*, *ST*, vol. 7, 307 (f. 5a3).

14 *tha mal zhen pa bzlog pa'i phyir* in *DZ* and *ST* makes much more sense than the tengyur editions (P and CT) of *tha mal shes pa bzlog pa'i phyir* (in order to reverse the ordinary mind).

15 A similar quote from *Stages in the Path of Illusion: The Commentary*, *ST*, vol. 6, 747–48 (f. 7a6–b1), commenting on verse 10, is attributed to *Actualization of Timeless Awareness*:

> All things are appearance and emptiness inseparable.
> Creation and completion and their unity;
> there is not a single phenomenon that is not creation and completion.
> This is the way that enlightenment is taught.

16 The tengyurs have *sngags* (mantra, praise) but *DZ* and *ST* have *sgra* (sound).

17 The three poisons (*dug gsum*) are the three main afflictive or toxic emotions of desire, anger or aggression, and stupidity or ignorance. The editions in *DZ* and *ST* mistakenly have "three times" (*dus gsum*) here.

18 *ma spangs 'dzin med*: although both *DZ* and *ST* have *ma yengs 'dzin med* (undistracted without fixation), the commentaries suggest that "without rejection" is correct.

19 This note in the canons (P and CT) says *gti mug ngo bo rtog pa chos sku*, but it makes more sense as it is explained in Gyaltsen Bum's *Guidance Manual of Infallible Three Integrations*: "Stupidity is nonthought. Knowing nonthought to be dharmakāya will undoubtedly bring liberation from the three poisons." *ST*, vol. 7, 313 (f. 8a2).

20 *bzung 'dzin bral ba* (free of dualistic fixation) in CT should be *sgyu 'dzin bral ba* (free of fixation on illusion) as in *DZ, ST,* and Gyaltsen Bum's *Guidance Manual of Infallible Three Integrations*. Ibid., 317 (f. 10a6).

21 *bde gsal phyag rgya chen po* (bliss-clarity mahāmudrā) in the tengyurs should be *'od gsal phyag rgya chen po* (lucid clarity mahāmudrā) as in *DZ, ST,* and Gyaltsen Bum's *Guidance Manual of Infallible Three Integrations*. Ibid., 318 (f. 10b4–5).

22 Gyaltsen Bum explains in the *Guidance Manual of Infallible Three Integrations*: "Now immediately all qualities actualize directly in myself, quickening the path. The 'path of direct actualization' (*mngon sum lam pa*) means that this is superior to all other instructions." Ibid., 319 (f. 11a6–b1)

Notes to Chapter 5, Immortal and Infallible

1 Tāranātha, *Supplement to the Lineage Stories of One Hundred Guides*, *DZ*, vol. 18, 105 (f. 4a1).

2 rMa lo tsā ba Chos 'bar (1044–1089) was a Tibetan translator who studied in Kashmir and India with various great masters. He was married to the female master Machik Zhama (Ma gcig Zha ma, 1062–1149), important in the Lamdre tradition. Roerich, *BA*, 219–20. The colophon in *DZ* mistakenly has "Marpa Lotsāwa" as the translator, and this mistake is also copied in *ST*, but Kongtrul makes it clear that it is in fact Ma Lotsāwa in the *Beryl Key*, *GK*, vol. 10, 485 (f. 14a6) and elsewhere.

3 The text *Spiritual Power of Amṛita*, translated by "Enadeva." In the *Beryl Key*, Jamgön Kongtrul also mentions a commentary to this text: *'Chi med grub pa'i 'grel pa*, in *ST*, vol. 6, 234. This must be Virūpa, *Spiritual Power of Immortality Commentary* in the Peking Tengyur (5026) (not included in the Derge Tengyur). The colophon of this commentary states, "the paṇḍita known as the South Indian Cemetarian (rGya gar lho phyogs pa Dur khrod pa), Kāmarūpa or Etewa (E te ba) or Gyadrepa (rGya 'gres pa) and Ma Lotsāwa translated it in the cemetery of Tete." In that text, the lineage is traced as follows: Vajradhara, Chinnamuṇḍa (dBu bcad ma), Virūpa, the Black Brahmin (Bram ze nag po, probably Kāla Virūpa or Virūpa the Younger), Black Cemetarian (Dur khrod nag po, Edewa/Lalītavajra?; see Stearns, *Luminous Lives*, 224), Latö Gönpo (La stod mgon po), and then to Sangye Nyentön (Sangs rgyas gnyan ston or Ri gong pa, 1175–1255), the sixth "jewel" in the Shangpa one-to-one lineage and presumably the one in whom the two transmissions of Immortal and Infallible converge. In the *Beryl Key*, *GK*, vol. 10, 468 (f. 5b1), Kongtrul states that the instructions were given to Sangye Nyentön *either* by the Cemetarian (bLa ma Dur khrod pa) *or* by Latö Gönpo (bLa stod pa Shes rab mgon po). See Zangpo, *Timeless Rapture*, 282–85, for more about Sangye Nyentön.

4 See the comments by Jamyang Khyentse Wangchuk, translated in Stearns, *Taking the Result as the Path*, 133. For the story of Virūpa the Younger, see Tāranātha, *The Seven Instruction Lineages*, 17–18.

5 *Catalogue*, 434 (f. 27b1–4).

6 *Glorious Immortal Great Timeless Awareness/ Immortal Natural Freedom* (*dPal 'chi med ye shes chen po* or *'Chi med rang grol*).

7 This is how the Sanskrit reconstruction appears within the text in P and CT, although it seems to be a word-for-word rendering of the Tibetan. In the contents of the Peking canon, it is listed as *Śrī-mahāmāra-jñāna-nāma*. Yet another version appears in *DZ* and *ST*: *Śrī-amāra-mahājñāna-nāma*.

8 Although the tengyurs have *tshe gcig* (one life) here, it is *rtse gcig* (one-pointed) in all other editions and commentaries and makes sense as such with the interlinear notes that relate the three levels of individual capacity or faculties to the three time periods of seven days, months, or years.

9 The generation of a deity in creation stage practice involves a number of steps: five, four, three, or all at once. The three rites (*cho ga gsum*) refer to three main stages of

visualizing the seat with the seed syllable, then the emblem or implement, and then the complete form of the deity. Instantaneous (*skad cig*) creation is the complete form present all at once.

10 The canon editions have only *hūṃ* in the notes, but in *DZ* and *ST* and in commentaries, there is both *hūṃ* and *baṃ*. These are the seed syllables for Chakrasaṃvara and Vajrayoginī, respectively, and are visualized consecutively as the source of purifying light.

11 *gnyid* (sleep) in the canons is clearly a mistake for *nyid* (itself), as in other editions, and follows the commentary in Gyaltsen Bum, *Guidance Manual of Immortal Mind, by the Wise and Venerable Gyaltsen Bum*, *ST*, vol. 7, 91 (f. 3a6) where it says, "Inside is empty, outside is refined into clarity itself" (*nang stong pa/ phyi gsal ba nyid du sbyangs pas*), and in Tāranātha, *Essence of the Last Four of the Golden Dharmas Taken from Tāranātha's Teachings*, *ST*, vol. 7, 122 (f. 7b5–6), where it is described as, "whatever is struck by the light rays becomes more bright and clear, while flesh, blood, and bones and such subtle and gross particles are refined away."

12 Or, as put succinctly by Gyaltsen Bum in the *Guidance Manual*, 175 (f. 5a2–3): "The meaning of immortal great timeless awareness is that the cause of awakening does not exist. Keep meditating as long as you are not sure of that."

13 The canons have *'chi kha'i tshe 'di'i dus gzhan du* (at the point of death [and] other times of this life), but the more likely version found in other editions is simply *'chi kha'i tshe'am dus gzhan du*. CT has a further interlinear addition of *'chi kha'i* ***ma*** *tshe*, and the *DZ* and *ST* versions have *'chi kha'i* ***do*** *tshe'am*, both of which are incomprehensible to me.

14 *Ye shes rgya mtsho'i rgyud*. This is one of the primary sources of the Shangpa teachings and is often quoted, but has not been located. A long shot would be the *Ocean of Ḍākas* (*Ḍākārṇava*), a Chakrasaṃvara explanatory tantra with several chapters on "cheating death" (*'chi ba blu ba*) and a first chapter entitled "Entering the Ocean of Timeless Wisdom" (*ye shes kyi rgya mtsho la 'jug pa*).

"Fourfold vajra verse of immortality" (*'chi med rdo rje'i tshig rkang bzhi*) refers to the above quatrain, beginning with "Thus, the cause of Illness . . ." Bodong labels it "pointing out immortality by means of the fourfold verse." *Guide to One's Mind Naturally Liberated as Immortal*, 385. It is also quoted from the tantra in Gyaltsen Bum, *Guidance Manual of Immortal Mind, by the Wise and Venerable Gyaltsen Bum*, *ST*, vol. 7, 98–100. There it is described as the realization of one's mind as the deity's form being clarity, its essence being empty, and its nature their unity, unseen by buddhas of the three times yet appearing unhindered without truly existing, and hence one becomes free of all concepts of (1) illness, (2) death, (3) samsara, and (4) nirvana.

15 *gsal bar ma gyur*, but in *DZ* and *ST* it is *dran par ma gyur* (not remembered).

16 That is, the instructions and practice of these teachings. The canon editions have *sngags kyi gnad* (vital points of mantra) rather than *sngar gyi gnad* (previous vital points) in this verse.

17 According to Bodong's *Guide to One's Mind Naturally Liberated as Immortal*, 391, the three examples are as follows: the catapult is an example of the power of one's previous meditation, which is like a cannon and a machine; throwing stones into a clear pool is an example of the constancy of one's equipoise; and the sun setting at the same time as the moon rising on the fifteenth day of the lunar month is an example of the unity of immortality and timeless awareness.

18 *bde chen* (great bliss) here (*ST*) but *bde stong* (bliss-emptiness) in other editions (*DZ*, CT, and Bodong, *Guide to One's Mind Naturally Liberated as Immortal*).

19 Seven generations would be from Vajradhara until Sangye Tönpa, as has been mentioned before. "Three" is explained in Bodong's *Guide to One's Mind Naturally Liberated as Immortal:* "After seven generations, the guru who was thus predicted by the guru [Khyungpo Naljor] and the ḍākinī [Niguma] will bestow this on three [kinds of] disciples: those of highest faculty who develop the belief that the guru is dharmakāya, the middling ones who develop certainty [even in] the ordinary, and the least, who mentally abandon the world and meditate." 395 (f. 23a4–6).

20 This line, "translated by Lendarma Lodrö and ascertained by himself and . . ." is missing in the canons, where only Rinchen Zangpo is credited.

Notes to Chapter 6, Chakrasaṃvara

1 *rnal 'byor bla med kyi rgyud*, with the Sanskrit is given as *anuttarayoga-tantra*. The schema of four divisions of tantra, of which anuttarayoga-tantra is the last or "highest," was not developed until the later spreading of the dharma in Tibet in the tenth to eleventh centuries. The lineages resulting from that propagation and its translation efforts are now called Sarma (*gsar ma*) or "new ones," which includes the Shangpa tradition. Yoginī tantra is an earlier category and may be connected with an even earlier designation of ḍākinī tantra. See Gray, *The Cakrasamvara Tantra*, 5–11.

2 As David Gray says in his incredible study and translation, "The text was written so as to require commentary. This was no doubt due to the imperative of secrecy, which the text itself repeatedly demands of its adepts. Only initiated adepts were to receive the Root Tantra (*mūlatantra*), and they would have required oral instructions from their gurus in order to understand it." Ibid., 15.

3 For instance, in Tāranātha, *Supplement to the Lineage Stories of One Hundred Guides*, *DZ*, vol. 18, 104 (f. 3a7–b2). For the *Jewel Ocean Tantra*, see note 123 of the introduction. It is admittedly confusing when it is stated that these particular texts are the source and at the same time that Niguma heard the teachings from Buddha Vajradhara, but of, course, all tantras are ultimately buddha-word.

4 Roerich, *BA*, 390: *Śrī-Ḍākārṇava-mahāyoginītantrarāja* (Toh. 372). For a list of the nine major Chakrasaṃvara explanatory tantras, see Gray, *The Cakrasamvara Tantra*, 16.

5 Mokchokpa et al., *Brief Life Story of Lama Khyungpo Naljor*, *ST*, vol. 1, 91; and Tāranātha, *Clearing Up Darkness of the Mind*, *T-CW*, vol. 17, 458.

6 Gray, *The Cakrasamvara Tantra*, 7; and Davidson, *Indian Esoteric Buddhism*, 236–92.

7 Gray, *The Cakrasamvara Tantra*, 35–37 for a discussion of the term.

8 Ibid., 56.

9 Shaw, *Passionate Enlightenment*, 108.

10 Niguma, *Mandala Ritual of Glorious Chakrasaṃvara*. In *ST*, the title page reads: "Empowerment Conferral of Meditative Absorption in Chakrasaṃvara" (*'Khor lo sdom pa'i ting 'dzin gyi dbang bskur*). The empowerment ritual found in Jamgön Kongtrul's *The Treasury of Precious Instructions* is by Tāranātha: *Chakrasaṃvara Five Deities Empowerment Ritual in Nigu's Tradition* (but called *Mandala Ritual* there). It is more commonly used because, as is pointed out in the colophon, there

are many missing components and those that are available are mixed up. *DZ*, vol. 11, 285.

11 The interlinear notes in the *Shangpa Texts* edition adds that this is done by sweeping and setting up covers and canopies. The translation here is from the tengyur in the Peking Canon and only those notes that are there are included in the translation, appearing in smaller font. Additional notes from other editions will be added as footnotes.

12 *ba'i rnam lnga* or *ba byung lnga*: dung, urine, milk, curd, and butter (*lci ba, chu, 'o ma, zho, mar*).

13 This is called the support (*rten*) mandala as indicated in the note in the Shangpa edition.

14 *Hūṃ* is at the center (*lte bar hūṃ*).

15 Several lines are added here in the *Shangpa Texts* edition, including both large and small print. It reads: "Do from finding the freedom and endowments [of the precious human life] and death and impermanence, the common and special going for refuge, engendering the two aspirations of wishing and engaging, together with the trainings, giving in generosity, gathering thoughts, the five branches of the path, the scarcity of the occurrence of secret mantra, bestowing the three sacred pledges, entering the mandala, and so forth."

16 "in the basin" (*nang gi mchod pa bzed zhal du 'bul*). *ST*, vol. 7, 449 (f. 3a6).

17 *'dab ma bzhi* added from *ST*, vol. 7, 450 (f. 3b5), where it appears integral to the text.

18 Spelled simply *a* in the tengyurs, but *āḥ* in *ST*.

19 Heruka is in this context a name of *Chakrasaṃvara* . For a discussion on the history of this term and the "Heruka origin myth," which sets the stage for the Chakrasaṃvara teachings, see Gray, *The Cakrasamvara Tantra*, 39–54.

20 "adorned by five" bone ornaments. *ST*, vol. 7, 452 (f. 4b6). The six bone ornaments that represent the six perfections are bone earrings (patience), bone necklaces (generosity), bone bracelets, armlets, and anklets (morality), bone belt (perseverance), bone wheel worn on the head (meditation), and bone ashes, smeared on the body or marked on the forehead (wisdom). The first five are associated with skillful methods of the masculine principle. The sixth represents the feminine principle of wisdom, and is therefore absent here because the deity itself is feminine.

21 *bde ba chen po*, referring of course to Chakrasaṃvara. The notes in *ST* add that this encounter will include the entourage. *ST*, vol. 7, 455 (f. 6a2).

22 The notes in *ST* paraphrase this: "mind-itself as appearance-emptiness and bliss-emptiness inseparable."

23 *sDom pa rgya mtsho'i rgyud*, not located, possibly *Śrī-Ḍākārṇava-mahāyoginītantrarāja* (Toh. 372).

24 *Swift Accomplishment of Glorious Chakrasaṃvara*. The full title literally is *The Method of So-Called Swift Accomplishment of Glorious Chakrasaṃvara* . The heading in the canons is "Saṃvara secret practice" (*bde mchog gsang sgrub*).

25 *srid pa gsum*: above, on, and under the earth; that is, the beings in the heavens, on the earth, and in the underworlds (such as nāga).

26 A khaṭvāṅga is a three-pointed staff carried by tantric adepts and representing the secret masculine consort and transformation of the three poisons. It is called *rtse gsum* in Tibetan, but the Sanskrit is often retained, as here.

27 Taking *dmigs pa stod* as *dmigs pa stad*, although it is spelled *dmigs pa bstod* (praise the visualization) in Bodong's edition. A note also indicates that it refers to the visualization above the crown of the head. I can find no comment on the dream reference.

28 This time the light is red. Bodong's edition notes: "the three existences [as] the red palace of great bliss."

29 *gar dgu'i nyams*: the nine sentiments or expressions of dance and dramatic art: erotic, heroic, disgusting, furious, humorous, frightful, compassionate, wonderful, and tranquil (*sgeg pa dpa' ba mi sdug pa/ rgod dang drug shul 'jigs su rung/ snying rje rngam dang zhi ba'o*).

30 In the tengyur editions here and in the following paragraph, the word is *man chad*, "up to" or "below," while in the *ST* and Bodong editions it is *yan chad*, "down to" or "above," although both words that are seemingly opposites can also be understood as "up to and including". The point anyway is that the elixir flows down through the top of the crown to the point that is specifically being purified, flowing further down each time—first to the head, then to the throat, and then to the heart.

31 It should be mentioned that *thugs* means both mind and heart, the same thing, located at the heart.

32 An obscure interlinear note here reads *shangs pa rngu* (or *rgu*) *pa*.

33 This word is written as *rjed dor* (P), *rjod thor* (CT), *brjed thor* (*ST*), and *rjed thor* (Bodong). I am interpreting it as "notes" or, literally, minor (*thor*) expressions (*rjod*).

34 These last two lines are found only in the *Shangpa Texts* edition, not in the tengyurs or Bodong

Notes to Chapter 7, Hevajra

1 Panchen Sonam Dragpa, *Overview of Buddhist Tantra*, 50.

2 *Nine Emanated Deities of Hevajra* (*dGyes rdor sprul pa'i lha dgu*) and the *Hevajra Tantra in Two Parts* (*brTag gnyis*) are listed in Mokchokpa et al., *Brief Life Story of Lama Khyungpo Naljor*, *ST*, vol. 1, 91 (f. 17a5–6) and in Tāranātha, *Clearing Up Darkness of the Mind*, *T-CW*, vol. 17, 458. They are not mentioned in the *Blue Annals*.

3 *bKa' babs bdun ldan*. See David Templeman's translation in Tāranātha, *The Seven Instruction Lineages*, 64 and n. 199.

4 *Stainless Union*. The author's name in the tengyur is given as Dhaṅkadāśa, which is also spelled Taṅkadāsa, and is identified as the Old Scribe (Kāyasthavrddha). This is a later translation by Vimalashrībhadra and Lodro Tenpa (bLo gros brtan pa).

5 Tāranātha, *Five Tantras' Mandala Method of Accomplishment*. This practice concerns thirteen deities of Hevajra as the basis of a sādhana of the five deities' mandala (*sgyes mdzad rdo rje drag po gdan can gyi bskyed pa'i rim pa la gzhi byas nas rgyud sde lnga'i dkyil 'khor gyi sgrub thabs nyams su len pa'i tshul ni 'di yin te*). *ST*, vol. 5, 452–53 (ff. 1b4–2a1).

6 Tāranātha, *Supplication to the Lineage of Five Tantras in the Shangpa Tradition*. There the lineage is Vajradhara, Nairātmyā, Doṃbīheruka, Ngotsar Dorje (mNgo mtshar rdo rje), Garbharipa, Gyalwa Pal (rGyal ba dpal), Ḍākinī Gongyal Kadawa (mGon rgyal dKa' zla ba; Durjayacandra?), Ratnākara, and Vajrāsana. *ST*, vol. 5, 440 (f. 1a1–4).

7 Niguma, *Mandala Ritual of Glorious Hevajra.* I did not have access to the Peking edition of this text, so this translation is based on the single edition in the Derge Tengyur, with some reference to source texts for the verses.

8 "Hundred thousands" refer to the mantras of the principal deity and "tens of thousands" to those of the retinue.

9 The vase in the center represents the deity (*lha bum*) and the one in the northeast is the "activity vase" (*las bum*) used during the ceremony.

10 bDud rtsi 'khyil pa (Swirl of Elixir): the name of a deity that appears in various contexts, or emanations, such as one of the four gatekeepers in the set of a hundred peaceful and wrathful deities, or one of the five classes of awareness deities for accomplishment, and as the central figure in a sādhana of the Namchö tradition. Here it is the deity visualized inside the vase, the embodiment of the holy amṛita, or elixir, contained therein.

11 *rtog pa bsdu ba*: that is, the concepts of oneself as ordinary.

12 The second verse here can be found in *Ḍākinī Vajra Tent Tantra*, an Hevajra explanatory tantra, ACIP, rgyud, vol. Ka, 415B.

13 This is from the same tantra, continuous with the last quote.

14 *'od du 'dus*: it seems that the eight Nairātmyās dissolve into one, and that one then unites with Hevajra in the center. Possibly the original Tibetan was *'ub du 'dus* (SKT).

15 These seed syllables of the purifying elements are more commonly in the order *raṃ yaṃ kaṃ* (fire, wind, water), and may be a mistake here.

16 From *Hevajra Tantra in Two Parts*, part 2, chap. 8, f. 57a1–3, in the Rumtek edition. It is translated from the Sanskrit in Farrow and Menon, *The Concealed Essence of the Hevajra Tantra*, 272–73. There are some differences in the Tibetan with the Niguma text. The only one that is significant in meaning is where the Niguma text has *mnyam med kye'i rdo rje ston*, "teacher incomparable Hevajra," the source text (Rumtek edition and ACIP, rGyud Ka, 374b) reads *smyo med kye yi rdo rje ston*: literally "teaching Hevajra unintoxicated" (sober Hevajra?). The commentary by Jamgön Kongtrul explains this as referring to the person carrying the sacred pledge, who is "not intrinsically reckless, with unrestricted conduct of the three doors, whose mind does not rest in its native state due to being bloated with pride over their clan lineage." Rumtek edition, ff. 299a4–300a5. This is omitted in the Farrow and Menon translation, though it appears to be in the Sanskrit: *kulajanmānumādi samayi hevajradeśakaḥ*.

Notes to Chapter 8, The Ḍākinī's Personal Instructions: Five Short Texts on Yogic Techniques

1 See, for instance, David-Neel, *Magic and Mystery in Tibet*.

2 Tāranātha, *Nigu's Yogic Exercises, Root and Commentary*, *ST*, vol. 6, 159–160 (f. 9a5–b5).

3 Khungpo Naljor, *Natural Liberation through Grasping Illusory Body and Sixfold Illusory Body*.

4 These are the *Shangpa Catalogue* and *The Beryl Key Catalogue to Fully Open the Precious Treasury of the Golden Dharmas of the Glorious Shangpa Kagyu*.

5 This instruction probably represents the source of the two methods for opening the central channel that constitute the thirteenth and fourteenth methods in Niguma's

eighteen yogic exercises, described in Tāranātha's *Nigu's Yogic Exercises, Root and Commentary*, *ST*, vol. 6, 153–54 (f. 6a5–b3).

6 *rnam snang gi chos bdun:* this position is described as the legs in full lotus, the spine straight, the shoulders broadened, the neck slightly bent, the hands in the gesture of equanimity, the tip of the tongue touching the palate, and the gaze placed in the direction of the nose.

7 This is also just known as *rLung 'don* in Sangye Tönpa et al., *Natural Liberation through Grasping Illusory Body and Sixfold Illusory Body*. *ST*, vol. 8, 742–44. This is probably the source of exercises 5, 6, and 7 in Niguma's eighteen yogic exercises. See Tāranātha's *Nigu's Yogic Exercises, Root and Commentary.*

8 *rlung gi 'khor lo thur du bshig*. In Tāranātha's commentary, the apparently equivalent phrase reads "Scare down the downward-clearing [prāṇa] and draw up the life-force [prāṇa]" (*mthur sel mthur du bsdig pa dang/ srog [rlung] steng du drang*). *ST*, vol. 6, 150 (f. 4b6). This brings together the two kinds of prāṇa ("downward clearing" and "life force") in the middle, a very common yogic method. Here it is expressed as joining the two wheels of prāṇa and fire. It is a puzzling use of the word *bshig*, literally "to destroy" or "demolish," and I can only assume that it is an alternate usage meaning roughly "to bear down" or "push." The exact wording is also used in another of Niguma's instructions for straightening the channels in the collection of yogic exercises in the *Shangpa Texts*, but without the intervening line concerning placement of the hands. *ST*, vol. 8, 740 (f. 62b5–6).

9 *a ba dhu ti*, left in transliterated Sanskrit; it is the name for the central channel (Tib. *rtsa dbu ma*).

10 Here *tsangs bug*, but more properly *tshangs pa'i bu ga*, Skt. *brahmarandra*: the opening at the top of one's head, the path of which leads to the higher realms.

11 *ST* has *drag po bdun bdun 'then par bya*, which seems to be preferable to the tengyurs' *drag po lan bdun bden par bya*.

12 *rdo rje gar*: In Tāranātha's *Nigu's Yogic Exercises, Root and Commentary*, the vajra dance is said to consist of the fifteenth, sixteenth, and seventeenth of Niguma's eighteen yogic exercises, that is, the exercises to help insert, guide, and gather the vital essence into the central channel. Sometimes the two exercises for opening the central channel are also included in the vajra dance, but that does not seem to be the case here. *ST*, vol. 6, 155 (f. 7a5–6).

13 In CT, vol. 42, 954–56 (2528) as *Ḍaki'i zhal gdams dug gsum zhi byed* (*Ḍākinī's Personal Instruction on Pacification of the Three Poisons*). These exercises altogether correspond to the eighteenth of Niguma's eighteen yogic exercises as described in Tāranātha, *Nigu's Yogic Exercises, Root and Commentary*, where they are called "Yogic Exercises for Clearing away Afflictive States." *ST*, vol. 6, 156–59.

14 These headings are added for clarification based on Tāranātha's commentary, *Nigu's Yogic Exercises, Root and Commentary.* As is often the case in Tibetan literature, there are issues with the enumeration. First of all, the title in CT, *Ḍākinī's Personal Instruction on Pacification of the Three Poisons*, clearly involves a miscount since there are more than three poisons. Then, in Tāranātha's text, which includes what might be taken as the source text, it is clearly stated that the last or eighteenth exercise in Niguma's eighteen yogic exercises can be divided into eight parts, and if added separately then there are said to be twenty-five in all. The only problem is that Tāranātha presents nine divisions, and that is how it is currently practiced in the lineage. In the

text here, one might count only eight if numbers five and six are not separated, as they appear not to be in the original (without reference to Tāranātha's commentary). But in order to offer a practical correspondence to the current tradition, I have used the nine exercises here.

15 *'dug stangs*: Although the term for "sitting position" is used here, which would normally mean the sevenfold posture of Vairochana, Tāranātha's description of these exercises specifies "mudra" (hand gesture) in this and the following exercises. *Nigu's Yogic Exercises, Root and Commentary*, *ST*, vol. 6, 156 (f. 7b2).

16 *mnyam bzhag phyag rgya*: this is also known as the mudra of Amitābha, as it is called by Tāranātha, *Nigu's Yogic Exercises, Root and Commentary*, *ST*, vol. 6, 157 (f. 8a5).

17 *'dom gsum chod pa*, but in Tāranātha's version it is "eight": *'doms 'jal brgyad*. Ibid., f. 8b3.

18 *lkog gis langs*, is spelled variously as *kag gis langs* or *kog gyis langs* (this last one with its meaning of "suddenly" makes the most sense). "With a hop," though not in the dictionary, comes from the oral tradition and must be the meaning of the phrase. Tāranātha adds that *kog langs* is in fact the name of this exercise.

19 In *ST*, vol. 8, 745–46 as *rkyang bskum* (*Extend and Contract*). These instructions seem to correspond to exercises 8 through 12 of Niguma's eighteen yogic exercises, although the first two are no longer in use in this form.

20 Concerning these exercises, which correspond to exercises 8 and 9 of Niguma's eighteen yogic exercises, Tāranātha comments: " It says in the source that these two, the eighth and ninth, [involved] first grabbing hold of a staff with one hand and then afterward grabbing hold with two and lifting off to a distance, so it was considered "pole vaulting" (*dbyug mchong byed pa*). However these days this practice is not done." *ST*, vol. 6, 152 (f. 5b 3–5). The description here, then, represents the earlier practice and is not thus described in later works, making it impossible to verify my interpretation.

21 *pus mo'i gnyan gong dag tu sbyar* (*ST*) is better than *pus mo snyan gong dag du sbyar* (join the knee to the ear)! CT.

22 *bu chung 'khrul 'khor*, also called *bu chung tshul* (the manner of a small child), is the eleventh of Niguma's eighteen yogic exercises, involving rotating the head.

23 *lag gsum* (CT) should be *lan gsum* (*ST*). Sometimes to hit the ground with the heels (*rting pa sa la brdab*) refers to standing in place, raising up on the toes, and then falling back hard on the heels. Sometimes it refers to leaping up and landing on the ground in a cross-legged posture

Notes to Chapter 9, Niguma's Aspiration Prayer

1 Entitled "The Sovereign of Noble Aspirations" (*'Phags pa smon lam gyi rgyal po*) in the tengyur, it is known as "Sealed Word" (*bKa' rgya ma*) in the *Shangpa Texts* and with practitioners. This translation is based on five versions: P rgyud 'grel, vol. Pu, 201a7–203a8 (4650), CT, vol. 42, 959–63 (2530); *ST*, vol. 6, 233–43; *DZ*, vol. 12, 459–62; and a separate xylograph copy in the translator's possession, ff.1a–3b.

2 This verse is missing in the Peking Tengyur edition and in the CT reprint of it.

3 *sbyin ba rnam bzhi* : four kinds of gifts—of items, dharma, relief from fear, and love (*zang zing, chos, mi 'jigs pa, byams*).

4 *chags thog med pa*: desireless and unobstructed means free from the two obscurations (*sgrib gnyis*) of afflictive emotions and cognitive limitations, respectively.

5 *slob pa gsum*: ethical discipline, meditation, and wisdom.

6 There is a significant difference in the several versions of this verse. *ST* and my xylograph edition, which I have translated here, read: *sems can khams dang rgya mtsho'i gting mtha' dang/ nam mkha'i mtha' dang chos dbying tshad med ltar/ bdag gi smon lam ting 'dzin phrin las rnams/ gting mtha' dpag med tshad bzung med par shog*. The tengyur editions read: *sems can khams dang rgya mtsho'i gting mtha' dang/ nam mkha'i khams dang chos dbying dbyer med lta/ bdag gi shes rab smon lam ting 'dzin rnams/ gting mtha' dpag med tshad bzung med par shog.* This could be translated as: "May my knowledge, aspirations, and absorptions be boundlessly deep and vast, impossible to measure, see the realms of beings and the depths and reaches of the oceans, the realms of the sky and the realm of reality inseparable."

Abbreviations

ACIP — Electronic files of the Asian Classics Input project, www.asianclassics.org.

ATG — Ācārya Tenpa Gyaltsen.

BA — 'Gos lo tsa ba gzhon nu dpal, *The Blue Annals* (*Deb ther sngon po*). Translated by George N. Roerich. 2nd ed. Delhi: Motilal Banarsidass, 1976. Originally published 1949 in Calcutta.

BD — *Bod rgya tshig mdzod chen mo* (Big Tibetan-Chinese Dictionary). Edited by Zhang Yisun et al. 2 vols. Beijing: Mi rigs dpe skrun khang, 1985, 1987.

Catalogue — *Catalogue of the Treasury of Precious Key Instructions, a Collection of the Ripening and Liberating Essence of the Eight Great Chariots of the Practice Lineages: An Ocean of Auspicious Renown* (*sGrub brgyud shing rta chen po brgyad kyi smin grol snying po phyogs gcig bstus pa gdams ngag rin po che'i mdzod kyi dkar chag bkra shis grags pa'i rgya mtsho*). *DZ*, vol. 18, ff. 381–547.

CT — Collated Tengyur (bstan 'gyur: dpe bsdur ma). Beijing: krung go'i bod kyi shes rig dpe skrun khang, 1995–2005.

Dg.K. — Derge Kangyur (sDe dge bka' 'gyur): Derge edition of the Tibetan canonical collection of sutras and tantras.

Dg.T. — Derge Tengyur (sDe dge bstan 'gyur): Derge edition

of the Tibetan canonical collection of commentarial treatises.

DZ — Jamgön Kongtrul Lodrö Thayé, *gDam ngag rin po che'i mdzod* (*The Treasury of Precious Instructions*). 18 vols. Paro, Bhutan: Lama Ngodrup and Sherab Drimay, 1979.

GD-CW — Lochen Gyurme Dechen's Collected Works (gsung 'bum/_'gyur med bde chen), TBRC: W2DB16431.

GK — Jamgön Kongtrul Lodrö Thayé, *rGya chen bka' mdzod* (*The Treasury of Extensive Teachings*). 20 vols. Paro, Bhutan: Ngodup, 1975–76.

JIABS — *Journal of the International Association of Buddhist Studies.*

P — *The Tibetan Collected Words of the Buddha and Its Commentaries* (Tripitaka). Peking Edition, 168 vols. Tokyo-Kyoto: Suzuki Research Foundation, 1955–61. http://web.otani.ac.jp/cri/twrp/tibdate/Peking_online_search.html.

RY — Rangjung Yeshe Online Dictionary, www.nitartha.org/dictionary_search04.html.

SKT — Surmang Khenpo Tsering Gyurme.

ST — *Shangpa Texts (Shangs chos)/ Indian Source Texts of the Dharma Cycle of Five Golden Dharmas of the Glorious Shangpa (dPal ldan shangs pa'i chos 'khor gser chos rnam lnga'i rgya zhung).* Edited by Karma Rangjung Kunkhyab (Kalu Rinpoche). Sonada, India: Samdrup Darje Ling Monastery, n.d. 11 vols. This collection is based on the Palpung edition. Reprinted by Lama Tsengyur Rinpoche, Kagyu Kunkhyab Chuling, 1982.

TBRC — Tibetan Buddhist Resource Center, www.tbrc.org.

T-CW — Tāranātha's Collected Works (rje btsun Tā-ra-nā-tha'i gsung 'bum), Dzamthang edition, 23 vols. Dzam thang Dgon, Sichuan, 1996 (as per colophon in vol. 12:1025).

THDL	Tibetan and Himalayan Digital Library (now THLIB).
Toh.	*A Complete Catalogue of the Tibetan Buddhist Canons (Chibetto Daizōkyō Sōmokuroku).* Edited by Hakuju Ui, Munetada Suzuki, Yenshō Kanakura, and Tōkan Tada. Sendai: Tōhoku Imperial University, 1934.
TOK	*The Treasury of Knowledge/Infinite Ocean of Knowledge (Shes bya kun khyab mdzod/Shes bya mtha' yas pa'i rgya mtsho)* 3 vols. Beijing: Bod mi rigs dpe skrun khang, 1982.
TTG-S	*Supplemental Texts to the Collected Works of Thang-stong-rgyal-po Series, Volume 1.* Grub chen thang stong bka' 'bum gyi rgyab chos ni gu chos drug pod dang pa. Royal Government of Bhutan Publishing House (dPal ldan 'brug gzhung dpe mdzod khang), n.d.

Bibliography of Works Cited by the Author

Canonical Works

Actualization of Timeless Awareness [Extensive Tantra]
Jñānābhyudaya
Ye shes mngon par 'byung ba['i rgyud rgyas pa]
Not located

Array of Sacred Oaths/ Array of the Sacred Oaths of the Five Families/ Array of Sacred Oaths Subsequent Tantra
Dam tshig bkod pa/Rigs lnga'i dam tshig bkod pa/ Dam tshig bkod pa'i rgyud phyi ma
Not located

Ḍākinī Vajra Tent Tantra
Ārya-ḍākinīvajrapañjara-mahātantra-rājakalpa-nāma
'Phags pa mkha' 'gro ma rdo rje gur shes bya ba'i rgyud kyi rgyal po chen po'i brtag pa
Dg.K. rGyud 'bum, vol. Nga, ff. 30a–65b (Toh. 419) (P11)

Dense Array of Adornments Sūtra
Ghanavyūha Sūtra
'Phag pa rgyan stug po bkod pa zhes bya ba theg pa chen po'i mdo
Dg. K. mDo sde, vol. Cha, ff. 1b–55b (Toh. 110)

Flower Ornament Sūtra
Āvataṃsaka Sūtra/Buddhāvataṃsakanāmamahāvaipulyasūtra
Sangs rgyas phal po che zhes bya ba shin tu rgyas pa chen po'i mdo
Dg.K. Phal chen, vols. Ka, Kha, Ga, A (Toh. 44) (P761)

Translation: Thomas F. Cleary. *The Flower Ornament Scripture: A Translation of the Avatamsaka Sutra*. Boston: Shambhala Publications, 1993.

Fully Illuminated Essence Sūtra
sNying po rab tu gsal ba'i mdo
Not located

Hevajra Tantra [in Two Parts] /Two Part Exposition Tantra
Hevajratantrarājanāma
brTag gnyis bshad rgyud
(Part I) Kye'i rdo rje zhes bya ba rgyud kyi rgyal po
Dg.K. rGyud 'bum, vol. Nga, ff. 1b–13b (Toh. 417)
(Part II) Kye'i rdo rje mkha' 'gro ma dra ba'i sdom pa'i rgyud kyi rgyal po
Dg.K. rGyud 'bum, vol. Nga, ff. 13b–30a (Toh. 418)
Xylograph: Rumtek, Sikkim: Rum brtegs karma chos sgar, 1970? ff. 1–64.
Translations: D. L. Snellgrove, *Hevajra Tantra: Parts I and II.* London: Oxford University Press, 1959; repr. 1971.
G. W. Farrow and I. Menon, *The Concealed Essence of the Hevajra Tantra*. Delhi: Motilal Barnarsidass, 1992.

Highest Intention Tantra
dGongs pa bla na med pa'i rgyud
Not located

Highest Timeless Awareness Tantra
Ye shes bla na med pa'i rgyud
Not located

Illuminated Timeless Awareness Latter Tantra
Ye shes gsal (or *gsang*) ba'i brgyud phyi ma
Not located

Journey to Lanka Sūtra
Laṅkāvatārasūtra
Lang kar gshegs pa'i mdo
Dg.K. mDo sde, vol. Ca, ff. 56a–191b (Toh. 107)

Translation: D. T. Suzuki. *The Lankavatara Sutra*. London: Routledge, 1932.

Latter Ocean Tantra
rGya mtsho'i rgyud phyi ma
Not located. Possibly the same as *Ocean of Timeless Awareness.*

Meaningful Discipline Tantra
'Dul ba (or *'dus pa*) don yod pa'i rgyud
Not located

Meeting of Father and Son
Ārya-pitāputrasamāgamana
'Phags pa yab dang sras mjal ba
Dg.K. dKon brtsegs, vol. Nga, ff. 1b–168a (Toh. 60)

Ocean of Timeless Awareness
Ye shes rgya mtsho'i rgyud
Not located. Possibly the same as *Latter Ocean Tantra.*

Perfection of Wisdom in Eighteen Thousand Lines
Ārya-aṣṭadaśāhasāsrikā-prajñāpāramitā
Khri brgyad stong pa/'Phags pa shes rab kyi pha rol tu phyin pa khri brgyad stong pa
Dg.K. Shes phyin, vols. Ka, Kha, and Ga (Toh. 10)

Questions of Four Girls
Bu mo bzhi zhus pa
Not located

*Questions of Matisambhava Sūtra**
bLo gros 'byung gnas kyis zhus pa'i mdo
Not located

Saṃvara Ocean Tantra
sDom pa rgya mtsho'i rgyud
Possibly *Ocean of Ḍākas Tantra:*
Śrī-Ḍakārṇava-mahāyoginītantrarāja
Dg.K. rGyud 'bum, vol. Kha, ff. 137a–264b (Toh. 372)

Secret Ḍākinī Tantra
Śri-ḍākinīguhyajvala-tantrarāja
dPal mkha' 'gro ma gsang ba 'bar ba'i rgyud kyi rgyal po
Dg.K. rgyud 'bum, vol. Ga, ff. 245b–247a (Toh. 408)

Secret Moon Drop Tantra
Śrī-candraguhyatilaka-nāma-mahātantrarāja
dPal zla gsang thig le zhes bya ba rgyud kyi rgyal po chen po
Dg.K. rGyud 'bum, vol. Ja, ff. 247b–303a (Toh. 477)

Sections on Grounds Sūtra
Sa sde'i mdo
Not located

Stainless Essence Sūtra
Dri med snying po'i mdo
Not located

Sublime Absorption Sūtra
Samādhyagrottama
Ting nge 'dzin mchog dam pa
Dg.K. mDo sde, vol. Na, ff. 179a–187b (Toh. 137)

Sublime Golden Light Sūtra
Suvarṇaprabhāsottama-sūtrendrarāja-nāma-mahāyānasūtra
gSer 'od dam pa/Phags pa gser 'od dam pa mdo sde'i dbang po'i rgyal po zhes bya ba theg pa chen po'i mdo
Dg.K. rGyud 'bum, vol. Pa, ff. 151b–273a (Toh. 556)
Translation: R. E. Emmerick, *Sūtra of Golden Light*. Pāli Text Society. Sacred Books of the Buddhists, vol. 27. London: Luzac, 1970.

*Sūtra of Bodhisattva Dṛdhramati**
Byang chub sems dbang blo gros rab brtan gyi mdo
Not located

*Sūtra of Brahmānanda**
Tshangs pa kun dga'i mdo
Not located

*Sūtra of Kumāraprabha**
Khye'u rab snang gi mdo
Not located

Sūtra of Teaching the Unimaginable
bSam gyis mi khyab pa bstan pa'i mdo
Not located

Tantra of Total Nonabiding
Rab tu mi gnas pa'i rgyud
Not located

Vajra Garland Tantra
Vajramālā/Vajramālābhidhāna-mahāyogatantra-sarvatantrahṛdaya-rahasya-vibhaṅga
rDo rje phreng ba/rNal 'byor chen po'i rgyud dpal rdo rje phreng ba mngon par brjod pa rgyud thams cad kyi snying po gsang ba rnam par phye ba
Dg.K. rGyud 'bum, vol. Ca, ff. 208a–277b (Toh. 445)

Vajra Peak Tantra
Vajraśekhara-mahāguhyayogatantra
gSang ba rnal 'byor chen po'i rgyud rdo rje rtse mo
Dg.K. rGyud 'bum, vol. Nya, ff. 142b–274a (Toh. 480)

Vimalakīrti Sūtra
Ārya-Vimalakīrtinirdeśa-sūtra
'Phags pa dri ma med par grags pas bstan pa
Dg.K. mDo sde, vol. Ma, ff. 175a–239b (Toh. 176)

White Lotus of Great Compassion Sūtra
Ārya-mahākaruṇā-puṇḍarīka-sūtra
'Phags pa snying rje chen po'i pad ma dkar po
Dg.K. mDo sde, vol. Cha, ff. 56a–128b (Toh. 111)

Treatises

Maitreya (Byams pa)

Mahāyāna Highest Continuum/Jewel Affinity
Mahāyānottaratantraśāstra/ Ratnagotravibhāga
Theg pa chen po rgyud bla ma'i bstan bcos
Dg.T. Sems tsam, vol. Phi, ff. 54b–73a (Toh. 4024)

Ornament of Clear Realization
Abhisamayālaṃkāra
mNgon par rtogs pa'i rgyan
Dg.T. Sher phyin, vol. Ka, ff. 1b–13a (Toh. 3786) (ACIP TD3786)
English translations: Edward Conze, *Abhisamayālaṃkāra.* Serie Orientale Rome. Rome: Istituto Italiano per il Medio ed Estremo Oriente, 1954.
Karl Brunnhölzl, *Gone Beyond: The Prajñāpāramitā Sūtras, The Ornament of Clear Realization, and Its Commentaries in the Tibetan Kagyü Tradition.* Ithaca, NY: Snow Lion Publications, forthcoming.

Ornament of the Māhayāna Sūtras
Mahāyānasūtrālaṃkāra
Theg pa chen po mdo sde'i rgyan
Dg.T. Sems tsam, vol. Phi, ff. 1a–40b (Toh. 4020)
Translation: L. Jamspal et al. *The Universal Vehicle Discourse Literature (Mahāyānasūtrālaṁkāra).* Editor-in-chief, Robert A. F. Thurman. Treasury of the Buddhist Sciences. New York: American Institute of Buddhist Studies, Columbia University, 2004.

Saraha

Song of Dohā Treasury
Dohākoṣagīti
Do ha mdzod kyi glu
Dg.T. rGyud 'grel, vol. Wi, ff. 70b–77a (Toh. 2224)
Translations: Herbert V. Guenther, *Ecstatic Spontaneity: Saraha's Three Cycles of Dohā.* Berkeley: Asian Humanities Press, 1993.
David L. Snellgrove, "Saraha's Treasury of Songs." In *Buddhist Texts*

through the Ages, ed. Edward Conze, 224–39. New York: Harper and Row, 1990.

Roger R. Jackson, *Tantric Treasures: Three Collections of Mystical Verse from Buddhist India.* Oxford: Oxford University Press, 2004

Reference Bibliography

Canonical Works

Abhidhānottaratantra
mNgon par brjod pa'i rgyud bla ma
Dg.K., rGyud 'bum, vol. Ka, ff. 247a–370a (Toh. 369)

Buddhavaṁsa
Khuddaka Nikāya, chap. 14, Pāli Text Society, ed. N. A. Jayawickrama, 1974, 1995.
Translation: I. B. Horner, "The Chronicle of Buddhas and Basket of Conduct." In *Minor Anthologies* 3, 2nd ed., Bristol: Pāli Text Society, 1975.

Collated Tengyur
bsTan 'gyur: dpe bsdur ma
Beijing: krung go'i bod kyi shes rig dpe skrun khang, 1995–2005.

Diamond Sūtra
Ārya-vajracchedikā-nāma-prajñāpāramitā-mahāyānasūtra
'Phags pa shes rab kyi pha rol tu phyin pa rdo rje gcod pa zhes bya ba theg pa chen po'i mdo
Dg.K. Shes byin, vol. Kha, ff. 121a–132b (Toh. 16) (P739)

Drop of Timeless Awareness
Jñānatilaka/ Śrī-jñānatilaka-yoginītantrarāja-paramamahādbhuta

Ye shes thig le/ dPal ye shes thig le rnal 'byor ma'i rgyud kyi rgyal po chen po mchog tu rmad du byung ba
Dg.K. rGyud 'bum, vol. Nga, ff. 96b–136b (Toh. 422)

Four Seats Tantra
Catuḥpīṭha-mahāyoginītantrarāja
rNal 'byor ma'i rgyud kyi rgyal po chen po dpal gdan bzhi pa
Dg.K. rGyud 'bum, vol. Nga, ff. 181a–231b (Toh. 428)

Ocean of Ḍākas Tantra
Śrī-ḍakārṇavamahāyoginītantrarāja
dPal mkha' 'gro rgya mtsho rnal 'byor ma'i rgyud kyi rgyal po chen po
Dg.K. rGyud 'bum, vol. Kha, ff. 137a–264b (Toh. 372)

Perfection of Wisdom in Eight Thousand Lines
Ārya-aṣṭasāhasrikā-prajñāpāramitā-sūtra
Phags pa shes rab kyi pha rol tu phyin pa brgyad stong pa'i mdo
Dg.K. Shes byin, vol. Ka, ff. 1b–286a (Toh. 12)
Translation: Edward Conze, *The Perfection of Wisdom in Eight Thousand Lines and Its Verse Summary*. Bolinas, CA: Four Seasons Foundation, 1973.

Questions of Akṣayamati Sūtra
Ārya-akṣayamatiparipṛcchā-nāma-mahāyānasūtra
'Phags pa blo gros mi zad pas zhus pa zhes bya ba theg pa chen po'i mdo
Dg.K. dKon brtsegs, vol. Cha, ff. 175b–182b (Toh. 89)

Stainless Union
Śrī-hevajratantrarājaṭikā-suviśadasaṃpuṭa
Kha sbyor dri med/ rGyud kyi rgyal po dpal kye'i rdo rje'i 'grel bshad kha sbyor shin tu dri ma med pa
Dg.T. rGyud, vol. Kha, ff. 61a–294a (Toh. 1184)

Sūtra of the Vast Display
Ārya-lalitavistara-nāma-mahāyānasūtra
'Phags pa rgya cher rol pa zhes bya ba theg pa chen po'i mdo
Dg.K. mDo sde, vol. Kha, ff. 1b–216b (Toh. 95)
Translation: Gwendolyn Bays, *The Voice of the Buddha: The Beauty of Compassion*. Translated from the French. 2 vols. Berkeley: Dharma Publishing, 1983.

Sūtra on the Ten Grounds
Daśabhūmikasūtra
Sa bcu pa'i mdo
Dg.K. Phal chen, vol. Kha, ff. 166a–203a (Toh. 44)
This is chap. 31 of the *Flower Ornament Sūtra (Avataṃsaka)*.

Sūtra That Unravels the Intent
Ārya-saṃdhinirmocana-nāma-mahāyānasūtra
'Phags pa dgongs pa nges par 'grel pa zhes bya ba theg pa chen po'i mdo
Dg.K. mDo sde, vol. Ca, ff. 1b–55b (Toh. 106)
Translation: John Powers, *Wisdom of Buddha: The Saṃdhinirmocana Mahāyāna Sūtra*. Berkeley: Dharma Publishing, 1995.

The Tibetan Collected Words of the Buddha and Its Commentaries (tripiṭāka)
Peking Edition, 168 vols. Tokyo-Kyoto: Suzuki Research Foundation, 1955–61.

Treatises and Commentaries

Asaṅga (Thogs med)
Bodhisattva Grounds
Bodhisattvabhūmi
Byang chub sems dpa'i sa
Dg.T. Sems tsam, vol. Wi, 1a–213a (Toh. 4037)
A section of the Yogāchārabhūmi

Compendium of the Mahāyāna
Mahāyāna-saṃgraha
Theg pa chen po bsdus pa
Dg.T. Sems tsam, vol. Ri, 1b–43a (Toh. 4048)

Bodong Chokley Namgyal (Bo dong Phyogs las rnam rgyal)
The Compendium of Suchness
De nyid 'dus pa
Encyclopedia Tibetica, or Collected Works of Bodong Chokley Namgyal, 137 vols. New Delhi: Tibet House. (TBRC W22103)

Guide to One's Mind Naturally Liberated as Immortal
Rang sems 'chi med rang 'grol kyi khrid
In *Heart of the Path*, in *The Compendium of Suchness*, Collected Works of Bodong Chokley Namgyal, vol. 103, 360–396, New Delhi: Tibet House.

Heart of the Path: Esoteric Instructions on Immortal Great Timeless Awareness
Lam gyi snying po 'chi med ye shes chen po'i man ngag
(Includes empowerment, Vajra Lines, and Guide, and Zab lam 'chug med lam khyer kyi man ngag bshad pa)
In *The Compendium of Suchness*, Collected Works of Bodong Chokley Namgyal, vol. 103, 351–423, New Delhi: Tibet House.

Dharma Mati (Chos kyi blo gros)
Extensive Outline of the Vajra Lines of the Six Dharmas
Ni gu chos drug gi sa bcad rgyas pa
ST, vol. 7, 719–31

Gampopa Sonam Rinchen (sGam po pa bSod nam rin chen)
Ornament of Precious Liberation: A Wish-Fulfilling Gem
Dam chos yid bzhin nor bu thar pa rin po che'i rgyan
Xylograph: Rumtek Monastery, n.d.
Translations: Herbert V. Guenther, *The Jewel Ornament of Liberation*. Boston: Shambhala Publications, 1986; Ken and Katia Holmes, *Gem of Dharma, Jewels of Freedom*. Scotland: Altea Publications, 1995.

Gö Lotsāwa Zhonnu Pal ('Gos lo tsā ba gZhon nu dpal)
The Blue Annals
Deb ther sngon po
2 vols. Chengdu: Si khron mi rigs dpe skrun khang, 1984.
Translation: G. N. Roerich, *The Blue Annals*, 1949; repr., Delhi: Motilal Banarsidass, 1976.

Gyaltsen Bum ('Jag pa rGyal mtshan 'bum)
Guidance Manual of Immortal Mind, by the Wise and Venerable Gyaltsen Bum Sems 'chi med kyi khrid yig bzhugs/ mKhas btsun rgyal mtshan 'bum gyis mdzad pa, also called in the colophon "Commentary to One's Deathless Mind Naturally Liberated" (Rang sems 'chi med rang grol gyi 'grel pa), signed sNgags 'chang Dhvadza Laksha, a Sanskrit reconstruction of rGyal mtshan 'bum.
ST, vol. 7, 87–108

Guidance Manual of Infallible Three Integrations
'Chug med lam khyer gsum gyi khrid yig, signed Dhvadza Laksha.
ST, vol. 7, 299–321

Gyurme Dechen, Lochen (Lo chen 'Gyur med bde chen/sKad gnyis smra ba)
Complete Explanation of the Vajra Lines of the Six Dharmas: Glorious Gift of Liberation
Chos drug rdo rje'i tshig rkang gi rnam bshad grol ba'i dpal ster
ST, vol. 8 (Nya), 469–615;
gSung 'bum/'gyur med bde chen, vol. 2, 453–574 (a) (TBRC: W2DB16431)

Jewel Mirror in Which All Is Clear: A Biography of the Glorious Accomplished Lord Tsöndru Zangpo.
dPal grub pa'i dbang phyug brtson 'grus bzang po'i rnam par thar pa kun gsal nor bu'i me long
Bir: Tibetan Khampa Industrial Society, 1976.

[Questions concerning] the Instructions of Glorious Niguma, Mighty Kecharī

mKha' spyod dbang mo dpal ldan ni gu ma'i zhes pa
gSung 'bum/'gyur med bde chen, vol. 2, 612–14 (ke) (TBRC: W2DB16431)

Transference of White Kecharī
mKha' spyod dkar mo'i 'pho ba
ST, vol. 3 (Ga), 315–23
gSung 'bum/'gyur med bde chen, vol. 2, 605–6 (Ku) (TBRC: W2DB16431)

Vajra Lines of the Six Dharmas of Niguma (editor)
Chos drug rdo rje tshig rkang
gSung 'bum/'gyur med bde chen, vol. 2 (Ha), (5 unnumbered folios; TBRC: W2DB16431)

Jamgön Kongtrul ('Jam mgon kong sprul bLo gros mtha' yas)
Beautiful Necklace of Clear Thought: A Brief Mention of the Sources of All Doctrines
Ris med chos kyi 'byung gnas mdo tsam smos pa blo gsal bgrin pa'i mdzes rgyan
GK, vol. 9, 69–99

The Beryl Key Catalogue to Fully Open the Precious Treasury of the Golden Dharmas of the Glorious Shangpa Kagyu/ Catalogue of Shangpa Teachings
dPal ldan shangs pa bka' brgyud kyi gser chos rin po che'i mdzod yongs su phye ba'i dkar chag bai ḍūrya'i lde'u mig/ Shangs chos dkar chag
GK, vol. 10, 459–99; *ST*, vol. 6 (Cha), 51–141

Catalogue of the Treasury of Precious Instructions, a Collection of the Ripening and Liberating Essence of the Eight Great Chariots of the Practice Lineages: An Ocean of Auspicious Renown
sGrub brgyud shing rta chen po brgyad kyi smin grol snying po phyogs gcig bstus pa gdams ngag rin po che'i mdzod kyi dkar chag bkra shis grags pa'i rgya mtsho
DZ, vol. 18, 381–547

Deciphering the Literal Meaning of Glorious Hevajra King Tantra in Two Parts: Disclosing the Secret of the Invincible Vajra
dPal dgyes pa rdo rje'i rgyud kyi rgyal po brtag pa gnyis pa'i tshig don rnam par 'grol ba gzhom med rdo rje'i gsang ba 'byed pa
Xylograph: Rumtek, India: Dharma Chakra Centre, n.d. (1970?)

Essence of Profound Meaning: A Recitation Manual for Five Tantras Condensed into the Main Figure
rGyud sde lnga gtso bsdus kyi bsnyen yig zab don snying po
GK, vol. 8, 433–52

Five Ḍākinīs' Method of Accomplishment and Empowerment Blessing
mKha' 'gro sde lnga'i sgrub thabs rjes gnang dang bcas pa
ST, vol. 2 (Kha), 755–68

Garland of Udumbara: Supplications to the Lives of the Wonderful Lineage of Jewels, the Masters of the Glorious Shangpa Instruction Lineage
dPal ldan shangs pa bka' brgyud kyi ngo mtshar rin chen brgyud pa'i rnam thar la gsol ba 'debs pa udumbara'i phreng ba
DZ, vol. 12, 389–447

Increasing Enlightened Activity: The Feast Offering and Concluding Rites of White and Red Kecharī in the Shangpa Tradition
Shangs lugs mkha' spyod dkar dmar gnyis kyi tshogs mchod dang rjes chog phrin las yar 'phel
ST, vol. 3 (Ga), 297–313

The Melody of Timeless Awareness: A Supplication to Niguma, the Ḍākinī of Timeless Awareness
Ye shes dāki ni gu ma la gsol ba 'debs pa ye shes sgra dbyangs shes bya ba (f. 4a) in *A Garland of Udumbara*
DZ, vol. 12, 393–95
Translated in Zangpo, *Timeless Rapture*, 231.

Ocean of Song/ The Collected Dohā, Vajra Lines, and Songs of the Glorious Shangpa Kagyu: An Ocean of Blessings Meaningful to Hear
mGur mtsho/dPal ldan shangs pa bka' brgyud kyi do ha rdo rje'i

tshig rkang dang mgur dbyangs phyogs gcig tu bsgrigs pa thos pa don ldan byin rlabs rgya mtsho (compiled by Jamgön Kongtrul)
DZ, vol. 12, 463–558; *ST*, vol. 5, 225–437

Practice in a Single Sitting: The Condensed Guide of Niguma's Root Six Dharmas, the Personal Advice of the Dākini of Timeless Awareness
rTsa ba ni gu chos drug gi khrid bsdus stan thog gcig ma'i nyams len ye shes ḍāki'i zhal lung
ST, vol. 2, 513–77

Radiant Light of Timeless Awareness: The Guidance Manual for the Practice of Four Deities Combined
Lha bzhi dril sgrub kyi khrid yig ye shes 'od 'phro
ST, vol. 3, 163–89

Releasing the Central Knots: The Practice of White and Red Kecharī, from the Five Great Guides of the Shangpa's Golden Dharmas
Shangs pa'i gser chos khrid chen rnam lnga las/ Me tog mkha' spyod dkar dmar gyi nyams len dbu ma'i mdud grol
ST, vol. 3 (Ga), 191–235

Shangpa Catalogue: A Key to Open the Door of the Vast and Profound
Shangs chos dkar chag zab rgyas chos kyi sgo 'byed lde mig
ST, vol. 9 (Ta), 43–70

The Treasury of Extensive Teachings (GK)
rGya chen bka' mdzod
20 vols. Paro, Bhutan: Ngodup, 1975–76.

The Treasury of Knowledge (TOK)
Shes bya mdzod
rDo rje rGyal po and Thub bstan Nyi ma, eds. 3 vols. Beijing: Mi rigs dpe skrun khang, 1982/1985.

The Treasury of Precious Instructions (DZ)
gDams ngag rin po che'i mdzod
18 vols. Paro, Bhutan: Lama Ngodrup and Sherab Drimay, 1979.

Katok Rikdzin Tsewang Norbu (Kaḥ thog rig 'dzin Tshe dbang nor bu)
Biographies of Some Holy Ones, such as Marpa, Mila, Gampopa, Atisha and Sons
Mar mi dwags po jo bo rje yab sras sogs dam pa 'ga' zhig gi rnam thar sa bon dus kyi nges pa brjod pa dag ldan nyung gsal
Selected Writings of Ka-thog rig-'dzin Tshe-dbang nor-bu, vol. 1, 669–705. Darjeeling: Kargyud Sungrab Nyamso Khang, 1973.

Khachö Wangpo, Zhamarpa II (Zhwa dmar pa mKha' spyod dbang po)
Earring of Accomplishment: The Life of the Glorious Jñānasiddhi [Nāropa]
dPal dznyā na sidhi'i rnam par thar pa grub pa'i rna rgyan
Vol. 1, 101–85, in *The Collected Works of Khachö Wangpo* (mKha' spyod dbang po gsung 'bum), 4 vols. Gangtok: Gonpo Tseten, 1978 (TBRC: W23928).

Khedrubpa (mKhas grub pa Shangs ston) and Khetsun Gyaltsen Bum (mKhas btsun rGyal mtshan 'bum)
Collection of Essential Directives on the Six Dharmas of Niguma
Ni gu chos drug gi zhal shes dgos rnams kyis lhan thabs
ST, vol. 8 (Nya), 311–68

Khyentse Wangpo (mKhyen rtse'i dbang po)
Guru Yoga in Connection with Six-Armed Protector Dwelling in the Heart/ Secret Precept
mGon po phyag drug pa snying bzhugs dang 'brel pa'i bla ma'i rnal 'byor/bka' rgya ma
DZ, vol. 12, 747–57

Khyungpo Naljor (Khyung po rnal 'byor)
Clear Lines of the Six Dharmas; Directory; Layout of the Ground, Path and Fruition; Fifteen Especially Exalted Instructions of the Ḍākinī of Timeless Awareness; and the Sixfold Illusory Body
Chos drug gi tshig gsal dang/ thems yig dang/ gzhi lam 'bras bu'i

rnam bzhag dang/ khyad 'phags kyi gdams pa bco lnga/ sgyu lus drug ldan rnams
ST, vol. 7 (Ja), 525–43

Directory of the Vajra Lines of the Six Dharmas
Chos drug rdo rje tshig rkang gi them yig
ST, vol. 7 (Ja), 533–35

Fifteen Especially Exalted Instructions of the Indian Ḍākinī
rGya gar mkha' 'gro'i khyad 'phags kyi gdams pa bco lnga
ST, vol. 7 (Ja), 538–42, also vol. 6 (Cha), 186–90

Instructions for Unerring Three Intermediate States
'Chug (or 'Phyug) med bar do gsum gyi gdams pa
ST, vol. 8 (Nya), 187–207

Natural Liberation through Grasping Illusory Body and Sixfold Illusory Body
sGyu lus 'dzin pa rang grol dang sgyu lus drug ldan
ST, vol. 8 (Nya), 617–33

The Story of Sukhasiddhī, "Spiritual Powers of Bliss"
Sukhasiddhī bde ba'i dngos grub lo rgyus
ST, vol. 1 (Ka), 49–58

Kinnaur Shangpa Texts
(published as) *Śaṅs-pa Bka'-brgyud-pa Texts: A Collection of Rare Manuscripts of Doctrinal, Ritual, and Biographical Works of Scholars of the Śaṅs-pa Bka'-brgyud-pa Tradition from the Monastery of Gsan-sngags-chos-glin in Kinnaur*
Sumra, Himachal Pradesh, India: Urgyan Dorje, 1977 (TBRC: W23708).

Kunga Drolchok, Jonang (Jo nang Kun dga' grol mchog)
Guidance on Niguma's Six Dharmas
Ni gu chos drug gi khrid
ST, vol. 7 (Ja), 545–59

Hundred Guides of Jonang
Jo nang khrid brgya
DZ, vol. 18, 1–380

Lineage History of the One Hundred Guides
Khrid brgya'i brgyud pa'i lo rgyus/ Jo nang khrid brgya'i lo rgyus
DZ, vol. 18, 67–98

Lama Zhang (bLa ma zhangs g.Yu bra pa brTson 'grus grags pa)
Life Story of Glorious Nāropa
dPal nā ro pa'i rnam thar
In 'Gro ba'i mgon po zhang g.yu brag pa'i gsung mdzad pa rnam thar gyi skor, vol. 1, 119–39, in *Collected Works of Zhaṅ brTson 'gru grags pa*. Kathmandu, Nepal: Khenpo Shedup Tenzin and Lama Thinley Namgyal, Sri Gautam Buddha Vihara, 2004 (TBRC: W26673).

Longchenpa Drimey Özer (kLong chen pa Rab 'byams pa Dri med 'od zer)
An Excellent Chariot: The Commentary to the Great Completion Natural Ease in Illusion
rDzogs pa chen po sgyu ma ngal gso'i grel pa shing rta bzang po
In *Trilogy on Natural Ease* (Ngal gso skor gsum)
Xylograph: vol. Tha, 47–219. Bhutan: Dodrup Chen, n.d.

Great Completion Natural Ease in Illusion
rDzogs pa chen po sgyu ma ngal gso
In *Trilogy on Natural Ease* (Ngal gso skor gsum)
Xylograph: vol. Tha, 1–45. Bhutan: Dodrup Chen, n.d.

Trilogy on Natural Ease
Ngal gso skor gsum
Xylograph: 3 vols. Bhutan: Dodrup Chen, n.d.
Translation: Herbert Guenther, *Kindly Bent to Ease Us*. 3 vols. Emeryville, CA: Dharma Publishing, 1975–76.

Losang Chökyi Nyima, Tukwan Lama (bLo bzang chos kyi nyi ma, Thu'u bkwan bla ma)
Collected Works of bLo bzang chos-kyi nyi-ma
10 vols., Lhasa: Zhol Par khang Gsar pa, 2000 (TBRC: W21507).

The Origin of Kagyu Tenets from the Clear Mirror of Tenets
Grub mtha' thams cad kyi khungs dang 'dod tshul ston pa legs bshad shel gyi me long las/ bKa' brgyud pa'i grub mtha' byung tshul
In *Collected Works of bLo bzang chos-kyi nyi-ma*, vol. 2, part 4, 123–78.

Mikyö Dorje, Karmapa VIII (rJe brgyad pa Mi bskyod rdo rje)
Noble One's Resting at Ease: A Commentary on Ornament of Clear Realization
mNgon rtogs rgyan gyi kar tīka rje btsun ngal gso
In *mDo sngags gzhung chen brgyad*, 2 vols.
Seattle: Nithartha *international* Publications, 2003.

Mipam Gyamtso, Ju ('Ju Mi pham rgya mtsho)
Complete Explanation of the Intended Meaning of "Ornament of the Mahāyāna Sūtras": A Feast of the Supreme Vehicle's Elixir
Theg pa chen po mdo sde'i rgyan gyi dgongs don rnam par bshad pa theg mchog bdud rtsi'i dga' ston
Vol. 2 of Collected Works (gSung 'bum) (27 vols.). Paro, Bhutan: Lama Ngodrup and Sherab Drimey, 1984–1993 (TBRC: W23468).

Mokchokpa (rMog lcog pa) (Rin chen brTson grus or Kun dga' 'Od)
The Life Story of Buddha Vajradhara
Sangs rgyas rdo rje 'chang gi rnam par thar pa
In *Golden Rosary of Shangpa Biographies*, *ST*, vol. 1 (Ka), 6–36.

The Life Story of Niguma, Ḍākinī of Timeless Awareness
Ye shes kyi dāki ma ni gu ma'i rnam thar
In *Golden Rosary of Shangpa Biographies*, in *ST*, vol. 1 (Ka), 37–48.
Xylograph: Karma sGrub brgyud and Kar-lu.
Also in *Kinnaur Shangpa Texts*, vol. 1, 529–35.

Mokchokpa et al.
Brief Life Story of Lama Khyungpo Naljor
bLa ma khyung po rnal 'byor gyi rnam thar zur tsam
Based on four life stories written by Mokchokpa, Zhangom Choseng (rTogs ldan Zhang sgom Chos seng), Meutonpa (bLa ma rMe'u ston pa) and Rinchen Dorje (Nye gnas Rin chen rdo rje). In *Golden Rosary of Shangpa Biographies*, *ST*, vol. 1 (Ka), 59–143. Also in *Kinnaur Shangpa Texts*, vol. 1, 417–65.

Nāgārjuna (sLob dpon kLu sgrub)
The Five Stages
Pañcakrama
Rim pa lnga pa
Dg.T. rGyud, vol. Ngi, ff. 45a–57a (Toh. 1802)

Root Verses of the Middle called Wisdom
Prajñānāmamūlamadhyamakakārikā
dBu ma'i rtsa ba'i tshig le'ur byas pa shes rab ces bya ba
Dg.T. dBu ma, vol. Tsa, ff. 1b–19a (Toh. 3824) (P2663)
Translations: Stephen Batchelor, *Verses from the Center: A Buddhist Vision of the Sublime.* New York: Riverhead Books, 2000; Jay L. Garfield, *Fundamentals of the Middle Way.* New York: Oxford University Press, 1995.

Nāropa
Vajra Lines of the Hearing Lineage
Karṇatantravajrapāda
sNyan brgyud rdo rje'i tshig rkang
Dg.T. rGyud, vol. Zhi, ff. 302b–304b (Toh. 2338) (P4632)

Niguma
Aspiration Prayer of the Sealed Word/ The Sovereign of Noble Aspirations
Ārya-praṇidhānarāja-nāma
sMon lam bka' rgya ma/ 'Phags pa smon lam gyi rgyal po
P rGyud 'grel, vol. Pu, ff. 201a7–203a8 (4650); CT, vol. 42, 959–63

(2530); *DZ*, vol. 12, 459–62; *ST*, vol. 6 (Cha), 233–43; *Kinnaur Shangpa Texts*, vol. 1, 399–403.

Channel Chakras of One's Body
Svaśarīra-nāḍī-cakra
Rang lus rtsa yi 'khor lo
P rGyud 'grel, vol. Pu, f. 201a (4649); CT, vol. 42, 957–58 (2429) as Daki ma'i zhal gdams; *ST*, vol. 8 (Nya), 745–46 as brKyang bskum

Esoteric Instructions on Opening the Channel
Nāḍī-vikāsanopadeśa
rTsa kha 'byed pa'i man ngag
P rGyud 'grel, vol. Pu, f. 199a (4645); CT, vol. 42, 948–949 (2525) as Dāki'i zhal gdams; *ST*, vol. 8 (Nya), 746–47

Glorious Immortal Great Timeless Awareness/ Immortal Natural Freedom
Śrī-mahāmara-jñāna
dPal 'chi med ye shes chen po/ 'Chi med rang grol
P rGyud 'grel, vol. Pu, ff. 160b–161b (4639); CT, vol. 42, 864–67 (2529); *DZ*, vol. 11, 24–27; *ST*, vol. 6 (Cha), 225–31; *Kinnaur Shangpa Texts*, vol. 1, 287–91; Bodong, vol. 103, 356–60 as 'Chi med rdo rje'i tshig rkang/Lam gyi snying po 'chi med ye shes chen po'i man ngag

Mandala Ritual of Glorious Chakrasaṃvara
Śri-cakrasaṃvara-maṇḍala-vidhi
dPal 'khor lo sdom pa'i dkyil 'khor gyi cho ga/'Khor lo sdom pa'i dbang chog
P rGyud 'grel, vol. Pu, ff. 158a–160a (4638); CT, vol. 42, 859–63 (2518); *ST*, vol. 7 (Ja), 445–55, as 'Khor lo sdom pa'i ting 'dzin gyi dbang bskur

Mandala Ritual of Glorious Hevajra
Śrī-hevajramaṇḍalavidhi
dPal dgyes pa rdo rje'i dkyil 'khor gyi cho ga
P rGyud 'grel, vol. Za, ff. 60a–61b (2426); Dg.T. rGyud, vol. Ta, ff. 187a–188b (Toh. 1296)

Meditation on Channels, Prāṇa, and Such
Nāḍyādi-bhāvanā
rTsa rlung la sogs sgom pa
P rgyud 'grel, vol. Pu, f. 199a–b (4646); CT, vol. 42, 950–51 (2526) as Ni gu ma'i gdams pa; *ST*, vol. 8 (Nya), 742–44 as rLung 'don

Meditation on Inner Heat in the Path of Methods
Upāya-mārga-caṇḍālikā-bhāvanā
Thabs lam gtum mo sgom pa
P rgyud 'grel, vol. Pu, ff. 199a–200a (4647); CT, vol. 42, 952–53 (2527) as Ḍāki ma'i zhal gdams; *ST*, vol. 8 (Nya), 747–49

Naturally Free Mahāmudrā
Svayaṃmukti-mahāmudrā
Rang grol phyag rgya chen po
P rGyud 'grel, vol. Pu, ff. 162b–163a (4641); CT, vol. 42, 871–72 (2521); *DZ*, vol. 12, 468–69

Stages in the Path of Illusion
Māyādhanakrama
sGyu ma lam rim/sGyu ma lam gyi rim pa/sGyu ma lam rim dri med snying po
P rgyud 'grel, vol. Pu, ff. 165a–176a (4643); CT, vol. 42, 878–99 (2523); *ST*, vol. 6 (Cha), 705–33; Ume edition, scanned from an original microfilm copy of an dbu med manuscript, n.d. TBRC, W1CZ1161, ff. 1a–6b (incomplete); *Kinnaur Shangpa Texts*, vol. 1, 29–49 as sGyu ma lam rim gyi rtsa ba (rdo rje tshig rkang); Bodong, vol. 57, 359–74

Stages in the Path of Illusion: The Commentary
Māyādhvanakramavṛitti
sGyu ma lam gyi rim pa'i 'grel pa
P rgyud 'grel, vol. Pu, ff. 176a3–199a2 (4644); CT, vol. 42, 900–947 (2524); *ST*, vol. 6 (Cha), 735–98; Ume edition, TBRC, W1CZ1157, ff. 1a–19b (incomplete); *Kinnaur Shangpa Texts*, vol. 1, 161–99; Bodong, vol. 57, 376–409

Swift Accomplishment of Glorious Chakrasaṃvara
Śrī-cakrasaṃvara-sādhana

dPal 'khor lo sdom pa myur du sgrub pa zhes bya ba'i thabs
P rGyud 'grel, vol. Pu, ff. 155a–158a (4637); CT, vol. 42, 855–58 (2517); *ST*, vol. 7 (Ja), 361–67; Bodong, vol. 93, 6.2–10.6/ 3b2–5b6

Three Dharmas to Integrate on the Path
Dhana-dharma-treya/ Mārgga-karya-tridharma
Lam khyer gyi chos gsum
P rgyud 'grel, vol. Pu, ff. 163a8–164b8 (4642); CT, vol. 42, 874–77 (2522); *DZ*, vol. 11, 15–17; ST, vol. 6 (Cha), 196–203; *Kinnaur Shangpa Texts*, vol. 1, 333–36

Three Kāya Integration and Three Kāya Abiding Nature
Kāya-traya-dhanakra
sKu gsum lam khyer dang sku gsum gnas lugs
ST, vol. 10 (Tha), 277–90

Vajra Lines of the Amulet Mahāmudrā
Mahāmudrā
Phyag rgya chen po ga'u ma'i rdo rje'i tshig rkang
P rGyud 'grel, vol. Pu, ff. 161b–162b (4640); CT, vol. 42, 868–70 (2520) as Rang shar phyag rgya chen po'i rdo rje tshig rkang; *DZ*, vol. 11, 13–15; *ST*, vol. 6 (Cha), 192–96

Vajra Lines of the Amulet Mahāmudrā (with Notes)
Mahāmudrā
Phyag rgya chen po ga'u ma'i rdo rje'i tshig rkang
P rGyud 'grel, vol. Pu, ff. 144a–145a (4634); CT, vol. 42, 846–48 (2515) as Rang shar phyag rgya chen po'i rdo rje tshig rkang; *ST*, vol. 8 (Nya), 799–803

Vajra Lines of the Six Dharmas
Ṣaḍdharma-vajragāthā
Chos drug rdo rje'i tshig rkang
P rGyud 'grel, vol. Pu, ff. 142b–144a (4633); CT, vol. 42, 842–45 (2514); *DZ*, vol. 11, 1–27; *ST*, vol. 6 (Cha), 161–232; GD-CW, vol. 2 (Ha), 439–48; *Kinnaur Shangpa Texts*, vol. 1, 211–14; Bodong vol. 57, 140–53

Yoga of Meditation in the Path of Methods
Upāya-mārga-bhāvanā-yoga
Thabs lam sgom pa'i rnal 'byor
P rGyud 'grel, vol. Pu, f. 200a5–b8 (4648); CT, vol. 42, 954–56 as Ḍāki'i zhal gdams dug gsum zhi byed; *ST*, vol. 8 (Nya), 749–52

Padma Gyurme Gyatso (Padma 'gyur me rgya mtsho)
Yogic Exercise Root Verses of Nigu's Six Dharmas: Great Bliss Reward
Ni gu chos drug gi 'khrul 'khor rtsa tshig bde chen 'dod 'jo
ST, vol. 10 (Tha), 613–24

Rāhula, Lama (Rāhulaguptavajra)
Lama Rāhula's Personal Instructions on Five Tantras
bLa ma ra hu la'i rgyud sde lnga'i zhal gdams
Kinnaur Shangpa Texts, vol. 1, 352–55

Rangjung Dorje, Karmapa III (Karma pa Rang byung rdo rje)
Kagyu Golden Rosary
bKa' brgyud gser phreng
Collected Works of Rangjung Dorje, vol. 4, 1–83
(biographies of Telopa, Nāropa, and Marpa [incomplete])

Rinchen Namgyal, Lhatsun (Lha'i btsun pa Rin chen rnam rgyal)
The Amazing, Wonderful Life of Nāropa
Paṇ nā ro pa'i rnam thar ngo mtshar rmad 'byung
In *Songs of Esoteric Experience of Ran-rig ras-chen*, 333–467 (TBRC: 01GS47725)
Translation: Hervert V. Guenther, *The Life and Teaching of Nāropa*. Boston: Shambhala Publications, 1986.

Rwalung Kagyu Golden Rosary
Rwa lung bka' brgyud gser gyi 'phreng ba
Vol. 1 (Ka). Thimpu, Bhutan: Tango Monastic Community, 1982.

Sangye Bum (Sangs rgyas 'bum)
Life Story of Marpa the Translator

sGra bsgyur mar pa lo tsā'i rnam par thar pa/sKye mchog mar pa lo tsā'i rnam thar dri med mthong ba don ldan (colophon title, 155)
Rwalung Kagyu Golden Rosary, vol. 1, 131–60

The Life Story of the Supreme Learned Nāro Paṇchen
mKhas mchog nā ro paṇ chen gyi rnam thar
Rwalung Kagyu Golden Rosary, vol. 1, 87–129

Sangye Palzang (Sangs rgyas dpal bzang)
Releasing the Knots of the Vajra Lines: A Guide to Amulet Mahāmudrā
Phyag rgya chen po ga'u ma'i khrid yig rdo rje'i tshig gi mdud grol
ST, vol. 9 (Ta), 99–173

Sangye Tönpa et al. (Sangs rgyas ston pa)
Collection of Necessary Oral Advice on Niguma's Six Dharmas
Ni gu chos drug gi zhal shes dgos rnams kyi lhan thabs
ST, vol. 8 (Nya), 311–68

Natural Liberation through Grasping Illusory Body and Sixfold Illusory Body (and Other Texts)
sGyu lus 'dzin pa rang grol dang sgyu lus drug ldan
ST, vol. 8 (Nya), 617–809

Shangpa Texts/ Indian Source Texts of the Dharma Cycle of Five Golden Dharmas of the Glorious Shangpa (ST)
Shangs chos/ dPal ldan shangs pa'i chos 'khor gser chos rnam lnga'i rgya zhung
Edited by Karma Rangjung Kunkhyab (Kalu Rinpoche). 11 vols. Sonada, India: Samdrup Darje Ling Monastery, n.d. This collection is based on the Palpung edition. Reprinted by Lama Tsengyur Rinpoche, Vancouver: Kagyu Kunkhyab Chuling, 1982.

Tangtong Gyalpo (Thang stong rgyal po)
Collection of the Essentials: Words on the Vital Points of the Hearing Lineage of the Ḍākinī Niguma

mKha' 'gro ni gu ma'i snyan brgyud kyi gnad yig snying po kun 'dus
DZ, vol. 12, 147–79; *TTG-S*, vol. 1, 241–336

Guiding Instructions on Nigu's Branch Practice, Amulet Mahāmudrā
Ni gu'i yan lag phyag chen ga'u ma'i khrid
DZ, vol. 12, 181–87; *ST*, vol. 3 (Ga), 683–94; *TTG-S*, vol. 1, 337–52

Guiding Instructions on Nigu's Branch Practice, Immortal Body and Mind
Ni gu'i yan lag lus sems 'chi med kyi khrid
DZ, vol. 12, 192–98; *ST*, vol. 3 (Ga), 703–13; *TTG-S*, vol. 1, 369–86

Guiding Instructions on Nigu's Branch Practice, Three Integrations on the Path
Ni gu'i yan lag lam khyer gsum gyi khrid
DZ, vol. 12, 187–92; *ST*, vol. 3 (Ga), 694–703; *TTG-S*, vol. 1, 353–67

Source of All Qualities: Entry to Nigu's Six Dharmas
Ni gu chos drug gi 'jug sgo yon tan kun 'byung
TTG-S, vol. 1, 1–67

Supplemental Texts to the Collected Works of Thang-stong-rgyal-po Series, Volume 1 (TTG-S)
Grub chen thang stong bka' 'bum gyi rgyab chos ni gu chos drug pod dang pa
Thimphu: Royal Government of Bhutan Publishing House (dPal ldan 'brug gzhung dpe mdzod khang), 1984.

Tāranātha, Jonang (Tā ra nā tha, Jo nang; a.k.a. sGrol ba'i mgon po)
The Amulet Mahāmudrā or Threefold Letting-Go Guidance Manual
Phyag chen ga'u ma'am rang babs rnam gsum zhes bya ba'i khrid yig
Tāranātha's Collected Works (rJe btsun Tā-ra-nā-tha'i gsung 'bum) (*T-CW*), Dzamthang, vol. 20, 563–78; *ST*, vol. 3 (Ga), 655–82

Chakrasaṃvara Five Deities Direct Realization Manual in Nigu's Tradition
Ni gu lugs kyi bde mchog lha lnga'i mngon rtogs
T-CW, vol. 12, 809–23

Chakrasaṃvara Five Deities Empowerment Ritual in Nigu's Tradition
Ni gu lugs kyi bde mchog lha lnga'i dbang chog
T-CW, vol. 12, 769–808; *DZ*, vol. 11, 255–85 (as Ni gu'i lugs kyi bde mchog lha lnga'i dkyil chog)

Clarifying the Profound Meaning: The Complete Explanation of Chakrasaṃvara Five Deities Method of Accomplishment in the Shangpa Tradition
Shangs lugs bde mchog lha lnga'i sgrub thab skyi rnam par bshad pa zab don gsal byed
DZ, vol. 11, 297–331

Clearing Up Darkness of the Mind: The Origins of the Dharma Cycles of the Glorious Shangpa, in the General Context of the Precious Doctrine of the Victorious One
rGyal ba'i bstan pa rin po che spyi'i rnam bzhag las 'phros pa'i dpal ldan shangs pa'i chos skor gyi 'byung khung yid kyi mun sel
T-CW, vol. 17, 417–535

Ḍākinī's Personal Instructions That Clarify the Three Integrations on the Path
Lam khyer gsum gyi gsal byed ḍāki'i zhal gdams
ST, vol. 10 (Tha), 393–417

Elixir Rain of Spiritual Powers: The Sources of the Dharma Cycle of Glorious Six-Armed Wisdom Protector
dPal ye shes kyi mgon po phyag drug pa'i chos skor byung tshul dngos grub bdud rtsi'i char 'bebs
ST, vol. 1 (Ka), 717–48

Essence of the Last Four of the Golden Dharmas Taken from Tāranātha's Teachings
gSer chos phyi ma bzhi'i snying po rje btsun tā ra nā tha'i gsung las byung ba'o
ST, vol. 7 (Ja), 109–24

Five Ḍākinīs' Method of Accomplishment and Empowerment Blessing in the Shangpa Tradition [extracted from *Mine of Jewels*]

Shangs lugs mkha' 'gro sde lnga'i sgrub thabs rjes gnang dang bcas pa
ST, vol. 2 (Kha), 755–68)

Five Tantras' Mandala Method of Accomplishment
rGyud lde lnga'i dkyil 'khor sgrub pa'i thabs
ST, vol. 5 (Ca), 451–539

Heap of Gold: The Path of Methods of the Adepts of Shangpa Kagyu
Grub thob shangs pa bka' rgyud kyi thabs lam gser gyi phung po
T-CW, vol. 20, 265–94

Mine of Jewels
Rin chen 'byung gnas/Yi dam rgya mtsho'i sgrub thabs rin chen 'byung gnas
T-CW, vol. 15, 3–744 and 1141–1238

Nigu's Condensed Guidance Manual
Ni gu'i 'khrid yig bsdus pa
T-CW, vol. 12, 957–72

Nigu's Yogic Excercises, Root and Commentary
Ni gu ma'i 'khrul 'khor rtsa 'drel
DZ, vol. 12, 137–45; *ST*, vol. 6 (Cha), 143–60; *T-CW*, vol. 12, 1013–26

Profound Meaning Expanded: A Guidance Manual for the Six Dharmas of Niguma ("Tangdalma")
Ni gu chos drug khrid yig zab don thang brdal ma/ Thang brdal ma
ST, vol. 3 (Ga), 335–512; *T-CW*, vol. 12, 825–955, as Zab lam ni gu chos drug gi 'khrid yig zab don thang mar brdal ba zhes bya ba bklags chog ma

Supplement to the Lineage Stories of One Hundred Guides
Khrid brgya'i brgyud pa'i lo rgyus kha skong
DZ, vol. 18, 99–118

Supplement to the Mamo's Collection of Source Guides on the Profound Path of Nigu's Six Dharmas
Zab lam ni gu chos drug gi gzhung 'khrid ma mo'i lhan thabs kha skong
ST, vol. 2 (Kha), 579–654; *T-CW*, vol. 12, 973–1011

Supplication to the Lineage by Negu, Letter 'A' Dharma Source
Nee gus brgyud 'debs a yig chos 'byung ma
T-CW, vol. 20, 595–604

Supplication to the Lineage of Five Tantras in the Shangpa Tradition
Shangs lugs brgyud sde lnga'i brgyud pa'i gsol 'debs
ST, vol 5 (Ca), 439–44; *T-CW*, vol. 12, 603–8, as rGyud sde lnga'i brgyud 'debs dngos grub rol mtsho

Tilopa/ Telopa/ Tillipa
Esoteric Instructions on the Six Yogas
Ṣaḍdharmopadeśa
Chos drug gi man ngag
Dg.T. rGyud, vol. Zhi, ff. 270a–271a (Toh. 2330)

Tsangnyön Heruka (gTsang smyon he ru ka, Rus pa'i rgyan can)
The Life of Marpa the Translator, Meaningful to Behold
sGra bsgyur mar pa lo tsā'i rnam thar mthong ba don yod
N. Kalsang, ed. 1970.
Translation: Nālandā Translation Committee, *The Life of Marpa the Translator*, Boulder: Prajñā Press, 1982.

Vajrāsana/Dorjedenpa, Loppön (rDo rje gdan pa, bsLob dpon)
Indian Source Text of the Glorious Five Tantras Method of Accomplishment
Pal rgyud sde lnga'i rgya gzhung/dPal rgyud sde lnga'i sgrub thabs (also called dPal rgyud sde lnga bla med rigs lnga'i sgrub thabs/ De kho na nyid bsdus pa)
ST, vol. 9 (Ta), 543–49

Vasubandhu (dByig gnyen)
Abhidharmakoṣa-kārikā
Chos mngon pa'i mdzod kyi tshig le'ur byas pa
Dg.T. mNgon pa, vol. Ku, ff. 1b-26b (Toh. 4089) (P5590)

Explanation of the Ornament of the Sūtras
Sūtrālaṁkāravyākhyā

mDo sde'i rgyan gyi bshad pa
Dg.T. Sems tsam, vol. Phi, ff. 129b–260a (Toh. 4026)

Virūpa
Spiritual Power of Amṛita
Amṛtasiddhimūla
bDud rtsi grub pa'i rtsa ba
Dg.T. rGyud, vol. Zhi, ff. 142b–145a (Toh. 2285)
same as:
Spiritual Power of Immortality
Amārasiddhimūla
'Chi med grub pa zhes bya ba'i rtsa ba
DZ, vol. 11, 19–24; *ST*, vol. 6 (Cha), 210–25

Spiritual Power of Immortality Commentary
Amṛtasiddhavṛtti/ Amarasiddhivṛtti[sanātanasiddhi]
'Chi med grub pa'i 'grel pa/ 'Chi med grub pa'i 'grel pa g.yung drung grub pa
P rGyud 'grel, vol. Yu, ff. 210b–213b (5026); *ST*, vol. 6 (Cha), 221–34

English Sources

Bays, Gwendolyn, trans. *The Voice of the Buddha: The Beauty of Compassion*. Translated from the French. 2 vols. Berkeley: Dharma Publishing, 1983.

Brunnhölzl, Karl. *Gone Beyond: The Prajñāpāramitā Sūtras, The Ornament of Clear Realization, and Its Commentaries in the Tibetan Kagyü Tradition, Volume 1.* Ithaca, NY: Snow Lion Publications, 2010.

_____. *In Praise of Dharmadhātu: Nāgārjuna and the Third Karmapa, Rangjung Dorje*. Ithaca, NY: Snow Lion Publications, 2007.

Buddhaghosa, Bhadantācariya. *The Path of Purification: Visuddhimagga*. Translated by Bhikku Ñāṇamoli. Kandy, Sri Lanka: Buddhist Publication Society, 1956.

Buswell, Robert E., Jr., and Robert M. Gimello, eds. *Paths to Liberation: The Mārga and Its Transformations in Buddhist Thought*. Honolulu: University of Hawaii Press, Kuroda Institute, 1992.

Campbell, June. *Traveller in Space: Gender, Identity, and Tibetan Buddhism.* Rev. ed. New York: Continuum, 2002.

Chattopadhyaya, Alaka. *Atīsha and Tibet.* Delhi: Motilal Banarsidass, 1999.

Chok Tenzin Monlam. "The Life and Works of Bodong Chokley Namgyal." *Tibet Journal* 30, no. 3 (2005), 91–102.

Conze, Edward. *The Perfection of Wisdom in Eight Thousand Lines and Its Verse Summary.* Bolinas, CA: Four Seasons Foundation, 1973.

Cook, Elizabeth, trans. *Light of Liberation: A History of Buddhism in India.* Crystal Mirror Series, vol. 8. Berkeley: Dharma Publishing, 1992.

Dagpo Tashi Namgyal. *Rays of Light from the Jewel of the Excellent Teaching: A General Summary of the Mantra-Vajrayāna.* Translated by Peter Alan Roberts. In *Mahāmudrā and Related Instructions: Core Teachings of the Kagyü School.* Library of Tibetan Classics, vol. 5. Boston: Wisdom Publications, in association with the Institute of Tibetan Classics, forthcoming.

David-Neel, Alexandra. *Magic and Mystery in Tibet.* London: Souvenir Press, 1967.

Davidson, Ronald M. *Indian Esoteric Buddhism: A Social History of the Tantric Movement.* New York: Columbia University Press, 2002.

Dayal, Har. *The Bodhisattva Doctrine in Buddhist Sanskrit Literature.* New York: Samuel Weiser, 1978. First published 1932 by Molital Banarsidass.

Dharmachakra Translation Committee, *Middle Beyond Extremes: Maitreya's Madhyāntavabhāga with Commentaries by Khenpo Shenga and Ju Mipham.* Ithaca, NY: Snow Lion Publications, 2006.

Dudjom Rinpoche, Jikdrel Yeshe Dorje. *The Nyingma School of Tibetan Buddhism: Its Fundamentals and History.* Translated and edited by Gyurme Dorjé and Matthew Kapstein. 2 vols. Boston: Wisdom Publications, 1991.

Dutt, Nalinaksha. *Buddhist Sects in India.* 2nd ed. Delhi: Motilal Banarsidass, 1978.

Dzogchen Ponlop Rinpoche. "The Ten Bodhisattva Bhumis." From Mahāyāna Path Curriculum, MAH350. Seattle, WA: Nalandabodhi, 2005.

Emmerick, R. E., trans. *Sūtra of Golden Light*. Sacred Books of the Buddhists, vol. 27. London: Pali Text Society, 1970.

Farrow, G. W., and I. Menon, trans. *The Concealed Essence of the Hevajra Tantra*. Delhi: Motilal Barnarsidass, 1992.

Ferrari, Alfonsa, ed. *Guide to the Holy Places of Central Tibet*. By 'Jam-dbyans Mkhyen-brtse'i-dban-po. Compiled and edited by Luciano Petech, with the collaboration of Hugh Richardson. Serie Orientale Roma 16. Rome: Istituto italiano per Il Medio ed Estremo Oriente, 1958.

sGam.po.pa [Gampopa]. *The Jewel Ornament of Liberation*. Translated and annotated by Herbert V. Guenther. Boston: Shambhala Publications, 1986.

Garfield, Jay L., trans. *The Fundamental Wisdom of the Middle Way: Nāgārjuna's Mūlamadhyamakakārikā*. New York: Oxford University Press, 1995.

Gray, David B. *The Cakrasamvara Tantra (The Discourse of Śrī Heruka) Śrīherukābhidhāna: A Study and Annotated Translation*. New York: American Institute of Buddhist Studies, 2007.

Guenther, Herbert V. *Ecstatic Spontaneity: Saraha's Three Cycles of Dohā*. Berkeley: Asian Humanities Press, 1993.

_____, trans. *Kindly Bent to Ease Us*. 3 vols. Emeryville, CA: Dharma Publishing, 1975–76.

_____. *The Life and Teaching of Nāropa*. Boston: Shambhala Publications, 1986.

Gyatso, Janet. *Apparitions of the Self: The Secret Autobiographies of a Tibetan Visionary*. Princeton: Princeton University Press, 1998.

_____"The Literary Traditions of Thang-stong rGyal-po: A Study of Visionary Buddhism in Tibet." PhD diss., University of California at Berkeley, 1981.

Hanson, Judith, and Mervin V. Hanson. "The Mediating Buddha." In *Soundings in Tibetan Civilization*, edited by Barbara Nimri Aziz and Matthew Kapstein, 296–303. New Delhi: Manohar Publications, 1985.

Harrison, Paul. "A Brief History of the Tibetan bKa' 'gyur." In *Tibetan Literature: Studies in Genre*, edited by José Ignacio Cabezón and Roger R. Jackson, 70–94. Ithaca, NY: Snow Lion Publications, 1996.

Huntington, C. W. Jr. *The Emptiness of Emptiness: An Introduction to Early Indian Mādhyamika*. Translation of the *Madhyamakāvatāra*. Honolulu: University of Hawaii Press, 1989.

Inagaki, Hisao. *Nāgārjuna's Discourse on the Ten Stages (Daśabhūmika-vibhāṣā)*. Ryukoku Literature Series 5. Japan: Ryukoku Gakkai, Ryukoku University, 1998.

Jackson, Roger. R. *Tantric Treasures: Three Collections of Mystical Verse from Buddhist India*. Oxford: Oxford University Press, 2004.

Jamgön Kongtrul Lodrö Thayé. *Creation and Completion: Essential Points of Tantric Meditation*. Translated by Sarah Harding. Boston: Wisdom Publications, 2002.

_____. "The Presentation of Grounds, Paths, and Results in the Causal Vehicle of Characteristics" from *The Treasury of Knowledge*. Translated by Karl Brunnhölzl for Nitartha Institute. Unpublished manuscript. 2002.

_____. *The Treasury of Knowledge: Book Eight, Part Four: Esoteric Instructions*. Translated by Sarah Harding. Ithaca, NY: Snow Lion Publications, 2007.

_____. *The Treasury of Knowledge: Book Eight, Part Three: The Elements of Tantric Practice*. Translated by Elio Guarisco and Ingrid McLeod. Ithaca, NY: Snow Lion Publications, 2008.

_____. *The Treasury of Knowledge: Book One: Myriad Worlds*. Translated by the International Translation Committee of Kalu Rinpoché. Ithaca, NY: Snow Lion Publications, 1995.

_____. *The Treasury of Knowledge: Book Six, Part Four: Systems of Buddhist Tantra*. Translated by Elio Guarisco and Ingrid McLeod. Ithaca, N.Y.: Snow Lion Publications, 2005.

_____. *The Treasury of Knowledge: Book Six, Part Three: Frameworks of Buddhist Philosophy*. Translated by Elizabeth Callahan. Ithaca, NY: Snow Lion Publications, 2007.

_____. *The Treasury of Knowledge: Books Nine and Ten: Journey and Goal*. Translated by Richard Barron (Chökyi Nyima). Ithaca, NY: Snow Lion Publications,2010.

Kalu Rinpoche (Karma Ranjung Kunchab). *The Dharma That Illuminates All Beings Impartially Like the Light of the Sun and the Moon*. Albany: State University of New York Press, 1986.

_____. *The Sādhana of the Five Deities of Cakrasamvara in the Shangpa*

Tradition (shang lugs bde mchog lha lnga'i sgrub thabs). Translated by Sarah Harding. Santa Fe, NM: Kagyu Shenpen Kunchab, 1986.

Kapstein, Matthew T. "Chronological Conundrums in the Life of Khyung po rnal 'byor: Hagiography and Historical Time." *Journal of the International Association of Tibetan Studies*, no. 1 (October 2005): 1–14. Available online at the Web site of the Tibetan and Himalayan Library, www.thlib.org.

_____. "The Illusion of Spiritual Progress: Remarks on Indo-Tibetan Buddhist Soteriology." In *Paths to Liberation: The Mārga and Its Transformations in Buddhist Thought*, edited by Robert E. Buswell Jr. and Robert M. Gimello, 193–224. Honolulu: University of Hawaii Press, 1992.

_____. "The Journey to the Golden Mountain." In *Religions of Tibet in Practice*, edited by Donald S. Lopez Jr., 178–87. Princeton: Princeton University Press, 1997.

_____. "Kong-sprul Rin-po-che on the Shangs-pa bKa'-brgyud." Carmel, NY: The Institute for Advanced Studies of World Religions, 1978.

_____, ed. *The Presence of Light: Divine Radiance and Religious Experience*. Chicago: University of Chicago Press, 2004.

_____. "The Shangs-pa bKa'-brgyud: An Unknown Tradition of Tibetan Buddhism." In *Tibetan Studies in Honour of Hugh Richardson: Proceedings of the International Seminar on Tibetan Studies*, edited by Michael Aris and Aung San Suu Kyi, 138-44. Warminster, England: Aris and Phillips, 1980.

_____. "The Strange Death of Pema the Demon Tamer." In *The Presence of Light: Divine Radiance and Religious Experience*, edited by Matthew T. Kapstein, 119–56. Chicago: University of Chicago Press, 2004.

Kaul, Advaitavadini. *Buddhist Savants of Kashmir: Their Contributions Abroad*. Kashmir: Utpal Publications, 1987.

Khenpo Könchog Gyaltsen. *The Great Kagyu Masters*. Ithaca, NY: Snow Lion Publications, 1990.

Khenpo Tsültrim Gyamtso. *The Sun of Wisdom: Teachings on the Noble Nagarjuna's Fundamental Wisdom of the Middle Way*. Translated and edited by Ari Goldfield. Boston: Shambhala Publications, 2003.

Levinson, Jules. "The Metaphors of Liberation: Tibetan Treatises on

Grounds and Paths." In *Tibetan Literature, Studies in Genre*, edited by José Ignacio Cabezón and Roger R. Jackson, 261–74. Ithaca, NY: Snow Lion Publications, 1996.

Lopez, Donald S., Jr. "Paths Terminable and Interminable." In *Paths to Liberation: The Mārga and Its Transformations in Buddhist Thought*, edited by Robert E. Buswell Jr., and Robert M. Gimello, 147–92. Honolulu: University of Hawaii Press, 1992.

Makransky, John J. *Buddhahood Embodied: Sources of Controversy in India and Tibet.* Albany: State University of New York Press, 1997.

Mar-pa Chos-kyi bLo-gros. *The Life of the Mahāsiddha Tilopa.* Translated by Fabrizio Torricelli and Āchārya Sangye T. Naga. Edited by Vyvyan Cayley. Dharamsala: Library of Tibetan Works and Archives, 1995.

Martin, Dan. *Tibskrit: A Bibliography of Tibetan Philology.* Edited by Alexander Cherniak. Jerusalem, 2006. Available widely in electronic version only, www.eecs.berkeley.edu.

_____. "The Woman Illusion? Research into the Lives of Spiritually Accomplished Women Leaders of the 11th and 12th Centuries." In *Women in Tibet*, edited by Janet Gyatso and Hanna Havnevik, 49–82. New York: Columbia University Press, 2005.

Monier-Williams, Monier. *A Sanskrit-English Dictionary.* Rev. ed. Delhi: Marwah Publications, 1986. Originally published in 1899.

Mullin, Glenn H., trans. *The Dalai Lamas on Tantra.* Ithaca, NY: Snow Lion Publications, 2006.

_____. *Selected Works of the Dalai Lama II: The Tantric Yogas of Sister Niguma.* Ithaca, NY: Snow Lion Publications, 1985.

Namdak, Neldjorpa Tsultrim, trans. *Hagiographies de Nigouma et Soukhasiddhi.* Combaudet, Evaux-les-bains, France: Éditions Yogi Ling, 1997.

Namkhai Norbu. *The Crystal and the Way of Light: Sūtra, Tantra and Dzogchen.* Edited by John Shane. New York: Routledge and Kegan Paul, 1986.

Naudou, Jean. *Buddhists of Kaśmīr.* Translated from French by Brereton and Picron. Delhi: Agam Kala Prakashan, 1980. Originally published 1968 by Presses Universitaires de France.

Obermiller, E., trans. *The History of Buddhism in India and Tibet by*

Bu-ston. Delhi: Sri Satguru Publications, 1986. First published 1932 in Heidelberg.

Padmakara Translation Group, trans. *Introduction to the Middle Way: Chandrakīrti's "Madhyamakāvatāra" with Commentary by Jamgön Mipham*. Boston: Shambhala Publications, 2002.

Padmasambhava, and Jamgön Kongtrül. *The Light of Wisdom: Vol. 1*. Translated by Erik Pema Kunsang. Boudhanath: Rangjung Yeshe Publications, 1999.

Pagel, Ulrich. The *Bodhisattvapiṭaka: Its Doctrines, Practices and Their Position in Mahāyāna Literature*. Tring, UK: The Institute of Buddhist Studies, 1995.

Panchen Sonam Dragpa. *Overview of Buddhist Tantra: General Presentation of the Classes of Tantra, Captivating the Minds of the Fortunate Ones*. Translated by Martin J. Boord and Losang Norbu Tsonawa. Dharamsala: Library of Tibetan Works and Archives, 1996.

Peking Tripitaka Online Search. Kyoto, Japan: Otani University, The Shin Buddhist Comprehensive Research Institute. web.otani.ac.jp/cri/twrp.

Powers, John, trans. *Wisdom of Buddha: The Saṁdhinirmocana Mahāyāna Sūtra*. Berkeley: Dharma Publishing, 1995.

Rahula, Bhikkhu Telwatte. *A Critical Study of the Mahāvastu*. Delhi: Motilal Banarsidass, 1978.

Riggs, Nicole. *Like an Illusion: Lives of the Shangpa Kagyu Masters*. Eugene, Ore.: Dharma Cloud, 2001.

Ringu Tulku. *The Ri-me Philosophy of Jamgon Kongtrul the Great: A Study of the Buddhist Lineages of Tibet*. Edited by Ann Helm. Boston: Shambhala Publications, 2006.

Roberts, Peter Alan. *The Biographies of Rechungpa: The Evolution of a Tibetan Hagiography*. London: Routledge Taylor and Francis Group, 2007.

_____. *Mahāmudrā and Related Instructions: Core Teachings of the Kagyü School*. Library of Tibetan Classics, vol. 5. Boston: Wisdom Publications, in association with the Institute of Tibetan Classics, forthcoming.

Roerich, George, N., trans. *The Blue Annals*. 2nd ed. Delhi: Motilal Banarsidass, 1976. Originally published 1949 in Calcutta. Page references to the 2nd ed.

Samuel, Geoffrey. *Civilized Shamans: Buddhism in Tibetan Societies.* Washington: Smithsonian Institution Press, 1993.

Schmidt, Erik Hein, and Marcia Binder Schmidt. *Blazing Splendor: The Memoirs of Tulku Urgyen Rinpoche.* Hong Kong: Rangjung Yeshe Publications, 2005.

Schoening, Jeffrey D. *The Śālistamba Sūtra and Its Indian Commentaries.* Vienna: Arbeitskreis für Tibetische und Buddhisticsche Studien, Universität Wien, 1995.

Shaw, Miranda. *Passionate Enlightenment: Women in Tantric Buddhism.* Princeton, NJ: Princeton University Press, 1994.

Smith, Gene E. *Among Tibetan Texts: History and Literature of the Himalayan Plateau.* Boston: Wisdom Publications, 2001.

Snellgrove, David L., trans. "Saraha's Treasury of Songs." In *Buddhist Texts through the Ages*, edited by Edward Conze, 224–39. New York: Harper and Row, 1990. Originally published 1954 by B. Cassirer.

Stearns, Cyrus. *King of the Empty Plain: The Iron-Bridge Builder Tangtong Gyalpo.* Ithaca, NY: Snow Lion Publications, 2007.

_____. "The Life and Tibetan Legacy of the Indian Mahāpaṇḍita Vibhūticandra." *JIABS* 19, no. 1 (1996): 127–71.

_____. *Luminous Lives: The Story of the Early Masters of the Lam 'Bras Tradition in Tibet.* Boston: Wisdom Publications, 2001.

_____. *Taking the Result as the Path: Core Teachings of the Sakya Lamdré Tradition.* Boston: Wisdom Publications, 2006.

Suzuki, D. T. *The Lankavatara Sūtra.* London: Routledge, 1932.

Tāranātha. *Essence of Ambrosia: A Guide to Buddhist Contemplations.* Translated by Willa Baker. Dharamsala: Library of Tibetan Works and Archives, 2005.

_____. *Tāranātha's History of Buddhism in India.* Translated by Lama Chimpa and Alaka Chattopadhyaya. Edited by Debiprasad Chattopadhyaya. Delhi: Motilal Banarsidass, 1970.

_____. *See also* Tāranātha, Jo nang.

Tāranātha, Jo nang. *The Origin of Tārā Tantra.* Translated and edited by David Templeman. Dharamsala: Library of Tibetan Works and Archives, 1981.

_____. *The Seven Instruction Lineages.* Translated and edited by David Templeman. Dharamsala: Library of Tibetan Works and Archives, 1983.

_____. *See also* Tāranātha.

Templeman, David, trans. *Tāranātha's Life of Kṛṣṇācārya/Kāṇha.* Dharamsala: Library of Tibetan Works and Archives, 1989.

Thomas, Edward J. *The Life of the Buddha: As Legend and History.* London: Routledge and Kegan Paul, 1927.

The Tibetan and Himalayan Digitial Library (THDL). www.thlib.org.

Tibetan Buddhist Resource Center (TBRC). www.tbrc.org.

Tsangnyön Heruka. *The Life of Marpa the Translator.* Translated by the Nālandā Translation Committee. Boulder: Prajñā Press, 1982.

Tucci, Giuseppe. *The Religions of Tibet.* Translated from the German and Italian by Geoffrey Samuel. Berkeley: University of California Press, 1980.

Tulku Thondup Rinpoche. *Buddhist Civilization in Tibet.* New York: Routledge and Kegan Paul, 1987.

Tulku Urgyen Rinpoche. *Rainbow Painting.* Translated by Erik Pema Kunsang. Boudhanath: Rangjung Yeshe Publications, 1995.

Waldron, William S. *The Buddhist Unconscious: The Ālaya-Vijñāna in the Context of Indian Buddhist Thought.* London: RoutledgeCurzon, 2003.

Watanabe, Shogo. "A Comparative Study of the *Pancavimsatisahasrika Prajnaparamita.*" *Journal of the American Oriental Society* 114, no. 3 (1994): 386–96.

Wayman, Alex. *Yoga of the Guhyasamājatantra.* Delhi: Motilal Banarsidass, 1977.

Williams, Paul. *Mahāyāna Buddhism: The Doctrinal Foundations.* London: Routledge, 1989.

Wylie, Turrell V. "A Standard System of Tibetan Transcription." *Harvard Journal of Asiatic Studies* 22 (1959): 261–76.

Yangchen Gawai Lodoe. *Path and Grounds of Guhyasamaja according to Arya Nagarjuna.* Translated by Tenzin Dorjee. Dharamsala: Library of Tibetan Works and Archives, 1995.

Yeshe Tsogyal. *The Lotus-Born: The Life Story of Padmasambhava.* Translated by Erik Pema Kunsang. Boston: Shambhala Publications, 1993.

Zangpo, Ngawang, trans. *Jamgon Kongtrul's Retreat Manual.* Ithaca, NY: Snow Lion Publications, 1994.

_____. *Sacred Ground: Jamgon Kongtrul on "Pilgrimage and Sacred Geography."* Ithaca, NY: Snow Lion Publications, 2001.

_____. *Timeless Rapture: Inspired Verse of the Shangpa Masters.* Compiled by Jamgön Kongtrul. Ithaca, NY: Snow Lion Publications, 2003.

Index

abiding base, 88
  See also all-base (*kun gzhi*, Skt. *ālaya*)
acceptance, level of (*bzod pa*), 61, 65, 106–7, 280n127
Accumulation, Path of, 56–60, 98–103
  four absorptions on, 59–60
  four foundations of mindfulness on, 56–57
  greater, 101–3
  intermediate, 100–101, 103
  lesser, 98–100, 103
  renunciation on, 57–58
  signs on, 60
accumulations, two, 74, 77, 82, 98
action, genuine completed, 71, 113–14
action-mudra, 111
Actualization of Timeless Awareness Extensive Tantra, 94, 96–97, 276n74
  on illusion, 87–88
  on level of warmth, 105
  on realization on the Path of Seeing, 111–12
"Adorned with Bone Ornaments," 5, 259n21
afflictive emotions/states (*nyon mongs pa*, Skt. *klesha*)
  on bodhisattva grounds, 76, 77, 275n64
  on eightfold path, 113, 114
  ethical discipline and, 78
  imputed, 111, 115, 282nn139–40
  level of warmth and, 103
  mindfulness and, 107
  nonvirtue of, 94
  pacifying, 58
  primary and secondary, 277n97
  purification in Immortal and Infallible, 163
  and purity, undifferentiated, 81
  renouncing, 101
  on ten grounds, 84
afflictive mentation (*nyon yid*), 88, 93, 277n93
aggregates (*phung po*, Skt. *skandha*), 277n90, 282n141
  countering by illusion, 63
  as five families, 96
  fully ripened body as, 162, 199–200
  in Uncommon Calm Abiding and Higher Insight, 36
aggression
  illusion, recognition as, 60
  isolation from, 107
  in mahāmudrā, 151
  meditative absorption, lack of fixation through, 64, 107
  pacifying, 58, 101
  renunciation of, 58, 60, 101
  in six dharmas, 140, 141
agitation, clearing up, 189
Akaniṣṭha, 73, 117
  buddhahood in, 130–31

perishability of, 132, 287n191
three kinds, 287n191
all-base (*kun gzhi*, Skt. *ālaya*), 44–45
clarity of, 91
as illusion-like realm of phenomena, 87–88
as indeterminate awareness, 88–89
Kalu Rinpoche on, 199–200
ripening of habitual patterns in, 90
as seed of everything, 89–90
synonyms for, 91, 92–93
Amoghasiddhi, 189
Amṛtabhāvana, 20, 263–64n69, 263n67
Amṛtakuṇḍalī, 179, 302n10
Amulet Mahāmudrā, 32, 143
four faults, liberation from in, 145, 146, 148
grounds and paths in, 147, 150
kāyas in, 145, 146, 147, 148–49, 150
ordinary mind in, 145, 147, 148, 150
threefold letting-go, 145, 148
See also *Naturally Free Mahāmudrā*; *Vajra Lines of the Amulet Mahāmudrā*
Ānanda, 3
anger
clearing up through yogic techniques, 190
on Five Paths, 111, 115
pacifying through Chakrasaṃvara, 175
in six dharmas, 32, 139
in three-kāya integration, 157
Anupama (Peme, dpe med), 3, 20, 21, 258n9
anuttara yoga tantra. *See* highest yoga tantra (*rnal 'byor bla med kyi rgyud*)
appearance
as creation phase, 157
and emptiness, unity of, 55, 96–97
in Immortal and Infallible, 163–64
on ten grounds, 79–82
three integrations and, 155, 156–57, 158
appearance-emptiness, 82, 112, 117
Application, Path of, 61–66, 103–8
dream recognition on, 62–66
five faculties of, 61
five powers in, 64–65
arhants
miraculous emanations of, 75, 275n63
path of as dream/illusion, 50–51
Array of Sacred Oaths of the Five Families/Array of Sacred Oaths Subsequent Tantra, 95, 96, 97, 278n103, 278n107
Āryadeva, 41, 270n7
Asaṅga, 44
See also *Bodhisattva Grounds*
Aspiration Prayer of the Sealed Word, 25, 193–97
aspiration prayers
of Mokchokpa, 22
of Niguma, 193–97
aspirations
characteristics of, 122
at death, 195
ten grounds and, 77, 78
two kāyas and, 73, 116
Atayavajra, 36, 270n131
Atīsha Dipaṃkara Shrījñāna, 33, 137, 268n115, 288n5, 288–89n8
attachment
illusion as antidote to, 37
meditative absorption, freedom through, 107
worldly, 63, 66
See also desire
attainment, subsequent, 146, 148
avadhūti (*rtsa dbu ma*). *See* central channel
Avalokiteshvara, 36
Āvataṃsaka Sūtra. See *Flower Ornament Sūtra*
Avṛha, Mount, 17, 262n58
awakening
aspiration for, 150, 155
time frames for, 139, 155, 157, 290n17
two kāyas and, 73, 116
awareness
and dharmakāya, attaining, 74
on Path of Accumulation, 56
of things as they are, 146, 149
See also timeless awareness
awareness-wisdom empowerment, 139, 290n21

Baker, Willa, 27
base constituent (*gzhi khams*), 91
See also all-base (*kun gzhi*, Skt. *ālaya*)
Basis of Everything, The (Kalu Rinpoche), 199–200
Bhairava, 171, 173, 175
blending and transferring, 62, 273n50
Blessing of Constant Four Deities, 35–36
bliss
in lucid clarity, 141
nondissipating, 146, 149, 164
in physical yogic techniques, 186, 190–91
pure realm of, 166
as saṃbhogakāya, 97
three integrations and, 155, 156, 296n13
three kāyas and, 55
bliss-emptiness, 82, 117
mind as, 133
three kāyas of, 142
bliss-warmth, 139–40
Blue Annals (Gö Lotsāwa Zhonnu Pal), 4, 5
English translation of, 26
on six dharmas, 6
bodhichitta (*byang sems*)
in Chakrasaṃvara practice, 174, 175, 301n30
in Hevajra practice, 180
in six dharmas, 140, 291n26
bodhisattva(s), 42, 271n22
activity of, aspiration for, 196–97
and buddhas, differentiated, 83–84, 133
Niguma as, 13
qualities of, 47–48
Bodhisattva Grounds (Asaṅga), 46
Bodong Paṇchen Chokley Namgyal (Bo dong paṇ chen Phyogs las rnam rgyal, 1376–1451), 24, 264–65n80
See also *Collected Works of Bodong Chokley Namgyal*; *Compendium of Suchness*
body, physical
arising of, 199–200
as basis of rainbow body, 10–11, 261n44
as illusory form, 156
as means, 135, 139–40, 290n19
mindfulness of, 56, 98–99
natural resting of, 145, 148, 294n8
in tantric practice, 168–69
wheel of in Chakrasaṃvara practice, 173–74, 175
as yidam, 155, 156, 158, 163, 164
Body of the Tathāgata, 99, 121
body of union (*zung 'jug gi sku*). *See* rainbow body (*'ja' lus*)
Bokar Rinpoche, 26
bone ornaments, 172, 300n20
Brahmā
aperture of, 186–87, 303n10
voice of, 196
Brief Life Story of Lama Khyungpo Naljor (Mokchokpa et al.), 16–18
bubbles, metaphor of, 67–68, 151
buddha(s), 117
and bodhisattvas, differentiated, 83–84, 133
bodies/dimensions of, 14 (*See also* kāyas)
as dharmakāya, 73, 116
Niguma as, 21
path of as dream/illusion, 50–51
pleasing, 108
on twelfth ground, 83
buddha families. *See* five families
Buddha Indraketu, 130, 286–87n184
buddha nature (*bde bar gshegs pa'i snying po*, Skt. *sugatagarbha*), 54, 92, 199–200, 276n77
See also all-base (*kun gzhi*, Skt. *ālaya*)
Buddha Shākyamuni
in Niguma's hagiography, 3
path as example, 43
Vajradhara as aspect of, 14
buddhadharma, path as, 43
Buddhaghosa. See *Path of Purification, The*
buddhahood
delusions obscuring, 124
grounds and, 47
illusion-like, 51, 54, 87
levels of, 9

Path of Consummation as, 72
traditions of understanding, 130–31
Buddhaśrī, 137, 138, 289n9
Buddhism
defilements, examining in, 49
gender issues in, 15
illusion in, 50–51
in Kashmir, 3
path in, 43
burglar's pointing-out, 149, 295n11
burning mudra, 189

calm abiding
higher insight and, 75, 113
as path, 47, 55
Uncommon, 36
Catuḥpīṭha (*gDan bzhi*). See *Four Seats Tantra*
central channel, 185–86, 188, 303n9
certainty, 68, 108–9, 137, 148, 299n19
Chakdrukpa. *See* Mahākāla, six-armed
chakras
in Chakrasaṃvara practices, 168, 171–72, 174
in Hevajra practice, 178
in physical yogic techniques, 191–92
in six dharmas, 139–40
in transference, 33
Chakrasaṃvara, 31, 163
in Five Tantras' Deities, 34
and Hevajra, compared, 177
practices in, 168
saṃvara, definition of, 168
See also *Mandala Ritual of Glorious Chakrasaṃvara*; *Swift Accomplishment of Glorious Chakrasaṃvara*
Chakrasaṃvara Tantra (root), 167, 168–69, 299n2
Chandrakīrti. See *Entry into the Middle Way*
Channel Chakras of One's Body, 191–92
channels
central, opening, 185–86
chakra, 191–92
relaxing, 145
three, 139–40
characteristics (*mtshan ma*), clinging to, 123, 286n176
Chinnamuṇḍā, 161
Chöd lineage, 143
clairvoyance, 110
of arhats, 75, 275n63
on Path of Seeing, 69
clarity
in Amulet Mahāmudrā, 146, 149
apprehended as other, 199
and emptiness, unity of, 70
in Immortal and Infallible, 163, 164
in lucid clarity, 141
as nirmāṇakāya, 97
on Path of Seeing, 68
three integrations and, 155
three kāyas and, 55
See also lucid clarity
clarity-emptiness
in dreams, 70
on Path of Consummation, 72–73
in peak [experience], 104
and subtle obscurations, eliminating, 116
clear awareness, 10–11
Clearing up Darkness of the Mind (Tāranātha), 1
Cloud of Dharma (*chos kyi sprin*, tenth ground), 72, 77, 82
characteristics of, 120
delusions obscuring, 124
in *Life Story*, 9
Niguma's attainment of, 21
realization on, 125
signs on, 121, 130
code-language, 7–8
cognitive obscurations
on Path of Consummation, 72
on tenth ground, 83
Collected Dohā, Vajra Lines, and Songs of the Glorious Shangpa Kagyu: An Ocean of Blessings Meaningful to Hear. See *Ocean of Song*
Collected Works (Tāranātha), 25, 265n88
Collected Works of bLo bzang chos-kyi nyi-ma (Tukwan Lama), 4, 5

Collected Works of Bodong Chokley Namgyal, 24
Collection of Necessary Oral Advice on Niguma's Six Dharmas (Sangye Tönpa), 135–36
Collection of the Essentials (Tangtong Gyalpo), 19, 25, 136
Commentary to Stages in the Path of Illusion. See *Stages in the Path of Illusion: The Commentary*
compassion
 in guru yoga, 155
 of Niguma, 21
 nonreferential, 76, 80
Compendium of Suchness (Bodong Chokley Namgyal), 24, 264–65n80
Complete Explanation of the Intended Meaning of "Ornament of the Mahāyāna Sūtras" (Mipam), 284–85n163
Complete Explanation of the Vajra Lines of the Six Dharmas (Gyurme Dechen), 154, 289n13
completion phase (*rdzogs rim*)
 deity's form in, 96–97
 dharmakāya and, 74, 117
 four empowerments as support for, 94
 Illusory Body in, 41
 Immortal and Infallible in, 162
 Niguma's emphasis of, 169
 rainbow body in, 11, 12
 as source of six dharmas, 135
 See also creation phase (*bskyed rim*)
concepts, 67, 68, 151, 200
conduct
 absorption of, 59, 102, 279n114
 in level of warmth, 105, 279n121
 of supreme dharma, 108
consciousness
 aggregate of, 199
 appropriating, 92, 277n90
 six kinds of, 200
 Third Turning understanding of, 277n94
 See also all-base (*kun gzhi*, Skt. *ālaya*); transference (*'pho ba*)
Consummation, Path of, 72–75, 115–18
 rainbow body at, 12, 261nn46–47
 signs on, 75
 subtle fixation on, 72–73
cosmology, 168–69
creation phase (*bskyed rim*)
 in Chakrasaṃvara practices, 170–71
 and completion, unity of, 55, 157
 deity's form in, 96–97
 four empowerments as support for, 94
 in Immortal and Infallible, 162
 three rites (*cho ga gsum*) in, 163, 297–98n9
 two kāyas and, 73, 116, 117
creation-completion inseparable, 74
cyclic existence (Skt. *samsara*), 146, 148
 discarding, 63
 as root of suffering, 60
 See also samsara

Dagpo Tashi Namgyal (Dwags po bKra shis rnam rgyal, 1512–1587), 12, 261n47
daily activities, four, 149, 156, 296n10
daily life
 as dreams, 63
 three integrations in, 153
dākinī code-letters (*mkha' 'gro brda' yig*), 7
dākinīs (*mkha' 'gro ma*), 2–3, 5–6, 33
 bone ornaments of, 172, 300n20
 in Chakrasaṃvara practice, 171–72
 code-language of, 7–8
 flesh-eating, 16–17, 262n56
 implements of, 173–74, 300n26
 and kāyas, relationship to, 15
 rainbow-like quality of, 10
David-Neel, Alexandra, 174, 301n29
death
 aspirations at, 195
 causeless, 165–66
 light or appearances at time of, 142, 293n40
 rainbow body at, 11
 transference at, 33
deities
 in dreams, 112

form of, 96–97
one's own body as, 150, 155, 156, 158
deities, Body of
as illusion, 54–55
in intermediate state, 141, 142
on Path of Application, 65
on Path of Seeing, 68
on ten grounds, 79–82
translation, difficulties with, 273n41
delusion
double, 140, 291n32
and illusion, distinguished, 78–79
Dense Array, Akaniṣṭha of, 132, 287n191
Dense Array of Adornments Sūtra, 89, 90, 91, 92, 93, 276n77
Derge Tengyur, 23–24, 177, 264n75
desire
illusion, recognition as, 60
pacifying, 58, 101
See also attachment; passion
desire realm, 111, 115, 282n143
determination
absorption of, 59, 102
in dreams, 62, 63
genuine effort and, 114
habitual pattern of, 60
renunciation and, 57–58, 100–101
devotion
aspiration for, 193
in dreams, 62
in Immortal and Infallible, 163
in mahāmudrā, 146, 149, 150–51
on Path of Seeing, 68
on paths and grounds, 96
in six dharmas, 140, 141, 291n29
in three integrations, 155, 158
dharma, perverse, 65, 142
dharma cognition (*chos shes pa*), 281n131
dharmakāya
in Chakrasaṃvara practices, 172
endowed with two purities, 73, 74, 116
mahāmudrā and, 143, 147, 151
mind as, 151, 165
as nonthought, 157, 296n19
recognizing, 146, 148
threefold essence of, 118
dharmas, thirty-seven. *See* enlightenment, factors of
dharma-source, 171, 172
Diamond Sūtra, 38
Difficult to Overcome (*sbyang dka' ba*, fifth ground), 76, 80
characteristics of, 119–20
delusions obscuring, 123
realization on, 125
signs on, 121, 127
diligence
absorption of, 59, 102
branch of enlightenment, 67, 109
characteristics of, 122
faculty of, 104
genuine effort and, 114
power of, 61, 64, 106
renunciation and, 100–101
as sign on Path of Accumulation, 60
ten grounds and, 77, 78
direct actualization, path of (*mngon sum lam pa*), 158, 297n22
Directory of the Vajra Lines of the Six Dharmas, 142, 293n43
disease, yogic methods of healing, 189–91
doubt, 60, 105, 279n120
dough-kneading mudra, 190
drama, nine modes of, 174, 301n29
Dṛdhramati. See *Sūtra of the Bodhisattva Dṛdhramati*
dream yoga, 17, 69, 136, 139, 140–41, 274n57, 291–92nn32–33
dreams
in Amulet Mahāmudrā, 149
as great bliss clarity-emptiness, 70
integrating illusion in, 158
lucid, 68
nine unfailing vital points of recognizing, 62, 273n46
on Path of Application, 62–66, 105–6, 107
on Path of Seeing, 112
as similes, 38
Drogön Sangye Tönpa. *See* Sangye Tönpa (Sangs rgyas ston pa, 1207–1278)

dullness, pacifying, 101
Dwelling in the Heart. See *Guru Yoga in Connection with Six-Armed Protector Dwelling in the Heart*
dzogchen tradition, 9, 11, 12

earth-touching mudra, 145, 148, 294n7
eclectic movement (*ris med*), 23
effort
  genuine, 71, 114
  renunciation and, 57, 100–101
  See also diligence
"Eighteen Physical Trainings, The" (*lus sbyong bco brgyad pa*), 184
  See also yogic techniques (*'khrul 'khor*)
eightfold path, 45
  bodhisattva path and, 47–48
  grounds of, 123
  on Path of Meditation, 70–71, 113–14
elements, five, 199
eleventh ground, 83, 125, 131, 291n30
elixir
  in Chakrasaṃvara, 171, 301n30
  in Hevajra, 179, 180, 181
  in Hollow Interior of *A*, 31, 290–91n24
  in physical yogic techniques, 186, 189
empowerment(s)
  into absorption, 169
  from ḍākinīs, 17, 19
  on eleventh ground, 83
  in Five Golden Dharmas, 30–31, 267n106
  of the tenth ground, 82–83
empowerments, four
  in Chakrasaṃvara practices, 171, 172
  on eleventh ground, 131
  grounds and, 140, 291n30
  in Hevajra practice, 180–81
  in *Stages of the Path*, 55, 94
emptiness (*stong pa nyid*, Skt. *shūnyatā*)
  apprehended as self, 199
  as completion phase, 157
  contingency and impermanence of, 38
  of four noble truths, 108
  illusion and, 37
  and māyā, development of understanding, 40–41
  on Path of Seeing, 67
  of phenomena, 99–100
  of self and phenomena, 114
  three integrations and, 155
  See also under appearance
Encyclopedia Tibetica, 24
  See also *Compendium of Suchness*
energy currents (*lung*, Skt. *prāṇa*), 140, 186–88, 191–92, 291n24, 303n8
enlightened activities
  aspirations for, 195, 197
  five (*phrin las lnga*), 55, 273n42
  mastery over, 77
  on tenth ground, 125
enlightenment
  aspiration for, 193
  causes of, 108–9
  manifest appearance of, 15
  seven branches of (*byang chub kyi yan lag bdun*), 66–67, 109–10, 281n133
enlightenment, factors of, 42, 45
  chart of, 53
  deity's Body as, 55
  and illusion, nonduality of, 51, 95–97
Entry into the Middle Way (Chandrakīrti), 46
environment, outer, 63
equanimity (branch of enlightenment), 67, 110
equipoise
  free of fixation, 110
  in mahāmudrā, lack of, 153
  mudra of, 190, 304n16
  of powers of absorption, 79, 82
Esoteric Instructions on Opening the Channel, 185–86
Essence of Ambrosia (Baker), 27
ethical discipline (Skt. *shila*), 44
  aspiration for, 195
  characteristics of, 122
  on Path of Accumulation, 60, 100
  ten grounds and, 77
  vice and, 58
Excellent Chariot, An (Longchenpa), 41–42, 281n132, 283n146, 287n191

Excellent Intelligence (*legs pa'i blo gros*, ninth ground), 77, 81–82
  characteristics of, 120
  delusions obscuring, 124
  realization on, 125
  signs on, 121, 129
Explanation of the Ornament of the Sūtras (Vasubandhu), 284–85n163

faith
  faculty of, 104
  one-pointed, 102
  on Path of Accumulation, 60, 103
  power of, 61, 64, 106
father tantra, 130–31, 136
faults, four, 145, 146, 148
fearlessness, lion throne of, 82
fears, five, 69, 110, 126
feast, 16, 17, 19
  in Chakrasaṃvara practices, 173
  in Hevajra practice, 179, 181
Five Ḍākinīs (*mkha' 'gro sde lnga*), 35
five faculties (*dbang po lnga*, Skt. *pañcendriya*), 104–5, 279n118
five families, 55, 96
Five Golden Dharmas, 28, 30–33
  Amulet Mahāmudrā in, 31, 143
  Immortal and Infallible instructions in, 33, 161
  Khecharī, White and Red in, 30, 33
  six dharmas in, 31–32, 135
  three integrations in, 32, 153, 154
five paths (*lam lnga*, Skt. *pañcamārga*), 45–46, 98
  chart of, 52
  devotion and, 55
  as illusion, 54, 87–88
  rainbow body on, 12
  See also individual path
five powers (*stobs lnga*, Skt. *pañcabala*), 64–65, 106–7, 279n118
Five Stages, The (Nāgārjuna), 87, 275–76n72
Five Tantras' Deities (*rgyud sde lha lnga*), 23, 31, 34–35, 178
Five Tantras' Mandala Method of Accomplishment (Tāranātha), 178, 301n5
fixation, freedom from, 146, 148
Flower Ornament Sūtra, 110, 122–23, 133, 282n137
form realm, 111, 115
formless realm, 111, 115, 283n153
Four Deities Combined (*lha bzhi dril sgrub*), 35–36
four noble truths, 43, 108–9, 111
Four Seats Tantra, 6, 259n22
fourteenth ground, 131, 140, 291n30
fruition, 83–84
  actual and nominal, 13
  as illusion, 51
  rainbow body and, 11
  time frames for, 155, 157
  See also buddhahood; Consummation, Path of
Fully Illuminated Essence Sūtra, 88, 89–90, 91
fury, clearing up, 188

Gayādhara, 137
gazes
  in mahāmudrā, 145, 146, 148, 149
  in physical yoga techniques, 189, 303n6
Gendun Gyatso (second Dalai Lama), 26–27
generosity, 69, 274n58
  characteristics of, 122
  on Path of Application, 105
  ten grounds and, 77
Ghanavyūha Sūtra. See *Dense Array of Adornments Sūtra*
gifts, four kinds, 194, 304n3
Glorious Immortal Great Timeless Awareness, 137, 162, 163–66, 288–89n8
Gö Lotsāwa Zhonnu Pal ('Gos lo tsā ba gZhon nu dpal, 1392–1481). See *Blue Annals*
goddesses
  in Chakrasaṃvara practice, 173, 174
  in Hevajra practice, 180
gold offerings, 17, 30, 142, 147, 159, 166, 262n57
Golden Rosary of Shangpa Biographies (Mokchokpa et al.), 1, 2, 16, 19, 26, 36

Golden Tengyur, 24
Gone Far (*ring du song ba*, seventh ground), 76, 81
  characteristics of, 120
  delusions obscuring, 124
  realization on, 125
  signs of, 121, 128
Great Transfer, 12
greed, clearing up, 190–91
ground of everything. See all-base (*kun gzhi*, Skt. *ālaya*)
grounds (*sa*, Skt. *bhūmi*), 46–47
  chart of, 52
  devotion and, 55, 96
  empowerments and, 140, 291n30
  essence of, 118
  etymology and meaning of, 46–47, 119, 284–85n163
  factors to be eliminated on, 123
  as illusion, 54, 87–88
  names and characteristics of, 47, 75–77, 119–20
  of Path of Meditation, 70, 72
  perfections and, 48, 77–78, 79, 122, 272n34
  pure and impure, 8–9, 16, 83
  rainbow body on, 12
  realizations on, 124–30
  signs of, 120–22, 125–29
  in *Stages*, 75–83
  twenty-one delusions on, 78–79, 123–24
  See also Cloud of Dharma (tenth ground); Difficult to Overcome (fifth ground); eleventh ground; Excellent Intelligence (ninth ground); fourteenth ground; Gone Far (seventh ground); Illuminating (third ground); Immovable (eighth ground); Manifest (sixth ground); Radiant (fourth ground); Stainless (second ground); thirteenth ground; twelfth ground; Very Joyful (first ground)
Guge kingdom, 137
Guhyasamāja, 34
Guhyasamāja Tantra, 136
Guidance Manual of Immortal Mind, by the Wise and Venerable Gyaltsen Bum, 298n14
Guidance Manual of Infallible Three Integrations (Gyaltsen Bum), 296n19, 297n22, 298n12
guru(s)
  blessings of, 147, 150
  female, 18
  integration of, 155, 156
  kindness of, 111
  meditation on in yogic techniques, 185, 186
  role in tantra, 31, 55
  role of in Immortal and Infallible, 166
  three integrations and, 155
guru yoga, 96, 155, 278n104, 290n23
  Four Deities Combined as, 35
  of six-armed Mahākāla, 36, 270n132
Guru Yoga in Connection with Six-Armed Protector Dwelling in the Heart (Khyentse Wangpo), 36, 270n132
Gyaltsen Bum ('Jag pa rGyal mtshan 'bum, 1261–1334). See *Guidance Manual of Infallible Three Integrations*
Gyatso, Janet, 8
Gyurme Dechen, Lochen (Lo chen 'Gyur med bde chen/sKad gnyis smra ba, 1540–1615), 136–38, 288n4, 289n13, 293–94n44

habitual patterns
  in all-base, 89, 90, 200
  application of on Path of Accumulation, 60
  four types of, 62, 273n47
  of ordinary beings, ripening, 90
hagiography, Tibetan and Indian traditions of, 2, 13–14
happiness, 60, 194, 196, 197
harm-doers, expelling, 189–90
healing, aspiration for, 196
heart-prāṇa, 188
heroic sitting posture, 191

Heruka, 170, 171, 179, 300n19
Hevajra
  in Five Tantras' Deities, 34
  Niguma in lineage, difficulties with, 178, 301n6
  practice of, 177–78
  textual tradition of, 23, 26, 177
  without consort, 180
  See also *Mandala Ritual of Glorious Hevajra*
Hevajra Tantra, 135–36
Hevajra Tantra in Two Parts, 177
Hidden Yogin (sBas pa'i rnal 'byor), 35, 269n126
higher insight
  calm abiding and, 75, 113
  as path, 47, 55
  supramundane, 118
Highest Intention Tantra, 116, 117, 283n157
Highest Timeless Awareness Tantra, 116–17, 132–33, 283–84n158
highest yoga tantra (*rnal 'byor bla med kyi rgyud*), 299n1
  buddhahood in, 130–31
  Chakrasaṃvara Tantra in, 167
  rainbow body in, 12
Himalayan Buddhism, 2–3, 22–23
Hinduism, 3
hollow interior, 31, 140, 290–91n24
hostility, aspiring to pacify, 195
Hundred Guides of Jonang (Kunga Drolchok, Jonang), 25, 265n87
hungry ghosts, practice for satisfying, 189

ignorance, 43, 111, 115, 199
Illuminated Timeless Awareness Latter Tantra, 112, 283n144
Illuminating (*'od byed pa*, third ground), 76, 79–80
  characteristics of, 119
  delusions obscuring, 123
  realization on, 124
  signs on, 121, 126–27
illusion
  appearance without attachment, 70
  aspirations for, 196
  in Buddhist tradition, 37–42
  creativity of, 68
  definition of, 38–39
  dreams as, 62–63
  existence of, 67
  integration of, 158
  lucid appearance of, 69
  mindfulness and awareness of, 64
  naturally arising, 79
  nonconceptual, 70
  path as, 50–51, 95
  on Path of Seeing, 112
  recognition of, 40–41
  role in Niguma's hagiography, 3
  similes of, 38
  space as, 54
  three integrations and, 155
  without fixation, 78–79
illusory body (*sgyu lus*)
  empowerment for, 17
  four levels of, 41
  Immortal and Infallible and, 161
  nonreferential, 68
  practice in *Vajra Lines*, 139, 140, 291n29
  in *Stages in the Path of illusion*, 42
  and three integrations, relationship to, 153
immeasurables, mindfulness of, 114
Immortal and Infallible (*'chi med 'chugs med*)
  benefits of, 164–65
  practices of, 162, 163––164
  sources of, 33, 161
  three examples in, 165, 298n17
immortality, 164, 298n12
Immovable (*mi g.yo ba*, eighth ground), 77, 81, 120
  characteristics of, 120
  delusions obscuring, 124
  on Path of Meditation, 70
  realization on, 125
  signs on, 121, 128–29
impermanence, 38, 139, 155, 170
India
  ḍākinī lore in, 16–17, 262n56

female gurus in, 18
six dharmas in, 135
Indian Buddhism, translation of, 22–24
Indian Source Text of the Glorious Five Tantras (Vajrāsana), 34
Indian Source Texts of the Dharma Cycle of Five Golden Dharmas of the Glorious Shangpa. See *Shangpa Texts*
Indrabhūti, King, 14
inner heat (*gtum mo*), 31, 267n109
in *Hevajra* tantra, 136
in physical training (*lus sbyong*), 183, 186, 190–91
(*See also* yogic techniques (*'khrul 'khor*))
practice in *Vajra Lines*, 139–40, 291n28
rainbow body and, 11
See also Meditation on Inner Heat in the Path of Methods
instantaneous mentation (*de ma thag pa'i yid*), 277n93
Integrating the Nature of Three Kāyas, 153
integration, Amulet Mahāmudrā and, 146, 149
integrations, three, 32, 142, 293n39
of guru, 155, 156
of illusion, 158
integration, defined, 153
sources, difficulties with, 154–55
of yidam, 155, 156–75
See also *Three Dharmas to Integrate on the Path*
intellect
in Amulet Mahāmudrā, 146, 148
illusion beyond, 37–38, 66, 75–76, 77, 79, 82, 164
limitations of, 136
on ninth ground, 120
intention, meditative absorption of, 102
See also mind, meditative absorption of
interdependent origination, 80–81
intermediate state
nirvana in, 112
practice in *Vajra Lines*, 139, 141–42, 293nn38–41
recognition in, 65
saṃbhogakāya, awakening as, 165
in *Stages in the Path of Illusion*, 68
isolation, 107

Jambudvīpa, 29, 266n100
Jamgön Kongtrul ('Jam mgon kong sprul bLo gros mtha' yas, 1813–1900), 26
on Amulet Mahāmudrā, 143–44, 145
on authorship of Niguma's *Life Story*, 20, 262–63n62
on ḍākinī code, 7
on Five Tantras' Deities, 34
on Four Deities Combined, 35
on illusory body, 41
on Immortal and Infallible, 162
physical yogic techniques, absence in catalogues of, 185
on rainbow body, 12–13
on transference, 33
on translation of *Vajra Lines of the Six Dharmas*, 137, 138
works of, 25
See also *Ocean of Song*; *Treasury of Extensive Teachings*; *Treasury of Instructions*; *Treasury of Knowledge*
Jamgon Kongtrul's Retreat Manual (Zangpo), 27
Jatang Kunga Yeshe (Bya btang Kun dga' ye shes), 20
"Jewel Mirror in Which All Is Clear," (Dechen), 18–19
Jewel Ocean Tantra, 30, 136, 167, 267n103, 269n123
Joining, Path of, 66
See also Application, Path of
Jonang tradition, 25
Journey to Lanka Sūtra, 91, 93, 94, 118, 276–77n87, 284n162
joy
branch of enlightenment, 67, 109
on Path of Seeing, 69, 110
in peak (of Path of Application), 64
joys, four
in Chakrasaṃvara practices, 172
dissipating and nondissipating, 139, 141, 290n20, 290n22

Kadampa, 143
Kagyu (*bka' brgyud*) tradition, 11, 23, 29, 36, 143
See also Shangpa Kagyu
Kālachakra tradition, 11, 12
Kālarātri, 171, 173, 175
Kalu Rinpoche, Khyabje (1905–1989), 25–26, 27, 36
See also Basis of Everything, The; *Shangpa Texts*
Kalu Yangsi Rinpoche, 26
Kambhalapāda, 6–7, 260nn24–25
kangyur, 22
Kapstein, Matthew, 26
karma, 89, 117
See also habitual patterns
Karma Kagyu, 29, 36
Karma Rangjung Kunchab. *See* Kalu Rinpoche, Khyabje
karmamudra, 131, 177
Kashmir, 1, 3, 4, 6, 20
Kāshyapa, 3, 20
kāya(s), 14, 73, 116
four, in Amulet Mahāmudrā, 144, 145, 146, 148
mahāsuka, 131, 146, 148
nonconceptual, 82
nondissipating, 21
rupa, 118, 165
of unity, 162
kāyas, three
in Chakrasaṃvara practice, 168–69
form of deity and, 97
grounds and, 14–15, 125
inseparability of, 146, 149
mahāmudrā arising as, 148–49
naturally arising, 55
on Path of Consummation, 73–75
relationship between, 117–18
six dharmas and, 139, 142, 289nn14–15
spontaneous presence of, 147, 150
three integrations and, 32, 153, 155, 156–57, 158
three poisons as, 157, 296n19
Kāyastha, Aged, 178, 301n4
khagamukhā, 139, 290n21
Khechara, realm of, 22, 33
Khecharī (*mkha' spyod ma*), White and Red, 4, 19, 33
Khyentse Wangpo (mKhyen rtse'i dbang po, 1820–1892). See *Guru Yoga in Connection with Six-Armed Protector Dwelling in the Heart*
Khyungpo Naljor (Khyung po rnal 'byor), 13, 15
amulet of, 32, 143, 144, 176
biography of, 10, 16–18, 27–28, 29, 266n98
Chakrasaṃvara empowerment of, 167–68
colophons of, 84, 133, 142, 147, 150, 154, 159, 166, 173, 176
dates of, 266n95
hagiography of, compared with Niguma's, 2
Hevajra commentary, request for, 178
instructions and empowerments received, 17–18, 21–22, 23, 28, 262n60
names of, 27, 266n94
six dharmas and, 6, 31, 135, 137, 138, 142
three integrations and, 154, 295n5
King of the Empty Plain (Stearns), 18–19
Kinnaur (Himachal Pradesh), 24
Kunga Drolchok, Jonang (Jo nang Kun dga' grol mchog, 1507–1566), 25, 265n87
See also *Hundred Guides of Jonang*
Kunga Ö (Kun dga' 'Od). *See* Mokchokpa, Kunga Ö

Lalitavistara. See *Sūtra of the Vast Display*
Lamdre tradition, 23, 161
Laṅkāvatāra Sūtra. See *Journey to Lanka Sūtra*
Latter Ocean Tantra, 106, 280n126
Lavāpa, 1, 6, 260n28, 260nn24–26
Lendarma Lodrö, Lotsāwa (Lo tsā ba gLan dar ma bLo gros), 84, 133, 137, 142, 159, 166, 173, 178, 182
liberation, path of, 143, 162, 184

Life and Teaching of Nāropa, The (Guenther), 4–5
Life of Marpa the Translator, The (Tsangnyön Heruka), 5
Life Story of Buddha Vajradhara (Mokchokpa), 20, 261n49
Life Story of Niguma, Ḍākinī of Timeless Awareness, The (Mokchokpa), 6–7, 9
Life Story of the Supreme Learned Nāro Paṇchen, The (Sangye Bum), 258–59nn12–13, 258n8, 263–64n69
light(s)
  in Buddhism, 10–11
  in Chakrasaṃvara practices, 170, 171–72
  empowerment by, 82
  five, 199
  in Hevajra practice, 180
  in Immortal and Infallible, 163, 298n10
  in transference, 141–42, 293nn40–41
Light of Wisdom, The (Padmasambhava and Kongtrul), 7
Like an Illusion (Riggs), 27
Lion-faced dākinī, 35
livelihood, genuine, 71, 114
Longchenpa Drimey Özer (kLong chen pa Rab 'byams pa Dri med 'od zer, 1301–1363). See *Excellent Chariot, An*; *Natural Ease in Illusion*
Lopez, Donald, 44
Lotus Sūtra. See *White Lotus of Great Compassion Sūtra*
Lotus-endowed (twelfth ground), 83, 112, 282–83n145
lucid clarity, 68
  in Amulet Mahāmudrā, 146
  Immortal and Infallible and, 161
  in *Mahāmāya* tantra, 136
  mahāmudrā of, 143
  on Path of Seeing, 112
  practice of, 139, 141, 292nn34–35
  threefold, 149
  in transference, 141–42, 293nn40–41
  without increase or decrease, 89
lujong (*lus sbyong*), 183
  See also yogic techniques (*'khrul 'khor*)
luminosity, 10–11
  See also clarity

Ma Lotsāwa (rMa lo tsā ba Chos 'bar, 1044–1089), 161, 297n2
madhyamaka, 37
Madhyāntika (Nyi ma'i gung pa), 20, 263n65
magic show, simile of, 39–40, 42
magical power, aspiration for, 195
Mahākāla, six-armed (Chakdrukpa), 35, 36
Mahāmāyā, 34
mahāmudrā
  definition of, 143
  in Immortal and Infallible, 161, 162
  in three integrations, 158
  See also Amulet Mahāmudrā
Mahāvairochana, 130
Mahāvastu, 46, 271n22
mahāyāna
  body of light in, 12
  buddhahood in, 130–31
  illusion, development of understanding in, 41–42
  limitless classification in, 45, 48–49
  perfections in, 47–48, 272n34
  ten grounds in, 46–47
Mahāyāna Highest Continuum (Maitreya/Asaṅga), 92, 118, 277n88, 284n161
Maitreya, 44
  See also *Mahāyāna Highest Continuum*; *Ornament of Clear Realization, The*; *Ornament of the [Mahāyāna] Sūtras*
Maitrīpa, 32, 36, 267–68n112
Mandala Ritual of Glorious Chakrasaṃvara
  creation phase and offerings, 170–71, 172–73
  four empowerments, 171, 172
  fruition of, 172–73
  mandala of Five Deities, 171–72
  preparation, 170, 300n11

purpose of, 169
source of, 167
Mandala Ritual of Glorious Hevajra
creation and completion in, 179
dedication and aspiration, 181–82, 302n16
four empowerments in, 180–81
preparation, 178–79, 302n9
supplications in, 179–80
mandalas (*dkyil 'khor*)
in Chakrasaṃvara practices, 170, 171–72
in Hevajra practices, 177, 178, 182
of knowable things, 149
of knowledge, aspirations toward, 194–95
on Path of Application, 63
as wheels (*'khor lo*), 168
Manifest (*mngon du gyur pa*, sixth ground), 76, 80–81
characteristics of, 120
delusions obscuring, 123–24
realization on, 125
signs on, 121, 127–28
mantra
in Chakrasaṃvara practices, 170–71, 173, 176
in Hevajra practice, 178, 179, 181
in three integrations, 157
of Vajrasattva, 31, 170
See also seed-syllables
mantra tradition. *See* tantra; vajrayāna
Marpa, 5
Marpa Kagyu, 143
māyā, 38–39, 40–41
See also illusion
Māyā, Queen (Māyādevī), 39, 270n4
Meaningful Discipline Tantra, 131, 287n187
means, path of (*thabs lam*), 135
meditation
dharmakāya in, 14
in mahāmudrā, lack of, 149
yoga of, 189–91
Meditation, Path of, 70–72, 113–15
eightfold path on, 70–71
factors to be eliminated on, 115
grounds and, 70, 72
Meditation on Channels, Prāṇa, and Such, 186–87
Meditation on Inner Heat in the Path of Methods, 187–88
meditation-in-action. *See* integrations, three
meditative absorption (Skt. *samādhi*), 44
branch of enlightenment, 67, 110
faculty of, 104
on first ground, 123
four periods of, 102
genuine, 71, 114
miraculous activity, as support for, 59–60
on Path of Accumulation, 100, 101–3
on Path of Meditation, 70–71
on Path of Seeing, 66–67
power of, 61, 64–65, 107
on single seat, 140, 291n31
vajra-like, 72
vice and, 58
without reference point, 109
meditative equipoise, 146, 148
meditative stability, 77, 78, 122
Meeting of Father and Son, 130
"meeting the buddha," 13
memory, integrating, 157
mental agility, branch of enlightenment, 67, 109
mental attention, 57, 58, 114
mental consciousness (*yid kyi rnam par shes pa*), 88, 93–94
mental engagement, 100–101
mental fabrication, 146, 148
mental nonengagement (*yid la mi byed pa*), 32
mentation, 89, 199–200, 277nn93–94
afflictive, 84, 88, 93, 125
mahāmudrā and, 151
merit, 73, 116
merit kāya, 117, 283–84n159
See also saṃbhogakāya
methods, path of, 139–40, 162, 183, 189–91
Mikyö Dorje, eighth Karmapa (rJe

brgyad pa Mi bskyod rdo rje, 1507–1554). See *Noble One's Resting at Ease: A Commentary on Ornament of Clear Realization*
mind
absorption of, 59, 102
as Akaniṣṭha, 132–33
as all-base, 93
and deity, inseparability of, 157, 164
and guru, inseparability of, 156
homages to, 54, 87, 150
as illusionist, 40
in integration of illusion, 158
mindfulness of, 56, 99, 114
resting in Amulet Mahāmudrā, 145
subtle body and, 135
wheel of in Chakrasaṃvara practices, 175, 301n31
"Mind and Body, Immortal and Infallible." *See* Immortal and Infallible (*'chi med 'chugs med*)
mind-dharmakāya, 148, 294–95n9
mindfulness
branch of enlightenment, 66, 109
in dreams, 62
faculty of, 61, 104
four foundations of, 45, 56–57, 98–100
genuine, 71, 114
power of, 64, 106–7
Mine of Jewels (Tāranātha), 35
Mipam Gyamtso, Ju ('Ju Mi pham rgya mtsho, 1846–1912). See *Complete Explanation of the Intended Meaning of "Ornament of the Mahāyāna Sūtras"*
miraculous activity, four absorptions of, 59–60, 101–3, 278–79n113
mirages, 74
Mokchokpa (rMog lcog pa)
identity of, 19–20, 262–63nn62–63
Kunga Ö (Kun dga' 'od), 20, 262–63n62
Rinchen Tsödrü (Rin chen brtson grus, 1110–1170), 19–20, 29, 34
See also *Life Story of Buddha Vajradhara*; *Life Story of Niguma, Ḍākinī of Timeless Awareness*
mother tantra (*ma rgyud*), 299n1
buddhahood in, 131
Chakrasaṃvara in, 167, 168
Hevajra in, 177
six dharmas in, 135–36
mudra(s)
in physical yoga techniques, 189, 190, 304n15
of a woman, buddhahood by, 131
Mūlamadhyamakakārikā. See *Root Verses of the Middle called Wisdom*
Mullin, Glen, 26–27
multiplicity, knowledge of, 21, 99, 146, 149

nāda, Tangtong Gyalpo's instruction by, 19, 262n61
Nāgārjuna. See *Five Stages, The*; *Root Verses of the Middle called Wisdom*
nāgas, 3, 20, 263n66
Nairātmyā, 178, 179, 180, 181
Namkhai Norbu, 11–12
namtar (*rnam par thar pa*), 13–14
See also hagiography, Tibetan and Indian traditions of
Nāropa (Nāroṭapa), 21, 262n57
dates of, 258n11
hagiography of, comparing, 2
and Niguma, relationship to, 3–5, 6, 258–59nn12–13
Narthang Tengyur, 23, 24
native state, resting in, 151
Natural Ease in Illusion (Longchenpa), 41–42
Naturally Free Mahāmudrā, 144–45, 150–52
Naturally Liberated Immortality (*'chi med rang grol*), 161
See also Immortal and Infallible (*'chi med 'chugs med*)
nature of mind, 10–11, 32
natures, eighty, 142, 293n41
Ngari (mnga ris), 137
ngöndro. *See* preliminary practices (*sngon 'gro*)
Niguma, 6–10, 8, 9
birthplace of, 3, 258nn9–10

Bodong Chokley Namgyal and, 24
historicity of, 15
in Khyungpa Naljor's biography, 10, 16–18
Marpa and, 5
in Mokchokpa's biography, 20–22
names of, 1, 3
and Nāropa, relationship to, 3–5, 6, 258–59nn12–13
parents of, 1, 3–4, 21
rainbow body of, 1, 7, 13
role in Shangpa tradition, 23, 24
sources on, 1–3, 5
in Tangtong Gyalpo's biography, 18–19
teachers of, 6–7
textual sources of teachings, 167, 299n3
transmission lineage of, 29–30
Vajradhara, teachings and empowerments by, 8, 9, 13, 14, 21
works of, 23, 29–30, 153–54, 177–78, 267n104

Niguma's Aspiration Prayer. See *Aspiration Prayer of the Sealed Word*

Nigu's Yogic Exercises, Root and Commentary (Tāranātha), 184, 185

Nine Emanated Deities of Hevajra (empowerment), 23

nirmāṇakāya
appearance of, 14–15
in intermediate state, 141, 142
natural arising of, 73, 117
pure lands of, 132
sound and attainment of, 157

nirvana
all-base as support for, 91–92
enlightenment and, 109, 164
as genuine illusion, 42, 51, 70, 76
on grounds (*sa*, Skt. *bhūmi*), 80–81, 123
in intermediate state, 112
in mahāmudrā, 150
purity of, 181

Nirvirana Vishkambin, 96, 278n107

No More Learning, Path of, 283n154
See also Consummation, Path of

Noble One's Resting at Ease: A Commentary on Ornament of Clear Realization (Mikyö Dorje), 280–81n129

nonconceptuality
in Amulet Mahāmudrā, 146, 148, 149
as dharmakāya, 97

nondistraction, 147, 149–50, 151

nonmeditation, 147, 149–50

nonreturners, 70, 81, 110

nonthought, 55, 141

nonvirtue
in dreams, 62, 273n48
genuine mindfulness and, 71
of mental consciousness, 93–94
on Path of Accumulation, 100–101
ripening of, 90

Norbu Dondrup, 11

no-self, realization of, 111

Nyingma tradition, 8

obscurations
five, 105, 279n121
most subtle, 116

obscurations, two
freedom from, 195, 304–5n4
purifying by Amulet Mahāmudrā, 147, 150
purity of, 73, 116, 142

Ocean of Ḍākas Tantra, 167

Ocean of Song (Kongtrul), 145

Ocean of Timeless Awareness Tantra, 165, 298n14

one-to-one lineage (*gcig brgyud*), 29

ordinary mind, 145, 147, 148, 150

Ornament of Clear Realization, The (Maitreya), 46, 74, 274–75n61
on twenty signs on Path of Application, 108, 280–81n129
on warmth and peak, 105, 279n119

Ornament of the [Mahāyāna] Sūtras (Maitreya), 119, 284–85n163

Padmasambhava, 6, 12, 262n57

Pāli tradition, 47, 272n30

Palpung Monastery, 25, 26

pāramitās. *See* perfections (*pha rol tu phyin pa*)

passion, 33, 140, 141, 151

See also desire
path (*lam*, Skt. *mārga*), 42, 55, 98
complexity of, purpose for, 49–50, 272nn36–37
derivation of term, 46
devotion on, 96
dual functions of, 43–44, 49
as illusion, 50–51, 95
perfections and, 48
primordial unity of, 88
of unity, 95, 98, 278n101
See also five paths (*lam lnga*, Skt. *pañcamārga*)
Path of Purification, The (Buddhaghosa), 38, 45
Paths to Liberation (Buswell, Jr. and Gimello), 49–50
patience, 77, 78, 122
peak, level of (*rtse mo*), 12, 62, 64, 104–6, 105, 107, 279–80n124, 280n127
Peking Tengyur, 23, 24, 144, 177, 183
Peme (dpe med), 3, 20, 21, 258n9
perfection, total (*rnam byang*), 91, 104
perfection of wisdom (Skt. *prajñāpāramitā*), 37
Perfection of Wisdom in Eight-thousand Lines, 50–51
perfections (*pha rol tu phyin pa*), 42, 47–48
buddhahood in, 130–31
characteristics of, 122–23
chart of ten, 52
mindfulness of, 114
on Path of Accumulation, 103
phenomena
as Body of illusion, 81
branch of enlightenment, direct revealing of, 66, 109
as deity and guru, 55
direct application of mindfulness to, 99–100
equality of, 113, 152
equipoise and, 110
illusion-like, 40, 54, 102
just as they are, realization of, 78
knowing of, 108–9, 281nn131–32
mind as only, 151
mindfulness of, 56, 99–100
on Path of Seeing, 108–9
realization of on grounds, 79, 80, 81–82
physical training (*lus sbyong*). *See* yogic techniques (*'khrul 'khor*)
pointing-out, 149, 162, 295n11
poisons
five, 147
three, 156, 157–58, 199, 296n17
See also afflictive emotions/states (*nyon mongs pa*, Skt. *klesha*)
postures, 185, 186, 189, 190, 191, 303n6
power
characteristics of, 122–23
ten grounds and, 77, 78
prāṇa. *See* energy currents (*lung*, Skt. *prāṇa*)
prāṇa-mind, 187–88
pratyekabuddhas, 50–51, 56, 76, 120
preliminary practices (*sngon 'gro*), 31, 146, 149, 155, 163, 170, 295n12, 300n15
pride, clearing up, 190
primordial unity, 13, 88
Pullahari. *See* Puṣhpahari
Pure Domains, Akaniṣṭha of, 132–33, 287n191
pure lands/realms
aspiring to manifest, 195–96
perishability of, 132–33, 287n191
power over, 81
pure perception, 16, 194
purification
in Chakrasaṃvara practices, 169, 174
in Hevajra practice, 180
by nonfixation, 79
on Path of Seeing, 70
in six dharmas, 140, 290–91n24
See also preliminary practices (*sngon 'gro*)
"Purifier, Hollow Interior of *A*, The," 31
purity, eight kinds, 121, 285n170
Puṣhpahari (Pullahari), 4, 259n14

Questions of Four Girls, 107, 280n128

Questions of Matisambhava Sūtra, 109–10, 113–14, 281n134

rabbit (*ri bong*), 140, 291n26
See also bodhichitta (*byang sems*)
Radiant (*'od 'phro ba*, fourth ground), 76, 80
characteristics of, 119
delusions obscuring, 123
realization on, 124–25
signs on, 121, 127
Rāhulaguptavajra (Lama Rāhula), 28, 33, 34, 36, 135, 268n116
rainbow body (*'ja' lus*)
and grounds, correspondence with, 12–13, 261nn44–45
in illusory body practice, 41
of Lavāpa, 7, 10
in Tibetan tradition, 10–12
Ratnavajra (Rin chen rdo rje), 6, 21, 264n40
Rechung Hearing Lineage, 154
Releasing the Knots of Varjra Lines (Sangye Palzang), 143, 296nn12–14
renunciation
genuine, four aspects of (*yang dag spong ba bzhi*, Skt. *catvāri saṃyakprahāṇa*), 57–58, 60, 100–101, 278n112
meditative absorption and, 102
on Path of Accumulation, 103
Riggs, Nicole, 27
rimé. *See* eclectic movement (*ris med*)
Rinchen Namgyal, Lhatsun (Lha'i btsun pa Rin chen rnam rgyal, 1473-1557), 3–4, 20
Rinchen Zangpo (Rin chen bzang po, 958–1055), 137, 138, 142, 166
Roerich, George, 5, 26, 167
Root Verses of the Middle called Wisdom (Nāgārjuna), 42
rupakāya, 118, 165

sacred pledge, 31, 146, 149, 163, 181, 295n12
Samantabhadra, 132, 196
Samantabhadra Vajradhatu, 131
samaya (*dam tshig*), 31
See also sacred pledge
saṃbhogakāya
buddhahood in, 131–32
in Chakrasaṃvara practices, 172, 174
communication through, 14–15
eighth ground and, 81
in intermediate state, 142
on Path of Seeing, 68
rainbow body and, 11, 13
Vajradhara, 14–15
Saṃdhinirmocana. See *Sūtra That Unravels the Intent*
samsara
all-base as support for, 91, 199
on grounds (*sa*, Skt. *bhūmi*), 80–81, 123, 125
as illusion, 41–42, 51, 70, 76
in mahāmudrā, 148, 150, 151
purity of, 181
revulsion for, 293n39
See also cyclic existence
Saṃvara Ocean Tantra, 30, 34, 167, 173, 267n103, 300n23
Sangak Choling (gSang sngags chos gling), 24
Sangye Bum (Sangs rgyas 'bum, 12th or 13th c.?). See *Life Story of the Supreme Learned Nāro Paṇchen, The*
Sangye Nyentön (Sangs rgyas gnyan ston, or Ri gong pa, 1175–1247/1255?), 29, 297n3
Sangye Palzang (Sangs rgyas dpal bzang). See *Releasing the Knots of Varjra Lines*
Sangye Tönpa (Sangs rgyas ston pa, 1207–1278), 29, 135, 288n1, 293–94n44
See also *Collection of Necessary Oral Advice on Niguma's Six Dharmas*
Saraha, 87
secrecy, 183–84
Secret Ḍākinī Tantra, 94, 277–78n100
secret mantra (*gsang sngags*), 8, 92-93
buddhahood in, 130–31
empowerment in, 94
See also tantra; vajrayāna

Secret Moon Drop Tantra, 130, 287n186
Sections on Grounds Sūtra, 91, 92, 93, 276n84
seed-syllables
 in Chakrasaṃvara practices, 17–174, 170, 171–72, 175
 in Hevajra practice, 179, 180, 181
 of hollow interior, 290–91n24
 in Immortal and Infallible, 163, 298n10
 in six dharmas, 139
Seeing, Path of (*mthong lam*), 12, 66–70, 108–13
 factors to be eliminated on, 111, 282n143
 level of warmth and, 103–4
 lucid appearances on, 68–70
 and Path of Application, relationship to, 61
 seven branches of enlightenment on, 66–67
 twelve hundred qualities occurring on, 69
Selected Works of the Dalai Lama 2: The Tantric Yogas of Sister Niguma (Mullin), 26–27
self, 44–45, 114, 199
self-fixation, 60, 93
sensations, mindfulness of, 56, 99
sense consciousnesses, five (*sgo lnga'i rnam par shes pa*), 70, 84–85, 88, 93–94, 125
sense pleasures, 69, 151
sentient beings, 90
 all-base in constituent of, 89
 aspirations for, 194, 196, 197
 lifespan of, 74–75
 welfare of, 66
seven branches. *See* sevenfold service
Seven Instruction Lineages (Tāranātha), 6–7, 177, 178
sevenfold service, 156, 157, 296n12
seven-generation injunction, 22, 29, 142, 166, 293–94n44, 299n19
sexual practices, 131, 168, 177
Shaivite tradition, 3
Shangpa Kagyu tradition, 27-36
 Chakrasaṃvara in, 31, 35, 36, 169
 exceptional qualities of, 136
 extraordinary practices of, 36
 Five Golden Dharmas of, 28, 30-33
 founding of, 27–29
 Hevajra in, 23, 34, 177–78
 Immortal and Infallible in, 33, 161
 lineages of, 29–30
 literary tradition of, 23–27, 265n82
 mahāmudrā in (*See* Amulet Mahāmudrā)
 spiritual poems of, 145
 Tāranātha, role in, 25, 184, 265n88
 three integrations in, 32, 154
 See also individual practices
Shangpa Texts, 25–26, 137–38, 185
Shantibhadra, 5
Shantivarman (Zhi ba'i go cha, father), 1, 21
Shavari, 35, 36, 269–70n129
Shaw, Miranda, 169
shrāvakas, 56, 76, 120
Shrīmati (dPal gyi blo gros ma, mother), 1, 21
siddha movement, 168
Siddhārtha, Prince (rGyal bu Don 'grub), 130, 286n182
similes, use of, 41, 42
six dharmas
 acumen needed for, 140, 141, 291n29, 291n31, 293nn38–39
 in Five Tantras' Deities, 34
 formulation of, 139
 in *Hevajra Tantra*, 135–36
 Khyungpo's receipt of, 17–18, 142
 of Niguma and Nāropa, compared, 135–36
 physical training (*lus sbyong*) for (*See* yogic techniques)
 source of, 6
Six Dharmas of Nāropa, 31, 135
skillful method, 77, 78, 122
sleep, lucid clarity in, 149
small child yogic exercise, 192, 304n22
small vehicle, buddhahood in, 130–31
Smith, Gene, 26
Sonam Dragpa, Panchen, 177
Sosadvīpa (Sosaling), 6, 16

sound, integration of, 157
Sovereign of Noble Aspirations. See *Aspiration Prayer of the Sealed Word*
space
as all-base, 54, 91–92
on tenth ground, 82
and timeless awareness, indivisibility of, 73, 84, 116, 146, 149
speech
aspiration for, 196
genuine, 71, 113
natural resting of, 145
in three integrations, 158
wheel of in Chakrasaṃvara practices, 174–75
Spiritual Power of Amṛita/Spiritual Power of Immortality (Virūpa), 161–62, 297n3
spontaneous presence, 42, 74, 77, 145, 147
Śrījñāna (dPal gyi ye shes). See Niguma
Stages in the Path of Illusion, 24, 54–84
and *An Excellent Chariot*, resemblances, 42
path in, 46
titles of, 84, 272n40
Stages in the Path of Illusion: The Commentary, 28, 86–133
all-base in, 45
grounds in, 8–9, 46–47
homage and author's statement, 86, 87
outline of, 85
path in, 46, 51
saṃbhogakāya in, 15
Stages in the Path of the Three Types of Person, 27
Stainless (*dri ma med pa*, second ground), 76, 79
characteristics of, 119
delusions obscuring, 123
realization on, 124
signs on, 120–21, 126
Stainless Essence Sūtra, 88–89
Stainless Union, 178, 301n4
storehouse consciousness. *See* all-base (*kun gzhi*, Skt. *ālaya*)
stupidity
pacifying, 58, 101
yogic technique for clearing, 189
Sublime Absorption Sūtra, 94, 277n98
Sublime Golden Light Sūtra, 117, 119–20, 122
subsequent attainment, 146, 148, 152, 156
subtle body, 135, 162
in Chakrasaṃvara practice, 162
in Immortal and Infallible, 162
See also vajra body (*rdo rje sku*)
suchness (*de bzhin nyid*), 92, 131, 141
in mahāmudrā, 146, 149, 150, 151
Sudarshana (lta na sdug pa), 3, 21, 263n68
suffering, 57, 63
Sukhasiddhī, 18, 24, 32, 161–62
six dharmas of, 34
supreme dharma, level of (*chos mchog*), 64, 65, 66, 108
Sūtra of Brahmānanda, 112, 283n146
Sūtra of Kumāraprabha, 108, 124–30, 281n130
Sūtra of Teaching the Unimaginable, 115–16
on buddhas and bodhisattvas, differentiated, 133
on ten grounds, 120–22
Sūtra of the Bodhisattva Dṛdhramati, 98–103, 104–5, 278n110
Sūtra of the Perfection of Wisdom in Eighteen Thousand Lines, 95
Sūtra of the Vast Display, 39
Sūtra on the Ten Grounds, 46, 48
Sūtra That Unravels the Intent, 39–40
Swift Accomplishment of Glorious Chakrasaṃvara, 169, 173–76

Tangtong Gyalpo (Thang stong rgyal po, 1361?–1485), 10, 265n84
biography of, 18–19
in six dharmas transmission, 136
works of, 24–25, 265n85
See also *Collection of the Essentials*
Tangtong Gyalpo Tradition (*Thang lugs*), 24
tantra, 8, 30–31

Tantra of All-Victorious Nonduality, 132, 287n192
Tantra of Timeless Awareness Drops, 131, 287n189
Tantra of Total Nonabiding, 131
Tantra of Vajra Bliss, 131
tantric action, four modes of, 169, 176
Tāranātha, Jonang (Tā ra nā tha, Jo nang; a.k.a. sGrol ba'i mgon po, 1575–1635), 257n6
on amulet mahāmudrā, 32
on cohesion of Niguma's teachings, 29–30
on Immortal and Infallible, 161
role in Shangpa tradition, 25, 184, 265n88
on three integrations, 153
on *Vajra Lines of the Six Dharmas*, 137
See also *Clearing up Darkness of the Mind*; *Collected Works*; *Five Tantras' Mandala Method of Accomplishment*; *Mine of Jewels*; *Nigu's Yogic Exercises, Root and Commentary*; *Seven Instruction Lineages*; *Stages in the Path of the Three Types of Person.*
Tāranātha's History of Buddhism in India, 6–7, 10, 260n25
tathāgatas, 9, 83, 129–30
See also buddha(s)
tengyur, 22–24
Teto cemetery, 161, 297n3
theravādin tradition, thirty-seven factors in, 45
third turning of the wheel of dharma, 44–45
thirteenth ground, 12, 131, 261nn46–47, 291n30
Tholing monastery (Tho ling, mtho gding), 137, 142, 288n5
thoughts
genuine, 71, 113
integrating, 157
on Path of Seeing, 67–68
Three Dharmas to Integrate on the Path, 155–59
three gates (*rnam thar sgo gsum*), 98, 278n11
Three Kāya Integration, 153, 154
Threefold Letting-Go (*rang babs gsum*), 32, 143
See also Amulet Mahāmudrā
Tibet House publishers, 24
Tibetan Buddhist Resource Center (TBRC), 24
Tibetan Canon, 22–23
Tibetan script, 136–37
Tilopa/Telopa/Tillipa, 3, 6, 260n26
timeless awareness
all-base as, 199
of Amulet Mahāmudrā, 147, 150
buddhahood and, 114
fivefold, 84
four kāyas and, 148, 149, 295n10
as immortality, 164, 298n12
nonconceptual, 75, 113
nondissipating, 140, 291n27
of Path of Seeing, 66, 70
perfection of, 78, 123
power of wisdom and, 107
and space, indivisibility of, 73, 84, 116, 146, 149
in ten perfections, 122–23
of unimpeded confidence, 82
Timeless Rapture (Zangpo), 27
Todgál (*thod rgal*), 12
trainings, three, 195, 305n5
transference (*'pho ba*), 19, 33, 268n117
in *Vajra Lines*, 139, 141, 292–93nn36–37
Treasury of Extensive Teachings (Kongtrul), 25
Treasury of Instructions (Kongtrul), 25, 137
Treasury of Knowledge (Kongtrul), 27, 136, 284–85n163
treatises (*btsan bcos*, Skt. *shastra*), requisites for, 86, 275n70
trulkor. *See* yogic techniques (*'khrul 'khor*)
Tsadra Rinchen Drak, 25–26
tsampaka flowers, 121, 285n169
Tsangnyön Heruka (gTsang smyon he ru

ka, Rus pa'i rgyan can, 1452–1507), 259n21
See also *Life of Marpa the Translator, The*
Tukwan Lama (Thu'u bkvan bla ma, Blo bzang chos kyi nyi ma, 1737–1802). See *Collected Works of bLo bzang chos-kyi nyi-ma*
twelfth ground, 83, 291n30

Uncommon Calm Abiding and Higher Insight (*thun mong ma yin pa'i zhi gnas lhag mthong*), 36
unity, path of (*Lam zung 'jug*), 95, 278n101
universal monarchs, 121, 196

Vairochana, posture of, 185, 189, 303n6, 303n15
Vairochana Immense Ocean, 132
Vairochana Vajradhara, 73
Vairochanarakṣhita, 34, 268n119
Vajra Bodhichitta, 131
vajra body (*rdo rje sku*), 12, 31, 135, 162
See also rainbow body (*'ja' lus*)
vajra dance, 188, 303n12
vajra lines, distinctions in, 154
Vajra Lines of the Amulet Mahāmudrā
notes on translation, 144, 145
root text, 145–47
root text with notes, 147–52
Vajra Lines of the Six Dharmas, 25, 31, 289n11
empowerment in, 30–31
root text, 139–42
sources of, 135–36
translation of, 137–39
transmission of, 135
vajra seal of, 142, 293–94n44
Vajra Peak Tantra, 132, 287n190
vajra position, 189, 190
See also Vairochana, posture of
Vajra Seat, 130
Vajrabhairava, 34
Vajradhara
accomplishment of, 261n46
biography of, 13–14
buddhahood through empowerment by, 131
lineage of, 29
seven aspects of, 139, 289–90n16
as source of Immortal and Infallible, 163
as source of mahāmudrā, 145, 147
as source of six dharmas, 136, 139, 289n13
as source of three integrations, 154
Sukhasiddhī and, 34
vajra-like absorption, 83, 116
Vajrāsana/Dorjedenpa, Loppön (rDo rje gdan pa, bsLob dpon), 35, 268–69n120
See also *Indian Source Text of the Glorious Five Tantras*
vajrayāna, 12, 41–42, 47
See also secret mantra; tantra
Vajrayoginī
in Chakrasaṃvara practice, 168, 172
as preliminary practice, 31
in White and Red Khecharī practice, 33
Varāhi with the Severed Head, 161–62
Vasubandhu, 44
See also *Explanation of the Ornament of the Sūtras*
Very Joyful (*rab tu dga' ba*, first ground), 44, 76
characteristics of, 119
delusions obscuring, 123
Path of Seeing and, 69
qualities of, 112
realization on, 124, 126
signs on, 120, 125–26
vice, 56, 57–58, 98, 100–101
See also nonvirtue
victors. *See* buddha(s)
Victor's Body, mindfulness of body and, 56
view(s)
to be eliminated, 111, 282n141
genuine, 70, 113
obscuration of, 72, 274n59
Vimalā (Dri med pa or Vimalādīpī, Dri med sgron ma), 4

Vimalakīrti Sūtra, 97, 278n108
Vimalamitra, 12
virtue
  base of, 54
  as buddha nature, 92
  dedicating the roots of, 101
  in dreams, 62, 273n48
  generosity and, 77
  of mental attention, 58
  of mental consciousness, 93–94
  on Path of Accumulation, 56, 57–58, 98
  on Path of Application, 105
  ripening of, 90
Virūpa, 33, 34, 161, 268n118, 297n3
  See also *Spiritual Power of Amṛita/ Spiritual Power of Immortality*
visionary experiences, 120–22
visualization
  in Chakrasaṃvara practice, 169, 170, 171
  in Hevajra practice, 179, 180–81
  in physical yogic techniques, 183, 184–85, 186–87, 188, 190
Visuddhimagga. See *Path of Purification, The* (Buddhaghosa)
vital essence (*thig le*, Skt *bindu*), 171, 187, 188, 190–91, 303n12

warmth, level of (*drod*), 103–5
  dream recognition as, 62, 63–64
  signs of, 105, 279n122, 280n125
wealth, aspiration for, 196
Western Tsang, 28, 266n98
White Lotus of Great Compassion Sūtra, 130
wisdom (*shes rab*, Skt. *prajñā*), 44
  characteristics of, 122
  faculty of, 104–5
  on Path of Accumulation, 100
  power of, 61, 65, 107
  ten grounds and, 77, 78
  vice and, 58
wish-fulfilling gem, 54, 150, 152, 194
Wöntön Kyergangpa (or Chökyi Senge, 1143–1216), 29

yidams
  in mahāmudrā, 151
  three integrations and, 32, 153–54, 155, 156–57
  transference to, 141
  See also deities
Yoga of Meditation in the Path of Methods, 189–91
yogāchāra, 44–45
Yogi Chen, 26
yogic techniques (*'khrul 'khor*), 183–85
Yoginī Tantra, 167, 168, 299n1
  See also mother tantra (*ma rgyud*)
Zangpo, Ngawang, 27
Zhang-zhong (Zhangs zhongs), 28, 266n98

Six-Armed Mahākāla